RECKONING DAY

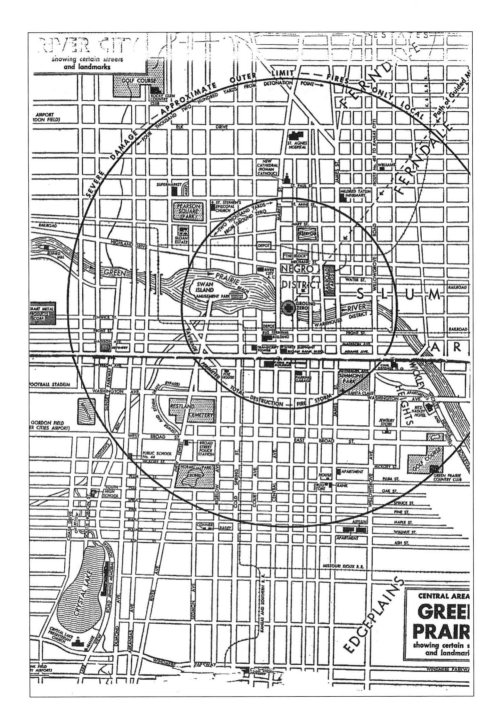

RECKONING DAY

RACE, PLACE, AND THE ATOM BOMB
IN POSTWAR AMERICA

Jacqueline
Foertsch

Vanderbilt University Press

NASHVILLE

© 2013 by Vanderbilt University Press
Nashville, Tennessee 37235
All rights reserved
First printing 2013

This book is printed on acid-free paper.
Manufactured in the United States of America

Library of Congress Cataloging-in-Publication Data on file
LC control number 2012035734
LC classification number E185.61.F64 2012
Dewey class number 323.1196'073—dc23

ISBN 978-0-8265-1926-9 (cloth)
ISBN 978-0-8265-1927-6 (paperback)
ISBN 978-0-8265-1928-3 (ebook)

Frontispiece from *Tomorrow!* by Philip Wylie.
© University of Nebraska Press, 2009.

Contents

Acknowledgments

Long ago, as the story often goes, this book was born through the reading of key texts with a group of engaged and intelligent students. In the case of *Reckoning Day*, the texts were authored by Pat Frank, Judith Merril, and Philip Wylie, all of whom play featured roles in this book's second chapter, and the students were members of my "Cold War Literature and Culture" class at the University of North Texas. While my debt to these authors and the many others joining this conversation is, I hope, implicit in each word that follows, this is the place to thank those smart students and the ones who have learned alongside me in succeeding semesters at UNT; their interest in our shared subjects and love of literature of all kinds inspire me daily.

I thank as well the terrific faculty and staff at UNT—the English Department's American Studies Colloquium, whose great speakers and panels are a constant source of intellectual stimulation; Chair of English David Holdeman, whose support and encouragement means so much; Diana Holt and Andrew Tolle in the English office, who expertly assisted in the provision of essential research and travel support; Kevin Yanowski, also in the office, for serving as my de facto research assistant numberless times; Learning Technologies adjunct faculty member Jonathan Gratch for his valuable technical guidance; and the Circulation and Interlibrary Loan staffs at Willis Library, who have quite simply never let me down. This book was also vitally supported through several Small Grants and two Research and Creativity Enhancement Grants, sponsored by UNT's Office of Research and Economic Development.

Further afield, I send my thanks to the talented staffs at the Schomburg Center for Research in Black Culture and the Stephen A. Schwarzman Building at the New York Public Library, the Tamiment Library and Robert F. Wagner Labor Archives at NYU, the Swarthmore College Peace Collection, and the University of Texas's Perry-Castañeda Library and Harry Ransom Center. Thanks also to Martha Campbell in Austin, and special thanks to the late Paul Boyer, who encouraged and inspired me for many years. Special thanks also to Russell Wyland and my helpful readers at the National Endowment for the Humanities, who awarded this project a Summer Stipend in 2010. I am grateful as well to the readers and editors at the *Journal of Modern Literature*, *Philological Quarterly*, and *Modern Language Studies*, which have each published excerpts of this work. Finally, I thank Eli Bortz, the editorial and production staffs, and my helpful anonymous readers at Vanderbilt University Press.

Back at home in Texas, I was encouraged constantly by dear friends and colleagues in UNT English and across campus. Special thanks to Alexander Pettit and Harry Benshoff who kindly read parts of this work; to Walton Muyumba for our long talks about African American literature and culture (and the Mingus reference essential to my conclusion); and to Deborah Needleman Armintor, Ian Finseth, Bonnie Friedman, Stephanie Hawkins, Eileen Hayes, Jennifer Jensen-Wallach, Jack Peters, Robert Upchurch, Kelly Wisecup, and Priscilla Ybarra for their marvelous friendship and ongoing interest in my work.

I thank other dear friends—Kathryn Stasio at St. Leo University and Annette Trefzer at Ole Miss—with whom I've shared the academic adventure from the start, and my beloved family, for whom I write always: Mom and Dad in Chicagoland, Christine and Mike in New York, my darling Aurora and Solana, who've made me the Happiest Aunt in America since the day they were born, and the amazing Terence Donovan, who has changed my life.

RECKONING DAY

Introduction

Mapping Ground Zero in Postwar America

Since the genre's inception in August 1945, atomic narrative has located its characters with painstaking precision with respect to the bomb. Most of the footnotes in Michihiko Hachiya's *Hiroshima Diary* (1955) record distances from various possible blast sites to the location of wounded friends and narrators; in *Hiroshima* (1946) John Hersey records the exact yardage between the point of impact and each of his interview subjects, their position behind windows, walls, or other buffers, and the life-saving (later, life-threatening) Ota River and Asano Park. Like many treating this subject, Hachiya and Hersey indicate that the worst position was not necessarily ground zero; the agonizing injuries (leading to permanent disability or eventual death) suffered by many in the mid-range between instant vaporization and the safe distance created the atomic era's first and most profound dilemma with respect to position: at this devastating moment in world history, who, and where, were the lucky ones? On the American home front, news of the two atomic flashes that ended World War II likely registered with each recipient in specific spatiotemporal detail: Where was I when I found out? What was I "in the middle of"? While the physical location of Hiroshima's blast victims was in every instance determinant of their survival and well-being, in America and elsewhere, the blast caused only a moment of paralysis, shortly giving way to the gyrations of victory. Yet that moment, for those still alive to remember it, remains powerfully present—"like it was yesterday"—or we might say that the recollectors themselves remain trapped in that particular past. Like the shadows of figures incinerated at Hiroshima's ground zero, they remain fixed then and there in their places, transfixed by the bomb's unprecedented horror and significance.

More broadly speaking, one's location in the American landscape when the bomb exploded—that is, during America's early atomic/cold war era—intersects with one's "place" in the American social hierarchy in significant ways. For the bomb presented Americans, especially those who have always enjoyed more freedom of movement, with a series of spatio-ethical dilemmas: where to go if the bombs should fall, who and what to leave behind. While the suburban boom of the immediate postwar period had myriad causes, one

1

significant reason was the strong sense that America's cities were the easiest and most likely of nuclear targets. Elaine Tyler May has examined the leafy, low-slung, spread-out qualities of American suburbs and has persuasively observed in these a response to atomic fears of urban verticality, congestion, and entrapment. For May it was especially the hunkered down, ranch-style home that "exuded this sense of isolation, privacy, and containment" (94). In atomic fictions of the period, the city is depicted as the site of conflagration; those characters lucky enough to find themselves in the suburbs or on the farm on "X-day" fare better and depend less on which way the wind blows during the fallout period.

While the suburban choice—again, for the white middle-class, for whom such choices were exclusively provided—seemed obvious, the decision with respect to whether or not to go underground, to build a bomb shelter and prepare to survive there in the atomic aftermath, was always a more fraught proposition. In the enmeshed social setting of the suburbs, how would it look to build a shelter when no one else was doing so? Kenneth D. Rose suggests that the lone suburban shelter-digger might seem not only eccentric (violating the cardinal rule of conformity) but also "immoral." "At issue," says Rose, "was controlling entry to one's personal or community shelter . . . to keep out radioactive fallout but also 'to prevent exceeding the maximum capacity of the shelter'" (93). How did one build to suit one's immediate family but not spaciously enough to include neighbors and passersby, or even parents, in-laws, aunts, and uncles from the "old country" (i.e., the urban birthplace)? The pointlessness of resurfacing in a ruined, depopulated post-nuclear environment may have dissuaded many from taking the plunge in the first place; others sought the furthest reaches of American civilization (and beyond) in their understanding that the key to nuclear survival was location, location, location.

We attach extremist notions like nuclear survivalism to a specific racial, classed position in the US—white (sometimes white-supremacist) lower-class place-holders who take to the hinterlands in order to reject not only the nuclear jeopardy in which America has placed its citizens from the cold war to the present but also much of what America represents (see, e.g., "Religious Group"). Such outward-boundedness positions one near the bottom of America's social scale, while downward-boundedness (bomb shelter-building) was a distinctly suburban (and, to some degree, urban) phenomenon and thus associated with America's middle class. In short, there was less stigma attached during the cold war to digging down than to lighting out, despite the seemingly more bizarre nature of the downward-digging: while survivalists thrive on the US's geographic and ideological margins into the twenty-first century, today no middle-class suburbanite would construct a bomb shelter in his backyard, so unorthodox an act would it be, and the two-hour commute has become more and more the norm. Perhaps, sixty years ago, a move to the suburbs was deemed so eminently respectable that included with the purchase of one's private lot was the right to go a little crazy in one's fenced-off backyard—to prepare for a post-nuclear life underground no matter how objectionable it was to some.

In America's "burnt out," "bombed out" urban cores, locales we have tagged with post-nuclear adjectives since the postwar period,[1] remained America's "undesirables"—African, Asian, and Latino Americans and other ethnic persons or immigrants with low incomes; poor whites; the elderly; gays and lesbians; the mentally disturbed; the otherwise socially delinquent. Ironically, their lives in inner city high-rises positioned these postwar Americans "at the top," while everyone understood that such physical superiority carried neither privilege nor security. If anything, the last place one wanted to be at this moment was up, and yet this particular sector of the American population had few other choices: the suburbs were closed to them, rural ties had been severed generations earlier, and the atomic threat found many of America's persons of color trapped at ground zero. Questioning "the Negro's relative exposure and immunity to nuclear annihilation" for *Negro Digest* in 1963, the sociologist and black studies founder Nathan Hare praised African Americans' emotional fortitude and resistance to physical travails—even the anticipated intense heat of atomic blast—due to their "cotton-chopping, cotton-picking backgrounds in the Southern sun and long years of tending ovens and furnaces in white kitchens and factories" (31). Yet Hare is intent on critiquing the demographic patterns of postwar society that have trapped the black community in northern ghettoes "near the centers or bull's-eyes of our big cities" (28). Citing racial residency patterns at that point, Hare notes that "a 10-megaton bomb on Washington, DC, or Chicago . . . would just about take care of the Negro community" (29). Hare's observations are echoed today by Katherine McKittrick and Clyde Woods, who decry America's long history of "uneven geographies," wherein "black and poor subjects are disposable precisely because they cannot move or escape" (3). This insight crystallizes the crisis faced by atomic-era African Americans, thought to deserve their fate for failing to meet the criteria for admission to the suburban safe haven.

Philip Wylie's novel *Tomorrow!* is a nuclear preparedness/survival fantasy that includes a map of the fictional sister cities that are its setting; these surround a "Negro District" that is dead-center during the climactic nuclear explosion. The story ends with its surviving characters, all of whom are white, viewing a scene of pristine, suburban-style rebirth. This vision resonates with those of postwar urban planners who could not but associate the bomb, despite its frightening implications, with their growing desire to revamp city life, specifically to "save the American city from 'the blight . . . gnawing at its innards'" (qtd. in P. Boyer 152). The National Paint, Varnish, and Lacquer Association produced a fright-mongering public service announcement in the mid-1950s that has achieved cult status in the intervening decades, *The House in the Middle*. As it opens, a disgusted narrator harangues against the combustible trash and rotting wood "you've seen in too many alleys and backyards—in *slum areas*" and crows about the destruction suffered by cluttered, littered, unpainted frame houses subjected to H-bombing at the Nevada Proving Grounds, images of which accompany his voiceover. Only the paint job of the lucky middle house saves it from the same fate, itself racialized, since "light colors" and "white" are recommended as the most light- and heat-reflective shades. Implicit in such texts, therefore, are visions of the nuclear-induced "urban renewal" that recent thinkers such as Martha A. Bartter and Dean MacCannell have broadly denounced, while Michele Birnbaum incisively reads the constructedness of racial identity thus: "we can describe one [race] only in terms of the other—a kind of Heisenberg principle of race in which racial difference is situational, provisional: it depends upon who is looking and who is next to whom" (3). As whiteness depends for its significance upon its position with respect to blackness (and vice versa), we see this supplemental relation repeated in the demographic shifting of the postwar US: African Americans, forced to remain in rapidly declining inner cities, maintained these locales as viable (i.e., populated) nuclear targets, creating in turn the relative safety of the "uninhabited" white suburban sanctuary.

GIVING (OR BUYING) SHELTER

Throughout the cold war period—but especially during the "shelter crisis" of the early 1960s (Weart 20)—cities pondered the pros and cons of "community" versus "family" shelters, a distinction that can be framed in terms of public/federally subsidized versus privatized, urban versus suburban, and racially integrated versus racially homogeneous modes of civil defense (CD).[2] In fact, experts agreed that better protection from many nuclear hazards (specifically, post-detonation firestorms and radioactive fallout) was to be found in the inner corridors and sub-basements of tall, sturdily built high-rises rather than in thinly-constructed single-family dwellings.[3] Yet these structural features would only provide such protection if the building in question survived the initial blast: positioned, as many were, in the direct path of enemy warheads, high-rise buildings, even their fortified basements, were as likely to fatally trap as protect their shelterees.[4] And how difficult would it be to retrofit potential shelter spaces with the necessary modifications and supplies? In a comment loaded with doubts and disclaimers, Martin Smith and William Eliason in *Family Survival Handbook* (1961) indicate the logistical issues related to converting one's apartment basement into a habitable shelter with 15 minutes' warning:

> The problem for the city apartment dweller is primarily to plan the use
> of existing space. Such planning will require the cooperation of other
> occupants *and of the apartment management.* The space available should

be identified and assigned to those who are to use it. The plan will work more smoothly if it is rehearsed. The owner of the building *may* find it necessary to modify the basement ventilation, water supply, and sanitation [or due to the costs of such renovations may much more likely do nothing at all].

You *probably* would have time to carry your family supplies from your apartment to the basement after an attack warning, before fallout arrives. (179, emphases added; see also Hagan 178–79)

In *Negro Digest* Hare questioned civil defense pamphlets that advised citizens to "close all windows and doors and draw the blinds." Such warnings, he said, failed to take into account the "broken and jammed windows and broken blinds ready to come tumbling down" in many tenement apartments, such that "many [Negroes] have taken a 'return-to-sender' attitude with regard to such pamphlets sent out by the Office of Civil Defense" (31–32).

In addition to the ultimately questionable structural and logistical superiority of high-rises, the benefits of community survival in the nuclear aftermath—skill- and labor-sharing, morale-boosting, and improved communication (Brelis 74, Fritz 147, Martin and Latham 270)—were undercut almost as soon as they were introduced: in the handbook *Strategy for Survival* (1963), Thomas Martin and Donald Latham point out that so much togetherness would lead almost immediately to "psychological problems, racial tensions, social stratification, 'leader' complexes, fear, neuroses, disciplinary problems, mental instability . . . in various community shelters." In addition, "[i]t would be almost impossible, particularly in target [i.e., urban] areas to regulate the number of shelterees to the designed capacity" (271). In the blunt phrasing of Mary E. Robinson of the Brookings Institute, "If [shelterees] think the law of the jungle is all that waits outside, that post-shelter survival will depend on every man fending for himself, then I think you can count on jungle behavior reaching into the shelter, too" (220).

While sheltering would thus be no picnic for any city-dweller, no matter how broadminded, African Americans in particular expressed alarm at the potential for segregated (separate and *un*equal) shelters in urban areas and even more so in the rural South or, worse, a whites-only shelter program that would exclude them entirely. These concerns were galvanized by President Truman's appointment of Millard Caldwell, a notoriously segregationist ex-governor of Florida, to head the newly formed Federal Civil Defense Administration (FCDA). NAACP leaders wrote and met with the administration, and, as I will demonstrate in Chapter 3, the African American press staged a prolonged and persuasive anti-Caldwell campaign. (See Grossman 92–97, McEnaney 141–46, and K. Rose 109–10.) While their protests, perhaps not surprisingly, fell on deaf ears—Caldwell remained in charge throughout Truman's term—in certain respects their fears, however valid, were misdirected: especially before the mid-1950s, when the dangers of fallout were yet to be fully realized (Oakes 60, 118), the focus of the FCDA was almost entirely on urban centers, especially in the North. Rural southern blacks (like their rural southern white counterparts) were perceived to be in the best possible position with respect to civil defense, even as they continued to suffer most greatly with respect to civil rights. Even once the danger of fallout was known, the noted disarmament advocate Roger Hagan suggested, "The Southern Negro may well wonder what fallout can do to him that the local police chief cannot" (qtd. in Brelis 154, Hagan 188; see also Weart, who considers civil defense entirely in terms of cities, and Martin and Latham chapter 5).

To that end, Caldwell, despite his segregationist background, championed a public urban shelter system (McEnaney 48), even as he and his successor under Eisenhower, ex-Nebraska governor Val Peterson, failed year after year to provide Congress with an affordable, realistic blueprint for such. The admittedly complex task of constructing adequate shelter space only fifteen minutes (about a quarter-mile) from every urban resident and commuter was never more than a drawing-board dream for civil defense planners during the cold war, despite the efforts of FCDA policymakers from three presidential administrations (Truman's, Eisenhower's, and Kennedy's) to gain congressional funding and public support. The potentially astronomical costs (though Congress rejected even modest funding proposals) caused these administrations to drift inexorably from public to privatized answers to the threat of nuclear war[5]—that is, to admit to the physical and economic impossibility of the (urban, racially and ethnically diverse) "blast" or bomb shelter and to place their hopes instead in the (suburban, white middle-class) "fallout" shelter—built and maintained at the expense and discretion of the individual suburban family. Ultimately, as the journalist Dean Brelis noted in 1962, "the shelter approach to the prospect of nuclear war . . . carries with it the built-in notice to millions of city dwellers that they are expendable" (118).

The privatized version of bomb-sheltering carried costs that many on the social margins would never have been able to afford. The exhortation to stockpile supplies, for instance, presumed a liquidity of cash flow from one month to the next that allowed the housewife in question to buy into the future, preparing two-week to six-month caches of medicine, soap, toilet paper, amusements for the children, water and foodstuffs from instant coffee (with one scenario suggesting five cups a day) to canned meat to hard candy. Ideally, these supplies would be rotated into the peacetime pantry and replaced with fresh stores on a regular basis, presuming ready access to these in the basement or backyard shelter, not a storage area twenty floors below. To encourage their readers toward do-it-yourself survivalism, Smith and Eliason downplay the costs associated with shelter stockpiling, insisting that storing large containers of water costs "nothing" (what about the containers themselves? the enlarged water bill?)

and that collecting supplies from camping equipment to extra bedding to paper plates will also cost "nothing"—"*if you have them all*" (29, emphasis added; see also Sharp 188–90). When Smith and Eliason advise the reader to "keep your car in top shape; battery charged . . . gas tank filled" (29), they presume not only the ownership of a car but the financial ability to keep it running and gassed up at all times. Despite the emphasis on shelter construction and maintenance throughout their book, they indicate here that the suburbanite's full tank of gas—his ability to escape to the hinterlands whenever it suited him and his family best—may elevate his prospects over those of his urban counterpart more effectively than the most fortified shelter. (See also McEnaney 55 and Sharp 205–09.) The costs of building the shelter itself were also significant: while many survival handbooks offered do-it-yourself guides for the cheapest and simplest types, all agreed that the more cash outlaid for sound materials and professional construction, the greater one's chances for survival; top-of-the-line models ran to $1700 in 1961 (Smith and Eliason 165), a cost equivalent of more than $15,000 today. The guides also agreed that bomb shelter construction would be cheaper if done at the time of new home construction (see Martin and Latham 124; Smith and Eliason 172). Yet again, suburbs and not cities were the sites of most new construction in this period, reinforcing the connection between adequate, affordable fallout-sheltering and the suburban alternative.

Despite the intensity of public debate surrounding these issues, there prevailed the sense of "total public disinterest in civil defense" (Martin and Latham 261), and the reality that "only about one in eight Americans took any practical war precautions during the crisis . . . [and o]nly about one in fifty had built even the crudest kind of fallout shelter" (Weart 25). As Hare observed, "With an average income about $2000 smaller than the average white family, and with more mouths per family to care for, the typical Negro couldn't afford a shelter if he wanted to" (30). We must observe, however, that the massive exodus to the suburbs conducted by white middle-class Americans during this period constitutes its own defensive, precautionary response to imminent nuclear disaster. Their very homes were multi-room, beautifully decorated "bomb shelters" whose comfortable kitchens stocked with the latest in long-lived canned and packaged foods provided a vital sense of security, however false that sense may have been. These suburbanites may have even availed themselves of the benefits of "communal" sheltering, stockpiling goodwill and owed favors amongst their close-knit neighbors, even as these bonds would have been of necessity broken in an every-family-for-itself post-nuclear scenario.

Awareness campaigns were a potentially more effective (and certainly much less expensive) means by which to prepare the public for nuclear attack, and the FCDA divided its efforts between lobbying Congress for funding (of urban, public shelters) and informing citizens as to the risks and responsibilities of American life in the atomic age. While this message was directed at urban and suburban, black and white, working- and middle-class populations, it was certainly better received by certain groups than others—especially white suburbanites, who possessed the means to respond. Andrew Grossman argues that "civil defense was aimed at postwar suburbia" (77), and representative of this claim is Smith and Eliason's warning, at the height of the cold war, that "CD . . . cannot make the necessary preparations to provide safety for your *own* household. That you must do yourself" (22). The cover of their 1961 text quotes John F. Kennedy preaching self-sufficiency to his listeners; during the Berlin crisis of 1961 Kennedy continued shifting the burden from the government to the private sector, "urging individuals to 'plan to protect their own families'" (Weart 22; see also Brelis 9–10 and K. Rose 2–5 and passim). Finally it was only those trapped outside the "outside" to ground zero—inner city residents whose federally funded shelter system never came together—who "failed" so perilously to heed the government's warning. The mass movement from the urban apartment to the suburban single-family home in the postwar period privatized not only the American lifestyle but American life itself; those who could not afford the costs of privatization faced dire consequences.

GETTING MOBILIZED

Even as national planners prepared for nuclear crisis by encouraging citizens to stay put (within communally assigned or privately constructed shelters), they published simultaneous and contradictory directives to get going no matter how. Early in his administration, Eisenhower abandoned the idea of an urban public shelter system for plans of mass evacuation instead, and staged various drills and simulations throughout the country, including one in Washington DC that required himself and 15,000 federal employees to move to a secret location outside the beltway (see K. Rose 27 and Gup). As was the case with public shelters, however, both blacks and whites viewed these evacuation schemes with suspicion: a disheartening incident occurred in Mobile, Alabama, during "Operation Scat," when rumors of racially targeted nuclear bombs—sent to avoid school de-segregation—flew through the African American community (see McEnaney 138 and K. Rose 110). Throughout the country, white and black urban populations caught up in these simulations failed to evacuate according to protocol in each instance; instead of orderly movement to the countryside, there was perfect gridlock on every highway, positioning evacuees as sitting ducks during any actual attack. As with the building of shelters, Americans by and large "could not be blamed for scoffing at the occasional mock raids held in the larger cities, raids reminiscent of the Keystone Cops—good for laughs but nothing else" (Brelis 10).

If contradictory exhortations to "sit tight" and "head for the hills" were not confusing enough, a third and equally insistent call to "run toward the fire" complicated matters further still. With an almost perverse disregard for its enormous campaign to promote shelter construction, stocking, and occupation for two weeks post-attack, civil defense planners sold with equal zeal a program of volunteerism that encouraged and trained these same shelter inhabitants to do whatever was necessary in the immediate nuclear aftermath: rescue and nurse the injured, put out fires, set up communication posts, maintain order. A Civil Defense short film from the early 1950s even equated evacuation with "treason" and "desertion" and challenged its viewers by asking whether they had "the guts" to stay and fight (*Our Cities Must Fight*). Regarding the drawing of women into such programs, Laura McEnaney notes that the government "did not set out consciously to feminize civil defense as a way to include women. Rather, they gradually realized that preparation and recovery from nuclear war was partly a welfare issue, which then led them to consider women's involvement more seriously . . ." (98).

Reviewing the various requirements of the immediate atomic aftermath—"temporary housing, soup kitchens, medical care (including psychological rehabilitation), short-term economic aid, care for orphaned children and the elderly, public health and sanitation services" (98)—McEnaney indicates the stereotypically feminine skills sought by civil defense planners. She also shows that civil defense programs drew a line between those who took care (i.e., those who had the financial, educational, and social wherewithal to do so) and those who were taken care of (i.e., the "welfare" recipients downtown scripted for home loss, psychological trauma, and massive physical injuries in the nuclear scenario).[6] In a rare reference to race in these early preparedness guides, Pentagon defense planner Richard Gerstell stresses equality, all the while segregating the roles of rescuer and victim: "plans have to be made for sick people, and those in mental institutions and prisons. And all this must be done without regard to race, creed, or color. If we let prejudice of any kind enter into the picture, the result can only make added trouble and possibly panic" (129–30). Note that those marked in Gerstell's imaginary by "race" and "color" belong solely to the victim category and become grouped with, even come at the bottom of the list of, society's other peacetime untouchables—sick people, crazy people, and prisoners.

In one of the only preparedness films surveyed that features an interracial cast, the cold war classic *Duck and Cover* pointedly integrates all of its classroom scenes.[7] Again, however, all of the African American actors in this film are of the civilian/victim variety and all are notably young—in the primary grades—while all of those cast as authority figures and first-responders (teachers, parents, civil defense officers, knowledgeable grown-ups on hand during an attack) are white. Reflecting the times it emerged from, when just about the only reliably integrated setting was the urban classroom of the northern states, the film plainly indicates that our children will shelter together without discrimination, even if none of the rest of us will. Yet from these several examples it is implied (or envisioned) that the only African Americans to survive a nuclear holocaust will be helpless or disabled, prepubescent, integration-minded, and profoundly indebted to white rescue.

LOCATING AFRICAN AMERICANS IN THE POST-NUCLEAR LANDSCAPE

Thus, perhaps not surprisingly, doomsday forecasting is an intensely political enterprise, with prevailing assumptions, hopes, and fears boldly on display. Specifically, the doomsday scenario described for its audience the horrible losses that would be incurred—or in a different vein, the unexpected gains bestowed—by all-out nuclear war. In one striking example, a report from the early Reagan administration envisioned an attack on US oil refineries that would result in the following unacceptable outcomes: "Gasoline rationing would at best severely curtail use of private cars; mass transit would be used to its capacity. . . . Demand for real estate would plummet in some areas, especially suburbs, and skyrocket in others, notably cities, as people moved nearer to work and stores" (Office of Technology Assessment 73). In addition, "All houses would be better insulated; more would use solar energy as fuel costs soared" (74). Of course what is depicted as an unlivable nightmare for the gas-guzzling suburbanite is simultaneously readable as the progressive's utopia: energy- and space-efficient, re-urbanized, and oil-free at last. Later it is lamented that "the livestock industry might be sharply curtailed" (Office of Technology Assessment 75), as grains and soybeans become more important as a cheap, efficient food source, a forecast sure to please the vegetarians in the audience. While this report provides a singular example of a nuclear war that even the pacifist Left could anticipate with joy, it, like dozens of other nuclear nonfictions written for government agencies, academic think tanks, and general audiences between the late 1940s and early 1980s, indicates in revealing terms the writer's view of what is most worth saving from total nuclear disaster, as well as the worst and best of what we might expect in the nuclear aftermath.[8]

In these scenarios, African Americans and other Americans of color were pictured idiosyncratically when they were envisioned at all. They were both visually and verbally absented in striking ways, present metaphorically on other occasions, and acknowledged as actual participants in the preparedness and recovery process only very rarely. Despite the gains made by postwar-era African Americans to establish themselves as free and equal members of US society, the tendency persisted throughout this period to envision America "in the aggregate" as it had always been: unthinkingly and overwhelmingly white, middle-class, religiously and politically homogenous, affluent, and united in opposition to a common enemy. What Patrick B. Sharp has observed about atomic-era fictions applies to its nonfictions as well: "Strategic fictions bought into the assumption that to be American was to be white" (154). Thus those scenarios assuming a multiracial but single-minded post-nuclear populace are as implausible as those that bar the presence of African American participants by the very logic and grammar of the writing itself. During these decades in US history, especially 1945 to 1965, the primary focus of this study, the role of African Americans, particularly, as per Birnbaum, vis à vis their white counterparts, was so complex and dynamic that assumptions of shared outlook and circumstance often did more harm than good.

Earlier I indicated that many preparedness analysts regarded the basements of urban high-rises (and the massive subway systems also part of the city setting) as better suited to blast sheltering than the light construction characterizing single-family postwar housing. In a telling exchange during a 1961 House Subcommittee meeting between Michigan Representative Martha Griffiths and Secretary of Defense Robert S. McNamara, Griffiths asks, "Under the system that you have set up marking out the shelters, would the inner city become the most protected place?" (qtd. in Brelis 78). When McNamara confirms her suspicions, Griffiths complains that her constituents in suburban Detroit would have to "rush back from [their outlying] homes to the city" on the occasion of a nighttime strike. Perhaps troubled by the assumption that the "inner city" is even more dangerous at night than during the day, Griffiths doubts that "anybody in his right mind at the time of the alarm would be willing to try for the interior of Detroit" (qtd. in Brelis 97).

In this exchange, Griffiths is clearly miffed that it is Detroit's downtown districts, and not the somehow more deserving suburban environs represented by herself, that have lucked into shelter designation (see also Smelser 227–28 and *A Realistic Approach* 16); likewise, she fails to acknowledge the existence of the millions of citizens who would not have to "rush back downtown" at all—the population, largely African American, who actually reside in downtown Detroit and would very likely fill the shelters themselves, such that suburbanites should not bother trying for the interior at any rate. While thus implied here is an attack scenario favoring black urban survivors, such a scenario is only implied, and implied only sixty years after the fact; in the original moment the officials debating the matter were literally unable to envision African Americans in their survival and recovery plans.

Similar blind spots limit the visual representations of urban shelters in other doomsday scenarios of the period, illustrating human figures with light skin and European features only (Bresee and Narver 201, 219). In one mock-up (Bresee and Narver 215), about a dozen white survivors rest or sleep on closely stacked bunks; the only upright, seated figure is a white male in a suit and tie (see figure 1). This image betrays several assumptions—that for maximum functionality, the shelters' tight sleeping quarters must be racially, even though not sexually, segregated, and that in such racially homogeneous circumstances, order would prevail, even to the extent of keeping one's tie in place. The prominent positioning of the businessman also indicates that shelter planners envisioned fortifying the basements of cities' business sectors, not their tenement neighborhoods. One map from this same period indicates a similar assumption: Manhattan's shelter zone is plotted for the lower reaches of Midtown, not Harlem (Bresee and Narver 213). To be sure, a zone map of Detroit (Bresee and Narver 209) confirms Rep. Griffiths's fears of placement in a rather rundown section of the "inner city," yet it has been located there to take advantage of the city's vast tunnel-grid system, where the converted shelters are once again illustrated to contain white survivors only (Bresee and Narver 208; see figure 2).

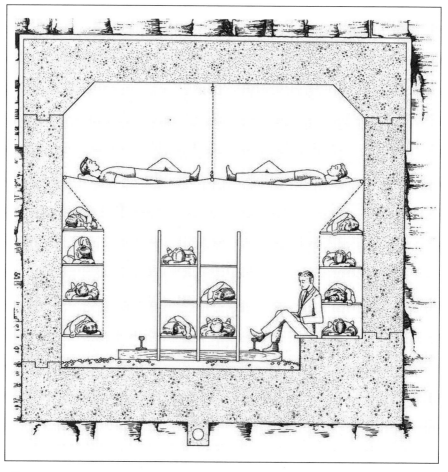

FIGURE 1: J. C. Bresee and D. L. Narver Jr. "Improved Shelters and Accessories." *Survival and the Bomb: Methods of Civil Defense.* Ed. Eugene P. Wigner. © 1989 Indiana University Press. Reprinted with permission.

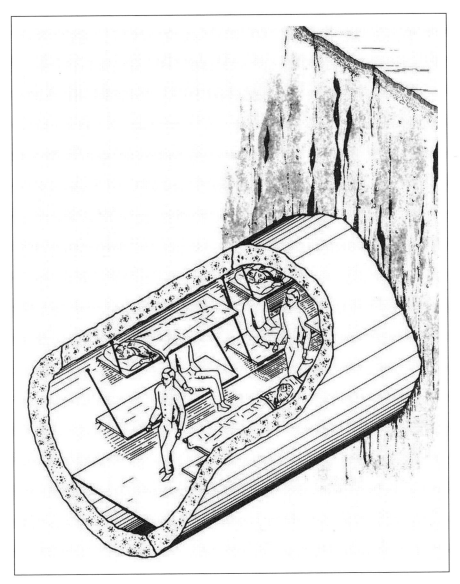

FIGURE 2: J. C. Bresee and D. L. Narver Jr. "Improved Shelters and Accessories." *Survival and the Bomb: Methods of Civil Defense.* Ed. Eugene P. Wigner. © 1989 Indiana University Press. Reprinted with permission.

Hardly surprisingly, mid-1950s newsreels of nuclear test sites included only white mannequins arranged inside their mock houses assembled for destruction. One reporter referred to these dummies as "Mr. and Mrs. America," and, as revealed in the last frames of the widely excerpted *Operation Cue*, each of these figures survives the blast intact. Illustrations of an implicitly segregated variety are supplied by the noted atomic physicist Ralph E. Lapp, who insisted that Manhattan and other *"such cities are cities of the past"* (85; see also Brelis 110 and Winkler 113). In his text *Must We Hide?*, whose title is a rhetorical question to be answered with a resounding "No" (see also P. Boyer 314), Lapp maps out variations on postwar suburban sprawl (most notably the "doughnut" or beltway model of the present day), each of which was a specifically white proposition in the postwar period (see also Sharp 186–87). If doomsday scenarists (e.g., Brelis 68) occasionally worried about the crisis of integrated shelters in the South, even shelters in so-called progressive northern cities were pictured in starkly segregated terms.

FANTASTIC FORECASTING

Comparisons of the yet-to-be-realized nuclear nightmare with other disasters of the remote and recent past are common in this canon: analysts have used the Black Plague, the Irish Potato Famine, the Cocoanut Grove fire of 1942, the Netherland Floods of 1953, even the Middle Passage, and of course the atomic bombings of Hiroshima and Nagasaki as models for panic behavior, sensory deprivation and overcrowding, tension between hosts and evacuees, anti-social behavior following catastrophe, and the physical effects of radiation, among other phenomena. Frequently, such comparisons have met with derision by anti-nuclear scenarists (e.g., Chazov and Vartanian 156; Dentler and Cutright 1–2; Sidel, Geiger, and Lown 1137) who insist that nuclear war of the multimegaton variety promised in the current day would be indescribably worse than any disaster that had ever befallen humankind. Still, those more confident in their ability to actually picture nuclear attack and recovery used such models regularly; in addition, the post-attack restoration of cherished American institutions—including the extremely loaded concepts of "democracy" and "freedom" but very likely such institutions as capitalism, segregation, and discrimination as well—was a subject obsessively returned to in the nuclear nonfictions. With remarkable pigheadedness, even into the final, tumultuous years of the 1960s, scenarists clung to the notion that America was a unified society with a "composite American personality" (Altman 166) and shared values, each of which would be reinstated with all due haste by every surviving American.

In 1969, for instance, Peter G. Nordlie, research director of Human Sciences Research, Inc., a DC think-tank prominent in the field of nuclear forecasting, wrote an essay on the subject of "Societal Recovery" that crawls with unfounded assumptions. For Nordlie, society is constituted by "identifiable patterns of behavior [that reflect] basic values and ideologies of the members. When we speak of the survival and recovery of a society, we refer not just to the people, but to their interrelationships, organizations, institutions, values, and ideology as well" (285; see also Klineberg qtd. in Vestermark 72; Vestermark 83). In his argument, Nordlie assumes either that Americans as a whole are in substantive agreement or that the only Americans worth recovery post-holocaust will be the likeminded, ideology-sharing collective he has defined as "society" but that would be more accurately defined as the majority, the establishment, or the bourgeoisie. To a certain degree, arguments such as this assume (and impose) the suppression of dissent during the preparedness era, just as disenfranchised Americans were enjoined during World War II to prioritize "unity" as the only means to "victory."[9] Never does it occur to Nordlie or to many others writing on this topic that anyone disinclined to rebuild America to its pre-nuclear specifications would be anything other than too psychologically damaged by his traumatic experience to participate. The notion that all would work for the restoration of democracy presumes, with egregious inaccuracy, that all shared in the benefits of democracy to begin with.

Notably, UC Berkeley analyst Neil J. Smelser correlated ethnic background and post-atomic survival: "In the period of initial emergence from shelters . . . , how will an individual's religious and ethnic identifications influence his behavior?" (217). Smelser advises allowing individuals to fall back amongst "their own kind" as a coping strategy in the immediate nuclear aftermath, although he admits that "this last suggestion is likely to be unpopular, since a very strong ideological force in contemporary America would downgrade the differences among ethnic and religious groups" (251). Also, "Insofar as these groupings become the basis of re-establishing cohesion, there will emerge a number of racial, ethnic, and religious cleavages of the sort that have created so many touchy political problems for American society in its recent history" (251).

Smelser's phrasing raises many questions, specifically regarding the identity of that "very strong ideological force" so intent to ignore racial and ethnic differences in the mid-1960s. Can he be referring to the Southern Christian Leadership Conference, who surely would have phrased their bid for equality very differently? To the Kennedy and Johnson administrations, which indeed worked to minimize the gaps between black and white with respect to education, healthcare, and voting rights? To color-blind white liberals who looked forward to the day when we could all "put race behind us" for reasons both altruistic and self-serving? His reference to "touchy" political problems contains its own ambiguities, with touchy construed either as "delicate" (i.e., requiring careful attention) or, as in more common usage, "oversensitive" or "fussy." Evidently, Smelser regards his own day's sectarianism a historical aberration, which is sure to revert to patterns of peace and agreeability well before nuclear doomsday tears apart the social fabric once more.

Yet it is implausible that societal-recovery analysts like Nordlie and Smelser failed to notice the conflicts between segregationists and integrationists, right-wingers and women's-libbers, anti-war protesters and the middle-aged establishment that burgeoned all around them in the mid- and late-1960s when many of these texts were written. More likely, their vision of the America specifically threatened by nuclear attack simply failed or refused to diversify "abstract" (i.e., white, propertied) notions of America that had prevailed since the penning of the Declaration of Independence. Perhaps there were optimists in the group who, flush with the promise of Johnson's Great Society and inspired by the gains made by the civil rights movement over the past decade, believed that at long last all citizens had come to share the bounty of the American enterprise and thus now equally embraced its values and institutions. This, of course, was a rose-tinted viewpoint never borne out by the facts of persistent poverty and demoralization experienced by many African Americans in urban and rural settings throughout this period. Finally in 1971, researcher Bruce C. Allnut came to the depressing but realistic conclusion that following nuclear war, "an increase in conflict between sections of the country, between advocates of varying war policies, and between urban and rural populations . . . would pose serious problems . . . [and] racial or class conflict as well . . ." (qtd. in Katz 222–23).

After a decade's worth of social upheaval and thoroughgoing indifference to same in the war-theorizing of its day, Allnut is among the first to admit that American society is so internally divided over race, social class, and the Vietnam War that nuclear catastrophe would only make such national disarray exponentially more unbearable. In agreement, and writing yet another decade later, Arthur M. Katz makes the fitting summation: "Ethnic, racial, regional, and economic conflicts present in pre-attack society, while minimized in the period immediately after an attack, will be heightened by the extent of the new deprivation and the resulting tensions after only a limited time. New antagonisms will develop between hosts and evacuees or refugees over the possession and use of surviving resources" (240). Like the rats and roaches predicted to survive in profusion in the post-nuclear landscape, race hostility will be dealt a temporary setback by the blast itself but burst forth with new vigor when the initial shock and its accompanying brief shining moment of universal goodwill wear away. On several occasions throughout this study, the cultural artifacts of the period will provide the implicit thesis that "it will take an atom bomb" to bring the races together; here, America's conflicting groups will be literally thrown together on X-day but reestablish and intensify old animosities during the lingering crisis.

Within scenarios acknowledging the prospect of racial conflict lies often the implicit coincident acknowledgement that nuclear attack would be less the founding occasion for said conflict than the long-awaited opportunity for two historically polarized social classes (i.e., the haves and have-nots marked variously by race and ethnicity) to slug it out to the death. Smelser predicted that ethnic and religious groupings would give way to one core opposition— between hosts and evacuees, though he conceded that this "fundamental conflict . . . would be assimilated to several pre-attack bases of cleavage—rural vs. urban, one region vs. another, and one ethnic group vs. another" (253). And in a fictional account written by Nan Randall for the US Office of Technology Assessment in 1979, "Blacks distrusted whites, the poor distrusted the rich and everyone distrusted the refugees as 'outsiders'" (132) in the weeks and months of continued deprivation (see also Katz 231–32). These authors raise the question whether race and ethnic division would exacerbate or ultimately submit to the new source of conflict between hosts and evacuees or shelter survivors.

In such evacuation scenarios, fleeing urban masses are described in terms frequently applied to pre-nuclear America's racial and social underclasses. Brelis refers to refugees from Southern California as "escapees" (63), and an unnamed Nevada official refers to this same group as "a swarm of human locusts [who would] pick the valley clean of food, medical supplies, and other goods" (qtd. in Stonier 95; see also Cousins 174 and Fleming, 30 September 1961 15). In Randall's fictional account, the refugees are infected by physical frailty and psychological paralysis; they are a drag on the host economy's meager resources and are soon turned against by the unaffected town to which they have fled (137). For unwilling hosts, the vision was of neither orderly procession nor stalled traffic but out-of-control, interracial mobs, overrunning outlying areas (McEnaney 49). As with the prospect of interracial conflict but also of interracial "mingling" enabled by the public shelter, the integration of white suburbs, through either federally mandated billeting of urban refugees or—more likely—post-nuclear chaos, itself constituted a form of nuclear "apocalypse" to certain hysterical whites, even as sheltering and evacuation plans were designed with the minimizing of nuclear disaster in mind. Due to the complexities and tragic misfortunes of race relations in pre-attack America's 400-year history, acknowledging the presence of disgruntled, disenfranchised citizens in the post-nuclear landscape is as fraught with unfounded assumptions and unanswered questions as are those attempts to ignore or failures to account for this same vital presence.

Throughout this discussion, I have tracked the terms of nuclear preparedness and racial injustice as they crossed the political spectrum. Robinson's comment earlier in this Introduction, for instance—regarding "jungle behavior"—is likely to have disconcerted anyone sensitive enough to wish a less racist expression had been chosen. When Otto Klineberg, hailed for providing scientific testimony during *Brown v. Board of Education*, makes his own post-nuclear forecast, he also resorts to phrasing whose connotations are hard to ignore. In the shelter, says Klineberg, "We may speak of social regression when a whole community behaves in a manner characteristic of primitive, archaic, even animal-like existence, almost to the point of creating a Hobbesian war of all against all" (qtd. in Vestermark 72). Reading Klineberg, nuclear scenarist S. D. Vestermark observes that "in this passage, the primal jungle emerges clearly" (73). Ironically, Robinson and Klineberg, writing from avowedly anti-nuclear positions, do their utmost to make nuclear reality look as dreadful as possible through terminology that has a degrading effect on the human figures in their forecasts but that has already had an equally degrading effect on the African American members of their own pre-nuclear society. Yet more ironically, it is often the apologists for nuclear confrontation who veer away from such dire and diminishing descriptions, opting to see the good in present-day humanity across the board and expressing confidence that such good behavior will prevail in the shelter and recovery settings. While it is the epitome of racist logic to dissuade fellow-Americans from nuclear nihilism by threatening that once in shelters we would all become "as the Negro," it is only sensible to argue that following nuclear war America's upper classes would know the deprivations and hardships of their impoverished fellow-citizens of color so thoroughly that that cherished and elusive American "institution"—democracy—would exist for the first time.

CONCLUSION: WHERE WOULD HARLEM BE?

Perhaps sensing the unspoken yet inevitable role for which they were destined, urban African Americans ignored requests to gear up for civil defense in droves (see Grossman 98, McEnaney 138–39). Yet as McEnaney points out, "if black citizens represented an intractable mobilization problem, then so did whites, for they, too, failed to volunteer to the FCDA's satisfaction. In fact, it seems that the obstacles to black participation did not differ dramatically from those which affected white participation" (140). Given these findings, it is curious that black citizens continued to be *perceived* as that much more "immobile" than whites: this perception certainly followed from racist stereotypes about "laziness" and "shiftlessness" but also reflected the rules of the enduring social order that made not only the atomic threat but also atomic preparedness and survival in so many ways a "white thing."

If CD propaganda all but promised that the proper training made one immune to nuclear attack, the opposite equation—indifference to civil defense was "asking for it"—was also implied: In an early interview conducted by the well-known African American journalist Lerone Bennett Jr., a white Atlanta official used frightening statistics and "vigorous arm thrusts" to scare up civil defense involvement. While the official makes no direct link between imminent mass destruction and indifference to civil defense in Atlanta's black neighborhoods, this link is implied throughout, such that the bombs aimed at "Auburn Avenue" and the "West Side" (two of Atlanta's predominantly African American neighborhoods) would be blacks' own fault for failing to join up ("Auburn Ave."). Countering misperceptions of African American disconnect to nuclear preparedness, New Jersey NAACP official Samuel A. Williams reminded Executive Secretary Walter White that African Americans served the public sector as admirably and essentially as did whites, that black "civil service employees such as teachers, fireman, policemen are pledged to civilian defense. Also doctors and nurses are pledged to the same thing." He added that, "I would rather see Negroes in every branch of this defense program, working to see that there is no discrimination in any form," not to mention "effectively harass[ing] Mr. Millard Caldwell and also Pres. Truman who made this very inept appointment" (qtd. in Grossman 97). These same citizens would have been sure to trouble the visions of doomsday forecasters and survival planners who failed on almost every occasion to picture African Americans as executive participants in the acts of post-nuclear recovery and reconstruction that became part of their official prescriptions.

In one of his remarkable "Simple" stories for the *Chicago Defender*, Langston Hughes's protagonist Jesse B. Semple ruminates over the frightening prospect of the notoriously racist Mississippi Senator Theodore G. Bilbo in possession of an atomic bomb. "Then where would Harlem be?" Simple asks, and his faithful drinking buddy answers, "Nowhere" ("Simple and the Atom Bomb.") Despite the comic tones of the exchange, Hughes voices here the deep-seated fears of a large sector of his readership, who had little trouble imagining racist white Americans turning the bomb upon fellow-citizens of color and literally wiping their historic neighborhoods off the map. As discussed throughout, the discursive absenting of African Americans from the nuclear policy-making of postwar bureaucrats repeats the violence of this frightening image on a less dramatic but no less significant scale. If Harlem was "nowhere" on the drawing boards of professional visionaries of nuclear survival, it was that much more likely to be turned into "nowhere" on annihilation day, due to its exposure and abandonment by national leadership during the preparedness period. It is little wonder that African Americans came to absent themselves from discussions of this matter or were considered by these same policymakers to care little about the nuclear issue.

Eugene Gordon was another columnist for the black weeklies, less famous than Hughes but equally talented and equally thoughtful about African American survival of a nuclear holocaust. While he wrote several columns on the subject, he produced as well an unfinished short story, "Fallout Shelter," where he raised many of the issues of import in this introduction and across this project as a whole: researching the piece, Gordon quotes the Reverend Angus Dun, who told the United Press International (UPI) wire service that private shelters were "immoral, unjust, and contrary to the national interest," because, in Gordon's phrasing, they would "put the question—the very fact—of survival on a selfish basis, discriminating against millions who cannot build shelters" ("Fallout Shelter" 1). Also making notes on Fr. L. C. McHugh, who famously advocated armed defense of one's shelter as allowable Christian behavior, Gordon reached the conclusion that a nuclear war, for the likes of

McHugh and his adherents, would be "a good way to get rid of undesirables, first chance we've ever had to do it without ourselves committing genocide" ("Fallout Shelter" 1). The "we" in the preceding quote is the white racist majority, whose perspective Gordon adopts in the opening scenes of the extant tale, set not this time in Harlem or even Manhattan but the upstate village of Newburgh, where, Gordon reports, an "official anti-Negro policy" was at that time in place.

As the white characters gather to discuss a possible community shelter, some espouse liberal views about a building large enough to include "rich and poor" but are soon interrupted: "I've been thinking that here, for the first time, America, *white protestant America*, has a chance to *cleanse* itself. To—." This hysterical character dismisses references to the UN convention on genocide, noting that this group is "ninety percent blacks, browns, and yellows—inferiors." In sum, shelter exclusions would enable white America to correct the mistakes of "Aug. 21, 1619," the day that the first European colonizers bought twenty slaves from the Dutch: "for the first time since then we've got a chance to build an America we should've built from the outset" ("Fallout Shelter" 4). For many white-authored texts to be discussed in this study, especially those in the time-traveling vein of science fiction, the bomb will be detonated to transport main characters to a setting indistinguishable from this whites-only version of the settlement-era past.

Yet another townsperson wonders "who'll do the dirty hard work when they come up [from the shelter following war] if they let all the Negroes be killed off," while another predicts that "unfortunately for us, there'll be black survivors" ("Fallout Shelter" 5). A debate erupts regarding who will be "the fittest" in a post-shelter death struggle between blacks and whites, and in a dramatic conversion, a one-time proponent of equal sheltering decides that if blacks are actually likely to "take possession of what's left in the world," then exclusion is a must: "If we go about this thing *now* the way we ought to, they *won't* survive like that [resentful and in force]. They'll be wiped out" ("Fallout Shelter" 6). Though the surviving pages of Gordon's notes move on to other issues—arms-bearing for each shelteree and a full-fledged narrative involving various named characters—the brief dialogue in this opening segment already broaches many of the important issues to be examined in this book: the location of African Americans on atomic D-day, master-servant roles (or interracial fights to the death) during post-atomic recovery, and competing visions of a post-atomic tomorrow.

Hughes's and Gordon's trenchant views on the location of African Americans at the moment of nuclear impact, despite their disparity in tone and content, both work to counter the white authorial take on the subject, such as that by satirist (and fellow-New Yorker) Jules Feiffer, who ultimately tosses off the role of the militant black maid Millie in his farcical romance *Crawling*

Arnold (1961). Millie informs a guest of her employers the Enterprises that she was caught on TV recently "rioting" at the UN and as a civil defense drill commences, she commandeers the family's fallout shelter and calls from within, "Let the white imperialists wipe each other out!" (54). Yet the meaning of shelter segregation—or shelter exclusion—is part of the joke here; Millie is portrayed as a complainer who is first insulted by wealthy Mr. Enterprise's offer to build her a separate shelter, then insulted by the prospect of having to share one with the family. To be sure, the pious refrain of the sappy visiting social worker—about her "great regard for the aspirations of your people" (50)—is also mocked. Yet finally it is Miss Sympathy's gradualist view—that we must "work . . . to reform laws [be they related to preparedness drills, acceptable adult behavior, or the assertion of civil rights] while continuing to *obey* them" (54), that "without those rules we'd have anarchy" (56)—that is endorsed by the play as a whole.

Millie's complaint is thematically and physically sidelined to make way for the romance between Miss Sympathy and the Enterprises' adult son: though Arnold's perverse crawling behavior is likened more than once to Millie's equally unorthodox and ungrateful militancy, the couple's flirtatious dialogue dominates the plot. Arnold is cured of his regressive tendencies by initiating sexual contact with Miss Sympathy (undressing her) as the curtain falls, while Millie has failed to accept and adapt. Notably, she is obscured behind the shelter door when she makes her anti-imperialist declaration, and the entire shelter sequence takes place off-stage. In fact it is Mrs. Enterprise who makes Millie's manifesto (also from off-stage) for the rest of the group, since Millie's own voice has become muffled behind the door. The last word regarding her comes from Mr. Enterprise, who informs his wife that she should "tell her to go to hell" (55).

All of what follows here explores the complex relationship of African Americans to the atom bomb in postwar America, their dynamic and various positions "on" the bomb that ran the gamut from "nowhere" (again, most often in depictions by white authors) to profoundly implicated in and committed to a peaceful and permanent resolution to the nuclear threat. In the first few decades of the atomic era, African Americans, both leading individuals within their ranks and as a likeminded class, drew closer to and farther from the bomb as the surrounding context—including the deepening cold war, the growing civil rights movement, and the shift from integrationist to separatist points of view—changed around them and around all Americans. The story told in this book is thus made up of actions and reactions; of subtle nuances, divided loyalties, and difficult dilemmas; and yet most often of the fruitful and productive give-and-take of two causes—nuclear disarmament and civil rights—that shared many features, strengthened each other rhetorically, and saw great success in this era.

As noted above, white authors of survival fiction and nonfiction depicted African American characters almost always as "elsewhere" to the nuclear threat, a term McKittrick and Woods use in their own work and read as part of a "spatial practice that . . . erases or obscures the daily struggles of particular communities" (4). In response, African American intellectuals, journalists, artists, and novelists throughout the postwar era knew that it was vital to locate oneself on the prospect of nuclear disaster—planted firmly in opposition lest it ever become a reality. Notably, these authors' depictions of African Americans as either victims of politicized spatial configuration (e.g., confined within substandard, endangered locations) or victorious claimants to their rightful turf in the atomic landscape (e.g., finding shelter where it is officially denied to them) function equally effectively as "protest literature" (see Trodd 224); they thus join the illustrious tradition of African American arts and letters aimed specifically at the winning of civil rights in postwar America.

PROJECT OUTLINE

"Reckoning Day" was chosen as the title for this project as an African American-inflected reference to the Second Coming, the end time at which millennia of injustice by human against human are to be rectified by divine judgment. African Americans and other oppressed groups in the western tradition have embraced the Christian doctrine of final reckoning as a consolation for centuries of oppression suffered at the hands of exploiters; narratives of deferred but inevitable divine retribution can help a beleaguered people survive the excruciating trials of earthly life. As already indicated, white text-makers of the postwar period envisioned the cleansing fires of atomic catastrophe as the key to urban renewal and the mass suburbanization of the American landscape; to cover fears of physical and social leveling, democracy at last and by total force, threatened by the bomb, these writers did their best to negate the survival of African Americans (or at least the survival of African American dissent) in their numerous visual and verbal omissions.

Yet African American authors returned the joust, as when Langston Hughes's Simple satirically dreamed of a bomb that would not penetrate dark skin ("Simple Supposes") and John Oliver Killens read the bomb with bitter seriousness as exemplifying the imminent fall of the white West. Despite their diverse approaches, both Hughes and Killens envision a bomb guided by cosmic forces against oppressor classes whose demise clears the way for the ascent of long-beleaguered African Americans. Much more often, however, African American intellectuals and civil rights leaders took a resolutely pacifist stand, as when both Lorraine Hansberry and Martin Luther King Jr. argued that the bomb was so dreadful a force *not* to be reckoned with that it must force a reckoning, a permanent reconciliation, amongst warring nations on earth and between warring racial groups in the US. Thus, both pacifists such as Hansberry and King and hawkish nuclear scenarists throughout the cold war era deployed the bomb in realization of their complex visions of a "better tomorrow," visions that often involved the vexing problem of (and solutions to) race relations. Yet these deployments varied enormously in their depictions, purposes, and results, and the remarkable spectrum of race-inflected responses to the bomb in the postwar era is the subject of this book.

In this book's subtitle, I reference the importance of "place" in this context—as discussed earlier, the hierarchy of social positions in the postwar US that correlated so thoroughly with the physical locations (inner city versus far-flung suburb, high-rise tenement versus family bomb shelter) thought essential to endangerment or safety from the atomic threat. Beyond the sociodemographic aspects of place, to which I will return throughout the chapters, placement as a political, intellectual, or aesthetic strategy will be even more germane to my argument. Thus I consider the location of African Americans—be these civil rights icons, leading intellectuals and artists, influential journalists, private citizens, or story characters in both white- and black-authored nuclear survival stories—with respect to the atomic threat. The realization that African Americans' physical location in overbuilt urban areas positioned them directly in the path of enemy attack caused many leading thinkers to take a position "on" the bomb, that is vigorously against the bomb, even as many others regarded the bomb as "elsewhere" to their main agenda—at best a side issue and at worst a dangerous distraction to the always-central struggle for civil rights. Often in what follows, I will examine the competing claims upon the time and energies of leading black intellectuals represented by the drive for racial equality and the escalating nuclear threat. Just as often, however, I will demonstrate the ways in which these causes came together in the words and actions of these same black leaders and writers, who argued forcefully for both nuclear disarmament and an integrated society with powerful rhetorics and artistic visions that hastened the advent of both.

Many black-authored depictions of survival in the face of (or in the aftermath of) nuclear catastrophe countered not only the realization of this very catastrophe but also myriad assumptions by white authors (and even some fantastical scenarios by black authors) that the nuclear threat and African Americans existed on separate planes of reality, that African Americans neither knew nor cared about the atomic threat and that their ignorance and indifference—or by contrast, their already thoroughly victimized position under the boot of white oppression—inexplicably shielded them from the bomb's historical significance and physical effects. By stressing both historical awareness and physical vulnerability, black writers on the bomb argued incontrovertibly for both their humanity and their equality with white fellow-citizens as equally threatened by nuclear proliferation and as equally committed to bearing witness to the permanent disarmament of the world's superpowers.

Broadly construed, texts of all kinds are spatial compositions, narrative landscapes, if you will, whereupon authors position characters and events in their essential places and move them into combinations that create tension, conflict, and resolution, not to mention reader interest and satisfaction. All of the textual landscapes examined in this study are of a specifically pre-, post-, or anti-nuclear variety, and characters traverse these nuclear spaces with their racial identities bearing almost always on their initial placement and ability to move (that is, both change locations and emotionally or intellectually change or grow). Too, the bomb itself is a textual element placed into a nuclear textual landscape for specific political and aesthetic purposes: some authors, such as dramatist Lorraine Hansberry (in her post-nuclear *What Use Are Flowers?*) and award-winning science fiction author Samuel Delany, set their atomic explosions decades or centuries in the narrative past, yet the vast majority in this survey will be sure to position their atomic explosions within their narrative landscapes, to maximize both the political impact and, we must add, the sensationalized entertainment value of their work. Doomsday authors Judith Merril, Pat Frank, and Robert Heinlein lead off with massive nuclear war in their survival tales, while the iconoclastic Philip Wylie treats readers to a full-scale, vividly rendered nuclear attack as a climax to his unforgettable *Tomorrow!*

Thus even staunch pacifists such as Hansberry and King may be seen to use their artistic license to "embrace" the bomb, to figure it centrally in their rhetorical statements and to regard it, ironically, as essential to their blueprints for better tomorrows. Not surprisingly—and not at all ironically—right-wing visionaries such as Robert Heinlein and fellow-SF writers, as well as white authors of atomic fiction and nonfiction of all kinds, positioned the bomb in direct opposition to the "tomorrow" of racial equality, so as to block the advance (or even the survival, or even the admittance) of characters of color within their post-nuclear textual landscapes. The films and popular music that come into view at the end of this project share a "pop" sensibility that centers the bomb in their textual landscapes most diversely of all: first and foremost atomic filmmakers and musical artists wanted audiences to get a "bang" out of their work. The sheer entertainment value of both the full-scale atomic conflagration and the delicately mixed atomic cocktail motivate the presence of the bomb in numerous popular works as often as does (progressive) political statement-making that, again due to film and music's pop context, meets almost always with mixed success.

Chapter 1 reconsiders many of the issues raised in this introduction, displayed in bestselling survivalist fiction of the period that politicizes, dramatizes, and indeed integrates the post-nuclear scenario in ways that the official nonfictions had only begun to do. Notable works in this canon, including

Judith Merril's *Shadow on the Hearth* (1950), Philip Wylie's *Tomorrow!* (1954), and Pat Frank's *Alas, Babylon* (1959) diversified their casts to a greater and greater degree as the civil rights decade of the 1950s wore on, in conjunction with and in a manner similar to "social problem" films of that period such as *Gentleman's Agreement* (1947), *Pinky* (1949), and *The Defiant Ones* (1958). Thus one observes issues of both racial integration and racial identity more and more prominently placed in white-authored '50s-era survivalist fiction. Notable, for instance, is Frank's post-catastrophe image of the disabled segregated drinking fountains in the southern town where the story is set. Following the bomb, implies Frank, neither black nor white will have access to traditional facilities— that is, to facilities that perpetuate shameful "traditions"—and so will have to work together to locate safe drinking sources. Yet even Frank's "employment" of black and Latino characters, as in the other works in this chapter, is mainly a post-nuclear broadening of their traditional "place" in the pre-nuclear land-scape, that of the faithful servant figure whose unstinting support of white life and liberty is more vital than ever. Frank's late-decade installment is as regret-table as its predecessors for positioning these characters, in their hearty servi-tude, as almost always "elsewhere" to the bomb's deleterious effects. To say the least, each story absents African Americans from executive roles at any point and from the scene itself as each narrative comes to a close. No matter how well-meaning an integrated survival tale may appear as it opens, as each wears on traditional cultural tendencies prevail, and characters of color appear in subordinate roles or disappear altogether in each story's final envisioning of a better tomorrow. Chapter 1 opens with brief discussion of George R. Stewart's survivalist parable, *Earth Abides* (1949), where a racially inflected "shiftlessness" settles on the largely white cast like a contagious disease following mass-scale catastrophe. This "social problem" is converted for the romanticized, mixed-race heroine into the traditionally feminine, traditionally servile "stoicism" that makes her little more than a rock of emotional support for her white husband.

Chapter 2 provides another look at white-authored, interracial nuclear sur-vival tales, this time bounded (and loosened) by the generic dictates of science fiction. As opposed to the realist narratives of chapter 1, SF has fantastic means at its disposal by which to position African Americans and the "problem" they represent at a safe distance from their white heroes and the journeys they un-dertake. In some stories (e.g., by popular pulp writers like J. T. McIntosh and Robert Sheckley) these heroes flee to distant planets to avoid the anxieties (in-duced by both nuclear brinksmanship and civil rights) of their earthly home, while others (e.g., by the iconic Heinlein) travel centuries into the future, meet up with a race of liberated, alien(ated) blacks, and deploy various tactics to return white characters and readers to the safety of the status quo, gradualist present. While the bomb blasts the races apart in a story by Ray Bradbury, it just as often throws them together—though almost always via racial allegory (yet another form of white flight; see also McKittrick and Woods 7), as a contest between nuclear-affected "mutants," frightening and dangerous to, but incontrovertibly born of and belonging to, the purer, pre-atomic race.

While the texts discussed in Chapter 1 evolved over time with ever-greater interest in exploring racial issues in the post-nuclear landscape, if anything the trend in the always-more-conservative world of SF went in reverse: Bradbury's early "The Other Foot" (1951) limits his black characters to dialect speech but provides them human dimensions and a legitimate platform for indignation, even revenge. Sheckley's mid-decade "Human Man's Burden" (1956) starkly racializes his clownish robot-servants, reproducing the devoted and harmless "darky" thirty years out of date. Heinlein's much later *Farnham's Freehold* (1964) presents a race of militant blacks as frightening as the nuclear war that empowered them, compounding for his white heroes and readers the horrendous impact of the bomb alone. If shamefaced whites turn up on black-owned Mars to beg forgiveness at the end of Bradbury's story, Heinlein's unapologetic right-wingers flee their encounter with the angry African descendants by handily leaping 2000 years back in time. Only Sheckley's hero happily totes his harmless racialized robots on his planet-hopping journey, and as discussed previously, the vast majority of these stories render difficult social problems harmless through the distancing mechanism of heavy-handed allegory.

Chapter 2 transitions at midpoint to the African American response, which it will investigate in-depth over the remainder of the book. Specifically, I read Ralph Ellison's canonical *Invisible Man* and Chester Himes's final installment in his Harlem detective series, *Plan B*, as belonging to the SF-related genre of Afro-Futurism, as they confront their readers with the prospect of a "tomorrow" pulled apart by cataclysmic racial conflict. Ellison's characters' most apocalyptic moments are also their most race-conscious and white-oppositional, while Himes's late-era vision of nuclear-threatened America seeks the same "critical distance" between the races as Heinlein did, and on the same terms: radicalized African Americans *are* whites' worst nightmare, though since time travel is not an option in this realist narrative, they are likely to fare much worse. The chapter concludes with consideration of the work of Samuel Delany, which belongs equally to the traditions of science fiction and Afro-Futurism and ties together numerous dilemmas considered but insufficiently solved earlier in the chapter.

Chapter 3 examines in detail the rich array of "angles" on the bomb presented by the postwar African American press. Once again issues of placement and position figure importantly, as the bomb appeared one week as a mere "sidebar" to more pressing civil rights or black-interest stories, one week as a front-page story or a topic of concern for the editorial staff, then for weeks or months disappeared entirely, as it did across the American media spectrum in periods of eased relations with the eastern bloc. Frequently, the black press itself took a position on the bomb starkly differentiated from that of the mainstream press: atomic-induced peace was not so "wonderful" if it meant the loss of thousands of war-era jobs, and diverse "American" setbacks in the arms race were construed as the embarrassing failures of the nation's white leadership, from which the black press could not but gain some measure of satisfaction. Focused on four prominent weeklies, the *Chicago Defender*, the *Pittsburgh Courier*, the *Baltimore Afro-American*, and the *New York Amsterdam News*, as well as other important African American newspapers and magazines across the nation, this chapter discusses the optimism, cynicism, and activism that characterized this body's response to atomic energy, weaponry, anxiety, and preparedness.

The African American press corps played a watchdog role whenever political appointments and preparedness campaigns—in addition to atomic industry employment trends—failed to account sufficiently for the black community. As also indicated in my reading of Hughes's columns, the bomb was an occasion for grim satire that flashed a bright light on white misbehavior in national and international arenas. Columnists smirked whenever the Soviets gained the upper hand, while editors angled cold war milestones such as the Sputnik launch and the Cuban Missile Crisis to intensify the significance of concurrent civil rights watersheds such as the Little Rock and Ole Miss integration stories. Though bomb coverage maintained an understandable "sidebar" status in the black press through much of the civil rights period, the diverse and meaningful treatment it did receive nicely undermines the notion that African Americans were only ever "elsewhere" with respect to the atomic threat.

Chapter 4 broadens this critique of African American indifference to the bomb, as the vigorous anti-nuclear statements penned by renowned civil rights leaders are examined for their remarkable rhetorical effects. Early advocates for peace and disarmament were W. E. B. Du Bois and Paul Robeson, joined shortly by the activist and organizer Bayard Rustin, the dramatist Lorraine Hansberry, and the all-around monumental Martin Luther King Jr., each of whom wrestled with this dual commitment and their sometimes divergent constituencies in remarkable ways. Though it may seem simple, sensible, and even unavoidable to take simultaneous positions against nuclear war and racial injustice, in fact these major figures sometimes found it as difficult as being in two places at the same time. Rustin especially campaigned staunchly against atomic weapons until the pressing needs of civil rights organizing forced him to choose the latter vocation over the former. While both King and Hansberry maintained their focus on both causes through their versatile written works, even King's dynamic and flexible metaphors found themselves occasionally stretched too thin to include racial equality and nuclear disarmament to equal effect. By the end of the 1960s, African American intellectuals of a more militant stripe took "anti-" and "post-" nuclear stances that differed from those of their integration-era predecessors: reading the bomb (and other shameful excesses of the postwar boom) as glaring indicators of the white West's corruption and decline, thinkers such as Elijah Muhammad and John Oliver Killens opposed the bomb not for the threat it posed but for its association with hateful whiteness, which they rejected in all permutations. Separatist writers such as Muhammad and Killens therefore envisioned "post" nuclear societies diametrically opposed to those dreamt up by the doomsday planners considered earlier: their survival scenarios included only liberated peoples of color, with all aspects of white society, from whites themselves to their wicked "tricknology," cast into the oblivion of yesterday.

Chapter 5 returns to the context of white authorship in nonfiction, fiction, and, for the first time, film, a medium that has in some respects been effectively "co-authored" by the presence of magnetic black leading men (and one leading lady) who confront their audiences with vital questions regarding interracial post-nuclear survival. All of these texts belong to this chapter because they involve the question of a "black Adam," or other African American male characters on hand when the issue of post-disaster regeneration arises. Though for centuries the white hysterical imaginary has feared black male sexuality as its own end-of-the-world-as-we-know-it, and though rampant sexual activity was often pictured in the postwar period as a direct first consequence of all-out nuclear war, numerous atomic survival narratives both serious and popular from the 1950s through the present day have cast attractive black actors as the capable, heroic "last man" to various blond, white, or otherwise racially off-limits "last women." Disappointingly, even very recent big-budget films perpetuate the centuries-old hysteria by barring the black lead sexual access to this "other" woman, planetary survival depend upon it though it may. In each text, the black hero may be said to sublimate his thwarted sexual longing into superheroic abilities that "charge" the scene in other ways—restoring lights, water, technological amenities, and food sources for himself and his white counterparts and figuring once more as the helpful-but-harmless servant figure from Chapter 1, who is now offering specifically sexual services that are rejected across the board. As these servant characters were positioned "elsewhere" to the bomb in white-authored survival fictions through their physical and emotional imperviousness to the bomb's effects, so here these heroes are cordoned off from the sexual prospects offered then rescinded in each narrative. Notably, the only black character located in these searches to engage in such restorative interracial sex post-disaster was a woman, Rosalind Cash, who starred opposite Charlton Heston in *The Omega Man*.

My conclusion draws upon a theme in African American popular music, including R&B, blues, gospel, and jazz, that interprets the atomic age from as many distinct positions as those adopted by African American journalists, artists, thinkers, writers, and filmmakers of the period. Whether the bomb is a likened to a sexy girl or God's saving power, whether it is loved as the perfect reply to the awful "Japs" or arrogant "Joe" (Stalin), or whether it is hated for making us "dig a hole" or "run, run, run like a son of a gun," the sentiments expressed in these songs reflect well upon this book's major themes and are audited in the Conclusion as a reprise. Specifically, I read the difference between songs that address the atomic threat literally and those that use it as little more than a trendy occasion to sing and swing; such diverse motivations replicate the tensions demonstrated by leading black intellectuals between callings, ideals, and interest groups throughout this book: occasionally, a song such as the Spirit of Memphis Quartet's "Atomic Telephone" effectively harmonizes vigorous anti-atomic sentiment with a devout Christian perspective. Meanwhile, more often we witness in these songs a contest between nuclear anxiety and diverse distractions from this: transporting faith in God, satiric humor about world politics, the chance to grab your "atomic baby" and dance the night away. As with the sermons, speeches, dramas, journalism, futuristic fiction, and film that shaped the African American response to the atomic threat throughout the postwar decades, so the popular music anticipates the dawn of atomic reckoning day with the diversity, passion, and promise that characterized America as a whole in that period.

"Extraordinarily Convenient Neighbors"

Servant-Savior-Savants in White-Authored Post-Nuclear Novels

In the introduction, I referred to a map positioned at the narrative moment of nuclear impact in Philip Wylie's *Tomorrow!*, which itself positioned the "Negro District" at the literal dead center of ground zero. This layout reflects the demographic realities of mid- and large-sized cities in the postwar period—an inner city inhabited mainly by persons of color surrounded by racially heterogeneous sections of commerce, industry, and, in the outlying neighborhoods, white residences—and reinforced the understanding during this period that should the bomb come, African Americans and other racial minorities would be the first, most severe, and most heavily represented among casualties. As World War II reached its highpoint, the second phase of the Great Migration drew African Americans by the tens of thousands from the poverty and hostility of the Jim Crow South to lucrative war-related jobs in the somewhat better integrated industrial North. Yet ironically, the war that had created this improving economic and political situation was abruptly concluded by a revolutionary class of weapons that now threatened these new arrivals to the great cities of the North along with all others who still lived and worked there.

As the ideological distinction between the new, modern, well-fortified, low-slung safety of the suburbs and the densely populated, rapidly declining core of the inner city sharpened in the postwar period, so those who remained there became doubly stigmatized: in the terrifying event of World War III, urban denizens were envisioned as both the mostly likely victims of nuclear annihilation and the hostile hordes of "escapees" (Brelis 63) from the blasted cityscape, hell-bent on commandeering the safe zones of white suburbia.

Anticipating the horror film zombies of later decades, which satirized both notions of post-apocalyptic survival and "the dawn of the dead" that is suburban existence (see Chapter 5), postwar African Americans were perceived by the hysterical white imaginary as both mortally threatened by nuclear conflagration and gruesomely rejuvenated by it, rising up to wreak vengeance on those who had done this to them—not the Soviet or Cuban enemy, but the white American scientists, generals, presidents, and suburban householders who developed or approved of these weapons in the first place. While white Americans may have used the atomic threat as an excuse to flee the racially heterogeneous urban centers they were in the process of vacating anyway, the bomb figured ironically as that which might blast these same racially marked undesirables into their restricted neighborhoods after all.

Such fears feed the racially inflected politics of place and space in the white-authored nuclear survival novels I examine here, each of which asks who is safely inside and who is dangerously exposed—and thus transformed into dangers themselves—when the bombs fall. Several of the authors discussed in this chapter enjoyed reputations additionally or even predominantly as writers of science fiction, yet each of the novels discussed in this chapter eschews the alternate-universe trappings and space-age hardware more characteristic of speculative fiction and opts instead for assiduously realist American backdrops to stories set not centuries but mere days or hours in the reader's future. While the nuclear threat is always the main theme (as are the attendant issues of civic-mindedness and nuclear preparedness), each story subtextually ponders the explosive potential of race, class, and gender relations in the struggle for post-nuclear survival, the social integrations and conflicts ignited by extreme circumstances and reflective of the challenges occurring in the historical environment that contextualized their origins. In the tradition of "social problem" films of the postwar era (such as *Pinky*, which explored racial conflict, and *Gentleman's Agreement*, which explored anti-Semitism), I classify these novels as "social problem" texts, to contrast with the more narrowly defined science fiction to be analyzed in Chapter 2.

While each of the novels considered here attempts a broadminded approach to class and racial difference, in each case this attempt is as half-enlightened and half-successful as that of the average social-problem film, limited as each was by the assumptions, misperceptions, and exclusionary definitions of the "happy ending" afflicting the postwar white mindset. Thus these doomsday novelists, in order to control the frightful prospects of nuclear-induced racial integration, depict African American characters not as gory victims or vengeful refugees but as the genial servant figures they had played in the media for decades, now essential to white survival and recovery following atomic war. All but the last of the texts discussed here will cast this savior figure as female, further diminishing the prospect of a threat and on one early occasion even transforming "mammy" into a romanticized, sexualized partner for the white protagonist and thus into the "mother" of a new race. As several film and media scholars have observed, after the storm of controversy generated by the racist characterizations in D. W. Griffith's *Birth of a Nation* (1915), film and literature from the 1920s through the '40s and television and advertising in the 1940s and '50s employed black figures in servant roles. The classic "toms" and "mammies" portrayed in foundational texts such as *Uncle Tom's Cabin* and *Gone with the Wind* influenced generations of media representation; examining kitsch collectibles from earlier decades and even recent reproductions, Patricia A. Turner notes that "[t]he most popular icons are those that contain safe, nonthreatening servile depictions of blacks or those that imply that inherent ineptness and imbecility will prevent the race from earning social and political parity" (12). Depending upon whether the genre in question was comedy or melodrama, the servant figures depicted in film and literature of the early twentieth century were inept, or sassy (in comic roles), or devoted, or treacherous (in melodrama). Often in melodramatic plots (*Birth of a Nation* being a paradigmatic example), "good" and "bad" (or, in another context, "house" and "field") servants were pitted against each other, by way of instructing disaffected African American audiences and ignorant northern whites in the wages of sin (see Bogle 11, 51). The post-apocalyptic narratives to be discussed here belong to the category of melodrama; instances of inept servitude are introduced for occasional comic relief, but primarily the service on display is dedicated, capable, and vital. In these works, black characters may hold a variety of positions before atomic D-Day but revert to roles of servitude in the survival scenarios that are the stories' main focus. Thus the atomic version of the "magical negro" tradition in popular representation functions in each instance as a servant-savior-savant; these characters exhibit terrific skills and rare knowledge that saves white lives following the bomb, yet they also remain subordinated to the white characters and central plotlines.

Many critics have analyzed the magical negro phenomenon in American culture; Krin Gabbard aptly describes "impossibly gifted black characters who only want to put their special powers at the service of attractive white people" (143), while Heather J. Hicks associates this phenomenon with "certain contemporary crises affecting white masculinity" (28). The preponderance of commentary on the magical negro is focused on films, and very recent ones at that, and while many egregious examples of magical-negro figures are located there (e.g., Michael Clarke Duncan's character in *The Green Mile* [1996] and Will Smith's in *The Legend of Bagger Vance* [2000]), they have been a feature of white-authored novels since Stowe's Uncle Tom (a saintly Christian Negro who miraculously saves Little Eva from drowning) and contribute significantly to the question of white survival of nuclear war in the postwar era. Specifically, black characters in this canon have the special power to prevail against nuclear holocaust when the author in question views the post-nuclear landscape as drastically reverted to primitive conditions, at which point the ancient folkways of a supposedly "primitive" people become "extraordinarily convenient" (Frank, *Alas Babylon* 139). Such characters maintain the well-being of white protagonists, using ingenuity and technical skill to restart the clock of civilization, yet few such servant figures are allowed to cross the threshold of modernity regained along with the whites. By contrast, those authors (such as Philip Wylie in *Tomorrow!*) who thought the bomb would thrust its survivors forward into a thoroughly reconstructed, ultra-modernized landscape of the future deployed devices by which to dispatch great numbers of African Americans at the point of impact, such that "tomorrow!" is always an overwhelmingly white proposition.

As various film scholars (e.g., Bogle 36; Harris, *From Mammies*; Manring 19, 31) have discerned the partially subversive yet partially recuperative nature of Hollywood servant characters, so the novels considered here attempt to advance a progressive thesis on race relations during and after nuclear catastrophe but only somewhat succeed: these white-authored depictions of blacks as saviors in some ways represent an empowering departure from the traditional disabling stereotypes and open the narratives containing them onto new territory (i.e., new in the 1950s) on the issue of racial equality. However, despite these figures' almost godlike properties (functions of both the "savior" role they play and the novels' apocalyptic context), they are rarely if ever released from their roles as servants: their talents and wisdom support the post-nuclear lifestyle (and enrich the narrative interest) of the white characters, while their own needs for such support are emphatically downplayed or, worse, denied through authorially mandated self-sacrifice.

Saidiya V. Hartman observes the phenomenon of "indebted servitude" (126) that characterized black-white labor relations since the end of the Civil War. Urged to keep in mind the "sacrifice" that had been made—the war itself—to win slaves their freedom, Hartman indicates that, in the one hundred years inaugurated by Reconstruction, black laborers were enjoined to spend their lives in compliant, poorly compensated service to former white masters. Hartman argues that "[t]he whip was not to be abandoned; rather, it was to be internalized" (140). Elsewhere, Michele Birnbaum discerns that the arena of inter-racial domestic service is fertile ground for feelings of friendship, romantic attachment, and erotic attraction that blur the distinction between service-purveyor and service-consumer and lead to exploitative, uncompensated transactions (17, 32). As Bogle helpfully phrases the situation, in film, "the servants were always around when the boss needed them. They were always ready to lend a helping hand when times were tough" (36). That servants were expected to lend or share their services, instead of name and receive a price for them, especially during the toughest time at all—the putative end of the world—is an assumption shared by these post-nuclear novels.

Significantly, Bogle observes that the servant figure's utter dependability was "used to reaffirm for a socially chaotic age a belief in life and the American

way of living itself" (36). Elsewhere, Thomas Cripps observes the "silent" figure of the Negro servant character and argues that this silence equals a sort of
stasis against the dynamics of white-oriented narrative movement, as well as
white lived experience: "[t]he white man's Negro on the screen [was] a tamed
image having little to do with changing reality. Black soldiers, labor organizers,
Pan-Africans, Zionists, cool cats, intellectuals, all the blacks who broke the old
molds in Northern ghettos, were unseen on the nation's screens" (115–16). Like
Bogle, Cripps notes that black actors functioned here—providing vital service
without uttering a line—to counterbalance and delineate white action; whether
such change be considered in terms of chaos (Bogle) or heroism (Cripps), the
frozen, enduring recurrence of black characterization was deemed vital to effectively showcasing and securing the white perspective. Most pertinent to my argument is James Snead's assessment: "Historical ambiguity requires some sense
of transhistorical certainty, and so blacks were as if ready-made for the task. . . .
[I]n films from King Vidor's 1929 *Hallelujah!* through Steven Spielberg's 1985
The Color Purple, blacks' character is sealed off from the history into which
whites have trapped them" (3). Krin Gabbard also observes, "As is so often
the case, black characters—magical or not—can be *in* the film but *outside* the
action" (156).

Emblematic of such an exclusion in the atomic context is an early scene in
Frank's *Alas, Babylon*, during which the protagonist Randy Bragg roams about
his large house and contemplates in alternating fashion his two most pressing, liberal-minded concerns: the atomic threat and the "Negro problem"—
specifically the state senate election he has recently lost to "Porky Logan, a gross
man whose vote could be bought for fifty bucks" (17), due to the Randy's out-
spoken if gradualist position in favor of integration. Thus Randy assumes the
role of the story's hero specifically for the singular stance he is willing to take
and the sacrifice it involves. Coming from a long line of illustrious politicians,
soldiers, and slave owners, Randy is the first "loser" in the family but represents
to the modern reader a refreshing break from dying traditions, an avatar of an
America of tomorrow, yet an America profoundly threatened by total destruction just as it begins to realize its most cherished democratic ideals.

Meanwhile, Randy's tendency to ruminate in two pastures—one containing past troubles (the lost election) and the other containing problems for the
immediate present (the escalating international conflict that provides the story's rising action)—keeps "the atomic" and "the African American" in separate
cognitive categories and confirms without challenging the damaging assumptions of this novel's original audience: that African Americans were less fellow-
citizens than a social "problem" like the atomic threat and that, confined to
the situation of *being* a problem, the significance of they themselves *having* a
problem—either with the bomb or with their second-class citizenship—was
never considered. As I will show throughout this discussion, white rendering
of black or ethnic nuclear-text characters almost always excludes them from the

history explosively unfolding around their white counterparts. Their imperviousness or obliviousness to the massive dangers that are the stories' primary themes removes them from the narrative action and from the very meaning of the bomb itself; they are, as Snead observes, "sealed off from the history into which whites have trapped them" (3). While they are sometimes drawn as physically or intellectually superior to the bomb's effects, freeing them to act more effectively than certain disabled or physically circumscribed white characters, they are primarily freed so as to serve and support. Their super-human qualities are simply dehumanizing, and their removal from history in these narratives reflects the wider reality of their absenting from the issues of nuclear preparedness and disarmament in postwar America.

PROLOGUE FROM THE LATE 1940S

Although the focus here is on three atomic survival narratives strewn across the 1950s, a decade marked by growing endangerment from nuclear war as well as growing enlightenment regarding the meaning and necessity of civil rights, I open with analysis of George R. Stewart's *Earth Abides*, published in 1949. Although earliest in the survey, its bold design not only includes but centralizes an interracial love story, while romantic attachment for the black characters in the later stories is de-emphasized or denied. Meanwhile, as we will see with the example of Rosalind Cash in the early-1970s film *The Omega Man* (Chapter 5), it is always more likely, as in Stewart's novel, that an interracial couple popularly represented will pair a white male with an African American female, not the other way around. Also notably, in *Earth Abides* traditional forms of black industry (making, building, and growing things) are not enthralled to the cause of white advancement at any point—and are notably missing from the main narrative altogether. Yet again, the romanticized heroine Em, while less a "mammy" than an Earth Mother figure, even the granddame of her tiny survivor community, is ever-expected to be stoical and self-sacrificing, to subordinate her emotional needs to those of her white husband.

The story tells of a vast epidemic that wipes out all but a hardy few and, significantly, leaves all vestiges of American infrastructure usable or functional for long duration. *Earth Abides* is thus not technically a nuclear doomsday tale, yet I include it here by way of enlarging the patterns discerned elsewhere in this chapter and extending these back to the late 1940s, when the traumas of Hiroshima, Nagasaki, and Russian detonation of an atomic bomb (also in 1949) were at their very freshest and when the rudimentary gains made by the civil rights movement intersect in a most curious manner with Stewart's vision. As Paul Boyer in his essential analysis of nuclear culture, *By the Bomb's Early Light*, argues that *Earth Abides* "is clearly a product of and comment upon the pervasive fears of the early atomic era" (262), so I will assume an analogy to nuclear catastrophe and pay special attention to the story's several African American characters.

Early in Stewart's story, the white protagonist Isherwood Williams tours by car the post-epidemic depopulated highways of America and encounters a small Negro collective made up of an older man, a pregnant woman, and a young boy, none of whom appear to be blood-related. They are lice-ridden and ragged, diffident in the face of Ish's questions and so oppressed by centuries of habit that they have not thought to vacate for finer digs than the ramshackle servants' quarters that it has always been their lot to occupy. Yet they tend "a luxuriant garden and a good corn-patch, and . . . a small field of cotton, although what in the world they expected to do with cotton [now that textile production has ceased] was more than Ish could figure out. . . . They had chickens in a pen, and some pigs" (63). Like the black servant characters located "outside the action" by Gabbard and other critics of twentieth-century film, these industrious Arkansans, says Ish, reap the earth's bounty because "they had merely carried on, doing the things that people in their world were supposed to do, and thus gaining a sense of security" (63). The narrative thus indicts this family for its naïve indifference to the radical changes that have befallen the rest of humankind, and Ish briefly considers exploiting their labors for his own gain: "'Here,' he reflected, 'I might be a king in a little way, if I remained. They would not like it, but from long habit they would, I think, accept the situation—they would raise vegetables and chickens and pigs for me, and I could soon have a cow or two. They would do all the work that I needed to have done'" (64). Wanderlust, not moral compunction, causes him to give up this offensive idea, and once back on the road, Ish contrasts his own situation to this group's, touching on the novel's key theme: "he began to think that the Negroes had really solved the situation better than he. He was living as a scavenger upon what was left of civilization; they, at least, were still living creatively, close to the land and in a stable situation, still raising most of what they needed" (64).

When Ish returns to the northern California neighborhood of his birth, he meets his future wife Em and establishes a tribe of well-meaning but minimally aspiring fellow-survivors. The dying art of "living creatively" is snuffed out by the group's overwhelming impulse to simply scavenge on—for decades—from the vast stockpiles of American ingenuity and prosperity that defined Stewart's late 1940s publication context. Since stores overflow with long-lasting canned goods and utilities are so gorgeously mechanized that they run unattended almost perpetually, it is a long while before even the lights and water go out and a longer while yet before the group will run out of food, clothing, and basic medical supplies. Stewart thus implicates the postwar glut of consumer goods for the mood of indifference and indolence that settles upon the group in the long aftermath of epidemic catastrophe; why indeed should anyone bother to innovate or return to the earth when the few remaining survivors can feast upon the already-existing fruits of mass production for decades to come? Yet at all points the hero does what he can to counter a race-inflected "shiftlessness" that is its own epidemic in the post-catastrophe context.

Shortly after she appears in the story as the dark-haired, deep-eyed heroine destined to become Ish's Eve, Em reveals her secret: "You looked at my hands and said they were nice. You never even noticed the blue in the half-moons" (129). Ish is stunned to realize what he should have seen all along, what in pre-epidemic times would have stood out immediately and disqualified Em as an object of sexual interest or at least marital prospects—the "brunette complexion, dark liquid eyes, full lips, white teeth, rich voice, and accepting temperament" (129) that evidently add up to Em's mixed-race identity. Ish has a good laugh about what-all this might have meant in olden times, then promptly commits to a life-long partnership with her. As their betrothal scene ends, Em is already being outfitted for the role of paragon of stoicism and fortitude she is destined to play. On this one occasion, when Ish is almost asked to forgive Em for her complicated racial background, "he . . . had been stronger than she" (130), while in all subsequent scenes, Em's superhuman aplomb repeatedly, thoroughly defines her.

Em's racial background is a non-issue in the remainder of this novel; aside from her one comment regarding "my people on the coast of Africa" (201), her minority status is never noted, let alone minded, by the all-white group she becomes part of, and when a visiting evil-doer leers at Em, it is recalled that she is the loveliest woman in the bunch, regardless of the darkness or lightness of her features. She is exactly as "shiftless" and "lazy"—and exactly as helplessly middle-class—as all of her white fellow-tribesmen and mixed-race children, such that her lack of initiative is neither singled out nor indicative of some "inferior" racial status. Stewart deserves credit for redrawing the lines of bigoted assumption in this manner, and yet Em is certainly minoritized to the degree that she is set apart in her superlative, allegorical role as "Mother of Nations" (297) and font of elemental wisdom. While more than once Ish regrets that "she has none of those things on which I used to count to so much—not education, not even high intelligence. She supplies no ideas" (298), yet her "greatness within and final affirmation" (298), her "courage and strength" (297), and the "rich loll of her voice [that] . . . seemed to cut in beneath the high-pitched almost yelping noises of the excited little crowd" (258) are prized by Ish and all the band as what sets her above and yet also sets her apart. It is Em who commissions the execution of the evil-doer in their midst, and Em who looks on with mute acceptance as various of her children succumb to untreatable afflictions. Finally it is this magnificent self-sufficiency that allows her to rest happily in her limited role as servant and sidekick; grieving over the loss of their fragile but intellectual son, Ish goes off alone, disregarding Em's need for a shoulder to lean on: "He did not worry about Em; she was stronger than he" (308), and even as she dies from some painful wasting disease late in the story "as it had always been, she was the one who comforted him" (332). In Stewart's novel the heroine-survivor Em and the Arkansas family met early on divide between them the roles of compliant support and remarkable (even miraculous) industry that will characterize the servant figures of the more traditionally defined atomic doomsday stories discussed in the remainder of this chapter.

A TRANSITIONAL DECADE

Judith Merril's *Shadow on the Hearth* (1950), Philip Wylie's *Tomorrow!* (1954), and Pat Frank's *Alas, Babylon* (1959), were published during the early, mid-, and late 1950s, respectively, coinciding with the increasingly tolerant, even progressive attitudes about race on display from one novel to the next, and coinciding as well with the increasingly visible and persuasive case made by African Americans for civil rights, especially school and housing desegregation, during this period. All three authors positioned themselves on the left, willing to risk popularity by politicizing their fiction and willing to oppose both nuclear brinksmanship and sexual and racial inequality in a markedly conservative era. In fact, all three succeeded in scaring their readership about the hazards of nuclear warfare (and the racial and class upheaval sure to follow) by succeeding with audiences as well as they did: Merril's and Wylie's novels attracted both science fiction and mainstream readerships; Wylie's spent several weeks at #5 on the *New York Times* bestseller list, and Merril's and Frank's were adapted for prestigious television "playhouse" series in the 1950s.[1] Frank's novel is featured today on many high school reading lists. In its own time *Alas, Babylon* received copious critical attention, even though Frank is the most obscure of the three authors now; Merril's and Wylie's novels received many fewer reviews, yet each has maintained a reputation, Merril in science fiction circles and Wylie among scholars of the mid-twentieth century who read his iconoclastic nonfiction with interest.[2]

Yet the question remains as to how successfully authorial politics transferred (even in a 1950s context) to literary output; while Merril, for instance, styled herself as an ultra-leftist deeply committed to women's sexual liberation, readers of her work (including *Shadow*) have considered it "sentimental . . . 'kitchen sink fiction,' practically devoid of character and pitched at 'a perpetual emotional screech'" (Atkins, quoting Morgan, 188). A devoted fan base of mainly SF readers refers to her with the loaded honorific "the little mother of science fiction;" this base regards *Shadow on the Hearth* as by far her best novel, yet it was written off in the *New York Times* as an implausible "chintzy account" (Poore 15 June 1950). Wylie, who like Merril saw himself as a radical, opposed primarily to the orthodoxies and hypocrisies of the Right, was castigated by feminists and other leftists for his attack on women (figured as acquisitive, controlling "Moms") in his bestselling, era-defining *Generation of*

Vipers (1942), and Momist characters abound in *Tomorrow!*. Frank and Merril were accused of creating characters in their atomic novels so fortuitously supported through their nuclear travails that "we wonder if [*Alas, Babylon*'s characters] are in Heaven or in Hell" ("Briefly Noted"). Despite the many progressive gestures in each story, likely missed by original readers but instructively in view today, in all three cases the conservative tendency of the times reasserted its influence by the final pages—that as the moment of resolution approaches, each narrative reverses itself on both the horrors of the atomic nightmare realized and the urgency of the issue of racial equality.

MERRIL'S MAGICAL ETHNICS

Judith Merril's post-nuclear *Shadow on the Hearth* in fact contains no African American characters, yet it presents an intriguing array of ethnic figures who support and sustain the white suburbanite Gladys Mitchell and her two daughters during their tedious, carefully confined days immediately following an atomic bombing. Because it appeared in the early years of the atomic age, Merril's novel betrays a rudimentary sense of the pervasiveness and lethality of "radiations;" in the story, therefore, who goes out and who stays in during the danger period are vital questions that bear on the novel's class and racial themes. Significantly, the story's main ethnic character—a domestic named Veda Klopak, whose vague central European background and sound health following a dose of fallout gets her branded a "saboteur"—is often read, especially by hastily processing undergraduates, as the traditional black maid. This misperception is aided by several factors, beginning with Veda's servant role and her residence in a dismal East Bronx tenement building, where she eccentrically wraps herself in warm blankets and stuffs "old stockings" (2) into the chinks around her door to sweat out a fever that befalls her just as the bombs strike. Situating Veda in the servant-savior role that I contend is typical for African American characters in this genre, we note that it is her "backward" folk remedy that not only saves her own life but Gladys's: it is borne out later in the narrative that, had Veda made it to work that day, Gladys would have been freed to attend a luncheon instead of forced to stay home, in the basement, doing laundry at the moment of the blast.

When she is well enough to venture north to the Westchester County suburb where Gladys and her daughters await her help and moral support, Veda appears in the hostile escort of two "white" police officers (they are dressed head-to-toe in pristine hazmat suits), her "[un]braided hair . . . dangl[ing] in stiff iron-gray waves" (88), her costume a ridiculous set of overalls and "cheap straw scuffs" (88) that reinforces her initial image as backward, "country," and for our students, black. Frightened and confused until this moment, Gladys speaks defiantly to the accusing officers; she gains strength in response to Veda's helplessness, though we see that in her weakness Veda is simply continuing to provide vital service to her mistress. Despite the seriousness of the situation, the episode's primary function is comic relief; Gladys and her elder daughter Barbara engage in a bit of slapstick about who has the notepad with necessary information, to the amusement of the two waiting authorities, and Veda's disheveled appearance and disoriented manner frame her as the clown. More comical yet (and most misleading of all) is this character's persistent use of a distinctly black dialect of speech (see also Atkins 191). Evidently, Merril was unable (or uninterested) to script a Russian or Polish accent, so settled for the typical dialogic tags of the unassuming black servant, like "jest" (for "just") "fer," "Missus," and "yestiddy." She is readable, therefore, as the story's single "black" character, even though her vaguely East-European origins will align her with the story's token Jew, Dr. Levy, elsewhere in the story.

As will be the case for black characters in other novels in this genre, Veda is "outside" the bomb and its significance in ways that empower but also dehumanize her, not to mention jeopardize the author's already flickering attempt to tell a scientifically accurate story. Evidently, the extraordinarily tight seal achieved in her inner city bedroom the morning of the bomb has provided Veda a sort of permanent immunity against its deleterious effects. She insists on tasting food for the family that might have become spoiled or contaminated after the blast (132) and is the only character in the novel—save Gladys's equally miraculously spared husband Jon[3]—to spend long intervals outside during the danger period (always on errands for Gladys and her family) without harmful repercussions. In fact, she is the only character, aside from Jon and Dr. Levy, to spend any time outside at all; Gladys and the girls are trapped in the house for almost the entire novel, while the patrolmen and technicians who visit are always zipped tightly inside their protective coatings. Thus, Veda is not only physically outside for much of the novel—i.e., exposed to radiation contamination in the service of her suburban family—but mysteriously "outside" of the toll ordinarily taken by radioactive fallout on human flesh. Her emotional strength and crude manner of speech translate into a bodily tough-hidedness that makes her half-animal, half-god, and impermeable to atomic effects. She is thus reminiscent of the implausibly strong black women analyzed by Trudier Harris: "These suprahuman female characters have been denied the 'luxuries' of failure, nervous breakdowns, leisured existences, or anything else that would suggest that they are complex, multidimensional characters" (*Saints* 12). Yet despite her hearty presence at novel's end and the family's devoted interest in her throughout the story, Veda's extended absences from the suburban home setting also mean that she is simply left out as much of the plot unfolds—that is, as a minor and thus largely expendable character. At one point, the family faces the prospect of evacuation and is informed that Veda's will be a specifically segregated fate: despite Gladys's protestations, she and her family will enjoy the uncontaminated safety of an upstate resort, while Veda is destined for the "detention camp" (204).

Not surprisingly, Veda's blood test late in the story shows normal values and type O blood; her "universal donor" status reinforces her role as not only servant but healer to all and echoes an inspired bit of subplot: reversing the typical perception (and likely outcome) of urban mortality distribution in the wake of the bomb, it is announced on the radio (neither phones nor electricity ever fail) that Manhattan's southern financial district is demolished, while the uptown neighborhoods of "125th Street" and "Washington Heights" have been converted into a hospital/decontamination center (35). In effect, Harlem has been commandeered as holding pen for the persistently contaminated and bomb-crazed survivors from Wall Street, who seek fresh blood in the suburban hinterlands and occasionally break through the *cordon sanitaire*. Gladys's hysterical neighbor Edie accuses Gladys of "want[ing] to let people out to spread radiation disease everywhere" (35); is it simply the silly neighbor's or the narrative's own viewpoint that radiation is spread like a contagious disease and that in the nuclear aftermath, Harlem would have to hold the line at all costs? On the topic of the racial *cordon sanitaire*, we learn later that Veda's blood is after all not necessary for transfusion into the veins of little Ginny, Gladys's younger daughter and the sickest character in the novel. Her mother's blood type matches the little girl's, and Veda is designated as donor for the ailing Dr. Levy, keeping with mid-century prohibitions against racial intermingling through blood donation. While Veda, for the reasons considered above, is readable as the novel's "black" character, she is equally discernible as "Jewish" or at least in league with this other ethnic figure due to their shared ancestry in north central Europe and to their both being branded as "reds" by local authorities; we recall, of course, that Veda's possible sentence to the detention camp at the end of the story not only segregates her in racial terms but figures her as both enemy subversive and Holocaust victim.

Developing the Jewish stereotype further, Dr. Levy is both a liberal pacifist and an intellectual, yet departs from type by being neither a money-oriented businessman nor an ineffectual nebbish. Holed up in the family basement when the authorities come canvassing, Dr. Levy corrects a leaky gas pipe and restores the family's hot water supply; later welcomed upstairs, he fends off an intruder and masterminds the bathroom blood lab that allows Gladys to determine whether or not Ginny has radiation poisoning. Tagged by Gladys with the suggestive pet-name Mr. Fixit, he is an obvious love interest should Jon never return[4] and easily bests his rival, a blustering block warden named Jim Turner. As opposed to the impervious Veda, Dr. Levy enjoys the authentically human status of radiation susceptibility, induced while leading his class on a fieldtrip during atomic attack. While Gladys's daughter Barbara, one of Dr. Levy's students, was also on this trip, she suffers no ill effects; their diverging physical predicaments mean that Barbara, to protect her health, must remain within the house until radiation danger passes, while Dr. Levy, who is already seemingly doomed, may spend as much time outside as he needs to. Like Veda then, Dr. Levy serves the Mitchell family by traveling outside at their behest—less often to run errands than to scout around and report back on the bigger picture, providing a service not only to the family but to the house-bound reader as well. While his fate is unresolved by novel's end, it is likely that, fortified by Veda's omnipotent blood, he will recover as miraculously as several other lethally exposed figures in the novel.

If Veda is the character most embedded in her ethnicity and thus mostly clearly marked as "outside" to the bomb, Dr. Levy wears his ethnic background more lightly (with even his waspish first name, Garson, indicating his semi-assimilated status) and is accordingly more "inside" (subject to yet dramatically realized by) the bomb. A final ethnic character, the dashing Dr. Spinelli, reinforces this pattern by being the most lightly coated by ethnic trappings of all—his soft, Italian last name seems almost an accident—and therefore more inside the narrative inner circle of white, suburban safety than all his ethnic counterparts. He is one of the white-suited technicians making periodic visits to Gladys's front door, yet acting as a foil to the arrogant Jim Turner. Like the other "whites" in the story, he has no natural tolerance for atomic fallout, so always wears a safety suit outside, but is helped in and out of this by the appealing Barbara whenever his visits extend beyond the normal time limits. Despite the more than ten years separating them, Pete and Barbara are a made match; while he is a "savior" figure in the story and functioning during the nuclear crisis as a public "servant," he is no servant figure (despite his ethnic designation) but a great catch for the elder daughter and thus fully included in the rapidly restoring family aggregate.

Although the effect seems entirely unintentional, Merril wrote a post-apocalyptic novel featuring female heroes that is ultimately as tedious and tightly circumscribed as women's lives actually were fifty years ago.[5] In classic devoted-housewife fashion, Gladys is so obsessed with clean laundry that she foregoes an important chance to lunch with some new friends the day of the attack and admits to being herself so utterly "outside" the bomb that she, a habitual non-reader of the papers, had no idea things had gotten so bad. Post-blast, she clings pathetically to her feminine wiles (hair-combing, lipstick-wearing) and her reliance on the absent Jon for *everything*, even now that a new set of behaviors is clearly in order. Long passages of dialogue in the novel (spoken mainly by the female characters) are circular, pressured, and pointless; whether she knew it or not, Merril's women are exemplary of the feminine-mystique victims so marvelously dissected by Betty Friedan a decade later. Yet their boring lives, while fascinating from a feminist standpoint, are simply boring from a literary one; without the emissaries from the outside—many of these ethnic in origin—arriving on a regular basis to enliven the perfect tedium of these women's homebound existence, this novel would be almost unreadable today. While many of these visitors (especially the male ones) threaten the women's well-being—Jim Turner is the classic predator, and even each opening of the door raised the indoor level of "radiations" to some degree—they are vital to these trapped women in many other ways and, again, to the reader as well. If even the falling of an atom bomb was not enough to get Gladys out of the house, it indeed opened the door to the wider world and allowed her the chance to know and recognize her utter dependence upon her ethnic New York neighbors. Meanwhile, though the ethnic men serve best as potential love interests for these kept women and are thus rewarded with survival and inclusion, the ethnic female in the narrative, whose clownish appearance and "black" dialect mark her not only as ethnic but "raced" in distinctive ways, is dispatched by white authorities at novel's end and had been largely written off by a countervailing white authorial viewpoint from the very beginning.

Wylie's Whites-Only "Tomorrow"

The only black character in Philip Wylie's densely populated *Tomorrow!* is yet another servant-savior-savant—Alice Groves, a nurse and hospital administrator whose clever dealings with white patrons before "X-Day" ensure the financial solvency of the story's black infirmary and whose deftly applied surgical skills in the immediate aftermath mark her as one of the story's two heroines.[6] Yet in addition to filling the typical savior role, she is a nicely dimensionalized character, as are most in Wiley's engaging cast—attractive, plucky, and manipulative of white power as it suits her needs, less a mother figure than a fun big sister to one of the novel's central white children, who is separated from her family on the day the bomb strikes. Mayhem ensues at the Infirmary that afternoon: "Alice . . . listened to the soughing of the fire wind and watched the jitterbug reflection on the painted wall, felt the tremor in the floors and listened intently to the groan that came up from the hot streets" as she prepares a needle for surgery (321) but interrupts herself to admit Minerva Sloan, the town's wealthiest woman and the Infirmary's white patroness, who is passed out in the street with a broken leg. While Minerva had slipped out from under Alice's attempt to rename the infirmary in her honor, here she is forced to "integrate" the hospital, having her life saved in the process. Meanwhile, it is significant that in the nuclear scenario, institutions once serving black needs are forced to turn their attention to whites, while no parallel scene—of a white hospital opening its doors to black casualties—is depicted.

Alice's striking personal qualities and accompanying financial wherewithal position her "outside" of ground zero (the Negro District) on X-Day; while she may in fact have had an apartment in the ill-fated District, she is shopping with a few fellow-nurses in the integrated commercial center on the other side of the river when the bomb hits, then makes her way to the Infirmary, well north of the 2000-yard radius that Wiley designates as hardest hit. As the novel is a vigorous polemic against the evils of overly concentrated urban development, Wiley gives Alice the brains and good fortune to shop and work outside the zone of total destruction, of course having himself already positioned the shops, the Infirmary, and many of his other favorite landmarks in the sensibly far-flung outer circles of his twin cities, River City and Green Prairie. It is the case, however, that Alice's countless nameless counterparts, the many "Negroes" occupying their "District" on X-day, are utterly destroyed; shortly before he meets his own fittingly horrible death, the insufferable Kit Sloan has, for himself, a utopian vision: "So they were on the move, on the way out of town, Polaks, Hunkies and Latwicks, Yids and Guineas and Micks. Not many Nigs. He even thought, racing past a bleeding family, there was a reason for the dearth of shines in the stampeded mobs: Niggertown was right at ground zero" (295).

Yet even as Wylie presents us with the accomplished Alice Groves and criticizes racist sentiment by making Kit a thoroughgoing ass, the author's politics with respect to racial and cultural mapping are a convoluted mix of progressivism and intolerance that calls such radical gestures into question. The novel is a preparedness parable, in which wise Green Prairie-ites stockpile, strengthen, and organize according to civil defense protocol during the pre-bomb period, ignoring the derisive chortling of their foolish neighbors to the north in River City. Not surprisingly, when the bomb hits, Green Prairie swings into cool-headed action while River Citizens simply lose their heads—and many other body parts—in a scene of total chaos. Wylie initially opposes Green Prairie's preparedness to River City's "isolationism" (48), a term attached to the self-serving, conservative mindset that has prevented the US from intervening in foreign conflicts unless its own economic interests were at stake.

As a domestic policy, "isolationism" is do-nothingism, a resistance to disrupting the status quo in order to avoid the "psychological contagion" of mass panic potentially set off by too much talk of doomsday. Sounding like Gladys's hysterical neighbor Edie, Wylie's newspaper editor Coley Borden asks, "If the nuts, the near-nuts, the neurotic, the criminal, the have-not people and the repressed minorities go haywire—why how many of the rest will *catch* it?" (120). But he is sharply informed by Henry Conner, the novel's middle-aged protagonist, that preparedness alleviates panic, does not spread it. Contrasting Coley's fear of the "have-not people" are the joiners attending CD meetings in Green Prairie as a democratic brotherhood of diverse classes (if not races) and professional backgrounds: If "most of the women were housewives" (the great leveling occupation for women), "men . . . employed in good positions" rubbed shoulders with "Ed Pratt . . . with his hat still on the back of head and a toothpick in his teeth" and "Joe Dennison, his broad backside propped on the windowsill and blue shirt open" (80). Ed and Joe bring to the table blue-collar skills (house-painting and bulldozing) as essential to the recovery effort as is the brain power to be supplied by Henry Conner and his upper-class cohort. In this patriotic commune, Wylie suggests, each will be called upon according to his abilities and each rewarded for his special contribution.

Later in the story, however, the two towns switch political personalities: River City's conservative "isolationism" gives way to a soft-hearted/soft-headed pacifism that is contrasted to Green Prairie's grasp of reality and common sense, virtues cultural conservatives like to reserve for themselves. Significantly, the river that divides these fictional towns also divides two states, which before the Civil War had been on opposite sides of the slavery question. Not surprisingly, it is the more conservative, southern town of Green Prairie that adopts preparedness wholesale, while the peaceniks to the north hide their heads in the sand. Also not surprisingly, the twin cities' entire Negro District is located just north of the river; almost like a magnet, it draws the bomb to a point of impact in the northern city, and the implicit criticism of the Negroes themselves—had blacks either stayed in scattered rural enclaves in the South or, crossing to freedom, not settled in a cluster so immediately to the north, they would have been spared their fate—is as difficult to ignore as it is entirely irrational.

Rationality is hardly essential to Wiley's vision, however; with the surgical precision of Alice Groves, the bomb spares all of his level-headed characters and picks off those whose behavior affront's Wiley's iconoclastic sensibilities: the pacifists and pinkos, the spineless men and the "Moms" who ruin them, snobs and racists like Kit, and bankers like his mother Minerva, whose influence has led to urban over-development and burnout. While Wiley might condemn both the racism and the urban development practices that have brought about the death of a large cast of unnamed Negroes, it is the case that these many characters remain nameless throughout—even his more tolerant white figures are always thinking favorably of "colored people" as an undifferentiated class (37, 94, 224)—and are therefore unable to be missed when the bomb strikes. Too, Wiley's own utopian vision, which closes off the novel, is of a new city built close to the ground and well spread out. Almost all of its former verticality is converted to one-story horizontality (never mind the logistics of building and occupying a single office building a mile wide), and green spaces, regularity, and "openness" are its hallmark features.

In other words, the vision provided is a thoroughly suburbanized one, within which there was simply no place for African Americans at this point in US history. Not surprisingly, Alice Groves, a minor character in the first place and easily forgotten in the radically depopulated final scenes, is nowhere to be found; ending as it does on such a redemptive note, the novel's implied thesis is that, for all its horrors, the bomb was the best thing that has ever happened to America—it was just the dose of strong medicine an ailing, overdeveloped society required—and that black characters, despite the role they may play as effective healers and saviors, have no place in this vision. Wylie's bomb is an example of what James Berger defines as an "apocalyptic cataclysm" that acts as "a means of banishing, symbolically obliterating, whatever the apocalyptic writer deems unacceptable, evil, or alien" (xv). It brings the "cleansing fire" that figuratively removes the morally decrepit amongst them but "bleaches" the face of the surviving American populace as well.[7]

FRANK'S HALF-HEARTED INTERRACIALISM

As Pat Frank's *Alas, Babylon* (1959) is the novel in this collection that treats most centrally and most consistently the issue of black survival in the post-nuclear setting, so it pushes the boundaries of racial equality further than any of the others—to the point of potentially alienating a large potential readership. If Stewart's northern California environs, Merril's New York, and Wylie's heart-of-America were each likely settings for a nuclear cautionary tale, for being so representative (if in such very different ways) of the US as a whole,[8] the north Florida locale of Frank's novel may have struck many as decidedly (yet also purposely) off-center to the action; likewise it might have attracted the specifically southern reader who expected southern authors (while not a Florida native, Frank spent many years there, including his final ones) to present the southern way of life (including its race relations) in traditionally conservative ways. However, Frank's novel is also the latest of the four considered; although only a few years separate the publication dates of the other novels, each year in this decade was a momentous one in civil rights history. The cumulative lesson absorbed at this point by well-traveled, well-read whites like Frank is evident in this story's relatively enlightened approach to the subject. Yet, of course, enlightenment is a relative, historically inflected proposition: what was daring fifty years ago appears to modern readers as a patronizing, ultimately limiting depiction of many of the black figures. While we may congratulate the novel's progressive steps, its several failures to fully integrate its post-nuclear utopia require our attention as well.

The novel's title is not only a quote from the Bible but from the sermons of a black preacher, Pastor Henry, overheard by the story's white protagonist, Randy Bragg, and his brother when they were boys. Listening to Preacher's lectures outside his ramshackle church, the boys develop a healthy respect for the apocalyptic perspective; growing up, "Alas, Babylon" became a code between them whenever a situation seemed hopeless. When early in the main action the adult Randy receives a telegram from his brother Mark, now a Strategic Air Command (SAC) officer in Omaha, with the words "Alas, Babylon," he understands that nuclear war is imminent and makes the preparations that will eventually save his extended family (including the Henrys who are his neighbors and employees) from post-nuclear destruction. Thus it is Preacher Henry's "long view"—his eye to the end of time, even should this occur tomorrow—that enables the heroism Randy eventually achieves.

Randy's devotion to Preacher and his family and his enlightening experience in the integrated ranks in Korea instill in him the respect for African Americans that doomed his integration-minded campaign for the state legislature months earlier. Meanwhile, he is independently wealthy and ultimately better off mulling his options in the Florida countryside, as opposed to losing his life at the hour of attack, as he would have if he had been working in the state capitol of Jacksonville, which is demolished along with all of the other major US cities. We recall that this same set of circumstances—the main white figure fortuitously sidelined on bomb day due to enmeshments with the serving class—opened Merril's *Shadow on the Hearth* as well.

In the days following "The Day," Randy desegregates his commune of neighbors and relatives despite the objections of the more bigoted among them (153). Randy's future father-in-law, who early on refers to African Americans as "dinges" (75), must function as "mechanic second class" (171) to Malachi Henry (Preacher's son) when the company's autos need repair and has his consciousness raised in the process. And despite the emotional trauma and newly restricted diet, Randy admits to himself after a few weeks of laboring alongside his black neighbors that "he was leaner and harder, and truthfully, felt better than before The Day" (181). As M. Keith Booker observes, "the book makes a point of arguing that racism has been rendered absurd in a the midst of such a crisis, when all right-thinking people need to work together" (87), and many months into their ordeal, the old social divides—and the city services that supported them—have dissolved. In town, Randy observes that "[t]here were two drinking fountains in Marines Park, one marked "White Only" and the other "Colored Only." Since neither worked, the signs were meaningless" (191). The meaninglessness of segregated drinking facilities, revealed to the town in the rocket-red glare of nuclear Armageddon, enables the spectacle of "Carleton Hawes . . . vice president of the county White Citizens Council" taking a drink from "a Negro's jug" (191). While the social order has not declined to such a degree that Randy knows the name and club affiliations of the generous "Negro," it is the case that the novel's "vision" of the post-nuclear world—to the degree that it is a vision, a fantasy come true—has its radical edge: recall that, where Wylie envisioned a racially, politically homogenous suburban new city in the wake of nuclear annihilation, Frank's post-bomb utopia features blacks and whites remaining within the ruined nuclear landscape yet sharing equally in its radical reconstruction.

In a dramatic later episode, Malachi drives a decoy truck that enables Randy and several other white characters to dispatch a band of deadly highwaymen. Seeing past the glimmer of hope represented by the interracial jug-sharing downtown, Malachi recognizes the persistence of racist sentiments on the highway and takes the wheel to provide an irresistible target to the violent marauders. Indeed, he has read his adversaries like a book and is fatally wounded in the take-down; his death results in the incapacitation of the last racist element in the narrative frame, furthering progress toward the inter-racial utopia Frank seems to be reaching for. We must note, however, that both Malachi and especially Preacher, despite their potentially subversive features, serve ultimately *as* servants, supporting the interests of white master figures around them. Acknowledging the somewhat enlightened qualities of Malachi, the Henrys otherwise abound in racial stereotypes, with Preacher as the classic Tom, his daughter (and Randy's maid) Missouri serving as the eternal Mammy, and her do-nothing, disaffected husband Two-Tone figuring as "the coon"—identified by Bogle (7–8) as another recurrent type in popular narrative.

The integrated Florida riverfront that is Frank's main setting is read nei-ther as a benefit to Negroes "lucky" enough to have landed in this superior neighborhood nor as a drawback to nearby property-owning whites. On the contrary, the friendly retired Admiral Hazzard, is pleased to snap up waterfront property at reduced rates, with the only drawback being "niggers for neighbors" (138). While the novel roundly condemns the racist sentiments of the white realtor who phrases the situation thus, it is the case that the Admiral capital-izes beautifully on his investment, at the Henrys' surely under-compensated expense:

> Sam Hazzard found that the Henrys were extraordinarily convenient
> neighbors. Malachi tended the grounds and helped design and build the
> dock. Two-Tone, when in the mood—broke and sober—worked in the
> grove. The Henry women cleaned, and did his laundry. Preacher Henry
> was the Admiral's private fishing guide, which meant that *the Admiral*
> consistently caught more and bigger bass than anyone on the Timucuan,
> and possibly all of Central Florida. (139, emphasis added)

Note the ways in which the Henrys' various labors are all for improving the leisure and "convenience" of the Admiral's life post-retirement. Especially sig-nificant is the arrangement by which Preacher's talents as a master fisherman, what McKittrick and Woods refer to as "black geographic knowledges" (7) are transferred to the Admiral to secure his catch (and his fame as a fisherman) in-stead of accruing in any way to Preacher's own benefit. Throughout the story, the Henrys will donate their skills and expertise—without complaint and with-out credit—to the cause of white well-being.

Following the blast, Randy approaches Malachi and announces matter-of-factly: "We don't have water in our house. I want to take up some pipe out of the grove and hook it on to the artesian system." Echoing the distinction made in *Earth Abides* between the "creative living" of the black Arkansas farmers and the shamefully ignorant Ish, Randy admits to white family members that he has no idea how execute this plan but that luckily "Malachi will know how to do it" (147).[9] At this fraught moment from *Alas, Babylon* Randy adopts the il-lusion of mastery of the situation, with Malachi and his brother enlisted only in supporting roles, and the Henrys have little choice but to play along. Later in the story, Preacher shares more of his knowledge of fishing to enable young, white, female Peyton Bragg to find fish that will bite, never receiving credit for the role he has played, since he is perceived, in his unofficial and inescapable servant capacity, to be only doing his job.

As their essential contribution to post-nuclear survival is persistently unacknowledged by the narrative's white viewpoint, so the black figures are depicted with marked regularity as was Veda in Merril's novel above—as oblivious and in some ways impervious to ("outside" of) the bomb's threat and the seriousness of the response it requires. Missouri, whom Randy calls by the childish name Mizzoo, cleans the Bragg household, "shuffling" as she goes (9) and fulfills various stereotypes with her jollity, size, and dialect speech. Early in the story, she polishes the floor by "dancing" with rags tied to her feet, her light manner as inappropriate to her eleventh-hour situation as was Gladys's ignorance of national news in *Shadow on the Hearth*. When she informs Randy that "nerves" have caused her to lose weight, it is not nuclear news reporting that makes her anxious but the demanding standards of another employer, Randy's future mother-in-law. (For a similar reading of Berenice in Carson McCullers's *A Member of the Wedding*, see P. Boyer 247.) Because Randy and Malachi were boyhood friends (even though Malachi now addresses Randy as "sir" and regards him as a boss), Randy shares with Malachi Mark's vital information regarding war's approach, yet Malachi is utterly unfazed: "Mister Randy, I've thought about it a lot, but there's not a doggone thing we can do about it. We just have to sit here and wait for it" (50). As opposed to the frantic but effective preparations engaged in by Randy throughout the novel's early chapters, Malachi is content to wait, sitting-duck style, for the bombs to strike, endangering his family by his fatalist (and "no-account") inclination to simply take it easy. Before divulging his secret to Malachi, Randy had wrestled with the prospect of doing so: unlike his white neighbors whom he has no intention of enlightening, but whom he assumes will fend well for themselves following attack, the Henrys are a "special problem"—beloved caretakers who deserve the information and also helpless "wards" (46) who will surely perish without his support. When Malachi rejects Randy's invitation to swing into panicky action alongside him, it is as if he and his family deserve any bad luck that befalls them. Malachi explains his indifference, presciently, by reminding his boss that "we [Henrys] don't need much" anyway (50), since their lack of most modern amenities, and total acceptance of this lack, suit them better than their white neighbors to any return to the "Dark Ages" that may befall them.

Indeed preparedness would have been wasted energy for the Henry family given their impossibly "isolated" position at the moment of attack. In a startling scene, Randy approaches the Henry farm immediately following the blasts and is transported back in time—to a pre-bomb, indeed prelapsarian, scene of rural contentment:

Fifty yards up the slope, Preacher Henry and Balaam [the mule] solemnly disked the land, moving silently and evenly, as if they perfectly understood each other. Caleb [Missouri's son] lay flat on his belly on the end of the dock, peering into the shadowed waters behind a piling, jigging a worm for bream. Two-Tone sat on the screened porch, rocking languidly and lifting a can of beer to his lips. From the kitchen came a woman's deep, rich voice, singing a spiritual. That would be Missouri, washing the dishes. Hot, black smoke from burning pine knots issued from both brick chimneys. It seemed a peaceful home, in time of peace. . . .

Randy walked over toward the back door and the Henrys converged on him, their faces apprehensive . . . Everything okay here? [Randy asked]

"Just like always" [Malachi replies]. (149–50)

As if their ignorance of and indifference to world affairs had miraculously preserved them against not only the bomb's physical effects but the emotional devastation that all feeling persons suffer at this point, the Henrys occupy an extra-temporal pocket-paradise of order and ease, but at the expense of their membership in history—in humanity—at this momentous moment. Randy's approach, the approach of awareness and action in the figure of the white master, elicits their "apprehension," indicating that the Henrys must now rely on Randy to reintroduce them to the passage of time itself, to the awful realities of their present and future. While Randy's yanking the Henrys into the post-nuclear present is a dubious favor to be sure, the Henrys' ability to help Randy and his white relatives adjust to "the past," the primitive mode of living that is the only option in the devastated post-nuclear environment, is a priceless gift that is barely acknowledged let alone adequately compensated.

One ethnic character—of the many surveyed in all of these works—stands out for her refusal to fill the servant's role, and for the consequences she pays as a result. As her Otherness stems from ethnicity (and class) instead of the more alien qualities of race, Rita Hernandez, a Minorcan siren from the rundown Pistolville section of town, is closer to Randy both before the bomb (they are lovers in the story's pre-history) and after: as opposed to the Henrys who serenely disregard the bomb's approach, and despite Randy's attempt to relegate her to his own pre-bomb adolescence by insisting that "Rita is part of the past" (200), Rita, like Randy, is keenly aware of the unfolding future and has been stockpiling wares against the day. Yet Rita's accumulation of resalable hard goods contrasts to Randy's pre-bomb hoarding in the name of protecting his family (especially his young niece and nephew), which is thus valorized in the narrative. With the advent of the waspy, marriageable Lib McGovern, Randy has cut Rita loose, and when she refuses to resign her role as sexual servant by pressing to legitimize their relationship instead, she is implicitly accused of not knowing her place, and the narrative turns against her. Her business acumen and fortified material position make her a figure of toughness and strength, who should be able to sustain a brush-off from Randy without lasting effect, while her aggressive, unkempt brother Pete reinforces our dislike of Rita and all her Pistolville clan. According to Pete, "Rita says this war's going to level people as well as cities" (156); Frank celebrated this interracial groundbreaking in the instance of white and black sharing the same liquor jug, but Rita's attempt to level the playing field, which threatens Randy's respectable union with Lib, is castigated.

Because of the large store of supplies she has maintained, armed and alert at all times, against the thieving gangs of Pistolville, Randy reencounters her during a goods exchange and is recaptivated by her seductive ways. Her crude assessment of Randy's current living situation—"I hear you've got two women in your house right now [Lib and his sister-in-law Helen]. Which one are you sleeping with?"—snaps him out of his spell, and he rebukes her. As Rita shares with Randy her plans to turn war-profiteer, her greed becomes as unattractive as her sexual voraciousness; fittingly, the diamond ring she shows off to entice Randy, demonstrating that she is both wealthy and spoken-for, is "hot" property, stolen from a jewelry store in south Florida that had been radiated by an atomic blast. Dan Gunn, the town doctor who accompanies Randy to the meeting, diagnoses radiation poisoning: "Her finger was marred by a dark, almost black circle, as if the ring were tarnished brass, or its inside sooty. But the ring was a clean bright white gold" (204). Concluding their visit, Dan observes to Randy that the Hernandez's stolen goods are "[i]mpregnated with fallout. . . . Suicide" (205). Cruelly abandoned by Randy in his position of white, male, middle-class superiority, Rita is forced to make symbolic marriage with the bomb instead, joining with it in her desire to achieve independent wealth and—as Dan's word choice implies—being thoroughly screwed in the process: having "gotten in bed" with its more dangerous properties, Rita is impregnated by the bomb not with a child but a monster: radiation poisoning. Her refusal to know her place, her sociosexual role, is the sin for which her terrifying dose of radiation exposure is supposedly just reward. As opposed to the impervious, oblivious Henry family, Rita has both a firmer grasp of the bomb's social significance and a normal ("human") physical reaction to the bomb's contaminating effects. If on this score she is *more* human than the ridiculously fortunate members of Randy's collective, who (with the exception of Malachi) fend off the realities of blast, fallout, and post-nuclear mob violence unscathed, it is only the reader who may regard her as the most tragic (and thus most heroic) figure in the story, since the story itself attaches her physical breakdown to her moral turpitude and bars her from the narrative inner circle therefore.

As the Henrys were a "special problem" for Randy in the beginning of the story, solved by their exploitative incorporation into the Bragg commune's early days of survival, they, along with Rita and her family, become the narrative's own special problem as it draws to its triumphant close. Malachi and

Rita's nasty brother Pete are the two minority characters who die in the story (Malachi heroically, saving white lives, Pete despicably, swathed in hot gold), yet all of them are pushed to the invisible margins of the story in its final pages, when—as with Wiley's vision—"tomorrow" is a zone of white middle-class familiarity. If Randy trades for honey as a treat for Ben Franklin and Peyton (the story's two white children) *and* Missouri's son Caleb, later in the story there is only typhoid vaccine enough for Peyton and Ben Franklin (248), the unvoiced assumption being that Caleb is hearty enough to withstand the infections threatening to more delicate systems. Following the Henrys' initial heavy infusion of folk wisdom into the Bragg collective, it becomes self-sustaining and there is less and less for a large cast of supporting characters to do. Again, their last service of any value is to simply fade away; neither the Henrys nor Rita make any appearance in the story's final episode: a surveillance/decontamination patrol arrives by helicopter and invites the family (and its white neighbors "the librarian and the telegraph gal" [315]) to vacate to safer turf. When Randy, on behalf of his familial collective, rejects the pilot's offer, he completes our understanding that the group has already reached, has created for itself, a zone of utopian safety, contentment, and "unmitigated hope" (Hager 323). Again, the Henrys' role at this point in the story is all but nonexistent; they are not referred to during the offer of evacuation nor consulted before the offer is turned down; their role from then on is one of complaisant invisibility.

CONCLUSION: PROBLEM-SOLVING IN THE DOOMSDAY NOVEL

Hal Hager observes that as he wrote, Frank was as caught up in headlines that told of school desegregation as in those that warned of atomic war (322); while the large role granted African American and other minority characters in this novel corroborates that argument, it is the case that for Frank, and for white authors and policy-makers in general, Negroes were a "problem," like the bomb, to be solved as expeditiously as possible; for white America, the answer in both cases was flight to the protected suburb, even as it knew in its fluttering heart that the solution was provisional at best. Racial integration was as looming a prospect as radioactive contamination, and in only the most farfetched geographic fantasies, Wylie's for instance, would one problem (the bomb) conveniently take care of the other (the Negroes trapped in their ground-zero inner cities).

As I argued earlier, to discern African Americans as "being" a problem in the nuclear-imminent landscape ignores the reality of their "having" a problem—the same one facing white America (and the world as a whole) at that moment—and the agency with which they would execute their own antinuclear protest, pre-nuclear preparedness, and, if necessary, post-nuclear survival. That is, while the black and ethnic servant figures examined here are terrifically effective solution-finders throughout the course of their stories, it is always the white characters who "own" the problem in question, be it blood contamination, disrupted water supply, or the bomb itself, and thus always the black characters who must have this problem introduced and explained to them and are tasked with (but not necessarily compensated for) finding its solution. While the novels read in this chapter each dimensionalize their nuclear scenarios by including characters of various ethnicities, races, and social classes, all tend toward the assumptions and conclusions dependent upon miraculously capable black servitude identified by film and cultural theorists to have been part of white-authored narrative since at least the end of the Civil War. In each of the novels discussed here, these characters' positions within the textual landscape are "below" (essential yet subordinated) and therefore "to the side:" physically and intellectually off-stage when the bomb drops, implausibly segregated from the bomb's detrimental effects, and whisked into marginalized invisibility as each narrative curtain falls.

CHAPTER 2

"Tomorrow's Children"

Interracial Conflict and Resolution in Atomic-Era Science Fiction and Afro-Futurism

In a remarkable story called "The Equalizer" (Williamson), published in *Astounding Science Fiction* in early 1947, a group of space-traveling scientists and military advisors return to Earth when an abrupt halt to communication from the home planet (attributed later to nuclear war) raises concern. The repatriated men land their space craft at "Fort America," where a president-dictator named Tyler (and likened in numerous ways to Hitler) had established his empire. At the edge of the abandoned urban stronghold, the explorers observe the warning, "Danger! Metropolitan Area" (see figure 3), but in the well-preserved rural countryside happy "peasants" engage in fulfilling farm work, dam construction, and (as the visitors note with admiration) copious energy consumption. Without provocation members of the peasant clan are gunned down by one of the crew, a maniacal "Squaredealer" who administers Tyler's interplanetary affairs. The villain's snide appellation takes a sniper's shot at the "Fair Dealers" and "New Dealers" who had been running the Truman and Roosevelt administrations for the preceding decade, yet when not associated with a fascist Truman, the Squaredealer's short stature, military garb, and slanted eyes suggest the other menace of the Axis era, General Tojo of Japan.

Thus the convoluted but ultra-right politics of the story's author, Jack Williamson, manifest in multiple forms, and Williamson contributes to the tradition of politicizing atomic-era spatial arrangements that is under investigation here: as seen on many occasions thus far, the city is the source of humanity's problems, while the bucolic countryside where all live blissfully with "simplicity, individualism, and complete personal freedom" (47) promises simultaneously the inevitable future and the physically impossible return to the past. Even the suburbs in this story, also destroyed in the atomic

FIGURE 3: Hubert Rogers. *Astounding Science Fiction* (March 1947). © 2012 by Penny
Publications LLC/Dell Magazines. Reprinted by permission of the publisher.

explosion (27), have gone to grass, yet the survivors' primitive enclave is incomplete without "the plastic dust and shavings" of their modern workshop,
the kitchen "fitted with shining gadgets to manufacture plastic dishes and syn-
thetic staples on the spot," and "the cold locker stored with a rich abundance of
frozen foods" (34). As one of the yeomen-survivors avers, "Most people didn't
live in cities by choice. They were huddled into them by the old division of
labor—specialized cogs in a social machine grown ruinously complex" (49);

"the cities were a product of the old technology, and they died with it" (51). In the eventful recent past, "criminals" were the last to leave (hence the signage prominent at the city gates and on Hubert Rogers's cover illustration), "a few men and women too stupid or too vicious to use the equalizer" (51). In another, somewhat earlier story from this magazine, "Beggars in Velvet," a merry band of "outcaste . . . outlaw" types (Kuttner and Moore 25) known as the Hedgehounds has waited in the wings for the bomb to lay waste to "New York and Chicago and a hundred other cities" that now "held only abnormal life" (14). One Hedgehound more or less blames overbuilt cities themselves for the bombs that innocently, unavoidably befell them, heat-seeking-missile-style, reminding his listeners that "the tribes that unified got dusted with the Eggs. We ain't unifying, brother!" (26).

And what is Williamson's "Equalizer," seemingly borrowed from another pulp genre, the hard-boiled detective story, if not a gleaming example of new technology with its own distinct political overtones: unique to this cultural debate, Williamson attempts to politicize atomic science itself; according to the truth-tellers thriving in the hinterlands, "the old technology of the Atomic Age had already reached the breaking point of over-complexity and super-centralization. . . . The old atomic pile, you know, was an enormously clumsy and wasteful and dangerous way of doing an extremely simple thing" (58). Instead, the equalizer is a model of atomic-age efficiency, providing each user with his own personally controlled, freely deployable atomic weapon: "Shaped very much like the huge guided missiles of Fort America, it was about six inches long" (53). Naturally, the weapon is used against the Truman-Tojo figure who shot the innocent peasants in the earlier scene, and any other question of racial difference is bracketed by the characters' time-traveling, not into the interstellar future but back to the Revolutionary-era past. As with the tricorn-sporting Tea-Partiers of America's present day, Williamson's post-atomic survivors live in an eighteenth-century North America where intrepid pioneers settle an "empty" continent and follow an ever-westward path that enables them to turn their backs on both the rapidly developing eastern seaboard and the messy horrors of southern slavery. Thus the only African Americans in the story implicitly figure in the urban "criminals" too stupid and vicious to learn the intricacies of equalizer operation. "They . . . tried to live by raiding and looting. They used the old military weapons" (51)—M1 carbines? over-centralized atomic bombs?—and were left to their own devices until they conveniently did themselves in.

While the racial shadings of this particular atomic-era contribution to the pulp science fiction scene are thus only suggested, in fact the genre of SF has explored themes of racial identity and conflict since the Morlocks stalked the Eloi through the pages of H. G. Wells's *The Time Machine* at the end of the nineteenth century. In the post-WWII period this tradition continued, inflected now with questions pertinent to its atomic and civil-rights contexts. If anything, the motif intensified, as the bomb was credited implicitly or explicitly with an explosion of mutant races across the interplanetary stratosphere—and within both ruined and recognizable American landscapes as well. Whether the mutant classes were depicted as beleaguered victims or unknowable enemies, their conflicts with more typically human types alluded unavoidably to the "race wars" between blacks and whites, doves and hawks, commies and patriots, being fought on home soil at that time as well. Out in the stratosphere, debates staged between those of a more civilized or intelligent race and those alien groups more backward or barbarous by comparison reflected the conflicts over voting rights, economic disparity, and equal education raging in real life on the American ground below. Despite the occasional sense provided in the stories themselves, that the purpose of science fiction was to ignore history and politics, the realities of postwar life—including questions related to urban survival and racial equality—shone through with remarkable regularity and deserve our attention at this time.[1]

Many of the atomic-survival novelists featured in Chapter 1 (i.e., Judith Merril, Philip Wylie, and Pat Frank) have produced texts more readily classified as science fiction as well. I, however, distinguish between the pointedly realist scenarios mounted in certain of their novels that are analogous to postwar "social problem" films and the intensely imaginative (yet scientifically plausible), frequently futuristic, alternate universes presented in traditionally conceived science fiction. Despite the generic differences, many of the science fictions considered here capitulate to the spatializing (that is, segregating) status quo by narrative's end, as did the realist novels of Chapter 1. While the black characters found in SF are servant figures, they may also be robots (see discussion of Sheckley in this chapter) or time travelers (as in Heinlein's *Farnham's Freehold*, also discussed in this chapter), in keeping with the genre's more imaginative scale. While many of the servant-saviors located in Chapter 1 were physically impervious and intellectually oblivious to the bomb's significance, in these science fictions, the phenomenon of atomic-induced genetic mutation is too dramatic a theme to ignore.

Though the genre is older than Wells, stretching back to include Shelley's *Frankenstein* (1818), fantastic journeys penned in the Renaissance era, and even More's *Utopia* (1516; see Clareson 7), in fact SF boomed in both popularity and respectability as a direct result of the atomic bomb. So accurately did the stories predict the design and use of atomic weapons that during the war even agents of the FBI became interested readers (see del Rey 108–09; see also Parrinder 43); in the frightening days immediately following the first atomic explosions, "Americans thought that they might find in those [science fiction] stories both some simple explanation of what had happened at Hiroshima and Nagasaki and a quick assessment of the consequences of entering the Nuclear Age" (Clareson 40). As the noted SF author Lester del Rey has observed, "the atom bomb had led—at least partially—to the acceptance of science fiction. . . .

[I]t made the former 'silly' stuff seem a lot less silly" (196; see also Parrinder xiii–xiv). More generally, David Ketterer remarks that in our age of rapid change and upheaval, "writers are drawn to science fiction; it is an outgrowth and expression of crisis" (24). As we will see shortly, the atomic theme lent itself to writers across the political spectrum: conservatives such as Williamson invented a personalized nuclear pistol after over-centralized, inefficient atomic piles had helpfully annihilated the urban masses, while more progressive writers such as Poul Anderson (in his early, left-leaning phase) and Carol Emshwiller looked bravely into the faces of a "race" of mutated children come nuclear tomorrow. In this chapter's second movement, I read the writing of African Americans representing the Afro-Futurist tradition of speculative fiction. While two of these authors—Ralph Ellison and Chester Himes—are not traditionally identified as science fiction writers, I am interested in the way a progressive, even radical, racial politics is advanced in their novels through the very gesture of progression—through the forcing of readers to confront an imminent, apocalyptic tomorrow rooted in the disparities and injustices of today. The third in this group, Samuel Delany, belongs in every respect to the top echelon of American SF writers as traditionally defined but has been saved for the end of this discussion as the author who succeeds with numerous dilemmas that emerge in this chapter.

In *Enemies Within: The Cold War and the AIDS Crisis in Literature, Film, and Culture*, I distinguished between spatial and temporal themes in crisis narratives from the heart of the cold war and the early AIDS era. In my research I regularly observed a conservative impulse to lie behind the tendency to spatialize the problem at hand—to draw a *cordon sanitaire* around a targeted population (the urban poor in an atomic context, gay men in the early days of HIV/AIDS) and construct outside this danger zone a utopia (almost always white and suburban) of pretended permanent safety and health. By contrast, those writers who worked with temporal themes—the impossibility of return to the past, the inevitably of our shared tomorrow—exhibited a more enlightened tendency to take individual responsibility for collective problems and seek solutions to them. I coined the term "eutemporal" to describe the authorial mindset committed to a tomorrow freed from the threat of both nuclear war and HIV infection and death—and that often produced graphic, horrific narratives of our worst nightmares realized by way of ensuring that said nightmares remained realized as text only.

In the science fiction and Afro-Futurist works to be discussed in this chapter, I discern by and large the same distinction at work: writers making statements about nuclear weapons and/or race relations in the postwar period deploy spatializing strategies (specifically the depiction of alternate universes or lands apart) to build fantasies of escape from a troubled planet or—by contrast—to act out conflict in an alternate zone while implicitly or explicitly excusing planet Earth from radical change. For such writers, the "tomorrow" of racial equality never actually arrives, while the "tomorrow" of atomic holocaust is never so unsurvivable as to actually signal the end of time, the inability to start again. By contrast, those science fiction authors who set their stories in recognizably American settings yet in a nuclear near-future environmentally and biologically devastating to its beleaguered survivors not only tell tales designed to shock their readers into renewed commitments to nuclear disarmament but also frequently meditate upon the crises that defined and disabled America's interracial "family" during the atomic era and certainly to some extent today. While he takes for granted, as I do not, the temporal features of science fiction across the board, Mark Rose draws a similar conclusion: "as a genre [science fiction] insists that [things] will and must be different, that change is the only constant rule and that the future will not be like the present. One might call fantasy a conservative form, whereas in principle science fiction might be called subversive" (*Alien Encounters*, 21). The Afro-Futurists to be discussed in this chapter likewise looked with progressive, even revolutionary, intent at an American tomorrow riven by these same interracial crises ramped up to apocalyptic dimensions. (And in contrast to Rose's contention, Delany often put science-fantasy to explicitly progressive use.) While the post-nuclear science fiction writers therefore depicted a land of mutant races now required to acknowledge their brotherhood in the wake of nuclear disaster, the Afro-Futurists presented a US society of the very near future whose dreams of interracial brotherhood are so horribly betrayed that only an apocalyptic race war can result.

ESCAPES FROM NEW YORK IN GOLDEN-AGE SF

As I remarked earlier, science fiction that appeared in the late 1940s and 1950s, the so-called Golden Age of magazine science fiction, sometimes perpetuated the genre's escapist traditions, offering its audience an intergalactic vacation from both stultifying ordinarity and the disturbing crises of contemporary history (see also Sontag 130–31). Published to large and devoted readerships of magazines like John W. Campbell's *Astounding Science Fiction*, Anthony Boucher's *Magazine of Fantasy and Science Fiction*, and, beginning in 1950, Harry Gold's *Galaxy Science Fiction*, as well as in dozens of shorter-lived series, such escapes might have well served readers who were so deeply agitated by the events of the day that SF was a much-needed respite, as well as readers (especially those from the white, suburban, middle class) who cared so little about civil rights or the atomic threat that the stories comfortably reflected their own tendencies toward race blindness and political indifference. In Thomas M. Disch's estimation, "By far the greater part of all pulp science fiction from the time of Wells till now was written to provide a [lower-middle-class] semi-literate audience with compensatory fantasies" (9). Even more pointedly,

Patrick Parrinder observes, "The estrangement-effect of the majority of SF stories is contained and neutralized by their conventionality in other respects. The result is that the familiar reality is replaced by an all too familiar unreality" (74; see also Huntington 166). On yet other occasions, the escape was less literary than literal—release from the urban hotbed of racial intermixing and "fascist" social-ism, as in Williamson's "The Equalizer" and in other stories whose pronounced anti-urbanism bespeaks, as per my argument from *Enemies Within*, a conservative fantasy of boundary-drawing, boundary-fleeing, and generalized spatial reorga-nizing similar to the postwar phenomenon of white flight.

This anti-urban bias coincided perfectly with the views of *Astounding*'s editor Campbell, a towering figure in SF publication throughout the middle twentieth century. As suburbanization—or "decentralization"—boomed in late-1940s America, Campbell wrote (from his snug berth on East 45th Street in midtown Manhattan) that New York City was the "unique" (might we call it even freakish or mutant?) product of its already-dying moment: "The super-giant city is a passing phenomenon of unstable culture. . . . [W]hen transpor-tation is good, fast, economical—then the city has no reason for existence" ("Megopolis" 5).[2] Ironically, Campbell discerns increasing "transportation" as the solution to urban "hardening of the traffic arteries," since his vision seems to include many fewer automobiles and many more "light plane[s, which] should help solve the average man's transportation problems" (5), provided there is adequate rural space to land the things. Though cities are currently the main targets of "the threat of atomic warfare" (6), Campbell's anti-urban bias goes beyond the exigencies of cold war politics. Even when the atomic threat has passed, "the super-giant city will be impractical. The same advanced science [that came up with a defense against atomic weapons] will, unquestionably, im-prove transportation, which is the death of cities" (6).

The theme of the dying city is intriguingly explored in an urbophobic fan-tasy by Robert Abernathy, "Single Combat," published in *Fantasy and Science Fiction* in early 1955. Echoing Mark Rose's observation that in SF and other romance genres the setting can be "more alive, will have more personality, than any of the characters" (*Alien Encounters* 8; see also "Introduction" 4 and Christopher 86), Abernathy taps into postwar paranoia by presenting the city as the formidable adversary. Just as Kuttner and Moore's Hedgehound blamed cities themselves for being so attractively "unified" that the approaching bombs could barely help themselves, so in Abernathy's story, the city stands accused of betraying its inhabitants to the vagaries of both tomorrow's atomic holo-caust and yesterday's declining infrastructure. It is thus rightfully challenged by the deranged hero who would beat the city to its punch by rigging an atomic bomb in a midtown basement and throwing away the key. Unnamed yet strongly suggestive of New York, Abernathy's city is poorly maintained, trash-strewn, and violent; it is plagued by interracial conflict and ringing with eth-nic slurs—"*Dirty nigger, dago, kike . . .*" (63, ellipsis in original)—such that the also unnamed hero seems to embark on a worthy mission to wipe out the inter-group hostility fomented in crowded urban spaces. Mainly, however, the human element figures as the unseen drivers of the careening, honking, exhaust-spewing cars and trucks strewn across the path of the hero's attempted exodus. That the vehicles themselves inflict their sensory damage almost without drivers at the wheels increases our sense that every element in this dangerous urban environment has come—in its death throes—uncannily to life.

Even as he exits his basement hideaway, the story's hero trips on a crumbling stair, and as he makes his frantic way to the city's edge, he must dodge a range of hazards—falling signage, tumbling cornices, open manholes, screaming subways, a flailing streetcar wire, a curb-jumping truck and the lamppost it snaps—simultaneously attributable to inevitable urban neglect and a much more purposeful and malevolent life force. Ironically, the city vanquishes its adversary only once he has reached a suburban scene of urban renewal; workmen are about to replace deteriorating housing with new construction—yet another assault on a city bent on preserving its tilting prewar monoliths—when the structure marked for demolition collapses on the man and has him "pinioned as if by the fingers of a gigantic hand." Confronted with dire circumstances, whereby "[t]hose fingers needed only to twitch . . . and his spine would snap" (69), our hero tells the workmen how to locate and defuse the bomb. Yet instead of the city's calling a truce, the "ponderous mass of masonry began to shift downward" (70) and snuffs out his life. The workmen look "into one another's white[-with-fear] faces" and acknowledge that "the city was merciless" (70). In the story's final urbophobic estimation, "growth" is likened to a "cancer budding from a few wild cells" (68) and the city itself to a voracious monster whose appetite for natural resources is as gross as its toxic excretions.

RACIALIZING WHITE-AUTHORED SCIENCE FICTION

Such stories also frequently "escaped" the significance of racial identity by pointedly ignoring it. Scores of tales published in the most popular pulps deployed references to fear-whitened faces (as in Abernathy) or much more often to "dark" persons to be read as mysterious, alluring, or villainous, not necessarily racially diverse. While a racialized reading of these stories is often possible, it is as useful to consider the ways in which racial difference was ignored in them, and is largely irrelevant to their most plausible interpretations, as it is to read the ways it was implicitly or inadvertently acknowledged. Thus in "The Equalizer," the color brown is positively, obsessively applied to one of the explorer-protagonists and to almost all of the farmer-survivors to suggest not Hispanic or African ancestry but only the values explicitly endorsed by the story as a whole: rugged masculinity, long hours spent outdoors (and the deeply tanned well-being this was once thought to provide), simple self-sustenance. In

Gordon E. Dickson's "Black Charlie," the titular character is racialized to the degree that he is the creator of unappreciated, "primitive" art yet hard to further interpret from this angle, due to his depiction as "more like a large otter, with flat, muscular grasping pads on the end of four limbs . . . , glossy, dampish hair all over it" (129), a low keening sound that is his only means of communication, and the ultimately minor role he plays.[3]

To a certain degree, it misreads August Derleth's "The Dark Boy" to insist upon a racial allegory in a story that applies the expression—ad nauseam, even after the boy's actual name has been established—mainly as a device of intrigue. In the one-room schoolhouse and its rural environs that set the story, no reference to racial identities is made, only universal whiteness implied. Instead, the boy's darkness suggests alluring mystery, as the story turns on the schoolteacher's figuring out that this boy is actually a ghost, the accidentally killed son of her emerging love interest, who refuses to give up his desire for learning. And yet the racial subtext (very likely never intended by the author himself) of this story of a "dark" boy who haunts an all-white schoolroom in February 1957—seven months before the Little Rock Nine would succeed in their historic integration attempt—is difficult to ignore. The "dark" scar on the boy's forehead, the result of the accident that took his life, eerily anticipates the many children's heads to be bloodied in the coming months and years by rocks and bottles, hurled in reaction to *Brown v. Board of Education*, just being enacted at this time.

In other stories the racial subtext was much more pronounced, and ran the gamut from overt hostility to grudging tolerance. In the offensive opinion of *Astounding* editor Campbell, "History strongly indicates that some populations of human beings want to be slaves" ("How to Lose" 8). Finn O'Donnevan's attempted comedy "Uncle Tom's Planet" corroborates this view when a spokesman for the downtrodden race of Aingoes tells a justice tribunal that his group is "very grateful" for their capture by the aggressive Delgens, that they spent all their days in unconstructive fighting before the Delgens came along, and that they frankly "don't care" whether they are enslaved or not (62). Where the bomb was credited with destroying racial hierarchy in Pat Frank's *Alas, Babylon* (see Chapter 1), in O'Donnevan's story it is discovered that excessive radiation emanating from the dying planet Aingo is actually responsible for its inhabitants' innate inferiority and "habitual state of imbecility" (63). Once "rescued" by the Delgens, they recover so fully that they wind up counter-enslaving their now-inferior masters, in a weak comic twist that does nothing to challenge misguided notions about the benefits of enslavement, nor mitigate the ugly racial depictions on display mid-story.

Only minimally less problematic is a "spare planet" fantasy by satirist Robert Sheckley, "Human Man's Burden," in which an attractive playboy stakes his claim in a conveniently uninhabited but paradisiacal world, fleeing suburban conformity and its attendant inanities and overcrowding. Edward Flaswell is the lone human (i.e., white) settler on a richly fertile plantation-planet, cared for by a robotic "mechanical" (read: menial) named "Gunga-Sam" who refers to Flaswell as both "massa" and "sahib." Illustrations depicts Gunga-Sam in dark tones with exaggerated racial facial features; he is the typical wise counselor who "understands human people better than anyone" (108). He and his fellow-mechanicals spend their off hours in "carefree songs and dances, interspersed with whispering and secret merriment" (98), are criticized by the humans for being "uppity" when their superior intelligence comes to the fore, and are described without irony on several occasions as having no soul. Sheckley attempts to modernize his antebellum fantasy by fueling his hero's enterprise with thorium, mined by the happy mechanicals whenever they are not harvesting fruits and vegetables, yet his reliance on stock situations and offensive racial humor marks the story as hopelessly outdated. Its setting is less a futuristic no man's land than a tropical island paradise, in keeping with Gauguin-esque fantasies of the postwar period. As per my argument from *Enemies Within*, Sheckley's story chooses a spatial solution—escape to a fortuitously uninhabited planet—to current problems (suburban conformity, modernizing race relations), emphasizing the white protagonist's right to colonize land at will, enjoy a role of mastery over the "non-humans" he brings with him, and increase his power via atomic-age technologies (e.g., thorium mining and energy production) whenever suitable.

One of the most famous genre writers in the business, Ray Bradbury, wrote a spare-planet fantasy so controversial that he was never able to place it in any American magazine, finally donating it to *New Story*, a Paris serial edited by a friend (Bradbury, "Introduction" viii). "The Other Foot" (1949) adopts the viewpoint of an African American citizenry now happily situated on Mars, primarily from the perspective of the race-conscious town leader, Willie Johnson, when white men arrive from Earth. As Willie's wife Hattie observes early on, "Right after we got up here, Earth got in an atom war. They blew each other up terribly. They forgot us" (40). Fortuitously, as per several of the "get-even dreams" enjoyed by African American journalists in the atomic period (see Chapter 3), the black community in this story makes a well-timed escape just as the whites and Asians start doing themselves in with their own wicked weaponry. The bomb not only slams the door on white America's ability to follow the blacks to Mars for the purpose of bringing them back or co-colonizing the planet with them, it also forces the whites to "forget" their animosity toward the civil rights struggle, since so many more important problems now loom. Where the bomb is credited in other stories in this study with bringing the races together, here it functions ironically to set them light years apart and to thus create the "peace" (44) that the story's black characters had never known back on their home planet.

Though Willie and many of his fellow-townsmen grab ropes and chains and prepare an immediate lynching, the white emissary who emerges from the landed craft is elderly and humble; in a sorrowful litany he runs through the list of hometowns large and small that have been destroyed in Earth's ensuing wars, causing deepening sorrow in his once-hostile audience. In a lengthy statement that requires hearing in full to interpret, he issues the survivors' apology:

> We've been stupid. Before God we admit our stupidity and our evilness. All the Chinese and the Indians and the Russians and the British and the Americans. We're asking to be taken in. Your Martian soil has lain fallow for numberless centuries, there's room for everyone; it's good soil—I've seen your fields from above. We'll come and work it *for* you. Yes, we'll even do that. We deserve anything you want to do to us, but don't shut us out. (51)

It may seem that the visitor has come to admit his guilt over America's two most grievous crimes against humanity, murderous racism—many of the Johnsons' own relatives were lynched in earlier times—and nuclear war, that the bomb has taught the handful of white survivors to see the error of *all* of their previous ways. Yet in fact the visitor describes the guilt of the nuclear belligerents—Chinese, Indian, British, etc.,—most of whom are not directly implicated in America's racial tragedies. Without offering a word of apology for America's history of racism *per se*, the visitor indicates that the nuclear survivors of these various northern nations ask to work for the black Martians by way of *atoning for* their nuclear sins alone. The humiliation of whites "even" having to stoop to blacks is read in this emissary's speech as a fate worse than death, and thus a fate only fitting for those nuclear death-dealers lucky enough to find themselves still alive. At no point in the story does this white character or the narrative voice acknowledge the evils of racism, nor the trauma that might have resulted in the black flight to Mars in the first place. Notably, none of Bradbury's black characters ever notices the visitor's missing apology, and instead Willie acknowledges that thanks to the bomb, there is "nothing [on Earth] left to hate"; the Martians lay down their ropes and welcome the wandering survivors. If Willie's revenge plots were originally frightening enough to keep this story out of American print, sixty years after the fact the story's failure to apologize to its black characters for white sins makes it discouragingly familiar.

INTERRACIAL FRATERNIZING ON THE FINAL FRONTIER

When the worlds discovered were not conveniently uninhabited, as they were in several of the comedies discussed above, a subgenre of interplanetary-travel stories from these magazines used an encounter—sometimes shocking, sometimes run-of-the-mill—with alien races to explore themes of interracial love and brotherhood. Meanwhile, though "change . . . in science, environment, attitude, morality, or the basic nature of humanity" is essential to the SF genre according to Lester del Rey (9; see also M. Rose 21), even the most transformed "environments" in this subgenre failed in the main to present truly modernized "attitudes": indeed, all such planet-hopping tales were set necessarily in the radically modified yet otherwise unspecified world of tomorrow, where much of the "not yet" and "someday" rhetoric of the postwar era forever deferred the arrival of racial equality and marriage as one pleased. Yet none of the stories discovered in my search could muster sufficient futurism to realize the dreams of interracial love and marriage that had been summoned as motivating themes. In J. T. McIntosh's "Eleventh Commandment," a cast of "mixed-race" couples (from diverse planets) celebrates the passage of a universal referendum in support of interplanetary marriage. Discussing race in science fiction, Robert Scholes and Eric S. Rabkin argue that "The presence of unhuman races, aliens, and robots certainly makes the differences between human races seem appropriately trivial" (188).

Yet McIntosh's story sacrifices this perspectival wisdom by pointedly cordoning off Earth, where with disappointing familiarity the anti-intermarriage "realists are in the majority" (90), distancing it from the interplanetary landscape where reform takes place. Without further elaboration, "[t]he [referendum] matter hardly concerns Earth. . . . Earth was the one world in a special position. For all the other worlds the poll meant something different" (106). Lacking the courage to complete the equation set up by its own terms, the narrative keeps the reader guessing as to why Earth receives this special dispensation from the pressing question of racial equality: because all of the racists still live back on Earth? Because all of the actually "raced" people do? Because on Earth the question is so charged that one might even change planets in an attempt to avoid it or safely allegorize it from the distance of sufficient light years? McIntosh's story suggests that no matter how far one goes into the immeasurable beyond, issues of racial identity and racial equality persist as worrisome problems whose resolutions are equivocal at best. As per my comments regarding the politics of space and time in these narratives, here again this tale's temporal dimension (its implied futurism) is subordinated to its spatial demarcations, the pronounced "thereness" of the conflict and resolution that spares the "here" of civil rights-era America from the disruptive trauma of actual change.

Thus the main problem with the ugly but kindly, telepathic "baldies" of Kuttner and Moore's "Beggars in Velvet," expressed once more in the gradualist rhetoric of the period, is that they are too many millennia ahead of their time: "If man hadn't used atomic power as he did, the mutations would have had their full period of gestation. They'd never have appeared until the planet was ready for them" (38). Despite their willingness, among all of the story's other post-nuclear "minorities" to "mingle on equal terms with the majority group" and their "desire . . . [for] racial assimilation" (28), they remain a persecuted minority due to their freakishly futuristic genetic make-up. As planet Earth remained throughout SF's golden age persistently unable to get "ready for" interracial marriage, so the hero of this story winds up alone and his attractive love interest winds up dead.

In this same disheartening vein, Poul Anderson's "Prophecy," published in *Astounding Science Fiction* in May 1949, presents a well-meaning and technologically advanced race from outer space that sends a diplomatic mission to Earth. Pointedly, the ambassadors "looked like very ordinary human beings of a curiously mixed race—dark skin, Mongoloid eyes of a light shade, thin Caucasoid noses, woolly hair" (54). While Anderson may go overboard in the racial hodgepodge his wise emissaries inhabit, it is nevertheless refreshing to encounter a "dark" face that actually indicates racial specificity and precedent-shattering to hear these intensely racialized characters described as "very ordinary human beings." Too, Anderson attempts to reverse the tradition of depicting the racially marked characters as technologically backward by hinging his story around the astronomically advanced intelligence of the visitors, who come from not only far away but from Earth's own distant future.

Yet discussing with their American hosts the many human races they have encountered on other planets, even these enlightened travelers cannot but succumb to the benighted mindset of half-baked postwar liberalism: "Oh, there are differences, of course, and *even races which look and think exactly alike could hardly be so similar as to make interbreeding possible*—but by and large the similarities exceed the differences" (55, emphasis added). Even in a story expressly designed to dispel myths of racial difference and racial inferiority, the proscription against intermarrying is the bedrock upon which the homily on brotherhood is safely built. Ironically, the 1500-year intelligence gap that the visitors are asked but refuse to close—since "Man . . . must learn, not only with his brain but with bitter and horrible and unforgettable experience," including, inevitably, "your atomic wars" (58)—contains a view on interracial marriage that mimics exactly primitive America's very own. Echoing a theme that has been implied in numerous texts throughout this study—that it will take an atom bomb to bring the races together—Anderson's emissaries from the future indicate that Americans dare not dream (or, conversely, need not worry) about racial "interbreeding" until well after the unthinkable day that nuclear Armageddon occurs.

MUTANT CHILDREN INTEGRATING THE POST-ATOMIC FAMILY

Notably, the post-nuclear setting enabled more sympathetic treatment of the interracial family, specifically the occurrence of mutant children born after the bomb to parents whose own birth in pre-atomic times ensures a more normal physical appearance—and again a racially homogeneous marital arrangement. In this specific context, the stigmatized races are mutated victims of atomic blast; their rendering is often sympathetic, and the prospects of interracial family-making are more freely explored. Through these portrayals of "tomorrow's children," postwar science fiction reached back to its roots in nineteenth-century gothic and horror fiction, two genres explicitly interested in the dissolution of the physical borders that kept human bodies normal and whole. Whether it be the stitched-together parts of Frankenstein's creature or the microbes invading Martian bodies at the end of Wells's *War of the Worlds*, gothic and horror writers present the prospect of bodily breakdown both subtle and grotesque and asked the moral and philosophical questions—for instance, what makes a human human?—attendant thereupon. Post-WWII, the genetic mutations on display in atomic-themed science fiction, not only in a character's offspring but often even in her surviving yet contaminated self, suggest the delusional nature of notions of racial purity or even a knowable racial identity— questions markedly relevant to these stories' civil rights context. Related to the social-problem novels discussed in Chapter 1, which measured the prospects of human survival and read the bomb as a "leveling" factor in political terms alone, the stories considered here intensify the inquiry by broaching not only social but also physical barriers. By considering the outcome when even seemingly inviolate biological categories give way, atomic-themed mutant fiction is able to challenge the societal status quo with regard to racial divides and racial difference down to the cellular level.

Thus, one of the only female-authored fictions located for this discussion, Carol Emshwiller's "A Day at the Beach," treats the issue of racially diversifying mutations across generations following atomic apocalypse, providing an atomic-era twist on crises of mixed-race (or wrong-race) children being born to women of a single (or other) racial background. As per the cover illustration on the August 1959 issue of the *Magazine of Fantasy and Science Fiction* (see figure 4), a "baldy" woman with exceedingly fair skin has birthed a "dark boy" into one of the most deprived and violent post-atomic environments on display in these magazine fictions. In his headnote, editor Robert Park Mills links Emshwiller's story of maternal devotion to Judith Merril's classic "That Only a Mother," published in *Astounding Science Fiction* in June 1948, in which a mother refuses to see the horrible atomic-induced mutations in her newborn child that her recently returned husband is horrified to discover. That story's oedipal subtext is on view in Emshwiller's as well.

Named no more than Littleboy (which is also, as David Seed points out, the name of the Hiroshima bomb [56]), the child is not only several shades darker than either parent but loaded down with atavistic features, including dark hair covering his head and body, "wide, blunt features and a wary stare" (37), a remarkable talent for tree-climbing, a lack of speech beyond the occasional "*Aaa, Aaa*" (37), and violent tendencies that include destroying his

FIGURE 4: *The Magazine of Fantasy and Science Fiction* (August 1959). © 1959 by Mercury Press. Reprinted by permission of Spilogale, Inc. Cover art by Ed Emshwiller.

father's glasses and biting his mother painfully on the collarbone. Thus "only a mother" could love this freakish brat, whose dark skin and wild, jungle-style behavior suggest unpleasant racial overtones as well. As physically ruined as are the boy's malnourished, alopecic parents, their high, fair foreheads and normal mental status connote a sort of purity against which the boy's glaring defects suggest an alarming species-wide decline: if this is the child born by these first-generation survivors of atomic catastrophe, what sort of sub-monster will he himself spawn when able to do so? While both Merril's fiction and this story by Emshwiller laudably depict nightmare scenarios, specifically parents' or mothers' worst nightmares, for the express purpose of confronting their audiences with realistic doses of atomic horror, the implicit comment here, that the nightmare consists mainly in the darkening of future generations, requires stringent challenge.

Despite Littleboy's many off-putting features, he embodies the optimism, hope, and survival motivation frequently accorded child characters in dystopia. He chiefly inspires his mother Myra's idea for a trip to the beach; while she herself longs to go, she is also keen to see her son romping on the sand and enjoying the waters as would any normal child in normal times. When the family is attacked by marauding thugs, Myra is spurred by loving maternal instinct to brace herself for mortal combat using a wrench hidden in the beach blanket. Most significantly, the danger, once averted, forges a bond between Littleboy and his father Ben that had been pointedly missing in the story's opening pages; Ben opposes the dangerous trip and in classic oedipal fashion resents Myra's attempt to use their son as an excuse to go. Once at the beach, he has a burst of sexual desire for his wife, who fends off his advances by reminding him that there are no doctors left should she become pregnant. Children born or unborn thus constantly frustrate Ben's own wishes, and, echoing the dictates of nineteenth-century mulatto melodrama, the boy's "mixed race" features alienate him even further from his white father by casting doubt upon the constancy of his white mother.

The story's meagerly happy ending arrives, therefore, in the image of the "tall, two-headed seeming monster walking briskly down the beach, and one head, bouncing directly over the other one, had hair and was Littleboy's" (42–43). Having chased off the thugs and retrieved his frightened son, Ben lays claim to Littleboy's monstrousness by setting his own monstrous head in close physical proximity. The family returns contentedly to their ruined, impoverished suburban home; relative to how disastrously things might have turned out, Myra can credibly insist, "we had a good day" since "Littleboy saw the beach" and no one was killed. As with Derleth's story "The Dark Boy," which ends with the teacher running her hand lovingly over the ghost-child's "thick dark hair" (63) and insisting to his estranged father, "If you could just get used to not being afraid of him, . . . you'd never notice him" (64), Emshwiller's story indicates that it is easier to incorporate a dark child into an atomic-era white family than to sanction the interracial marital and sexual relations suggested but ultimately rejected elsewhere in these pages.

Poul Anderson drew repeatedly on the subject of mutant children to present his readers an incontrovertible case against atomic war. As in Emshwiller's story, Anderson's "Logic" dares to depict human suffering *in extremis*; a gang of thieves intending violence on the barely recovering town where the story is set is yet made sympathetic by repeated references to their dire hunger and fatigue. As the gang's leader, Dick Hammer, points out to the story's hero, in terms with clear race and class implications for postwar America, "You an' your kind made us outlaws, drivin' us away when we come starvin' to you, houndin' us south an' then in your fat smugness forgettin' about us" (70). Despite this point scored, the gang's bloodthirstiness requires their being countered by the autistic-like mutant son of the protagonist with a mysterious ionizing weapon he concocts the morning they attack. Anderson deals obliquely with the subject of pitched battles between warring groups; "the South" (both the American southern states and Latin America), as per the regional stereotype, is where all those lacking the fortitude to "stick it out" (70) in the cold North fled in the immediate aftermath of atomic war. Like the ne're-do-wells dying off in the cities of "The Equalizer," those living in the South are made savage by overcrowding and deprivation and, for mysterious reasons, rarely threaten the rapidly reindustrializing northlands, recently unified into a single nation consisting of the northern US, Canada, and Alaska. Leaning hard on the politics of regional instead of racial difference, Anderson takes pains to integrate Hammer's gang, yet the thugs of color are identified by denigrating nicknames—"Mex" and "Sambo"—and play negligible roles. Although Hammer is a native of the town he attacks, he has clearly sustained a slide down the class scale in his geographical flight south, figuring upon his return as poor white trash. While Anderson is correct to suggest that the underprivileged members of currently conflicting racial groups would band together to take control of remaining resources in the post-atomic setting, he also supplies the reassuring thesis that even in such desperate circumstances, clear thinking and hard work win out as they should.

In the idyllic northern town itself, disrupting Anderson's dichotomy with the inexplicable name of Southvale, racial difference is allegorized in the conflicts between human and mutant classes, specifically children, whose intergroup skirmishes have the classically cruel repercussions. The normal children taunt the mutant ones with calls of "Mutie! Mutie!" (54), while the mutant children band together for protection, despite the fact that there are "no two alike" (54). Depicted as a motley band of freaks, they are also in animal fashion "shy of humans" (55) yet strong in their inevitably increasing numbers. As in "Beggars in Velvet," the mutant outcome is dominant now and in a racially loaded moment, the narrator remarks that "the older [mutant children] generally realized that *they* would inherit the earth, and were content to wait" (55). Starting with his SF-style name, the hero's son Alaric is even stranger than the other mutants, since he does not band with peers and is a noncommunicating enigma to his loving parents. While they wonder whether he can even read, his invention of the death-dealing gadget indicates his status as idiot savant and leads to the realization that "mutants can serve society as talented members" (72). The parents' bold embrace of their freakish child—his mother ends the story with the declaration "No, . . . no[t] human. But he's our son" (76)—is a radical claim for both disability and civil rights: referring repeatedly to the mutant generation as the end of humans' "racial existence" (53, 54), the guilty humans who allowed atomic war in the first place are (human) race traitors in the most damning sense, whose only honorable choice is to be race traitors once again: embrace their mutant children, whose devastation is their own fault, following atomic catastrophe.

Anderson's comment is even more pointed in his debut tale for the pulps (co-written with F. N. Waldrop), "Tomorrow's Children," where the president of the post-atomic United States and his chief census-taker debate the possibility of containing a national epidemic of mutant births. On his data-gathering duties, the hero, Drummond, visits every corner of the nation and returns with the sobering message that there is no place safe from radioactive dust, that genetic mutations are now so many and so diverse that they dominate the gene pool. The president, Robinson, expecting his own first postwar baby within days, goes into a fascistic panic, suggesting quarantine, euthanasia, and sterilization, in terms explicitly likened by the more realistic Drummond to the "*Herrenvolk*" (75) ethos of Nazi Germany. The story depicts race hatred as literal madness, as Drummond tries to calm Robinson's hysteria—even slapping him at one point, as per the melodramatic cliché—yet has little success. Drummond preaches a homily of acceptance, insisting that "the only way to sanity—to *survival*—is to abandon class prejudice and race hatred altogether" (75). Intensifying the effect created by the novels of Chapter 1, where the bomb was credited with pulling down mansions and disabling segregated drinking fountains, in "Tomorrow's Children" it is a radioactive attack—upon "[e]very breath that we draw, every crumb we eat and drop we drink" (78)—that has re-arranged the social order from the microbiological ground up.

And yet, despite taking this notable stand, Anderson's progressivism dead-ends into postwar neo-liberalism, just as in the social-problem novels; here Drummond's brotherhood message is expressly called into service to avert the likelihood of damaging "group" mentalities. Instead of a "separate class" of mutants making war against "lumped-together 'humans,'" survival belongs only to those who "work as individuals" (75) and "build a culture of individual sanity" (77). In some ways, the mutant child, for whom no mutation is ever the same as that which occurs in his siblings or playmates, is the ideal "*new* human" (74) in this libertarian schema—a genetically blueprinted "individual" with no opportunity or inclination to form a group identity, due to the unending, uncontrollable biodiversity that characterizes his generation. Nevertheless, the mutant child born to Robinson at the end of the story, whose "limbs were rubbery tentacles terminating in boneless digits" (78), is both reality check and divine retribution for the delusional Hitler figure. While David Seed interprets such mutant children as "scapegoats in a ritual purging of social guilt over the primal explosion" (57), they are equally readable as impossible to purge, as the lasting marks of their forebears' guilt that cause the adults a permanent state of anguish. As with the brown, simian child who belonged to the hairless but light-skinned parents in Emshwiller's "Day at the Beach," the tentacled infant that arrives at the end of this story is an inextricable mix of blessing and curse, whose narrative function points simultaneously backward to retrograde stereotypes about racial identity and bodily non-normativity and forward toward analysis and debunking of those same stereotypes.

HEINLEIN'S NOVEL APPROACH

The bestselling Robert A. Heinlein, who began his career as an author for *Astounding Science Fiction*, is widely credited with removing the genre's "pulp" stigma when he himself switched from short stories to novels in the late 1950s and early 1960s. In its opening and closing segments, his *Farnham's Freehold* (1964) resembles the survival fantasies by Pat Frank and Philip Wylie examined in Chapter 1 and is closest to Wylie's *Triumph* published a year earlier (to be discussed in Chapter 5). In these several stories, the bomb is ultimately construed as a boon to the societies depicted, which, divine-retribution style, destroys the soft-headed undeserving in its purifying flames and leaves only a tough-minded remnant to carry on. In the hopeful words of Heinlein's protagonist, "this may be the first war in history which kills the stupid rather than the bright and able . . ." (29), while his leading lady agrees that "killing the poorest third is good genetics" (30). In Heinlein's novel (and similarly, in Wylie's *Triumph*) a farseeing patriarch saves a band of disoriented and insufficiently grateful survivors from atomic doom by inviting them at zero-hour into his soundly constructed bomb shelter. Both novels include a racially diverse cast and address sexual themes, although what a difference separates the year (and their authors' respective "pulp" versus "slick" origins) between Heinlein's and Wylie's work: as we shall see, *Triumph* nervously hints at the prospects of shelter-bound sexual frustration and interracial union, its decorum in keeping with early-1960s audience expectations. In stark contrast, *Farnham's Freehold* lunges audaciously toward a late-1960s/sexual-revolution context, including frank (if laughably rendered) sexual situations and provocative statements on race relations.

While Wylie's novel will implicitly credit the bomb with landing its several male characters in the cat-bird's position of having multiple fertile women with whom to couple and reproduce, the aphrodisiac qualities of Heinlein's atomic blast are even more explicit: in the immediate aftermath, soaring temperatures in the shelter cause everyone to strip to her or his panties or undershorts, and Heinlein's middle-aged protagonist Hugh Farnham finds himself constantly confronted by nubile, topless women (including his own daughter) who present themselves as willing sexual objects (again, this includes his own buxom, perverted daughter) whom he at first resists with iron fortitude. To the orgasmic accompaniment of a second blasting, Hugh succumbs to the seductions of

Barbara (his daughter's friend) while his flabby souse of a wife snores on the cot next door. As it turns out, Hugh's daughter Karen is pregnant by a boyfriend from college, yet loses the child and is herself lost in a delivery episode that H. Bruce Franklin describes as "one of the most moving scenes that [Heinlein] has ever penned" (*Robert A. Heinlein* 152).

Yet, perhaps not surprisingly by now, despite the wealth of sexual candor in the novel's early scenes, *Farnham's Freehold* maintains a decorous reticence—though more likely a racist unwillingness—on the subject of the sexual needs of the group's only black survivor, the houseman Joe, who is nobly devoted to his cat and conveniently oblivious to the women's rampant nudity. "Joe ignores it so carefully," says one naked woman to another at one point. "Is that boy square!" (37). Joe literally "has [on] the only pants among us" (38), and Heinlein and his readers would have it no other way. Even the radical anti-nuclear statement of Karen's death is tempered to the degree that it also cuts off the radical prospect of her impending marriage—to dear but unexciting Joe, to whom she had earlier proposed as a matter of necessity after determining that "miscegenation" was only slightly less objectionable than "incest" (93). Thus, despite the seemingly liberal take on sexual subject matter, Heinlein's views on race and politics in general are markedly conservative. Patrick Parrinder (72) identifies Heinlein, as well as Jack Williamson, whose "The Equalizer" opened this chapter, as two SF authors whose values remained ultra-conservative throughout the ever more left-leaning 1960s (see also Blish 58).

If Joe's celibate reserve goes toward depicting him as a sympathetic, salvageable character for Heinlein's white readership, he undergoes radical revision in the novel's most SF-styled section, where it is revealed that the atomic blast that fell on Farnham's shelter was a direct hit so intense that it blasted the group twenty centuries into the future. Here the survivors find themselves prisoners of "the Chosen," future descendants of the Africans who survived the East-West War, then came north to take control of the US territories. While scientifically brilliant, they are cool-handed slaveholders with a taste for human blood, or, more specifically, the flesh of their young, white, female chattel. In the course of events, Joe is granted full citizenship, while Hugh remains a rebellious slave; his peevish son Duke is castrated for the purposes of social control, his wife a drugged courtesan in the royal household, and even Barbara a bamboozled bridge partner of the ruler until Hugh makes her see the incontrovertible value of personal freedom. In a late scene, Hugh confronts Joe for having turned coat, while Joe delivers a retort worthy of that era's Malcolm X and the rising black separatists he inspired:

> "I'm a respected businessman—with a good chance of becoming a
> nephew by marriage of some noble family. Do you think I would swap
> back, even if I could? . . . I was a servant, now you are one. . . ."

The younger man's eyes suddenly became opaque and his features took on an ebony hardness Hugh had never seen in him before. "Hugh," he said softly, "have you ever made a bus trip through Alabama? As a 'nigger'?" (208)

Reading this and related scenes, Franklin argues that "*Farnham's Freehold* expresses the most deep-seated racist nightmare of American culture. . . . [T]he novel appeals to the very worst terrors about Blacks lurking in the minds of the overwhelmingly white readership, already considerably frightened by Black uprisings in 1964 and the visions of Blacks in the white media" (*Robert A. Heinlein* 157, 158). Though this assessment is sound, in many respects Joe is undeniably right to put the blame back onto the patronizing Farnham, his outright racist family members, and the white readership receiving this narrative. One of the undeniable payoffs of the civil rights struggle and especially the black radical movements that followed was the forcing of whites to realize the ways in which "attitude problems" such as Joe's originated from centuries of mistreatment handed down by the white majority. Just as the outlaw Dick Hammer in Poul Anderson's "Logic" castigated the townsmen for the smug exclusionism that resulted in their own torment by the desperate marauders, so in Heinlein's novel there prevails a chickens-come-home-to-roost subtext to Joe's (and the Chosen's) triumph so many centuries in the future. Joe's most threatening words are also his most logically unassailable, indistinguishable from the sort of manifesto that black separatists of the mid- and late 1960s would and did proudly publish. His words, his characterization, and the role played by the Chosen throughout the novel are thus readable—as is Revelations' own "reckoning day"—as equal parts unimaginable nightmare and glorious righting of a world's worth of wrongs. Indeed, the Chosen's view is reinforced (intentionally or not) by the storyline itself: throughout, they retain the upper hand, easily recapturing Hugh and Barbara in an attempted escape and ultimately releasing the couple back to their own era—to relive the disaster but avoid a direct hit— only when they themselves deem it fitting to do so.

Indeed, Hugh and Barbara return to the present moments before the hit but flee to an abandoned mine instead of the shelter that they now know will be ground zero. Instead of blasting into the future, they and their infant sons emerge as free-holding survivors in the largely depopulated atomic aftermath of their own rightward-tending, whites-mainly present. Yet as has been the pattern of all the stories discussed in this chapter thus far, this present is simultaneously a return to the past, as the atomic slate-wiping reestablishes America's Revolutionary moment—or at least the militiamen mentality that prevailed therein. In an attempt to regenerate society, Hugh and Barbara open a bar and restaurant whose "welcome" sign warns customers to "advance with your Hands *Up*. Stay on path, avoid mines" (256) and is topped by a vigorously whipping American flag. As in all of the other atomic fantasies discussed in this project, the bomb here retains its status as ultimate boon to humankind, bringing a new day that corresponds perfectly to its author's and protagonist's political specifications.

I have also argued that the colonial past is the only temporal register in which conservatively oriented texts reside comfortably and that these texts are much more likely to adopt the "alternative universe," "spare planet," or "safe zone" modes of escape whenever the nuclear nightmare threatens and/or implicates its main characters too stringently. Yet again in Heinlein's rightist narrative, confrontation with the post-nuclear future must be avoided no matter how. Thus while the favor granted Hugh and Barbara—to return to the present whenever they wish, just as with Dorothy from Oz—is inexplicable from the Chosen's point of view, from Heinlein's it is essential: as opposed to more progressively-minded SF writers who send characters into the future to confront the reality of racial equality and racial interdependence, and as opposed to the Afro-Futurists to be examined shortly, who also picture a near-future moment wherein the tables are turned in favor of black revolt, Heinlein glimpses an atomic-induced future of corrected race relations and will have none of it. His narrative rejects the radicalizing effects of the temporal shift and forces a return to the status-quo present, where his white heroes will move forward, day by day, from atomic blast to an America of their own remaking.

"ALIEN" MEN IN ATOMIC AMERICA

In these stories the "mutant" is usefully distinguished from the "alien," yet another non-normative figure set in opposition to surviving humans in postwar science fiction adopting an atomic theme. In both of two popular scenarios—one in which aliens are encountered when humans ruin planet Earth with atomic destruction and must seek a homeland elsewhere (or vice versa; see Sontag 125) and another in which the setting off of atomic bombs during atmospheric testing draws the attention of citizens of a distant planet—the alien encounter is read as a fitting consequence for the promethean overreaching of scientists and politicians who act recklessly with atomic weapons and invite their planet's demise. For as opposed to the often sympathetic, victimized, and ultimately harmless mutant character, the alien is usually depicted as ineffable—closed off to human communication or issuing indecipherable commands (see Amis 13–14 and Sontag 127–28)—and motivated by malevolent intent. Wayne L. Johnson observes that "in the tradition of invaders throughout history, when we [Earthlings or Americans] are doing the invading, it is called 'colonization'" (34). Thus, even when the visiting aliens mean no harm, are simply on an innocent mission to "colonize" another world, the targets of this experiment feel quite unpleasantly invaded, such that the very term "alien" almost always connotes a figure from beyond whose ultimate aims are takeover, pillage, and destruction. Mark Rose (*Alien Encounters* 141) suggests a connection between alien figures spilling over the horizon in postwar science fiction and the Marxist concept of alienation—a sense of estrangement from one's own work, life, and self due to industrial compartmentalization and growing antagonism between management and labor classes since the mid-nineteenth century (see also Booker 16–17). In the late 1940s and 1950s, even this managerial class experienced a sense of alienation as veterans returned from the trauma of war only to enter a world of mind-numbing conformity at work and suburban banality at home. Such disconnect from one's ever more technically intricate work product can result, posit these critics, in the sort of accidents and overproductions that lead to nuclear war, which would attract (and even morally justify) the intrusive interest of alien visitors.

The racial aspects of postwar alienation are many and complex. Note, for instance, how the anti-conformity statement on display in Kurt Vonnegut's classic "Harrison Bergeron" (originally published in the *Magazine of Fantasy and Science Fiction* in October 1961) mutates imperceptibly into a biting critique of ideas that have been termed political correctness and affirmative action more recently. In the tale, the titular protagonist is a 14-year-old boy with obvious physical gifts. In the hysterically democratic society in which he lives, however, he, his cognitively superior father, and all others with skills or intelligence must wear weights, blinders, and distracting buzzers in their ears, to ensure that they are as physically inept and mentally dull as the most mediocre specimens of their breed, including Bergeron's addle-brained mother and the sourpuss harridan who rules the land. The story's blatant sexism and barely disguised racism, ethnocentrism, and intellectual elitism are thus of a piece with the otherwise progressively situated appeal to nonconformity; Vonnegut implies that the intellectually and physically superior are alienated by postwar trends toward suburban like-mindedness, marital "togetherness," and racial integration—even the dumbing down of the college curriculum required by the GI Bill—and may seek, ironically, the means to separate (alienate) themselves from the mediocre pack. Interpreting the closely related message of Ray Bradbury's *Fahrenheit 451*, M. Keith Booker paraphrases the Author's Afterword, "If minorities do not like his books, Bradbury haughtily proclaims, let them write their own" (83). Though corporate and suburban conformity were often targeted by the postwar Left for all manner of crimes against culture and individuals, in fact Vonnegut's anti-conformity satire is first cousin to Heinlein's individualist survival fantasy, and the alienation in both examples comes not from a sense of separation but from a suffocating sense of group-identity that reflected society-wide fears of communist takeover and racial equality in this period.

In a specifically civil rights context the mutant/alien distinction mirrors the integrationist/separatist divide. Throughout US history both white and African American authors have chosen between depicting African American characters as loveable and sympathetic (as with the post-atomic mutant victims) or as self-aware and dangerous (as with the alien invaders from outer space). As the mutants discussed in stories by Emshwiller and Anderson were often depicted as children, so childlike Negro figures were a staple of sympathetic (i.e., patronizing) treatments throughout the nineteenth and early twentieth centuries, and the idea that mutated children belonged nevertheless to the hubristic parents who bore and maimed them corresponds to ideas of family ties, fellow-feeling, and interracial responsibility that prevailed during the integrationist period. As with the horror-fantasy shadings of the mutant, whose radical genetic decline threated the integrity and viability of the human race, so African American victimization was the unpunished crime festering in the heart of American democracy and threatening postwar American claims to the position of leader of the free world. To rectify this imbalance, to cleanse the defect of racism and hypocrisy at the jeopardized core of the American experiment, reparations were promised and accepted between integrating American brothers of the period.

By contrast, the alienated Negro of white nightmares (such as Heinlein's *Farnham's Freehold*) and black-separatist manifestoes was fully grown, "highly intelligent," and inclined toward violent militancy. While the alienated white man in the grey flannel suit experienced the ennui of suburban conformity, the race-conscious African American of the same period experienced his alienation sometimes through exclusion from this exurban paradise but more often through increasing awareness of history and self that made the post-Reconstruction status quo no longer acceptable. Here, the classic example in both American literature and the more specific canon of Afro-Futurism is Ralph Ellison's invisible man who, as Booker observes, is "nothing if not alienated" (17). Yet as Aimable Twagilimana notes, "the Invisible Man's alienation allowed him to experience and critique American society. . . . Ironically, it is because America never sees him that Invisible Man truly sees America" (102). Finally, David Ketterer asks whether "a work describing a totally subjective, alternate reality qualif[ies] as science fiction" and that if so, then "Ralph Ellison's *Invisible Man* . . . qualifies as such an apocalyptic work." For Ketterer, Ellison's apocalypse consists of the novel's "culminating in riot and chaos, . . . the last loosing of Satan, with Bliss Rinehart in the anti-christ role." In addition, "this apocalyptic reality is an index of the extent to which the reader's consciousness is transformed by the realization that the black man, in a very real sense is invisible" (165; see also Leigh 193).

RALPH ELLISON'S *INVISIBLE MAN*

Ellison's masterwork from 1953, *Invisible Man*, serves as this project's fitting segue from white to black authorship, now in focus for the next several chapters. Its hugely canonical status might give it pride of place in any event, but

I am drawn to this work for other reasons—Ellison's description of his novel as "science fiction" for starters, as well as its absolute silence on the subject of atomic culture *per se*, all the while being deeply conversant with and a valuable contribution to the context of atomic fear, atomic humor, atomic politics, and atomic ambivalence that shaped the experience of inner-city life when the nuclear threat was greatest. My reading of Ellison's work therefore underscores many of the findings of my introduction and anticipates the observations to be made in Chapter 3 regarding bomb coverage in the African American press. As in Ellison's novel, the two audiences (and settings) of greatest import for the major black weeklies were the city from which each paper hailed and the rural locales where the recently migrated readers in those cities continued to have deep ties. Ellison's early-1950s rural South and New York backgrounds resemble the situation faced by actual African Americans during this "preparedness" moment in US history, when these citizens were made to feel invisible with respect to shelter-building, air raid siren audibility, and large-scale drills. In addition, since the dawn of the atomic era African Americans had experienced a deep sense of alienation—of dispiriting separation from one's work product—thanks to the bomb's abrupt curtailment of war-related jobs and opportunities for heroism in battle. In Mark Rose's estimation,

> Marx's discussion of alienated labor sounds almost like a prescription
> for science fiction, but this should not be wholly surprising. As a genre
> science fiction comes into being not only as a medium for expression of
> the feeling of separation from physical nature, the alienated senses both of
> space and of time, but also for expression of the feeling of social discon-
> nection that accompanied urbanization and industrialization. (*Alien
> Encounters* 141)

Ironically, Ellison's nameless protagonist moves to the industrialized, urban-ized north for the express purposes of finding work and fitting in; instead, he repeatedly experiences traumatizing invisibility to his fellow-humans alternat-ing with humiliating moments of all eyes on him—when he is reduced to a specimen under glass or freakish circus attraction—followed by his failure to deliver. To be sure, the black worker's relationship to his "work product" has been one of profound alienation since he was dragged onto US shores four centuries ago; never has he enjoyed an unadulterated craftsman period of the kind harkened back to in Marxist analyses, when individual cottage laborers gratify-ingly managed their own inventories and oversaw production at every stage. In fact, since emancipation, African Americans have sought avidly to obtain the kind of skilled and unskilled industrial labor that Marx denounced. During World War II, such jobs were held by African Americans in historic numbers, and *Invisible Man* was begun in the summer of 1945, only months before the atomic-induced end to the war-industry boom and during a period of Ellison's own non-employment, when he was furloughed from the Merchant Marines due to a kidney infection (Ellison, "A Special Message" 353).

Thus, as Ellison wondered about his professional future during this transitional moment in US history, so his protagonist may be described as a young man who spends the course of this epic narrative reviewing career options and finding that his all-purpose liberal arts education—as he explains to his foreman at the paint factory, he is "no engineer" (208)—has ill-suited him for anything in particular. He resembles a generation of shell-shocked, alienated World-War II veterans who wandered the pages of Sloan Wilson and Mickey Spillane and the screens of William Wyler, Billy Wilder, and Alfred Hitchcock in the late 1940s and 1950s; though not ordinarily construed as post-traumatic stress, the abrupt loss of job opportunities in home front industries and in the labor battalions where they chiefly served in the military proved as disconcerting to African Americans, and African American characters such as the invisible man, as did the sudden return to peace faced by white combat veterans of the period. To the degree that both black and white veterans suffered the twin fears of feeling invisible—overlooked or shunned, especially if they returned disfigured or mentally altered, by their home societies—and feeling like universal objects of pity and despair, Ellison's hero spoke for a generation of young men reborn into and at sixes and sevens within an alien and alienating postwar society. The novel itself is the result of an abrupt career shift due to the exigencies of the war's end: it began as "a prison-camp novel" ("A Special Message" 353) featuring a young black airman who eventually served as the hero of Ellison's well-known short story "Flying Home." For reasons remaining unclear, Ellison eschewed the path taken by young veterans such as Norman Mailer and Irwin Shaw, who charged onto the postwar literary scene by turning their war experiences into bestselling first novels. Now that the war had ended this theme no longer appealed to Ellison, and the postwar zeitgeist characterized by disillusionment, unemployment, uncertainty, and ennui pervaded the author's consciousness instead. As Ellison famously tells the story, he had a visitation from an alien(ated) presence who confronted him insistently with the novel's famous first line, "I am an invisible man," and committed to this unique speaker from that point.

It is important to speculate upon why Ellison referred to this novel as "science fiction" (xv) in the introduction he wrote to its reissue in 1981. Loosely, the term may refer to the other-worldliness of invisibility itself, or to the futuristic factory-hospital scene in which the invisible man is incubated in a glass-and-steel machine and reborn, a la Frankenstein's monster, as a deformed and defiant product of medical experimentation. Elsewhere, the magical white hat and dark glasses that cause all to misrecognize the invisible man as the charismatic and multifarious Bliss Rineheart belong to the fantasy tradition. Finally, the eerie alternate universe of the prologue and epilogue, the protagonist's underground cell of blazing light, is notably SF in theme and will be the special focus of my reading to follow. *Invisible Man* has been included by Kali Tal and others in the canon of Afro-Futurism, due likely to these several sci-fi elements, as well as the full-scale race-war that serves as the novel's dramatic climax—and as a warning about the "tomorrow" awaiting all Americans if change does not occur (see also Thomas, esp. xii).

As wordplay, "science fiction" may refer to Ellison's satire of the power of science in the novel. From the evil geniuses at the factory hospital to the doctrinaire "Brotherhood" member who—in textbook Marxist fashion—harps upon the fundamentals of "science," Ellison may have launched his science *fiction* as a bracing antidote to the controlling presence of science fact on the intellectual scene at that moment, or he could be cleverly conveying the sentiment that much of what passes as "science" in his era is in fact damaging "fiction." As Thomas Schaub argues, Ellison seemed to write in opposition to the scientific determinism on display in naturalist writings by Richard Wright and others influenced by social Darwinism, who depicted blacks and other members of the American underclass only ever as victims: "For Ellison, the rise of naturalism, with its emphasis upon the crushing influence of the environment, is a literary corollary of the growing influence of [quoting Ellison] 'contemporary science and industry,' which has obscured the 'full, complex ambiguity of the human'" (133). While Schaub argues that Ellison places the psychological in opposition to the sociological in his novel, by way of fully exploring the interiority and humanity of his black characters, in fact Freudianism itself was regarded as a hard-and-fast, supremely reliable, and informative "science" in the postwar period, and at certain points the psychoanalytic buzz-terms and boozed up, repressed housewives are as satirically treated in *Invisible Man* as are the references to sociology, medicine, and the hard sciences. Yet, as per Schaub, there is an undeniable power, and an illuminating psychological allegory, on display in the invisible man's iconic descent into the urban subconscious at the novel's climax and throughout its prologue and epilogue. When he issues his indelible final challenge—"Who knows but that, on the lower frequencies, I speak for you?" (581)—the invisible man echoes Fanon's remarkable summation in his own work during this period that the black man is the white man's subconscious, his irrepressible id. As opposed to the show-stopping arrivals made by other alien visitors in SF fiction and film of this period, the invisible man anticipates the insidious horror of the "body snatchers" tradition of the mid-1950s, silently burrowing into the brain (or heart or entrails) of the cultural adversary and taking control.

Admittedly, the atom bomb was a topic of rare interest in Ellison's writing[4] and as noted above gets no specific mention at any point in *Invisible Man*. In fact, the Second World War as a whole is barely cited, with the story's various direct or implied references to General Pershing, Marcus Garvey (refigured as the African-accented Ras the Destroyer), Booker T. Washington, union organizing, exploding dynamos, and the Harlem race riots of the 1930s and early

1940s seeming to set the scene in the early decades of the twentieth century, not the late 1940s and 1950s that are its actual context. Where atomic catastrophe blasted the characters in Heinlein's *Farnham's Freehold* two thousand years into the future, the atom bombings that actually ended the World War II evidently sent Ellison's novel hurtling into a prewar, Depression-era past. As Mark Rose defined science fiction as structured by a sense of alienation from both time and space, so Ellison may have rejected the anxieties of postwar uncertainty by relocating his story to the prewar era, while similarly his protagonist may have fled his contemporary space for the seemingly impervious-to-history shelter of his underground cell. Yet I contend that any reader taking up Ellison's novel in the early 1950s, when it was first published and received enormous critical and popular attention (see, e.g., O'Meally 3–5) would have found it difficult to ignore its generally postwar and specifically atomic-age implications, starting and ending with the "sub-urban" shelter-dweller himself and climaxing with an apocalyptic riot in Harlem that prefigures the urban incinerations feared by doomsday scenarists during the atomic period.

Significantly, the invisible man's underground phase is as subversive as it is surreal; while chased down a manhole by two white thugs with a baseball bat, he winds up glad to be safe from the firestorm raging above-ground and finds his best accommodations just outside Harlem, that is, holed up in the basement of a well-fortified, white-occupied high-rise apartment. Though he rails against "this passion toward conformity" and fears its manifestation in their "forcing me, an invisible man, to become white" (577), yet tucked into his cozy bower, he espouses in the epilogue the postwar suburbanite's mantra—regarding the need to get "away from it all" (573)—as his chief justification for having fled there in the first place. As per this suburban model, Thomas Heise describes the invisible man's cellar as a "space of individual privacy, heroic self-recreation, and writing" (*Urban Underworlds* 130; see also Allen; Morel). Of course African Americans dealing with anxieties about urban overcrowding, sprawling slums, and nuclear attack were rarely encouraged to get away from it all as were their white counterparts answering the advertisements of postwar suburban real estate developers. Thus the invisible man's integration of the sheltered white space, which he so handily renovates into convivial home space, is both a distinct triumph and perhaps the most science-fictional/fantastic element of the entire story.

As readers of the black press—and even some mainstream magazines and newspapers—would have known during that period, leaders of the black community frequently criticized white city leadership for failing to envision black neighborhoods in their shelter and preparedness planning. As per the communication breakdown between Congresswoman Griffiths and Secretary McNamara discussed in my introduction, entire communities went unnoticed—were rendered invisible—when the assumptions of white city planners and preparedness campaign managers prevailed. Notably, Harlem's widely read *New York*

Amsterdam News editorialized frequently in the early and mid-1950s on the lack of proposed shelter space in New York's black neighborhoods (see Chapter 3), questioning where Harlemites might be expected to run, with ten minutes' warning, in the event of nuclear attack. The invisible man's occupation of the urban basement at the height of an apocalyptic race riot is shot through with implications for this 1950s preparedness context: firmly ensconced within the city limits, the basement retreat is identical to the very apartment basements, sewer systems, and subway tunnels included in postwar urban planners' visions of survival following nuclear attack. At the same time, this space, pointedly located on the other side of a white boundary line, reframes Harlem itself as "the city" and the surrounding white sections of Manhattan as the better fortified, more commodious "suburbs." Subversively laying claim to this forbidden turf, the invisible man positions himself within what Zoe Trodd identifies as a centuries-long African American "literary landscape of manholes, coalbunkers, sewers, kitchenettes, shacks, and boxes" (224) whose "trope of confined spaces reveal[s] and challenge[s] this country's narrative of historical progress" (227).

As Trodd reads the "hole" or "box" that recurs in African American literary history, such containers are both shelter and confinement and are equally effective contributions to the protest tradition. Both protected and buried alive within his hole in the ground, the eeriest aspect of the invisible man's occupation is its notably long term. It is implied that he has maintained his subterranean existence for a period of months or even years, has taken his living space through drastic transformations, endlessly rides the subways, and as he contemplates reemergence is unsure even what season it is. His lengthy stay underground, therefore, strongly resembles that of the post-atomic shelter-dweller of many fictional, cinematic, and government-sponsored doomsday scenarios of the postwar period, for whom the dash below would be no short-term proposition. Using his nose to gather information, he observes that "there's a stench in the air, which, from this distance underground, might be the smell either of death or of spring—I hope of spring. But . . . there *is* death in the smell of spring and in the smell of thee as in the smell of me" (580). As the classic shelter-survivor emerged—alive but alone—into a world of death at the end (or beginning) of many doomsday narratives, so these same narratives emphasized the democratizing, leveling effects of atomic blast, just as Ellison references here the shared mortality of all mortals.

Once acclimated to his surroundings, the invisible man siphons electricity from the satirically named Monopolated Light and Power, to light and heat his shelter alcove with a fantastical 1,369 light bulbs (and counting). His marked success with this scheme anticipates the African American heroes of atomic survival narratives from the end of the decade, including Pat Frank's novel *Alas, Babylon* (see Chapter 1) and Ranald MacDougall's *The World, the Flesh, and the Devil* (see Chapter 5), who make life easier for themselves and their fellow-survivors by getting the lights back on, establishing a connection with remaining power sources. In the densely satiric environment of Ellison's novel, this re-empowerment is established to the nth degree; not only is each screwed in bulb another jab at the stingy landlords and greedy utility barons who have kept northern tenement dwellers in the cold and the dark for decades but the striking image itself—of the invisible man's once dark shelter space now ablaze with blinding light—is one of the most SF- and atomic-inflected in the novel (see also Wilcox). Ellison makes no attempt to place this remarkable image into a realist framework; the invisible man even claims that as soon as the walls and ceiling are covered with lights, he will set to work on the floor. While now assuming tall-tale proportions, with satiric payoff and perhaps little else, it is a traditional narrative form specifically updated for the modern age (see Ford 889–90). Its comic elements are plain, yet the image is likewise as scorching and blinding as an atomic flash.

Clearly aware of the lasting impression made by the spatial arrangements of his epic tale, Ellison's 1981 introduction to *Invisible Man* takes pains to map the novel's own production, specifically in terms of its vertical trajectory, its heights and depths. Conceived, Ellison says, in the "crowded subways" of New York and a "ground floor apartment on St. Nicholas Avenue" in Harlem, the novel was developed "in a fellow writer's elegant office" on the eighth floor of a Fifth Avenue apartment building, "symbolically and actually. . . . the highest elevation upon which the novel unfolded." While this pleasing little penthouse was "a long, far cry from [his own] below-street-level apartment" (viii), in fact Ellison feels more at home in this elevated place, since his stay-at-home-husband role led to raised eyebrows amongst his Harlem neighbors and saddled him with an "indefinite status" (ix)—caught between poles of racial, class, and intellectual identity—quite similar to his protagonist's own. Just as the invisible man's shelter is marked as white, due to its past-Harlem location and its blazing-white wattage, so Ellison finds "sanctuary in [this] predominantly white environment" (xi).

These eighth-floor offices shared space with a jeweler's establishment, and "the suite's constant flow of beautiful objects and its occupants' expert evaluations of pearls and diamonds, platinum and gold gave [Ellison] a sense of living far above [his] means" (*Invisible Man* vii). Here Ellison positions himself within the illustrious tradition in African American letters, of the black writer working on the borrowed funds and in the borrowed spaces of wealthy white patrons— "far above [his] means" although by virtue of his exceptional talent fully deserving such support, and thus "on the same level as" the other art objects that crowd the elegant environment. In addition he suggests ironically that what makes it to the top in US society—even if it is just an elegant eighth floor in a city full of skyscrapers—is often that which comes from deepest underground, the "natural resources" such as pearls, diamonds, platinum, and gold that must be mined from the depths of the land and waters of Africa and other regions in the global south. On at least two occasions in *Invisible Man*, the hero acerbically describes himself as a "natural resource" (303, 508) being mined by his handlers in the communist Brotherhood to promote their message amongst his fellow blacks in Harlem. In so doing, he correctly assesses his talents and his person as "precious" to advancing the Brotherhood's cause but also as an inert, insensate, and powerless mineral substance, a second cousin to dirt, that the Brotherhood feels free to shovel around in any direction. The atomic-age natural resources suggested by this trope are the powerful yet deadly plutonium, strontium, and cesium by which postwar modernity itself could not have advanced and whose fiery effects when properly detonated suggest the danger faced by the Brotherhood, and white society in general, when it manipulates its black "natural resources" recklessly. While the invisible man's role is ultimately quite small, the Harlem riot that occupies the novel's final movement explodes on his own behalf in the faces of the whites he has bridled against the entire novel.

While Ellison in his introduction suggests the traditional class-based cartography of US society, wherein the poorest inhabit the miasmic lower depths while the wealthy enjoy an unobstructed view from the top, the atomic-era inversion discussed in my introduction, whereby safety and affluence were relocated to far-flung, low-slung suburban dwellings, with vulnerable entrapment the plight of those remaining in urban high-rises, is exhaustively suggested throughout Ellison's novel. Here, vertiginous reversal of the comparative cultural values of north and south, up and down, constantly occur. The narrator contemplates whether he was better off at his historically black college in the Jim Crow South or in the hands of seemingly well-meaning northern white liberals with insidious agendas to fill—as one shell-shocked WWI veteran from his college town describes the dilemma, "out of the fire into the melting pot" (152). An advisor in the city informs him that he can help invert the current social order, even within the black community: "it's the ones from the South that's got to [change society], them what knows the fire and ain't forgot how it burns. Up here too many forgets. They find a place for theyselves and forgets the ones on the bottom" (255). As the invisible man exchanges his short-term jobs in the industrial sector for a journey through the ranks of the Brotherhood, the exoticism and luxury of this largely white and wealthy movement disorient him as to whether the career move constitutes an ascent or a selling-out; a state-of-the-art elevator to an early meeting "stops with a gentle bounce [such that] I was uncertain whether we had gone up or down" (300).

Too, the centrality of Harlem to the Brotherhood's expansionist plans is played off against the invisible man's banishment at one point to the nowheresville of "downtown," where he is further stigmatized by having to lecture on the Woman Question instead of more pertinent issues like racial protest and housing reform in the city's northern neighborhoods. In a powerful scene from the final riot episode, a local leader forms a kerosene bucket brigade with his enraged Harlem neighbors and, "work[ing with them] in silence now, like moles underground" (547–48), methodically sets fire to a tumble-down tenement that the city managers refuse to renovate. Despite the protests of certain residents who have nowhere else to go, the far-seeing Scofield insists that it is the only way to effect change; he here echoes multiple contemporaneous reports in the *Amsterdam News* about black New York neighborhoods that should stage atomic preparedness drills because they look as though they had been atom-bombed anyway. Indeed the detailed scene of the brigade's check for remaining inhabitants and their floor-by-floor ignition of the kerosene fire mimics the disaster drills actually carried out on "bombed out" Harlem real estate in this period. The small-scale destruction enacted in this scene reflects the absurdly limited scope of the various drills described in *News* reports. In both the slum clearance executed here and the preparedness exercises conducted by the Red Cross in 1950s Harlem, the gesture is more symbolic than realistic, suggestive of its ultimate futility.

Yet the drama of this scene is plain, and at the height of the chaos he has helped to create, the invisible man, fleeing through the stairwell of the house on fire, is warned to "Keep going man, it's hell upstairs" (548). The statement both perfectly encapsulates the inverted orders of bacchanalia-cum-apocalypse that reigns at the moment and pronounces upon the baseline hellishness of New York's upstairs—its northern Harlem neighborhood—on even an ordinary day. Again, it underscores the physical inversions of power and safety that characterized city life in the atomic era: in the doomsday scenario, it is the upstairs, the tallest buildings clustered in derelict uptown neighborhoods like Harlem, that explode into hellfire. In the estimation of Zbigniew Lewicky, "In Ellison's book, the black world goes through a series of apocalyptic ends until it is finally destroyed, but the white world remains intact. The mutual alienation of these two cultures seems to reach beyond temporal conflicts into eternal differentiation" (57). David J. Leigh agrees that Ellison's riots "become both racial and wider battles for power and identity within the nation, battles that reveal the chaos to be racial, societal, and ultimately moral and apocalyptic" (192).

THE FAILED FUTURISM OF *PLAN B*

Like Ellison, Chester Himes, a noted author of Harlem-based potboiler detective stories, is credited with a key work in the canon of Afro-Futurism, his surreal and provocative *Plan B*. Grouped with several other contemporaneous texts that Kali Tal dubs both "the black militant near-future novel" (66) and "kill-the-white-folks futurist fiction in the African American literary tradition" (67), *Plan B* is the final installment in Himes's detective series, drafted in the late 1960s but not published in France in its incomplete form until 1983, months before his death. Despite the novel's fragmentary state, its final movement makes sure to complete the series itself through the surprising murder of one of his detective heroes, Coffin Ed Johnson, by his once-loyal partner, Grave Digger Jones. Grave Digger is then dispatched by the mastermind behind the story's impending race war, whose plan Grave Digger has just killed his own partner to defend. Although an all-out war of blacks against whites is the futuristic premise upon which the novel is based, in fact Himes undermines the possibility of such an apocalyptic, revolutionary tomorrow at every turn, starting (or rather, ending) with this senseless black-on-black murder.

Throughout his body of work, including many short stories, interviews, and a two-volume autobiography, Himes developed a philosophy of absurdity to explain his approach to his craft and his outlook on life. As encapsulated in the opening statement of *My Life of Absurdity*, the second volume of his life story, "Racism introduces absurdity into the human condition. Not only does racism express the absurdity of the racists, but it generates absurdity in its victims. And the absurdity of the victims intensifies the absurdity of the racists, ad infinitum" (1). Later, "Realism and absurdity are so similar in the lives of American blacks that one cannot tell the difference" (109; see also Milliken 11–13). As the pointless deaths of the two heroes make clear, *Plan B* indeed presents a world of tomorrow that is patently absurd (yet see also Walters 210–13). It is a narrative so distracted by historical digressions, elaborate sex jokes with no bearing on the main plot, repeated loops of action, watered down folk humor, and a general atmosphere of inexplicable mayhem that its status as futuristic novel, with a complete and triumphant vision of tomorrow, comes under threat and ultimately succumbs. As per the scene described above, rapid-fire, self-inflicted (i.e., intraracial), counterproductive violence characterizes every attempt to even visit the novel's main theme—execution of "Plan B"—such that no actual reckoning day ever even dawns, let alone results in the achievement of social equality that it was fully within Himes's power, as a storyteller if not a revolutionary, to achieve. Aptly characterizing the experience of reading this novel, James Sallis observes, "Though he has often been labeled as such, [Himes] is not a protest writer, for that term carries an implicit sense of meliorism, of redemptive change, a sense rarely manifested in Himes's work. The sense one *does* receive is that of a vast pall of futility, a huge sea of inaction and impotence relieved by sudden islands of violent, random motion" ("In America's Black Heartland" 128). Ultimately, Himes rejected the crossing of one genre (detective fiction) with another (science fiction or even political fantasy) that would have provided his reader the get-even dream of racial retribution narrated with relish by many African American authors to be examined elsewhere this study. Despite the outlandish, fantastic, comic-book-style that characterizes the entire Harlem series and *Plan B* in particular, the reality of America's entrenched racial divide must have prevented Himes from using his authorial license to take his readers, both black and white, to the frightening but edifying land of tomorrow that *Plan B* presents with such intriguing promise at its outset.

The "B" in "Plan B" stands for the adopted last name of its enigmatic mastermind, Tomsson Black, who approaches center stage in this intricate plot over the course of 150 pages and 150 years. Himes interleaves a ribald narrative of Black's white and black ancestry with scenes from present-day—or, more accurately, day-after-tomorrow—Harlem, where high-powered automatic rifles are mysteriously delivered by unidentified messengers to unlikely Harlem residents. Yet of course the "B" stands not only for the last name of the story's hero but for blacks in general, who, Himes posits, will rise up as one in the very near future and take over where "Plan W," so to speak, has so miserably failed. The concept of a "plan B" is yet more broadly futuristic, suggesting a new social order destined to succeed a variety of "plans A" that were in the process of winding down into disappointment as Himes penned the initial episodes of his story: King's integrationism, Johnson's Great Society, and even the more militant response of the Black Power movement—its own "plan B" to the vision of interracial brotherhood envisioned by King, such that a better name for Himes's novel might have been *Plan C.* For Himes, even the black nationalists had failed on multiple counts, including power struggles within leadership circles, mercenary motivations, and an over-abundance of energy spilt against civil rights predecessors. Although the organizers of Himes's own "plan B" fail in just the way Himes critiqued the black nationalists for failing—that is, by being insufficiently organized—yet he had been describing clearly, for the preceding quarter-century, his vision for the next stage in the racial revolution that America so desperately needed.

In an essay published in *Crisis,* "Negro Martyrs are Needed," in May 1944, Himes boldly advocated the incitement of "revolution" based on well targeted "incidents" executed by Negro "martyrs." While one possible outcome of this revolution—"the overthrow of our present government and the creation of a communist state" (159)—was probably the notion that got Himes an FBI file opened on himself the very next month (see Fabre and Skinner x; Margolies and Fabre 182n16; and Sallis, *Chester Himes* 78), in fact in this early document, Himes seeks volunteers from the Negro middle-class whose well-staged incidents would spring from infringements on Constitutional rights, not, for instance, "an unjust accusation of rape [which will] serve no primary purpose other than to agitate or inflame. . . ." In fact, "in the event of a Negro American revolution it is hoped there will be no shooting" (174). While *Plan B* presents Himes's radical revision of the revolutionary blueprint—now replete with violent interracial sex and gun battles breaking out on every street corner—one proscription launched in "Negro Martyrs" remained a plank in Himes's platform throughout the later Harlem detective novels—that against purposeless, self-destructive riots. In "Negro Martyrs," written, let us recall, during a veritable craze for war-era race riots fought over jobs and housing in urban centers throughout the North, Himes distinguished the pointless energy expenditure of impromptu, emotionally charged rioting from well-planned, well-executed revolution. At the end of Himes's second-to-last Harlem novel whose deeply cynical title, *Blind Man with a Pistol*, says it all, Himes has a laugh at the expense of warring factions within the Harlem community (Black Power adherents, Black Jesus cult members, back-to-Africa charlatans) who erupt in pointless internecine warfare in the novel's apocalyptic finale (see Lundquist 131; Margolies and Fabre 144; and Muller 94–105). Himes's social critique in such renderings is clear: so long as members of the African American community expend violent energy against each other, a principled, premeditated response to white oppression cannot occur.

It is within this later, more violent vision of revolution that we locate the politics of weapons-wielding, what Michael Denning terms Himes's "ideology of violence" (156), that Himes also came to espouse, as well as identify the role played by the atomic bomb within his racially politicized arsenal. As in the estimation of radical writers examined later in this book, specifically Elijah Muhammad and John Oliver Killens (see Chapter 4), by the late 1960s, the bomb was no longer an attractive metaphor, or even the mobilizing device of get-even dreams, claimed by the integration-era generation of African American writers more neutral or even hopeful about the benefits of an atomic age. As will be the case with Muhammad and Killens, Himes consigned atomic power to the cache of icons that symbolized the corruption and decline—in Himes's specific register, the overwhelming absurdity—of white America, characterized by Himes on another occasion as a "burning house" no longer worth integrating (qtd. in Margolies and Fabre 135). For this and other reasons to be discussed shortly, Himes rejected the bomb as a weapon, even a futuristically retooled one, employed in the cause of black freedom and equality.

In *Plan B* the bomb crowns the campaign of ludicrous overkill launched by white society against black rebels at the height of the racial conflict taking place. In terms explicitly science-fictional (even science-fantastic) and identical to those dreamt up by white SF writers such as Jack Williamson with his hand-held "Equalizer," in Himes's novel "the white community petitioned Congress to suspend the manufacture and stockpiling of nuclear weapons, continental ballistic missiles, and Polaris submarines, and concentrate on developing atomic bombs that could be used to destroy one black bastard with a gun without subjecting the entire white community to danger" (137). Always for the SF writer, the non-discriminating messiness of atomic blast and subsequent radioactive contamination required authorial containment for the benefit of the sympathetic character or group. In his own futuristic novel, Himes mocks the attempts of white science fiction writers (and white US policy makers) to submit nuclear energy to such politicized, racist intent. When Himes describes the whites clamoring for "an atom bomb that could be carried in a policeman's pocket with his blackjack and which would not produce any radioactivity when it exploded" (137–38), he closes the circle opened by Williamson's straight-faced fantasy of exactly such a weapon and the indeed racially homogenizing work it would do in the hands of his hearty peasants. Himes extends the atomic gag by picturing "Geiger counters which reacted only to the combined pulsations from black skin and blue steel, for use in the location of black killers with guns" and stretches the scene to its preposterous limit with the invention of "anti-riot glue to immobilize rioters by sticking them together in balls of ten or twelve each" and "sneezing powders to incapacitate rioters with paroxysms of sneezing" (138). By the end of the 1960s, the atomic threat had receded so far in the national consciousness due to the resurgence of traditional warfare in Vietnam and the pressing concerns of civil rights issues at home that the bomb is little more than a joke for Himes, one of many absurd and embarrassing indicators of white racist animosity and hysteria.

Himes gets similar comic, and darkly satiric, mileage out of the military tank, brought in to blast away a lone gunman in two separate "incidents" in the course of the story. Each arrives in grand farcical style; in chapter 8, "coming up the middle of 8th Avenue" and looking like "some kind of strange insect from outer space" (63) and in chapter 21 not knowing "where to look" for the gunman so "shoot[ing] explosive shells at the black plaster-of-paris mannequins in a display of beach wear in a department store window" (180–81) instead. Each escapade turns grim quickly, however, as when in chapter 8, the tank's canon blows out the back wall of the shooter's already-rickety tenement, endangering those Harlemites seeking shelter from the crossfire in the first floor entry. The canon fire from chapter 21, set in the white environs of lower Manhattan, explicitly echoes the doomsday descriptions of atomic survival narratives—"The [tank's] concussion was devastating. Splintered plate glass filled the air like a sand storm. Faces were split open and lacerated by flying glass splinters. . . . Many other men, women, and children were stripped stark naked by the force of the concussion" (181)—and leads to society-wide upheaval: "the stock market crashed. The dollar fell on the world market. The very structure of capitalism began to crumble" (182). The dark absurdism in both incidents is clear; time and again, the narrative suggests, ludicrous displays of firepower are marshaled by white officialdom against a single black individual, resulting in collateral damage to black and white society of apocalyptic proportions.

By contrast, Himes's weapon of choice for his Harlem revolutionaries is the traditional, individually operated high-powered rifle, in keeping with the wide-scale revolution he envisioned for social change. In a key interview with his fellow-Afro-Futurist, novelist John A. Williams, Himes developed his idea by pointing out that "Even individually, if you give one black one high-powered repeating rifle and he wanted to shoot it into a mob of twenty thousand or more white people, there are a number of people he could destroy" ("My Man Himes" 45). In the populist sentiment expressed in his autobiography, "Deep in the heart of every American black person is the knowledge that the only way to fight racism is with a gun" (*My Life of Absurdity* 27). When Himes tells Williams that revolution must be "massively violent . . . as violent as the war in Vietnam" ("My Man Himes" 44), he argues for action that involves "the masses" on both sides of the conflict; the Vietnam analogy positions black citizens as an army of "foot soldiers" whose objective is to "kill the enemy and that's all" ("My Man Himes" 45). Where hysterical whites in *Plan B* called for the policing of black behavior down to forced ingestion of "white" foods such as rice and milk (138), reminiscent of the anti-communist loyalty oaths of the Truman era, in Himes's vision of revolution the joining of battle is itself such a pledge of allegiance that each revolutionary would make individually by taking up individual arms. The prospect of wide-scale destruction caused by one black general pushing one atomic button would cancel the need for this mass commitment and is therefore never entertained by Himes. And as per the hard economic realities of both the World War II and Vietnam eras, during which war was a chief source of employment for African Americans, Himes's one-man/ one-gun model of traditional warfare would also be a massive jobs program designed to occupy and enable disaffected blacks. In conversation with David Jenkins, Himes explicitly juxtaposed "100,000 blacks armed with automatic rifles" who would take, invisible-man style, to "the subways and basements of Manhattan," against white, atomic-style attack: "There would be no way, there is no weapon, to get them out. You could bomb Manhattan and all, and still not reach underground" (qtd. in Heise 504).

Yet despite its proudly proletarian association with traditional, infantry-style war technology, the guns proliferating across the pages of *Plan B* are also among its most futuristic, SF-inflected elements.[5] In the first scene, an automatic rifle comes mysteriously to the door of downtrodden T-Bone Smith, packaged innocuously in a florist's delivery box. Denigrated by the narrative for his generally Tomish ways, T-Bone is frightened by its arrival and even lacking the literacy to read its note of instruction, while his much more militant-minded woman Tang easily reads both the conspiratorial note and the weapon's future usefulness. The dispute over the gun in this eerie, futuristic opening scene also perpetuates a distinction—between mutants and aliens—located across the genre of science fiction in my earlier discussion; T-Bone's illiteracy, cowardice, and childish willingness to turn over the gun to the police are of a piece with his grossly exaggerated physical appearance, as is the case with many of the key figures in *Plan B* and across the series. Albinos, dwarves, transvestites, and strung-out junkies dot the landscape of each novel; even Coffin Ed— notably the more assimilation-minded throughout *Plan B* and especially its final scene, where he is done in by his more militant, alienated partner—is hit in the face with acid in the first installment in Himes's series and spends every subsequent novel "look[ing] as though [he] had been made up in Hollywood for the role of the Frankenstein monster" (qtd. in Cochran 27). In *Plan B*, T-Bone, with his "greasy black pants, . . . bare black torso . . . decorated with a variety of scars, . . . lips the size of automobile tires, and . . . eyes sticky with mucus" (3), is pointedly revolting, while his more intelligent counterpart Tang wears her slovenly ways as a badge and a threat: "she was just a lean, angular crone with burnt red hair and flat black features. . . . Only her eyes were alive: they were red, mean, disillusioned, and defiant" (4). While T-Bone's deformities are not readable as literal manifestations of radiologic mutation, his status as "mutie" in this largely warped and mutilated society bears out the predictions of Poul Anderson and others—that such shocking bodily deviations would become more and more the norm—and, as David Cochran has noted, undergirds Himes's "thesis that American racism severely deformed black personality and culture" (27).

Not only is the gun mysteriously delivered and freighted with fatal significance—within hours Tang is slashed to death by T-Bone due to their diverse views on how to proceed, and T-Bone is shot by Grave Digger to avenge Tang—its origins are utterly untraceable, try though New York's finest, the FBI, and the CIA may throughout the later episodes of the novel. All that is learned on first appearance is that it is some kind of "army gun" (8) yet lacking any kind of stamp identifying its military base of origin (15). The experts are baffled as well by its unlikely first recipient (46), and when the otherwise unidentified "Conspiracy" (135) emerges as the most likely source later, Himes presents a "shadow world" motif typical of many science fiction tales.

The technology of these weapons is as futuristic as their origin is fantastic, demonstrating the killing capability of a much larger and more complex gun. With obvious (and comic) phallic implications, the puny .38 caliber bullets fired by the police are no match for the "7.62 caliber slugs" (57) dealt out by the mysterious master-weapon in *Plan B*'s chapter 8. Here a lone gunman dispatches five officers with ease, then "chops [multiple] police cruisers apart systematically" (57); at the height of the action, thirty such patrol cars are held hostage before the window where the shooter fires and waits, miraculously impervious to ordinary ballistics, for the final outcome. With even greater success the solitary shooter of chapter 21, aiming his weapon through the poor box donation slot in a church, takes out "row after row of captains and lieutenants" in an all-white police parade being staged by Himes as an ironic, indeed absurd, show of "unity." Seemingly hundreds of marchers and spectators are laid low in gleefully gory detail—"nasty blobs of brains, hairy fragments of skull, . . . gristly bits of ears and noses, flying red and white teeth" (178)—before the necessary reinforcements arrive. While not verifiably attributable to the guns *per se*, both shooters enjoy a lengthy interval as "invisible men," long after the barrage issuing from their weapons would have revealed their whereabouts in a realist scenario; H. Bruce Franklin points to the irony of the chapter 21 shooter's strategic invisibility by noting that on this occasion of the all-white unity parade being cheered on by its all-white audience, "There is not a single Black person in sight" (*Victim as Criminal* 230). Thus Himes provides his Harlem characters their own manner of "equalizer"—a sleek, efficient, futuristic weapon that gives its user super-human abilities against multiple enemies, in both classic detective and SF fashion. As well, Himes capitalizes on the "invisibility" of his shooters, who turn a political liability into a revolutionary gain and remain so persistently unlocatable that their invisibility seems literal—and thus utterly fantastic.

Notably, however, such futuristically empowered weapons militate against Himes's broader revolutionary vision, creating some of the political contradiction and narrative gridlock that ultimately impair *Plan B*. In his *Crisis* essay from 1944, Himes read the isolated "incident" instigated by the individual "martyr" as only a stepping stone toward full-scale "revolution." If for Himes full-scale revolution would only be realized by the mass mobilization required by traditional forms of war, then super-weapons that did more than their physically plausible share of killing—be they futuristic rifles or magically targeted atomic bombs—would perpetuate the martyr model, whereby one actor creates broad-scale public disturbance but is ultimately gunned down by superior white weaponry, while the vast majority of the black population claims a position of safety and blamelessness in anonymous, silent bystanding. As Himes himself quips in the midst of the chapter 8 shootout, "All these black people, who had protested in one way or another against being considered invisible by the white citizenry, would have given anything to have been invisible then" (57). Echoing the deadly disagreement between T-Bone and Tang, "The guns were more dangerous as malignant objects then they were as offensive weapons. They were, in some ways, similar to sixteen pounds of radium. Just being near one was dangerous, and the wages of owning one were instantaneous death" (142). With this final reference to the negative aspects of atomic power, the narrative meanders into a modern-day "Mamlambo" tale, wherein Harlem residents try desperately to ditch their guns on street corners and into the possession of unsuspecting neighbors, only to have them rematerialize, like the magical poisonous snake of old, with fatal repercussions.

Such absurd infighting is the epitome of the disorganization that Himes decried, yet it is Himes himself who fails to provide the alternative of heroic mass action in scene after scene of *Plan B*. As Gilbert H. Muller argues, "Himes could not sustain his grotesque vision of a second American revolution or even figure out its metaphysics coherently." Muller suggests that, "unable to find a proper form or voice for his larger nationalistic fantasy" this unfinished novel in fact finished Himes's career as a fiction writer, with the focus thereafter on "the completion of his autobiography" (115–16; see also Margolies and Fabre 145–46; Tal 70). One reason for the ultimate failure of *Plan B* likely rises from Himes's profound cynicism with respect to realization of his revolutionary dreams; as he told Michel Fabre in an interview, "black people don't have the political maturity needed to band together into an effective force" (135), and "It was obvious to me that blacks had no chance in an armed confrontation, the odds being one to ten" (136).[6] Too, given all that is known about Himes's sexual biography and literary preoccupations, the image lone gunman super-figure, wielding his preposterous phallus of power,[7] may have been too tempting a comic and political statement not to exploit. Most meaningful, however, is Himes's observation elsewhere in the interview with Fabre that in *Plan B*, each of his black gunmen—almost as if acting on his own volition—"instead of waiting for an organization to form . . . begins shooting white people for his own personal reasons" (134).

The comment is seconded by Himes's hero Tomsson Black in the final scene of the novel, when he admits to Coffin Ed and Grave Digger that

> only a small percentage of guns had been distributed and their owners were running amok with them. . . . [He] would have liked to have had *the time* to organize the black race into effective guerilla units, and the units into an effective force, in order to add weight to the ultimatum. He would also have liked to have granted white people *the time* for reflection and consideration before they made their choice. Somehow it had gotten out of his control. (200, emphases added)

In other words, Black himself, the revolutionaries he tried to organize, the white society at their mercy, the readers of *Plan B*, and its very author never bore witness to the "tomorrow" of racial revolution (violent or otherwise) that the political crisis of lived experience and the generic conventions of science fiction in fact required. Harking back, ironically yet significantly, to the words of Martin Luther King Jr., who lectured his fellow-clergyman from his cell in the Birmingham jail against the rhetoric of forever waiting for a proper time for action and change, Himes's Harlem citizens refuse as well to wait for the opportunity tomorrow might promise or, due to the apocalypticism that yet characterized the upheavals of the late 1960s, might never bring. Their rejection of the "tomorrow" essential to the science fictions and sociological predictions[8] of both white and black futurists of the period results in mayhem and murder—or we might say, as the novel remains unfinished, results in nothing at all. Yet how can one blame Himes's rioting Harlemites (and the society of fed-up African Americans they so accurately represented) for ignoring the exhortation to place hope in tomorrow sent out by the novel's own protagonist and the futurist context toward which his version of this story inclined? At this apocalyptic moment in American history, patience had lost its last shred of virtue, and the time required to realize Himes's long-held vision of his community's move from incendiary incident (plan A) to world-changing revolution (plan B) simply ran out.

DELANY'S TRIUMPHANT TOMORROWS

The career of the prolific and influential Samuel R. Delany has spanned myriad social movements across the latter half of the twentieth century, including civil rights, gay rights, and HIV/AIDS awareness; a rare African American and an equally rare openly gay man in the pantheon of award-winning science fiction authors, Delany has boldly accomplished in various of his works what every other author discussed in this chapter has ultimately failed to do: envision a future that blithely, almost blandly—and frequently with the enabling back story of massive nuclear war—integrates the phenomenon of racial difference into both its basic workings and its lofty quests for the meaning of human existence. Where Himes struggled within the bounds of social realism (however stretched for satiric purposes they may have been) to effect his cataclysmic tomorrow, Delany's cataclysms occur centuries before his stories begin, and a chastened humanity (to use the term loosely) wisely, firmly rejects the political and psychological divides of old. Where Ellison's invisible man ends his story subversively transgressing in white territory, "irresponsibly" (*Invisible Man* 14) espousing the suburbanite's desire to "get away from it all," the "brown," androgynous hero of Delany's Nebula Award-winning *Einstein Intersection* (1967) serenely "[got] away from the it-all of the village" (25) with an ex-lover, planting flowers and enjoying life in the narrative's pre-history, and is now content to return to the community. Where many of the white science fiction authors from the Golden Age treaded carefully around themes of interracial marriage and child-bearing in their atomic mutant stories, Delany so complicates notions of inferiority, superiority, and "difference" that the terms become productively meaningless. In other words, Delany made a simple decision that most others examined in this discussion refused to make—he fully assumed the omnipotent mantle of SF authorship, creating worlds in accordance with his progressive but integrationist point of view and flourishing with readers and critics in the process.

In keeping with the scope of this study, my focus is on Delany's earliest work, including the debut *The Jewels of Aptor* (1962), the *Fall of the Towers* trilogy (1963–65), and the award-winning *Einstein Intersection* (1967). Many of these early novels borrow a technique on display in novels by Heinlein, where a character of color is designated as such in an offhand manner and with little to no bearing on his or her psychological make-up or dramatic function. Delany is an appreciative observer of this technique (see note 3 in this chapter and Delany, "Necessity," 30), and his own first novels likewise minimize the thematic significance of racial difference. The heroine of *Babel-17*, Rydra Wong, for instance, demonstrates little in her personality or outlook of Asianness beyond her last name; she is widely recognized as based on Delany's wife at the time, editor and poet Marilyn Hacker, whose own lack of an Asian background further indicates Delany's purposely loose commitment to racial designation in this period. As Jeffrey Tucker observes, "rarely, if ever, do characters make race the center around which their identities are constructed" (17–18), and as Delany himself describes it: "In most of my futures, the racial situation has changed, and changed for the better. . . . I wanted to write about worlds where being black mattered in different ways than it matters now" (qtd. in Tucker 18).

In keeping with the conventions of John W. Campbell's Golden Age, most of Delany's early heroes are in fact white—young, attractive men whose "blond" or "dark" hair falling onto their foreheads is an unassuming indicator of European extraction. In *Jewels of Aptor*, Delany even adopts the white authorial convention of racially marking only the lone "Negro" character—in this case, Iimmi, a castaway who falls in with the three white heroes and is further racialized by fetishized references to his "black shoulder" (61) and "black chest" (64), etc. The most even-handed departure from these traditions raised editorial hackles; notably, Campbell is famous for having rejected Delany's later *Nova* (1968) for serial installments with the comment "For Heaven's sakes, he's got a Negro for a protagonist! It's a good book, but our readers aren't going to be able to identify with that" (qtd. in Tucker 51 and see Delany "Racism" 387).

While the earliest novels therefore assign recognizably American racial identities to major and minor characters in fairly standard fashion, Delany instead uses the device of a large-scale nuclear holocaust occurring centuries prior to create an array of mutant characters with which to allegorize racial difference. In *Jewels* a four-armed mutant named Snake joins forces with the hero-human Geo and his lumbering, bear-like sidekick, appropriately named Urson. Though Urson displays prejudice against "Strange Ones" such as Snake, Geo retorts that Urson "could be one too. How many men do you know who reach your size and strength by normal means?" (26). Though Urson bridles at the accusation, in typical racist or homophobic manner, eventually Snake's intelligence and bravery are recognized and embraced by all. In this novel, Delany uses the radiation theme to achieve even more progressive ends: with implicit satiric reference to the dilemma of nuclear "armaments," not only are Snake's two extra arms directly attributed to post-nuclear genetic mutation but mid-novel Geo loses an arm due to prolonged radiation exposure, while both of Iimmi's black arms are bleached white in the same accident. As it is joked late in the novel that Geo should borrow a spare arm from Snake (158), so Iimmi seems to have "borrowed" a pair of white arms from Geo, such that the three men come together across both physical and racial divides. They recognize their shared status as non-normative, post-nuclear mutants in ways that unite, enlighten, and empower them. In this novel, Delany also handily solves the school integration crisis plaguing the nation at the time; with no fanfare whatsoever, Iimmi and Geo discover themselves to be former students at the same University (74) and look forward to "turn[ing] up in some of the same classes" (158) in the novel's upbeat conclusion.

Not surprisingly, Delany's is a relentlessly urbophilic vision, set against the urbophobia on display in numerous nuclear survival tales (both SF and mainstream) and in the mass relocation to the suburbs by America's white middle class in the 1950s and '60s. Cities are referenced in almost all of his stories, and reflecting its tri-partite structure, three cities play a prominent part in the

Towers trilogy: the "dead" city of Telphar, "embalmed by the radiation" of the pre-narrative nuclear war (Milicia xv); the declining Toron whose "fall" the trilogy documents; and most importantly, the City of a Thousand Suns, "beautiful on the lake's edge" (410), being constructed in the jungle by diverse malcontents and visionaries throughout the trilogy and rising up like a beacon of hope for the empire's beleaguered survivors at series' end. Opposing the suburban utopia sprawled at the conclusion of Philip Wylie's *Tomorrow!* and the rural sanctuary held down by hearty survivors in Pat Frank's *Alas, Babylon* (see chapter 1), Harlem native Delany refused to abandon the progressive potential of the urban model, despite cities' vulnerability to nuclear attack and interracial animosity during that period. For Delany, the solution to a "dead city" was not no city, but a new, communally constructed urban alternative; in the utopian city of Delany's vision, the only "alien" presence is alienation itself, the satanic "Lord of the Flames" who attempts to foment discord and ultimately fails.

In *The Einstein Intersection* the telepathic skills of the brown hero Lobey (yet another post-nuclear mutant) involve his equally unique musical gifts; likened throughout the story to both the Beatles' Ringo Starr and the mythic Orpheus, he can hear music inside others' heads and instantly play it on his remarkable flute. Also he once "saved a life" through the dexterity of his semi-opposable toes, and we moderns with our much less capable feet should therefore not "knock it" (6). In the phrasing of George A. von Glahn, "Life's real issue, as Lobey comes to discover, is whether one is to become a unique person (different) without at the same time moving completely outside group norms. Death is being under total control, having nothing uniquely individual to express or contribute . . ." (118–19). Despite his stated appreciation for Heinlein, in fact Delany tends to present his readers with a situation directly opposite that of *Farnham's Freehold*; staging atomic holocaust many centuries back, Delany, like Heinlein, blasts his readers into a post-atomic far-future where instead of white heroes confronting a race of frightening black dictators, the heroes are themselves brown-skinned, evolved for altruistic purposes, laid back, and loveable.[9]

Delany's tendency to include mythological and other fantastic elements (e.g., the Phaedra and Minos legends, dragons) in his stories has caused some to categorize them as science fantasy or space opera (see Parrinder 14). He (as a member of the late-1960s "New Wave") was famously lambasted by the 1950s SF icon James Blish at the 1968 Nebula Awards Banquet, where moments earlier Delany had received his best-novel prize for *Einstein*—and where moments later he would retake the stage to receive the award for the best short story of 1967, "Aye, and Gomorrah." As Delany tells the story, Blish came to the ceremony to gripe about "pretentious literary nonsense" ("Racism" 389), while Clareson adds that Blish complained that "The reliance on myth attempts to explain any resultant mythic world [quoting Blish] 'in terms of eternal forces which are changeless. The attempt is antithetical to the suppositions of science fiction, which center around the potential of continuous change'" (250). It is ironic that Blish came to the ceremony to fend off a threat to "continuous change" yet railed against the very change represented by Delany and other New Wave writers. If anything, what bothered Blish was a loosening of the genre's parameters, characterized for some as a "re-christen[ing] of the genre [of science fiction] as 'speculative fiction'" (Parrinder 17). Patrick Parrinder adds that the speculative inclinations of the New Wave "both reflected (and to some extent anticipated) popular disillusionment with scientific advance" (18; see also M. Rose 154). This comment links Delany directly with more militant black intellectuals from the late 1960s including Chester Himes, discussed earlier, and John Oliver Killens (see Chapter 4), both of whom read atomic technology as a sign of white Western decline, a banal vestige of yesterday uninteresting to a people hastening with confidence toward a more equitable tomorrow. Though Delany, as noted, puts the bomb to significant use in many of his novels, he likewise positions it well into his various narrative yesterdays and lacks the infatuation with the scientized gadgets that so preoccupied Golden Age writers. Parrinder himself comes out as a member of the old guard when he brands *The Einstein Intersection* "an artistic failure" (25) and the New Wave in general as frequently guilty of "irresponsible fantasy" (22).

Clearly it is Delany's position that less worry about strict extrapolation from scientific fact leads actually to greater change; his refutation, for instance, of the hard "facts" of racial difference (anticipating the scientific refutation of "race" by many decades) and the dispiriting sociological "facts" that accompany assignment to racially stigmatized categories struck 1960s-era readers (Campbell among them) as too fantastic to swallow. If Ellison's hero copped to the charge of irresponsibility for running from the prospect of revolutionary change, Delany would deny it categorically: for him it is the SF writer's, especially the African American SF writer's, main responsibility to provide readers of all backgrounds with futuristic works that indicate "what [an] 'improved racial situation' was actually going to look like" ("Necessity" 31). He told interviewers in 1980 that "As a young writer, I thought it was very important to keep an image of such possibility before people" (qtd. in Tucker 18), and in "The Necessity of Tomorrows," Delany explicitly critiques realist fiction such as that by Richard Wright (which Ellison himself thought too naturalistic) and even Chester Himes's debut novel, *If He Hollers, Let Him Go* (1945). These works about "well, history . . . said that the condition of the black man was awful [and] . . . precisely what made it so awful also made it unchangeable." Delany lamented the paucity of "moments of interracial rapprochement" (28) in these realist works, and of "images" that would show what the world would look like when, as he said above, race mattered differently than it does today. In this important essay, Delany champions science fiction as the genre that best provides "a profusion and richness of our tomorrows," since "we need images of tomorrow; and our people need them more than most" (35).

CONCLUSION: SF IN ATOMIC AMERICA

With regard to both white and black futurist writers from the postwar period, it is impossible to sum up the role of atomic fear, atomic hope, and atomic absurdity in a single closing statement. But in every case an SF or Afro-Futurist author's deployment of atomic weaponry has had deep political implications; from Williamson's and Kuttner/Moore's collective-busting equalizers and Heinlein's atomic blast into the racially inverted future; to Emshwiller's and Anderson's mutant children who confront parents (and their audiences) with themes of guilt, acceptance, and interracial unity; to Chester Himes's outright rejection of the atomic option as a vestige of the dying white power structure, the bomb in these stories rarely dropped straight down but came at its victims from a radically rightward or leftward direction. As with the atomic theme, an author's attitude toward racial unity (political, sexual, familial, or otherwise) came across plainly in the narratives depicted. From ugly racial stereotypes in the stories of O'Donnovan and Sheckley, to the failed attempts at apology and atonement issued from Bradbury's white space-wanderers, to the hesitant hopes for interracial marriage proffered by McIntosh's story "Eleventh Commandment," even the most progressively-minded white authors of science fiction flinched at the prospect of interracial coupling on Earth. Meanwhile the interracial sex depicted in Ellison and especially Himes add to the general mood of apocalypticism prevailing in their work and aggressively, valuably shove its black and white readership into the inevitable future. Delany's fairer tomorrows will resemble Lorraine Hansberry's optimistic life-affirmation in both her landmark *Raisin in the Sun* and her anti-atomic works (see Chapter 4),[10] though the emphasis shift between them is worth noting: Hansberry hated the bomb and sought to inspire her audiences toward courageous peace activism, while Delany, who dreamed as a boy of being a nuclear physicist (Peplow and Bravard 11), may have deployed atomic weapons in his novels as some physicists might atomic energy in the real world: as a tool with dangerous properties that when handled correctly bring light and power to all concerned.

Since its detonation day the bomb has been a world-historical phenomenon with profoundly alienating repercussions. Regarding the alienation effect as a feeling of profound and irreparable separation, the Hiroshima and Nagasaki bombs divided history itself into wartime and postwar periods, separated a contaminated and unfathomable post-blast Japan from the rest of the world, and, as the device chiefly responsible for ending the war, abruptly separated a generation of men from their roles as soldiers, destroyers, laborers, and builders with profound and permanent aftereffects. Even at Alamogordo, as it left the hand of its creator, J. Robert Oppenheimer described his utter alienation in his famous pronouncement, "Now I am become death, destroyer of worlds," and the bomb has been regarded as an alien presence in the human midst—How can mere man create such destruction? How can humans so threaten fellow-humans?—since its zero-hour. In postwar popular culture, the bomb has been depicted as the hubristic act that draws the malevolent attention of alien visitors from other planets and/or creates a race of guilt-inducing mutants within our ranks. It is the awful harbinger of the (reckoning) day-after, so rife with environmental, biological, and political implications that it simply can never come. The bomb was both the literal embodiment of all there was to fear in the postwar decades and a broader symbol of other end-of-world possibilities looming on the American horizon in the postwar decades. While white suburbanites celebrated boom times with a measure of oblivious enjoyment, returning veterans within this group, as well as millions of Americans whose racial or ethnic identity barred them from postwar mobility and prosperity, also experienced feelings of alienation. Pulp science fiction from white authors in this period, as well as major fiction by black authors with their own SF or Afro-Futurist elements, reflect the mood of alienation that prevailed however insidiously in this era and contemplated similar sets of questions regarding the make-up of the human family—and the human individual—in the postwar period. Their stories of tomorrow's children challenged readers to examine past misdeeds and improve the chances of planetary survival and interracial brotherhood however possible.

CHAPTER 3

Sidebar

Covering the Bomb in the African American Press

Across the front page of the *Chicago Defender*, 27 October 1962, James Meredith's heroic attempt to integrate the University of Mississippi predominates. Though the story had broken weeks earlier, the *Defender* probed further in this week's edition, including a recap of Meredith's first days on campus; a headline on Meredith's wife, now also to enroll at Ole Miss; and a serene photo from the University of Alabama, where the first Negro students since Arthurine Lucy[1] had applied for admission but not yet arrived. Bottom center is the title "Crisis Affects African Nations," and three short paragraphs—followed up at some length on page 2—regarding the reactions of newly independent African nations to the "crisis" in question: the showdown between John F. Kennedy and the Castro/Khrushchev alliance that had days earlier brought the world to the brink of nuclear-armed conflict. Unmoored to any copy save its caption is a photo mid-right of an African American serviceman on duty in Key West, where the military was massing troops and materiel in the event of war with Cuba. On that same date, coverage of the Cuban Missile Crisis in the *Pittsburgh Courier* was even more spare: the only front-page mention is a brief item regarding Castro's attempt to lure southern Negroes to Cuba with a "Radio Free Dixie" broadcast;[2] on page 1 of that day's *New York Amsterdam News*, where the Meredith story had already faded, "Harlemites Backing President's Stand" upper left, competes with the lead stories "Shades of Mississippi: Muslims Chained in N.Y. Courtroom" and "Sarah Vaughn Sorry Police Grabbed Hubby." On this date, the *Baltimore Afro-American* was entirely silent on the subject, reporting instead on the latest in the Meredith story, other school desegregation battles about to begin, and the Vaughn scandal.[3]

The editorial decisions made with respect to the selection and arrangement of stories on this historically significant front page reflect the role played by the African American press since its inception, and comment specifically on the way it adjudicated between this particular moment's competing dramatic narratives—the integration of US higher education and the closest the world has ever come to nuclear war. In *Jet* a few weeks later, Larry Still's article, "The Spotlight is Diverted, but Rights Fight Goes On," acknowledged that "last week, Americans of all complexions turned their attention from the mounting civil rights crisis in the South to the Cuban crisis 90 miles off the Florida coast" (14). The story quotes NAACP Executive Secretary Roy Wilkins, who urges his community to not let this disruption—however important it may be—slow the momentum enjoyed by the movement at this time: "We don't see any reason why in this emergency," Wilkins said, "we should not go full steam ahead" (15; see also Goodlett, "USA Peace"). From Still's report and Wilkins's statement, one observes that for some African American writers and readers of the period, the arms race, and even the prospect of nuclear war, posed as much of a threat to "the free world" as to the campaign for the freedom they were still very much striving to complete.

As placement and location have been themes of import since my opening pages, so the late-October-1962 front pages of the African American press present a dilemma faced by many in the broader black community: how prominently to position the Cuban story in the spectrum of African American news worth noting and whether this same narrative would, however temporarily, sideline the Ole Miss story and the rights struggle it crystallized at that moment. "Place" as well refers here (as it will in Chapter 4) to location on the political spectrum—to a complex understanding of "right" and "left" in the postwar African American context and to the realization that, as progressive as its tendencies ultimately were, every permutation of public opinion and ideological influence is to be found in this era's black press. As I observe these writers who spoke during this period for an American postwar nation within a nation, I echo the analysis of Eve Dunbar, who reads "blackness as the ultimate segregated region in the United States" and argues that "during the 1940s . . . blacks literally and literarily occupied a space outside the confines of mainstream white America" (188).

Of several postwar African American periodicals surveyed for this discussion, *Jet*'s response to the bomb, like that of its sister publication *Negro Digest*, was notably light. Yet another sibling in media mogul John H. Johnson's family of bestselling magazines, *Ebony*, aimed itself at the postwar African American bourgeoisie and played up the contributions of black soldiers and scientists to atomic science and industry.[4] Its opposite number was Shirley Graham Du Bois's elegant and erudite *Freedomways*, which approached the nuclear threat and the necessity of peace—including opposition to the Cuban blockade—from an international, far-left perspective. In this chapter African American magazine coverage of the bomb will be of interest whenever suitable, but the focus will be the weekly newspapers published by and for African Americans, specifically four well-funded, expertly-run, big-city papers that have been significant to press historians (e.g., E. Gordon, "The Negro Press" 208) and average readers since their beginnings: the *Chicago Defender*, the *Pittsburgh Courier*, the *Baltimore Afro American*, and the *New York Amsterdam News*.[5] Along with relevant citations from the *San Francisco Sun-Reporter* and the *Atlanta Daily World* (the only daily in the survey),[6] the material found in these pages represents black press coverage of atomic news as it was received by a wide sector of African American readers in the postwar period.[7]

The interest in things atomic within postwar black newspapers varied according to the moment in time and even more significantly according to the inclination of the editorial staff. The *Defender*'s continuing engagement with the bomb throughout the relatively low-threat decade of the 1950s, for instance, is largely attributable to Langston Hughes, or more specifically to Hughes's enduring fictional creation Jesse B. Semple and the Hughes persona who served as "Simple's" bar buddy and straight man. On the other hand, the *Pittsburgh Courier*'s renowned George Schuyler, took, like Hughes, a wide interest in world affairs but had little to say about the bomb after providing solid coverage and commentary in the *Courier*'s first post-Hiroshima edition. Between 1945 and 1962, the bomb was addressed in the black press primarily in the editorial pages and primarily when nuclear fears were an unavoidable national concern—immediately after the Hiroshima/Nagasaki bombings that ended the war and during the Cuban Missile Crisis. The African American journalist, historian, and Boston-based intellectual Eugene Gordon, in his syndicated column "Another Side of the Story," once chided "US Negro Newspapers" for this lack of interest: "Don't our editors and publishers want us to know that a generation of Negro children with bone cancer and blood disease would be less able to continue our fight for human rights? Or less able to enjoy those rights when won?" ("The Ashes of Death" n.p.) Gordon is correct that the bomb was a non-issue in the black press for months at a time during the postwar period; it is also the case, however, that mention when made was almost always a rich lode of political, cultural, and rhetorical significance. Even in non-crisis moments, these papers provided their readers with interesting (even sensational) updates on atomic science and industry; consistent coverage of the "race angle" on civil defense (its segregationist tendencies) and peace protest (its integrationist aspects); and rhetorically effective reference to the atomic bomb whenever the occasion suited. Ultimately the atomic metaphor was a popular device at the disposal of the African American press—a powerful weapon to be regularly deployed in the fight for equal rights.

The short shrift given a major story such as the Cuban Missile Crisis within the pages of the black press is unsurprising, since, as Donna Akiba Sullivan Harper points out, "For news of general interest, African Americans read the major daily papers and listened to their radios, as did whites" (26). Yet as Harper also notes, "In those general news sources . . . blacks in the 1940s found little about themselves" (26). Harper illustrates her point by contrasting main-stream press coverage of black figures—usually celebrities like Paul Robeson or outstanding members of the criminal element—with diverse reporting on all kinds of African Americans, the exceptional and the ordinary, in the black periodicals. She reads a cartoon from a 1945 *Defender* that pokes fun at this very discrepancy: "The cartoon showed a black patron at a newsstand that sold four or five different white daily papers, all of which proclaimed in banner head-lines, [the all-Negro] '92nd [division] RETREATS!' The black patron used a magnifying glass, however, to examine the Want Ad Section, where he read 'negro tank units trap 20,000 Nazis'" (28). Because mainstream publications were so overwhelmingly slanted toward white doings and away from the interests of African American readers, the black press presented only those stories with a significant African American angle and excluded almost everything else.

The editorial inclinations of white-oriented publications corroborate the contrast located by Harper. *Life*'s acknowledgement of the Meredith story is almost begrudging, as it merits only "Picture of the Week" treatment in the 5 October issue. In the photo, Meredith stands silent and motionless to the far right, as the unfolding drama belongs to two whites in suit coats—US Marshal James McShane and Mississippi Lieutenant Governor Paul Johnson—coming to blows over Meredith's right to matriculate. Despite the fact that controversy had been brewing for months, including a late-September attempt to register for class that led to a riot ending with two dead and hundreds injured, *Life* assumes that its audience has never heard of the situation, since it introduces its featured player as "A Negro named James Meredith, a former Air Force sergeant" (3). By late October coverage is more complete, though again the African American presence in this story is notably minimized: no citizens of color are photographed protesting, only one black soldier is pictured with a National Guard unit, and the only image of Meredith is of his face half-hidden behind a handkerchief to block tear gas. *Life*'s Cuban Missile coverage, com-mencing in dramatic front-cover fashion on 2 November and developed over several issues, leaves no room for follow-up of the Meredith story.

Thus the black press's intense and long-lasting focus on Meredith, almost to the exclusion of the Cuban affair, counters the white press's tendency to minimize the significance of the Ole Miss integration story and to sideline al-most entirely the role of black participants in the event, even Meredith himself. As the black papers inverted the emphases in the Meredith story as covered in the mainstream press, so their take on the atomic threat came often from an angle dramatically oblique to the standard response. Whether the topic was weapons technology, the morality of war, the Soviet threat, the supposed supe-riority of the American perspective, or the generalized contest between legiti-mate fear and trumped up hysteria played out in the atomic period, the views of the African American press often diverged sharply—and therefore in unique and valuable ways—from those found in mainstream media. Accordingly, this corps reliably positioned itself "elsewhere" on the bomb itself—vigorously, necessarily revising the representation it received in the mainstream press.

PEACE NOT SO WONDERFUL

This unique perspective is on display from the earliest moments of the atomic era. While the major news media emphasized the heady thrills of victory and homecoming at war's end, writers in the black press reminded their readership that peace, as the title of a *Defender* editorial cartoon put it, was "not so wonderful" (25 August 1945, 12); the Associated Negro Press's Dean Gordon B. Hancock quipped that in fact peace was "Blunderful!," since the bomb's abrupt end to war would now mean a severe curtailment in jobs and a clear threat to the Fair Employment Practices Commission (FEPC), which barred discrimination in war-industry hiring ("Peace" 6). As stated bluntly on the front page of the *Defender*'s 18 August 1945 issue, "Jap Peace Brings Unemployment Threat for Millions of Negroes." When Hughes's Simple complains that "Peace ain't wonderful when folks ain't got no job" ("Simple's Selfish Peace" 14), he points up the primary antagonism between peace and prosperity that few mainstream papers (or white readers) were willing to acknowledge at the time. The *Daily World* explicitly linked "the dropping of the atomic bomb" with the "danger of early termination" of the FEPC. It saw the problem specifically in terms of speed: the bomb's instantaneous ending of war meant that "the country [was] not prepared for reconversion and peace" and that the speedy end of war would mean an "equally speedy return to job discrimination" ("See Quick Peace"). In succeeding weeks fears increased as the *Defender*'s front page headline of 25 August blasted "400,000 FIRED IN CUTBACKS! See Million Jobless By Spring" (1). Lead articles on that same page included "FEPC Doomed, Gets Notice to Close Up" and "V-J Hilarity Sobered by Grim Prospects."

There is no question that the *Defender* and other papers of this era aimed at a working-class readership employed garish, tabloid-style sensationalism to attract newsstand passersby with eye-catching, often fright-mongering headlines, and that in this instance, as in all instances with news media, bad news meant good business; in Eugene Gordon's estimation, "yellowness marks [the Negro Press], and is flaunted as a badge of honor" ("The Negro Press" 207). Yet the economic crisis facing postwar African Americans was real and necessarily couched in dire terms: the FEPC died a slow, painful death over the course of the Truman administration, and spiking postwar unemployment among those "last hired" was one impetus to the civil rights movement, as well as one origin of the economic and social disparities suffered by many African Americans to this day. Thus the lack of "hilarity" on the part of black papers and black readers at war's end is understandable. While front-page reports celebrated the return of "Tan Yanks" from theaters of war and hailed African American scientists involved in the Manhattan Project, as always these papers' reliable emphasis on the economics of life in a racist society meant that the mood of heedless abandon characterizing mainstream papers of the moment was tempered here to a large degree. (See also "Now—The Battle," "Peace? It's Not so Wonderful," and Hughes, "VJ Night.")

Even the fantasies of atomic-enabled "mass leisure" (qtd. in P. Boyer 141) enjoyed by many in the mainstream press were cast in the black press as threats to employment. For African Americans, for whom jobs had always been difficult to come by, the threat of nuclear weaponry was only slightly more concerning than the threat of nuclear industry—an industry that would likely exclude them from skilled employment and would mean a general shutting down of blue-collar opportunity, once a package of atomic energy "no bigger than a woman's lipstick" (White, "Atom Bomb") could power an entire city or run a car for a year. On 18 August 1945, the *Baltimore Afro American* found that "Atomic Bomb Brings Fear of Cave Life, Joblessness" for the man (and woman) on the street. Mrs. Mary Hall expressed concern that "in times of peace, it will bring comfort but also unemployment for the masses" (17), and in fact many public intellectuals both black and white feared this very prospect. Hughes continued to worry a decade later that as atomic industry improved, Negroes would be fired from their heavy labors by the thousands. As Simple comically complains, "And all you will have to put in them machines will be just a little old grain of an atom. . . . So who do you think will be the first to be throwed out of work? Negroes!" Simple worriedly forecasts that when there is no more coal to dig, haul, or shovel, the only job left will be "lift[ing] a pin-head of an atom into a cupsized furnace. . . . That will be skilled labor—and one white man can do that. So far as I know, they don't let no Negroes touch no atoms nohow, nowhere, no place." While his dire prediction is met with protest by his better educated bar buddy, as usual Simple speaks unassailably for a large sector of the African American populace who felt in their hearts that "The atom belongs to white folks" ("When the Atom Comes" 11). Again, many in the general press feared similar loss of purpose when atomic power swept away the need to work for a living, yet African American newsmen and their audiences had special cause to think upon atomic joblessness with special concern—as a sign of return to the prewar status quo.

The bomb's abrupt end to war, opined these papers, would have political as well as economic repercussions. Several *Defender* cartoons derided the particularities of "peacetime reconversion." In one a black maid salaams to her white mistress and explains that she is "just practicing reconverting to peacetime employment, Ma'm!" (Jackson [15 September 1945] 15; see figure 5). Two weeks later, two poor whites, with shotgun and hound dog in the foreground, read a headline about "Negro Lynched" in another state's local paper and complain, "Florida done beat us convertin' to peacetime activities" (Jackson [2 November 1945] 5). For postwar African Americans peacetime was much less a new

FIGURE 5: Jay Jackson. *Chicago Defender* (15 September 1945). 15. Courtesy of the *Chicago Defender.*

chapter full of promise and growth than a dangerous invitation to home-grown fascists to return to their violent ways against fellow-citizens, now that the foreign enemy had been conquered and the vital roles played by Negro laborers and servicemen diminished.

CLAIMING ATOMIC POWER

Despite Simple's assertion regarding the atom "belong[ing] to white folks," many readers, and even reporters, of the black press really did think that peace was "wonderful" in a manner coincident with their white fellow-citizens at this time.

In his column of 25 August 1945, the *Afro American*'s Dwight Holmes embraces the advent of complete leisure feared by the citizens interviewed by his paper the week before. In Holmes's estimation, atomic power takes us "one step nearer a state of perfect freedom from beastly toil . . ." (4). Alfred Eisenstaedt's famous photograph "V-J Day in Times Square," in which a sailor passionately embraces a white-clad nurse in the midst of celebrating throngs, is replicated in the photo "V-J Day and the Atomic Bomb Kiss" in the 18 August edition of the *Amsterdam News*. Also captured in Times Square, the photo features an African American couple "celebrating the capitulation of the Japanese last Tuesday" by sharing an "'Atomic Bomb' kiss" so forceful that it rips the girl's shirt.

As was the case nationwide at this point, "atomic" became a trendy buzz-word in African American culture, as when GIs at Tuskegee Airfield dubbed band leader Lucky Millinder "the atomic maestro" ("Theater," see also "Atomic Entertainment"), and when a *Defender*-affiliated children's organization is described as "atomic in its moral force" ("Judge Wendell" 9C). The *Atlanta Daily World* reported the football scores of the YMCA's "atomic league" (who squared off at season's end in an "Atomic Bowl"), and ran an ad in 1947 for the Atomic Jivers' Social Club. An Edgecombe Avenue church group advertising in the *Amsterdam News* calls its fundraiser "Atomic Fashions of 1953," knowing that the term, still trendy in the mid-'50s, would draw an audience ("Atomic Fashion Show" 12). A decade later the Fallout Club, which ran regular ads in the *Sun-Reporter*, was a popular nightspot in San Francisco's Oceanview neighborhood.

The couple sharing the atomic kiss, however, caused others to worry, as one club woman put it, about a "moral lag in the atomic age" ("Friendship Women" 3). From notices in the black press, it is evident that church groups constantly programmed against the dangers (related to unlicensed sexual activity and other debauchery occasioned and excused by the putative end of the world) faced by youth in this modern "atomic" era. When one reads of "a day-long testimonial to youth in the Atomic Age" sponsored by Denson Temple ("Giant Youth Program") or a preacher discussing "what young Baptist [sic] can do to meet with problems of an Atomic Age" (Arnold), one sees that "atomic" had become for some a synonym for unbridled modernity itself (see also "Eleanor" and "Should Parents"). Meanwhile, when others discussed later in this chapter associate forward-looking atomic science with the inevitability of racial equality, the imminence of atomic modernity holds great promise. Incisively linking the atomic threat and the civil rights struggle, the *Sun-Reporter*'s well-respected opinion-maker Thomas C. Fleming observed in 1961 that "Negro youths [taking the lead in sit-ins and other protests in the South] . . . have recognized that since they might be living on borrowed time, they would like to achieve the status of human dignity before that time expires" (25 February 1961, 6). If for some the end-of-days aspect of atomic culture signaled an outbreak of youthful abandon to be preached against at every opportunity, for Fleming it handily fostered moods of nihilism and derring-do in youthful civil rights pioneers. The kiss pictured in the *Amsterdam News* seems to embody both the hysteria and the hope of the newly dawned atomic age for African American newsreaders of this period.

Alongside this implicitly mainstream response to atomic victory we find more explicitly conservative views published immediately following the Japan bombings. Racist sentiment tarnishes a column by William A. Fowles in the *Daily World*, who evinces a Western outlook through his superior attitude toward the Japanese. Where others in the black press worried that a rapid end to war would mean a rapid death for the FEPC, Fowles is concerned about the slow pace of the peace-signing and wonders in stereotypical fashion what the Japanese may be plotting in their delay: it is "just that their Eastern mind and ramifications of Oriental 'saving face' is [sic] incomprehensible to the western mind that is mine" ("Extended War" 4). Fowles critiques "the deeply embedded racial hatreds of the Japanese" against their enemies in the West, presenting himself as not only a fully-fledged Westerner, American, and war victor but also a foe of racism wherever he finds this—even in fellow-persons of color against the Western "race." In another *World* piece, Charles H. Loeb of the Combined Negro Press posited that Japanese surrender was less a result of the atomic bombings than "the plight of these little people who weren't quite westernized enough to tackle the greatest free nation on the Globe" (6, see also Kearney 124 and Doreski 179–80).

An editorial in the *Afro American* employs the ethnic slurs "Japs" and "Nips" that were ubiquitous in that era, even while taking the part of the former adversary based upon "the fact that the Japs are colored" ("Are We Prepared" 1). Another *Afro American* columnist, Ralph Matthews, sends a mixed message in his filing of 25 August; he refers to the "cold sweat" of terror induced by the bomb, fantasizes about the bomb in the hands of beleaguered Ethiopia, and reminds his readers, echoing Fowles, that while "the sabre-rattling Japs" are a colored race, their long-held conquest of China likens them to the Aryans with whom they had recently joined forces ("Watching the Big Parade" 4). He seems to welcome the advent of short wars fought while the average citizen is away on a fishing trip, but the forced comedy of this scenario requires us to read his final line—"Yes, the atomic bomb is a wonderful thing"—as deeply ironic. Two weeks later the literary critic, historian, and *Afro American* columnist J. Saunders Redding calls it correctly when he notes that "One reads accounts of the atomic bomb with confused emotions" (4); ultimately, one must characterize the black press's response to the bomb as diverse, complex, and deeply ambivalent.

RACIALIZING ATOMIC VICTIMS

Meanwhile, many black columnists commented acidly—as did many writers in the broader press—upon the racially charged ethical crisis unleashed by the Japan bombings. The *Afro American* editorial that simultaneously defended and slurred the recently vanquished Japanese observes that "Use of the atomic bomb for the first time against Japan, although it was reportedly possible to have ready for use against the Germans, has revived the feeling in some quarters that maybe the Allies are fighting a racial war after all" ("Are We Prepared" 1, see also Kearney 122). Reading the results of a survey, in which many would have happily kept bombing Japan into oblivion, the *Defender* remarks, "Perhaps the people . . . participating in this poll have the same prejudices against the Japanese that Southerners have against Negroes" ("A New Low" 14; see also P. Boyer 183). The Trinidadian activist and journalist George Padmore provided the view from Africa, where "Morals of Whites Dropped With Atom Bomb" ("Morals" 4). Padmore also reported on the hardships suffered by Congolese miners, largely responsible for supplying the Anglo-Saxon superpowers with the world's uranium supply ("Africa Holds" 4). On 15 September, the *New York Amsterdam News* lampooned the white West's "helping hands" as menacing claws of "imperialist power" reaching down to lift "uranium" and "Ethiopia's oil" off the back of the beleaguered laborer "Africa" ("Helping Hands?" 6A). Again the message is that in both production and consumption (i.e., detonation), the bomb targets only the darker nations of the world.

For many, the bomb threatened not only undefended peoples overseas but the equally defenseless African American population within the US. Many in the black press construed a relationship between the bomb and African Americans' war-era arch-nemesis, Mississippi senator Theodore G. Bilbo, who regularly spouted white-supremacist ideology from the floor the Senate and argued intensely against voting rights for African Americans in the South. He infamously filibustered an anti-lynching bill in 1938 and was a life-long member of the Ku Klux Klan. The black press followed Bilbo's antics closely and vilified his views on a regular basis, reading him as both the American Hitler and an atomic death-dealer. Likely playing up the consonance between "bomb" and "Bilbo," the press forged numerous associations between the two, as when, in response to a soldier writing a letter on this topic, it asked "Which is Greatest Menace, Bilbo or Atomic Bomb?" On other occasions it simply reported upon the statements of Bilbo himself, as when he told constituents that civil rights leaders in Mississippi should be "atomically bombed and exterminated from the face of the earth" ("The Man" 3; see also "Miss Voters"). Novelist and *Defender* columnist Earl Conrad likened Bilbo's tirades to the dropping of "an atomic bomb. The atoms split northward, covered the whole continent" ("Open Letter" 14). In that same issue, Hughes's Simple fearfully contemplates the prospect of "Bilbo with an atom bomb" and asks rhetorically, "Then where would Harlem be?" His barmate's answer—"Nowhere"—repeats the image of nuclear-assisted "urban renewal" envisioned by postwar urban planners and novelists such as Philip Wylie, who posited the "Negro District" as ground zero in his post-nuclear survival tale *Tomorrow!* (see Introduction and Chapter 1). Simple's only defense is broad-spectrum pacifism, including his dream of taking part of the $2 billion spent to build the bomb and using it instead to "educate Bilbo" ("Simple and the Atom Bomb" 13). Interestingly, Simple wants better schools not for poor blacks but for well-placed white southerners who are desperately in need of a refresher course on the US Constitution, modern science, and general Enlightenment principles. Bilbo's absurd propositions and the sardonic response of the black press suggest the scenario of an atomic race war within the US perpetrated unilaterally by terrorist whites.

DISOWNING ATOMIC RESPONSIBILITY

Others looked less with fear than disdain upon atomic power and read it as a product of white America *per se*, for which the African American nation-within-a-nation claimed no credit and took no responsibility.[8] In the column just referred to, Hughes's "I" and Simple argue this out:

> "Don't keep on saying 'they,'" I said. "You are a voter, too, and this is your government. That Two Billion Dollars that made those atom bombs came out of your income tax."
> "I HEREBY PROTEST!" said Simple. . . . Them atom bombs make me sick at the stomach." ("Simple and the Atom Bomb" 13)

Over at the *Courier* J. A. Rogers smirked that supremacist nonsense about the white man as the "climax and crowning glory of God's creation" might be true after all, since it is whites who will be responsible for ending civilization, having created the weapon that will return humanity to the caves ("Atom Bomb" 7). In his *Defender* column NAACP executive secretary Walter White looks forward to the day when "Russian or Chinese or Indian or Negro scientists may . . . independently learn also how to split atoms" ("Atom Bomb" 13, see also Du Bois, "Atom Bomb" 13). His designation "Negro scientists" refers implicitly either to scientists from African nations or to those belonging to the Negro "nation" within the US, who at this moment may feel more in common with their beleaguered Chinese or Indian brethren than they do with their white, war-mongering fellow-Americans (see also Kearney 126).

George Schuyler, in his *Courier* column of 18 August 1945, indicates his sense of alienation as he comments, "The atom bomb puts the Anglo-Saxons definitely on top where they will remain for perhaps decades. . . . This means that the Anglo-Saxons, led by the USA, will have their way in the world until other people discover and perfect a weapon more devastating than the uranium bomb" (7). With irony worthy of Mencken, who mentored Schuyler and to whom he was often compared, Schuyler casts a cynical eye even upon the "breath-taking" possibilities now enabled by atomic energy:

> We shall be able to do all the world's chores (if the earth survives indiscriminate use of atomic bombs) with practically no physical labor. Even the slaves in Africa, Russia, Germany, Siam, Java, and Mississippi will be able to loll at ease most of the day and have no duties except to be courteous and obedient to politicians and pro-consuls set over them. (7)

Even in the midst of a technological revolution, Schuyler is bitterly certain that the old disparities will prevail: "Negro insurance executives from Durham and Atlanta will be vacationing on the moon or Mars, albeit in the Negro section. NAACP executives will be sending television messages protesting against the failure of interstellar transport lines to provide adequate facilities for colored tourists" (7). As opposed, for instance, to Fowles's proud claims of membership in atomic-enabled Allied victory, Schuyler separates himself and his readership from the white West. He thus indicates his belief—a belief shared by many writers, editors, and readers of the black press during this period—that victory in Europe and Japan and sole possession of the atomic secret will boost white America to new heights of imperialist arrogance and cultural self-absorption, which can only spell trouble for this nation's second-class citizens. Yet again the bomb was seen as a weapon aimed however indirectly at African Americans by the white Western scientists and military men who had brought it into being.

EMBRACING ATOMIC INDUSTRY

Many who shared the race-conscious views of these journalists nevertheless sought a niche in America's atomic future through the maximization of employment in nuclear weapons and energy industries. In the early 1950s, Walter White noted the impending move, for civil defense purposes, of weapons-manufacture and other industrial installations from the enlightened North to the protected interior of the Jim Crow South and argued for a renewed commitment to the Fair Employment Practices Commission ("Race for Atomic Control" 7). Bearing out White, in this same period the *Courier* lambasted job discrimination at developing nuclear industry sites in Paducah and Savannah River ("Atom Bomb Bias," "Bomb and Bias," and Anderson, "H-Bomb Project"). These commentaries criticize discriminatory hiring practices that kept African American laborers confined to menial jobs and challenge federally sponsored installations to comply with Executive Order 9980, a postwar version of the FEPC. Even blackness "by association" evidently disqualified one from atomic industry employment, as when *Jet* reported that a white engineer was cut from consideration for a high-level job because he "associated too much with Negroes." The engineer was told that those with many Negro friends were regarded as "bad security risks" ("Negro Friends" 3).

The Oak Ridge story, which turned into the Oak Ridge scandal in the months and years following the war, contains many of the elements of the black press's response to the bomb already broached in this discussion. It includes both economics and politics (that is, lucrative war-industry jobs for African Americans that were nevertheless held in a harshly segregated setting), Pulitzer Prize-worthy exposure of a problem leading to real change that simultaneously reeked of overplayed exposé. While one paper (the *Afro American*) mainly congratulated black workers at the Oak Ridge nuclear weapons facility for their valuable wartime service, two others (the *Defender* and the *Courier*) emphasized the ugly reality behind the patriotic display and turned the outrage into a multi-week bonanza for hard-driving reporters and eager readers. Interestingly, in an 18 August article, the *Afro American*'s Paul S. Henderson considered these workers' race-based deprivations as *part* of their service and sacrifice, in the way that the black soldiers suffering war-induced hardship in France or North Africa would have been lauded in reports from the battlefield (1+). That same issue, the *Afro American*'s weekly feature "The Feminine Front" hailed black female Oak Ridge workers with a photo spread of smiling nurses at their post, student nurses reading together in their well-appointed cottage, and a cafeteria worker making her bed ("Behind the Men" 15).

As was the case in both black and generalist news publications in the immediate postwar period, war workers were given special mention for having maintained silence throughout the war regarding their highly sensitive doings behind closed industrial doors. Yet because of the top-secret nature of the work performed at Oak Ridge, the dirty secret of this planned community's purposefully constructed double-standard could not be told until the jobs African Americans gained there were already in danger of being lost. Even during the lush years of high employment for African American war workers, degrading conditions shaped their experience; in the words of memoirist Valeria Steele, "coming to Oak Ridge only reaffirmed one rude fact: that [African American employees] still lived in America, in the country that had always denied them freedom and equality" (199).

The inequities suffered by African American nurses and laborers at the facility since its inception in 1943 were indeed stunning, as the *Defender*'s Enoch P. Waters Jr., the *Courier*'s Trezzvant W. Anderson, and also the *Afro American*'s Henderson all took pains to point out. Henderson addresses the problem by the fourth paragraph of his report, where he noted that "There is no school for [the children of black Oak Ridge workers], although the whites have a high school, a junior high school, and eight elementary schools, employing 317 teachers." Also, "there are jim-crow wards in the million-dollar 800-bed hospital and a separate colored section in the 27-chair dental clinic" (1), and Abby J. Kinchy observes of this same article that each of its picture captions draws even more attention to the unequal living and working conditions at Oak Ridge (306).[9]

Although Henderson clearly deplores the inequities suffered by black workers at Oak Ridge, he seems also half-impressed with the sheer size and cost of the modern, state-of-the-art facility. His reliance on numbers and statistics "quantifies" the problem in a way that could be said to water down or mislay the glaring injustice at hand (see also McKittrick and Woods 6). His description of the million-dollar hospital and 27-chair dental office are of a piece with the general numerical description provided at the end of the article, and likely cribbed from Oak Ridge's own press release: "Oak Ridge has 5 restaurants, 9 cafeterias, and 3 lunchrooms. About 350 buses operate on the area and another 400 buses operate off the area, taking workers to their homes" (8). At least a few of Henderson's readers must have wondered how many of these restaurants and lunchrooms served Oak Ridge's black residents, how many of those buses traveled into the facility's black sections or had to be ridden only at the back.[10] When Henderson calmly runs through the housing types at Oak Ridge—"In addition to houses, apartments, and dormitory spaces, there are trailers, hutments, and barracks"—he glosses over a significant sore point of segregated life at Oak Ridge, the relegation of black workers to drafty, ramshackle, mud-embedded "hutments," that Waters and Anderson made a dramatic focus in their reports.

Waters was a war correspondent for the *Defender* and talented chronicler of events throughout the 1940s and 1950s. In his December 1945 coverage of Oak Ridge, he demonstrates a strong rhetorical flair, opening his exposé with a series of embarrassing contradictions pertaining to the government-run installation and late-realized centerpiece to America's wartime "arsenal of democracy":

> Here at the secret birthplace of the atomic age, some of the nation's greatest brains are engaged in exploiting the unknown future of atomic power but Negro children are denied the right to learn their ABCs.
>
> Here cloaked in mystery, inanimate gadgets of steel and glass are housed in concrete palaces where temperatures are controlled to a fraction of a degree but Negro workers must live in flimsy packing box structures set flush on the muddy earth.
>
> Here millions of dollars are marshaled to exploit atomic theory but not enough pennies can be corralled to provide for the welfare and comfort a few thousand Negro workers. ("Atom Bomb Birthplace" 1)

Waters contrasts a typical city's emerging slum areas, which decline through decades of neglect, to the shocking situation at Oak Ridge, "the first community I have ever seen with slums that were deliberately planned. The concept back of the planning and operation of this small city is as backward sociologically as the atomic bomb is advanced scientifically" ("Atomic Bomb Birthplace 1; see also Johnson and Jackson 22, 111–12).

Throughout his two-part report, Waters lays out the undeniable discrepancies related to white versus African American housing, schooling, recreation, dining, and hospital facilities; black school children of the wartime and immediate postwar years had no choice but to be bused to Knoxville, while white children had all of their schooling provided to them on-site. None of Oak Ridge's four first-run movie theaters admitted black patrons, even to their balconies; instead, African American Oak Ridgers were required to make do with old movies shown once a week at the under-appointed recreation and community centers constructed specifically for their use. Waters described the wretched living situation endured by the black nurses, clerks, maids, janitors, and laborers of Oak Ridge:

> Their homes are known as hutments. A hutment is nothing more than a 16×16 packing box, its floor set flush to the ground.
>
> It has four unscreened, unglassed apertures which serve as windows. They admit to the interior light, rain, flies, mosquitoes, and heat or cold depending upon the season. . . .
>
> For each group of 12 hutments there is a central bathhouse outfitted with four toilets, four wash basins, and four shower heads. The bathhouses have cement floors, are drafty, and often dirty. ("Inside Oak Ridge" 1)[11]

According to Walters, Oak Ridge's fourteen Negro nurses shared two dwellings so crowded that some were forced to sleep in the kitchen, where they were all also required to eat, being barred from the main dining halls.

Four years later, the *Pittsburgh Courier* picked up the trail, introducing their series with much fanfare: "Sensational . . . Shocking . . . Stunning," promised a teaser from the 2 April 1949 edition, immediately preceding Trezzvant W. Anderson's multi-part series. "Read the *Courier*'s Expose [sic] of How Negroes Live and Are Treated in the Atomic City" ("What Goes On"). The following week, Anderson opens with Murrowesque relish of the outrage he describes: "This is Oak Ridge! The birthplace of the atom bomb! . . . Yet in this very same city, things are happening which should make Uncle Sam hang his head in shame before the world" ("Government-Owned" 2). Throughout two multi-part reports, filed in April and October 1949, Anderson takes up where Waters left off, reporting that new injustices have emerged since 1945; Oak Ridge's only black councilman will likely never be replaced due to district gerrymandering ("New Dirty Deal" 1+), and two black businessmen have been recently outbid by white proprietors for almost all concessions in their community ("New Scandals" 1+). In an article for *Negro Digest*, Richard B. Gehman reported that by 1948 many of Oak Ridge's Negro workers had left the hutments but only for "drafty, cramped little buildings known as Victory Cottages" whose only victory, quipped one interviewee, "was over comfort" (5).

In keeping with the *Courier*'s hyped presentation of the series is Anderson's tendency toward exaggeration (comparing the hutment facilities to the death camps at Dachau) and soaring rhetoric: "the stench still lingers" ("Government-Owned" 2), "shocked, aghast, and amazed" ("New Dirty Deal" 4), and "the damnable double cross . . . will live forever as one of the blackest pages in American racial infamy" ("Hideous Housing" 6). His several reports owe some of their heft to repetitive descriptions, and in long passages Anderson abandons reportage for editorial rants, including at one point, the exasperated outburst, "Bah! . . . the United States Government is to blame" ("Hideous Housing" 6).

To its credit, the *Courier*'s noisier take on this subject reached more ears. In the third week of his first series, Anderson observed with well-earned pride that the local Oak Ridge paper had taken up the story, as had the *Cleveland Plain-Dealer* ("*Courier* Expose [*sic*]"); eventually, even a spokesman for the Atomic Energy Commission was forced to acknowledge the problem by responding to a series of questions sent by the *Courier* to AEC chair David Lilienthal (Graves). In fact, both Waters and Anderson as well as the *Courier*'s editorial staff made eloquent, irrefutable arguments regarding the travesty of Oak Ridge not as a traditionally segregated town in Dixie but a carefully planned, scientifically oriented, democracy-defending, government-run installation; Gehman described Oak Ridge as "an oasis of government-sponsored racial discrimination" (4). Here, these writers correctly point out, no policies of segregation and discrimination should have been allowed. Waters adds that the usual spurious defense mounted on such occasions—that even a federal facility must follow local custom—could not stand up to observation of the relatively liberal, integrated environs of east Tennessee and nearby Knoxville. As Russell B. Olwell observes, "The area in which Oak Ridge was located had been a checkerboard of black and white farms and communities for generations, but when the army built the city of Oak Ridge, it created separate 'Colored' and 'White' living areas" (21). According to Waters, the poor farmland in the area meant that in earlier times, large-scale plantations and the entrenched hostilities such institutions encouraged never took hold. During the Civil War, Tennessee "was the last state to withdraw from the union and the first to return" (Waters, "Atom Bomb Birthplace" 1); even white Knoxvillians were outraged when Oak Ridge's dirty segregationist secrets came to light following the war.

Anderson likewise hammers away at the hypocrisy of a federally owned and operated enterprise kowtowing to local custom. He targets AEC Chairman Lilienthal (as well as Lilienthal's boss Harry Truman) in almost every report, while an accompanying editorial from 23 April 1949 observes incisively that the top-secret nature of wartime Oak Ridge potentially liberated it from the history and limitations of its US southern context but that the government failed shamefully to capitalize on this potential: "As a matter of fact nobody in Tennessee or anywhere else knew what was going on in Oak Ridge, let alone demanding that jim crowism be the rule" ("The Oak Ridge Disgrace"). As will be discussed in detail later in this chapter, here the *Courier* aligns the power of atomic science (specifically its unprecedented top-secretiveness) with future-oriented, forward-thinking developments in the area of racial equality. As the editorial observes, Truman railed against Congress for failing to pass civil rights legislation, yet failed to take executive action when able to, such as banning discrimination at Oak Ridge (see also "Lilienthal, Liberalism, and Oak Ridge!"). Many years later, following *Brown v. Board of Education*, the *Courier* could report with relief that the schools of Oak Ridge had desegregated ("A-Bomb City"); eastern Tennessee's more liberal tendencies emerged as Oak Ridge schools were the first integrated in the state (Plant 385) and—unlike its notorious neighbor Clinton, where riots and bombings occurred—peaceably (Olwell 114).

THE PROMISE OF THE ATOMIC FUTURE

If African American press coverage of atomic industry had clear economic implications for its readership, appeals to a new era of rationalist, scientific thinking as heralded by the atomic revolution promised political gains. In classic (though only ever implicit) Marxist fashion, these writers contrasted the irrefutable principles of forward-thinking "science" to the "ideology" (and stupidity) of old-fashioned, racist ways. As Simple desired to spend whatever it took to "educate Bilbo," many columnists hailing wartime scientific breakthroughs hoped that the bomb would modernize the nation's mental climate, making Americans smarter, more sensitive, and thus more likely to discern the intellectual bankruptcy of bigotry and discrimination. In *Negro Digest* Fannie Cook advocates "An Atomic Approach to Racism," whereby "atomic" is a substitute term for "scientific" and social scientists renowned for their writings on race, such as Gunnar Myrdal and Melville Herskovits, take over the debate from "the blind, sullen, confused Southern reactionary" (23). In the *Courier* J. A. Rogers appealed to prevailing cold war sentiment when he listed "the hydrogen bomb, the guided missile, [and] the atomic-powered submarine" as prime examples of America's current "products of knowledge." Yet he laments the misplaced priorities of American high schools, "where the one most looked up to is the star football player while the budding scientist is ignored," and congratulates the Russians for clearing their minds of the "clutter" of religious superstition, the sort of "dead rubbish" that fills the minds of both white and black Americans ("History Shows" 9). Again, Rogers's Marxist-style argument (that is, his opposition of "religious superstition" to science) is not named as such, but in his estimation, the literal-minded, knowledge-loving Soviets are dangerously outpacing their western counterparts.

The *Defender's* Earl Conrad drew on biology and semantics to debunk the notion of races based on skin color or other physical characteristics. For Conrad, "race" is "the instrument of those who would divide us," since scientists cannot even agree on the exact number of "races" and since the field of hematology has demonstrated "there are only four blood types all over the world and they can all be found inside each 'race.'" Here Conrad touches on a wartime sore point fomented by the Red Cross, which capitulated to the military's insistence on segregating its blood supplies. It would continue this practice until 1950, and thus Conrad implicitly undermines the legitimacy of the Red Cross as an organization guided by scientific principles. When Conrad observes that "the atom is the same inside all skins" ("That Unscientific Word" n.p.), he suggests not only the shared cellular composition of all human beings but also the shared fate of all human "skins," should World War III take place.

DENOUNCING ATOMIC RESPONSIBILITY

Coverage of the bomb between Russia's first atomic detonation in 1949 and the Sputnik debacle of 1957 varied greatly from one publication to the next, according to audience and editorial inclination. Once more, geographic location seems a contributing factor: the southern-based *Afro American* had least to say of the four main newspapers; its relative distance from the issue of atomic attack and preparedness comes through in the blasé, almost impatient tones of its brief editorial from 1 October 1949: "Announcement that Russia has the atomic bomb is anti-climax as far as most of us are concerned. Few of us were naïve enough to believe that Uncle Sam could keep the secret for very long" ("Russia and the A-Bomb"). In stridently conservative fashion, the editorialist dismisses the prospect of "mass hysteria" as the product of "professional worriers" and "unreconstructed agitators"; he concludes by suing for "more developments in the constructive use rather than in the destructive use of atomic energy," downplaying the magnitude of both the Soviet achievement and American anxiety over same.

By contrast, the northern-based *Courier* made fine political hay of Russia's 1949 atomic detonation, as in Joseph D. Bibb's cleverly titled column of 8 October, "Gone with the Bomb." Here Bibb likens the newly inaugurated cold war to the Civil War, since now the "A-bomb" has wiped out the "aplomb" of master nations, "just as the autocratic Old South dissolved in the wind when Sherman and Sheridan rode over the slave plantations of Dixie" (17). Frightened though he admits to being—as are all Americans regardless of color at this moment—Bibb cannot but enjoy the hush of submission that has fallen over the "Anglo Saxon empire" and the at-least temporary end to "big talk, bombast, and truculence." While the mainstream press had stressed the equation between US atomic monopoly (specifically the Japan bombings) and world "peace," for black commentators who questioned this view in August 1945 and for Bibb four short years later, peace between the US and Russia and amongst all nations on earth was possible only now that the white West has been forced into parity with its erstwhile "inferiors."

On that same page, J. A. Rogers takes a lighter tone with "Each Time White Folks Get Into Trouble the Negro Gets Closer to His Goal." On this occasion, the goal is employment, specifically in the burgeoning atomic field of chemistry. In his *Courier* column a week later, city editor P. L. Prattis presents extensive critique of US foreign policy while making little if any effort to play up an African American angle. He uses folk humor to turn the tables—"This is a 'supposin'' piece. . . . Just suppose that Russia instead of us had perfected the atom bomb first" ("'Supposin'' Piece" 14)—then argues that America would have behaved, justifiably, just as has the USSR. His is a detailed, persuasive adoption of the eastern-bloc viewpoint during this immediate postwar period of US land-grabbing, arms-supplying, and arm-twisting. In a manner very likely to elicit an invitation from HUAC just a few years later, Prattis declares himself a proud American then spends the rest of his column putting himself in the shoes of Soviet leadership, justifying its gestures of self-defense (including developing its own bomb) and in general recasting the self-congratulating leaders of the free world as overbearing bullies on the international playground.

Meanwhile, the *Chicago Defender* and *New York Amsterdam News*, issued from two of America's top-tier urban nuclear targets, paid special attention to civil defense throughout the cold war period, especially as it furthered or threatened the prospect of African American survival of nuclear attack. At the first Soviet detonation, the *Defender* expressed a fervent wish for a more powerful, better organized United Nations ("Peace and the Atom Bomb" 6). With the advent, in early 1950, of the US's many-times-more-powerful hydrogen bomb, the tone was even more serious, verging on the apocalyptic. These papers opposed not only the escalated brinkmanship but the boost to white Western arrogance that resumption of top place in the arms race was sure to provide. In a column from October 1951, with Korea tensions high, even the *Atlanta Daily World's* Dean Gordon B. Hancock touted the end of the white primary in Louisiana but found it hard to stay on topic. "The rights of Negroes," he wrote, "are incidental to such matters" as the raging cold war, with gains made in the South only meager comfort: "So long as we seem headed for atomic war . . . it is just as well that we suffer as brothers and not as masters and slaves" ("Louisiana" 4). By 1954, with the testing of ever more powerful hydrogen weapons, all the *Amsterdam News* could do was throw up its hands in prayer: "Underground shelters are no longer regarded as adequate defenses against atomic rays. . . . Hope seems to be our only defense now . . ." ("The Hell Bomb" 18). These more urban journals' serious-minded response provides a useful counterpoint to the *Afro American*'s relative indifference and the *Courier*'s ironic resignation; with each issue, each member of the black press marked out its unique contribution to the opinion spectrum by its finely nuanced reaction to each development in the atomic saga.

QUESTIONING ATOMIC PREPAREDNESS

The *News*'s comment on "underground shelters" and their several limitations spoke to the preparedness craze that preoccupied the nation throughout the 1950s and early 1960s. As per my Introduction, Truman, Eisenhower, and Kennedy all attempted to develop plans for public or private shelter construction, mass evacuation, and post-attack recovery—each of which died in infancy from lack of congressional funding and public interest. Almost all bomb coverage in the black press of the early 1950s relates to civil defense—general information about pamphlets to acquire and pantries to stock, as well as cynical assessments of failed drills and shelter plans that pointedly excluded African American neighborhoods. The *Amsterdam News* had been thinking about New York's vulnerability since the dawn of the atomic age, when it warned its readers on 25 August 1945 that "17 Atomic Bombs Would Completely Destroy Boro." While such doom-casting seems sensationally premature, given that the only nation to even have atomic capability (its own) had already run out of bombs after dropping two, the *News* understood its role as an advocate for America's premier city and presented its dire measurements against the day when New York (or in this case, Brooklyn) would be struck first. The article discounts rumors of the Japan bombings causing weather change but plays up the intrigue surrounding "the M. W. Kellogg Company of 325 Broadway, Manhattan, which designed the Oak Ridge, Tenn., atomic bomb plant" ("17 Atomic Bombs" 1). Somber once more, the story concludes with the alarming account of Dr. Harold Jacobson, persecuted to the point of collapse by the War Department for broadcasting the danger of atomic radiation (see also Lifton and Mitchell 41–42).

At the start of the preparedness era, black press coverage tended toward open-mindedness: shortly before her appointment in 1951 as an advisory board member to the Civil Defense Administration, the noted civil rights activist and *Defender* columnist Mary McLeod Bethune enjoined her readers—especially her female readers—to prepare themselves and their homes for attack (6). The *Amsterdam News*'s assessment of "Our Underground Shelters" in August 1950 assumes in neutral tones that all neighborhoods will be provided for during air raids. It hails the city's shelter plan as "good news." While stressing the need for shelter in all neighborhoods, regardless of population density (a carefully worded alternative to referencing class or race), the editors commit their community to an active role in civil defense, asking that each neighborhood be represented "at all levels of function: advisory, administrative, and common worker" ("Our Underground" 6). That same year, the *News* published what looks to be a verbatim press release from the Atomic Energy Commission regarding its new pamphlet, "You and the Atomic Bomb." The *Courier* did its civic duty by reproducing "The A-Bomb and You," a government-sponsored press release—illustrated with white characters cowering under basement steps ("You Save These Rules" 13). Even in 1954, the *News* praised the newly installed interstate highway system, designed, among other purposes, to enhance traffic movement in the event of catastrophe such as nuclear attack. Without comment on the exclusionary aspects of an evacuation policy premised on private car ownership and receptive host territories, the editors observe instead that "A good, long, and safe speedway is one of the few places in America where first class citizenship is already a reality" ("Ike's Highway Program" 14). As late as 1959, the *Defender* published "Nuclear Attack Fallout Shelter Now Available," which was little more than an ad dressed in editorial clothing for a prohibitively expensive ($1500) welded steel model.

Early on, however, the African American press began also to realize that despite its own and its readership's willingness to cooperate, civil defense was proceeding around, not within, the black community. An article in the *Afro American*, "Civil Defense Ignores Medics, Other Leaders," presented the views of the National Medical Association, the African American counterpart to the American Medical Association (5). As *Jet*'s Simeon Booker observed, "The Defense Dept.'s $175 million radiation fallout shelter program is designed for suburbs and bub, you know how many of us live in those areas" (12). In *Negro Digest* sociologist Nathan Hare complained that "there would be no time to stage a hide-in or shelter-in, no NAACP to take [the case against shelter exclusion] to the Supreme Court" (30).

The *Amsterdam News* cited plans for five large shelters arranged throughout the city yet noted that "none of these are to be near the heart of Harlem, which is generally said to be around Seventh Ave. and 125th Street. . . . Most Harlemites would have to walk, run or drive, the latter virtually impossible, to one of the shelters during the brief period of warning before an A-bomb burst" ("Harlem Left" 5; see also "See Complete Annihilation"). Mocking the sentiment of some white authors of post-apocalyptic fiction, who depicted their black characters as impervious to atomic assault (see Chapter 1), this editor cracks, "Some people are saying that Harlem must be A-bomb proof" (5; see also "Harlem Shelters"). To indicate the absurdity of such assumptions, *Jet* repeatedly noted scientific studies that showed persons with darker skin more subject to heat and burns received during atomic blast than those with lighter skin ("Negroes Subject" and "Say Negroes More Prone"). One *News* editorial noted that even if shelters were more psychological comfort now than physical protection during an actual attack, "there are few places that need such morale uplifting more than the [*sic*] Harlem, Bedford-Stuyvesant section in Brooklyn and the Morrisania area of the Bronx, where thousands of people are now living in places that look like something the H-bomb disposed of long ago" ("Civil Defense in Harlem" 6).

Historians have remarked upon the ultimately poor response to civil defense, regardless of race or social class, during the postwar period (see the Introduction). When one reads the preparedness coverage provided by the black press, it is little wonder that African Americans—and Americans in general—viewed such displays with a jaundiced eye. Confusion reigned, for instance, when a group of housewives were told in October 1951 to stockpile food in the event of atomic attack but had to remind the Civil Defense Commissioner following his address that they were forbidden to "hoard" for the duration of the Korean conflict, also transpiring at that time ("Food" 10). Conflicting public service announcements published in the *Courier* and the *News* told motorists to roll up the windows if driving during an attack ("You Save These Rules") or to roll them down ("What Motorists Should Do"). Bomb survivors were told on one occasion to stay out of the way of emergency service providers ("You Save These Rules") yet on another to help out however possible ("State Issues"). In addition to the lack of adequate shelter space, the *News* complained that "the air raid warning sirens can scarcely be heard in [Harlem]" (Kennedy 2), while the *Defender* reported on one occasion that "Mock A-Bomb Warning Fizzles in Chicago," especially in "the Southside's ghetto," where yet again "sirens were so faint that few persons actually heard the warnings." Callers to the *Defender*'s office speculated that "maybe the sirens were not meant for Negroes" ("Mock" 12), making low participation in African American neighborhoods entirely understandable.[12]

Items published in the *News* in this period indicate the absurdly small scale on which some air raid drills were conducted—often in and around a single building. These notices also included the evening's agenda—start and finish times (usually only an hour apart), program highlights (e.g., rescuing a man from a roof), and featured performers (CD units, the local hospital, the Red Cross). When the public was invited "to witness these drills for their education value" ("Harlem's CD Units" 33), one cannot but assume that it would have been more their sheer entertainment value that drew appreciative onlookers. And despite Harlemites' sense that Civil Defense ignored their neighborhoods, ironically these seemed to have been frequently selected for drills because of the large stock of "bombed out" housing available as realistic disaster areas. One report refers to a building scheduled for demolition as the "'ruins' [that] were probed for other injured" ("'Air Raid' Reveals" 2-B), while a promotion for an upcoming exercise promises that the designated site in Queens "will be an actual simulated destroyed area" ("Harlem Escapes" 4).

THE SPECTER OF SEGREGATED SHELTERS

Both the *Defender* and the *News*, as well as the *Atlanta Daily World* and *Ebony*, railed against the appointment of Florida ex-governor and notorious segregationist Millard F. Caldwell to the post of top civil defense administrator. Florida native Stetson Kennedy filed with the *News* a thorough rundown of Caldwell's shameful record on civil rights, aptly titled "New Civil Defender is Old Jim Crower" (see also "Hit Caldwell" 8 and "A Look at Atom and Evil" 94). All four publications worried that Caldwell would legislate segregated bomb shelters with the usual disparities in quality. "If a bomb drops," the *Defender*'s editorial staff opined, "we do not want regulations that require citizens to run 10 blocks to a separate racial shelter when one marked 'for white only' is just around the corner" ("Memo" 6). The editors at *Ebony* argued that since "there is no Jim Crow in foxholes" (especially following military integration three years prior) and that since the entire nation, now in a shelter-digging frenzy, was turning itself into a giant foxhole, there could be no more segregation in the shelter-planning of US policy makers, nor in civil defense administration or atomic industry ("A Look at Atom and Evil" 3). The *Daily World* hailed the appointment of Bethune to Caldwell's staff, specifically to an advisory council populated by politicians and pressmen from the integrated North, who were likely to temper Caldwell's extremism (A. Anderson 1).

The *Defender* reported in 1951 the frightening remarks of New Orleans's chief air raid warden, to the effect that "Negroes [must] . . . stand on their own feet and take care of their own people as the whites are taking care of theirs" ("Hint Jim Crow" 1; see also "Separate Races" 3). It was a tumultuous decade later that readers might read with relief the *Courier*'s report from November 1962 that "N.O. Bomb Shelters Integrated." If evacuation was the more realistic scenario, the San Francisco *Sun-Reporter*'s Thomas C. Fleming cast a sardonic eye on the prospect of a "whites only" zone of refuge, specifically neighboring Nevada, whose lawmen promised to repel refugees from the racially mixed urban centers of California. For Fleming, the preparedness frenzy was a "national hysteria" that, however, "play[ed] hob with only one segment of the people. There is another segment of the population who have always been treated as pariahs who do not share this fear of destruction of the bomb." On the contrary, "such a moment of doom would equalize all of the people" (30 September 1961).

By the end of the preparedness era, and at the height of the integrationist phase of the civil rights era (the early 1960s) the *Courier* was able to provide its readers with the ironically encouraging view that "as we lived the grim reality of a nuclear war, none of us had time to think about the color of another human being's skin." This comment came from Pittsburgh-area resident Douglas Waters, the "Lone Negro" in a bomb shelter deprivation study, during which twenty volunteers including himself spent fourteen days in a 20″×12″ fallout shelter. Mr. Waters reports not only a general atmosphere of interracial harmony but good behavior across the board, including job-sharing, kidding around, and the saying of grace before meals ("Lone Negro" 9). As was predicted by several white novelists writing the interracial survival tales discussed in Chapter 1, the bomb (or in this case the mock-bomb) seems to have blasted away old hierarchies and caused this diverse gathering of guinea pigs to pull together. Several of the stories discussed here, however, imply the ironic obverse of such a view—that tragically an atom bomb must go off (or at least be threatened) before the races overcome their animosities. According to Mr. Waters, the experiment's stipulation against discussing race, religion, or politics "wasn't necessary. The horrible implications of the experiment became apart [sic] of us immediately" ("Lone Negro" 9; see also "Negro Sailor"). A year later, the *Courier* itself integrated a shelter experiment when it asked various Pittsburgh men on the street—both African American and white—to share their thoughts on shelter-building. Not surprisingly, the divergence in opinion was political, not racial; the *Courier* encountered several conservatives, both black and white, who thought the government should get out of shelter-building and plenty of progressives, again, both black and white, who thought either that the government should either take charge of shelter construction or admit that shelters would be no help at all ("Pittsburghers Speak Up").

WOMEN REPORTERS ON PREPAREDNESS AND PEACE

It cannot but strike the modern reader that all twelve of the "Pittsburghers" stopped for an interview on this occasion also happened to be men. As if it needed reinforcement, the notion that women's views were largely inconsequential in this period is pointedly indicated here, yet even at this time—and even in the pages of these African American newspapers—the evidence is clear that women had taken an active, essential role in planning and staging the integrated, international peace movement that led to the ban-the-bomb accord of 1963. In Chapter 4, I will discuss the role played by African American women in various sectors of the women's peace movement. In the black press, specifically in the *Chicago Defender*, the important chronicling provided by the Savannah-born, Chicago-based educator, organizer, and clubwoman extraordinaire Rebecca Stiles Dodson (aka Rebecca Stiles Taylor) in her "Federated Clubs" column proved this case again and again. Dodson had a long résumé in community service and feminist activism through her many decades as a club administrator at the highest and most complex national levels (see J. C. Smith). She championed causes related to women and children both nationally and internationally, and from one week to the next her column shifted from standard club fare—a women's luncheon in a fancy hotel—to coverage of world news, including Kikuyu women's role in the Mau Mau uprising ("African Women") and women delegates to an international Peace Conference ("Chicago Women").

Throughout the mid-1950s, Dodson highlighted the racially integrated women's response to the threat of atomic war; she reported on an upcoming meeting of the Chicago Women for Peace—not only the "beautiful prizes" to be raffled at their supper but also their petition to Georgia's Governor Talmadge to commute the sentence of Rosa Lee Ingram and her two sons,[13] as well as their agitation for atomic disarmament ("Chicago Women Act for Peace" 16). Anticipating Lorraine Hansberry's poignant plea for human survival in the nuclear age (see Chapter 4), Dodson titled one column "Women Want to Live" and asserted that "Women of the world are against the use of the BOMB" (15). Dodson quotes multiple peace groups, church leaders, and nuclear scientists (including Einstein) who were at that point (late 1954) urging an end to nuclear testing and weapons development. At other times she promoted the programs of peace-activist women and women's groups; one column was the verbatim speech of World Peace Council delegate Angiola Minella ("They Fight"); another quoted in full the eleven "steps for peace" published by Chicago Women for Peace ("Steps to Peace").

In the *Daily World*, Margaret Goss Burroughs of the Associated Negro Press supplied an editorial whose simple message—"Peace is Wonderful"—recast the victory cry of 1945 as a call to cease weapons- and war-making (see also Kinchy 301). In the *Sun-Reporter* an anonymous writer announced, "Women, It's Up To Us," and urged African American mothers to complain loudly against atmospheric test fallout endangering children's health. She premised her integration plea on freedom from nuclear fear: "If we don't have peace, and soon, we won't be living. There will be no one left to go to work, live in houses, go to schools, swim in pools . . ." (10). In terms traditional for the period, the *Sun-Reporter*'s Thomas C. Fleming challenged white female anti-nuclear activists to maximize their feminine influence over their warmongering mates—and to include African American women more fully within their ranks (see "Weekly Report" columns from 18 November 1961, 28 April 1962, and 22 December 1962). In other venues, the black press demonstrated that the peace movement was integrated with respect to both sex and race. In the *Afro American* Edward Peeks takes a plainly pacifist stance in his warm support for peace marchers who turned up in front of the White House "regardless of race, rank, or religion" (5). An accompanying photo of yet another group of integrated "Peace Picketers," this time in front of City Hall, creates the impression that interracial peace protest had become an unstoppable wave of human activity, taking place on every American street corner (see also "Protest Use" and Skinner).

SIMPLE'S CYNICAL VIEW

Yet again the great Langston Hughes weighed in on these issues as he illustrated themes of preparedness and peace-making over the course of many *Defender* columns published in the early to mid-1950s. While his columns addressed first and foremost his Chicago-based readership, he spoke always from the heart of and with regard to his beloved Harlem environs, such that his views on urban blight, segregated shelters, and the general dangers of atomic contamination addressed urban-based African Americans across the board. Of course one can never confuse Hughes's comic approach with indifference to or acceptance of the problems he discussed; his humor was instead searing in both its harsh critique and its indelible impression (see also D. Harper 62–64). James Smethurst reads Hughes's left-slanted cold war columns as challenging "the notion that [his] work during the 1950s was marked by a political quietude" (1226). In these pieces Hughes did not simply restate that day's news, since his colorful enactments of pressing problems made them evocative and nuanced in ways that straightforward editorial content could not. Simple himself was an avid reader of the daily papers, and his comic rendering of the headlines opened up the occasion for him and the Hughes persona, or for him and his girlfriend Joyce, to hash over breaking news in its most minute and meaningful terms.

As a typical member of the working class, Simple is at once superstitious and justifiably concerned about what he reads and hears: "Even the garbage is going to be radioactive," he reports to the Hughes persona one summer day in 1954 ("Charged with Atoms" 11); the following week, Joyce complains that "the papers is full of nothing but news about hydrogen bombs and atom bombs" ("Joyce Discusses" 11). In delightful local-color fashion, Joyce worries that her new spring hat would get blown off during an atomic blast and that the tuna fish she serves Simple has been "atomized" due to bomb testing in the Pacific. Her comic remarks, however, do not obscure the seriousness of her reference to the then-recent *Lucky Dragon* incident, during which a Japanese tuna boat trawling in the Pacific was inadvertently covered in deadly fallout during the Castle Bravo detonations, causing the death of one fisherman. While Joyce and Simple humorously worry about contaminated tuna threatening Simple's sexual potency, the underlying accusation—of government-sponsored sterilization of both African Americans and "them Japanese, fix[ed] so they can't have no more children"–is no joke. With dark irony, Joyce reassures Simple that New York should escape atomic bombing: "We make mostly women's clothes here, so nobody would want to bomb the garment center. And in Harlem we do not make anything" ("Joyce Discusses" 11). Ever suspicious of the world's white leaders, Simple still worries that "there is lots of folks who just do not like Negroes—which might give some of them a crazy notion to try that bomb on us, just like they tried it out first on the Japanese . . ." ("Joyce Discusses" 11).

While this column concludes on a note of gloom and persecution, many of Hughes's other Simple pieces end with a twist of sweet revenge—in the phrasing of Hughes scholar Melvin G. Williams, a "'get-even' dream" (qtd. in D. Harper 54)—that sends the reader away with a humorous perspective on the ironies and reversals to be realized on nuclear reckoning day, regardless of the mayhem that might also ensue. Scanning the news for the latest on segregated shelters, Simple complains that "white shelters would have everything—nice toilets, telephones, newsstands, Coco [sic] Cola machines—like the railroad stations down south—everything a man needs in the WHITE waiting rooms, nothing in COLORED." The Hughes persona tries to reassure his friend that "if the bombs start falling, white folks probably will forget all about segregation," yet Simple is sure that the only reason whites will "behave" is if, in an ironic reversal of fortune, "the atom bomb roasts them black. . . . in which case, then, they will get Jim Crowed right along with me" ("How Jim Crow" 11). In the "radioactive garbage" piece, Simple stretches his views of radioactivity to tall-tale proportions: if the garbage is radioactive, the cats that eat the garbage will get that way as well; when Joyce pets a stray cat, she will pick up the "charge" and pass it on to Simple, at which point, look out:

> suppose all the Negroes get atomized, charged up like hot garbage, who would serve the white folks' tables, nurse their children, Red Cap their bags, and make up their Pullman berths? . . . [If] I went downtown and punched that time clock where I work, the clock would be charged. Then a white fellow would come along behind me and punch his card in the time clock and he would be charged. . . . Atoms, they tell me, is catching." ("Charged With" 11)

At the comic highpoint Simple pictures himself walking through his own neighborhood, setting off doorbells and "atomizing" people (including his dreaded landlady) over the phone—"that is what you call a chain reaction"; yet atomization has mainly cross-racial implications, as Simple insists that Negroes can sustain radiation much more reliably than whites: "If Negroes can survive white folks," Simple zings at the close, "we can survive anything" ("Charged with Atoms" 11).

In a related piece, Simple supposes what would happen if "atoms wouldn't take on us . . . [if] them atom bombs that burn, scorch, and sizzle other folks . . . would not burn, scorch and sizzle colored folks at all." He imagines "white ladies down in Georgia . . . writing love letters to Bill Robinson and King Cole," so that the biracial products of their sexual union would have added protection in case of nuclear attack. When the bawdy humor has played itself out, Simple adds a parting shot on behalf of himself and his fellow racemen: "And if the bomb don't take on us, I am liable to go back to Africa, too, because Africa will be the most popular land in the world. . . . Africans will be walking around big and black and strong as ever" ("Simple Supposes" 6).

Several years later, Simple is once more poring over the papers and becomes justifiably frightened by news of an impending showdown with the Soviets. Equally concerning is the exclusion of Harlem from recently published atomic-emergency evacuation plans, yet Simple is able to turn the depressing image of white abandonment into another fantasy of sweet revenge: with whites gone, Harlem's legendary state assemblyman and current Manhattan borough president Hulan Jack "would be left setting in the City Hall to act for the Mayor while the Mayor was away. And [vaudevillian entertainer] Pigmeat [Markham] might be the only actor on Ed Sullivan's TV show that week, with maybe Leonard Reed as substitute MC, since everybody white would be gone to their hideaways." Simple himself would hole up at the Stork Club, where he has never been allowed to dine before; following the emergency, Simple dreams, whites would "have to beg me to evacuate" his newly gained turf ("Week by Week" 10). On even more grandiose occasions, Simple desires to rule the world, at which point he would either give the atomic secret to Negroes ("Simple and the Secret" 14), or—with yet more of Hughes's dazzling comic irony—make all nations get along peaceably, lest "I drop my atom bomb on you and wipe you out . . ." ("Simple Views the News" 10).

DETONATING THE ATOMIC METAPHOR

In each of these marvelous works, Hughes depicts his beleaguered African American community making a lemonade of survival and success from the lemons of white-generated nuclear catastrophe. Through these and other remarkable revenge scenarios dotting the pages of the atomic-era black press, one observes these writers' attempt to wrest "the atom" from the control of "white folks" by casting it as on the side of the oppressed, as bringing to them inadvertently or by grand cosmic design long-awaited equality and justice. Almost always there was humor in these "supposin'" pieces that envisioned the bomb as a weapon in the arsenal of civil rights: on the occasion of his one hundredth birthday, former slave Giles Tuggles tells the *Defender* that "We need [the bomb] worse than the Russians. Reckon nobody would discriminate against nobody who had the bomb" (Durham 1). Elsewhere, the wartime *Life* magazine reporter, 1950s-era city councilman, and long-time *Amsterdam News* columnist Earl Brown was racially harassed during a visit to Washington, DC, causing him to feel "like dropping an atom bomb on it" ("Timely Topics"), and a *Defender* editor facetiously suggests "Some Atom Bomb Targets," including the apartheid-ruled nations of South Africa and Australia. But the levity induced did not obscure the heartfelt portent of the writing in question; in each case, the speaker or writer would use atomic weapons to wipe out racism, to counter to any degree possible those already dropped upon fellow-persons of color at the end of the second world war and those used as threats against African Americans by racists like Senator Bilbo and civil defense administrator Caldwell.

Yet another defense against this threat was the figurative association of the bomb with racial equality, which these papers reported upon or forged themselves whenever appropriate. The *Courier* quoted novelist Lillian Smith, who told an integrated audience in South Carolina that "The dropping of segregation in the United Stage would have more effect on the world than dropping an atomic bomb on China" (Rivera 1). The *Amsterdam News* cited the ruling of a Flatbush magistrate against a race-baiter harassing a porter in a train station, commenting from the bench that "racial prejudice and hate" were akin to "the new and deadly atomic bomb" ("Judge Compares" 2-B; see also "Atom Bomb Forces" 9). The *Defender* found many ways to work the analogy into its own opinions, including an editorial days after Hiroshima called "Splitting the Atom of Race Hate" and a book review that same day by Ben Burns who commented that the "teaching of tolerance can be as devastating and precedent-shattering in keeping the peace as the atomic bomb is in waging war" (14). If Bilbo's racist filibustering was like an atomic bomb dropping, so also did the signing of Jackie Robinson to the Brooklyn Dodgers "have the impact of the atomic bomb on a few of the race prejudiced southern brothers" ("Hats Off" 14). Louis Armstrong on the disgrace of Little Rock had "both the timing and the explosive effect of an H-bomb" ("Ole 'Satchmo'" 10). In March 1963 an *Afro American* cartoon depicted the arm of "JFK" guiding a missile marked "Civil Rights Message" into "the heart of rural Dixie" and blasting a linen-suited elder labeled "racial voting barriers" on his backside ("On Target" 4). Thus atomic energy and even atomic weaponry were richly suggestive registers for writers and illustrators in the African American press, which supplied the arsenal of civil rights in a variety of ways: in a negative light, the bomb was likened to the disaster of US and international racism; repurposed into the service of justice for all, the bomb targeted hatred and prejudice—or, often in comic or folktale-fashion, even a few of the prejudiced themselves.

SPUTNIK AS SWEET REVENGE

The atomic-era black press also lit upon striking historical coincidences to emphasize the hypocrisies and contradictions involved in US claims to leadership of the "free world." At the outset of this chapter I indicated the concurrence—and the degree of political tension that resulted—between James Meredith's integration of Ole Miss and the Cuban Missile Crisis; some years earlier, the coincidence of the Soviet launch of Sputnik and the Little Rock school desegregation debacle proved a much more productive rhetorical occasion. Sputnik was less a full-fledged crisis than a political embarrassment—that is, less a dangerous distraction than yet another rich political opportunity that the African American press exploited in myriad ways. Like the first atomic detonation by Russia in 1949, and like the U-2 and Bay of Pigs incidents of the early 1960s, Sputnik was an atomic-inflected turning of the tables on the white Western power structure, a "get-even dream" come true whose ironies the black press was sure to remark upon. How the world had changed, however, between 1949 and 1957, with respect to the dramatic developments of the civil rights struggle. In 1957, freedom marches, bus boycotts, and school integration made daily national headlines, and the antagonism between Arkansas governor Orval Faubus and the Eisenhower administration broke onto the front page only weeks before the Soviets successfully orbited their surveillance satellite. As the weaponry itself became ever more "surgical" and precise, the Sputnik incident could be aimed at a specific target—the outrage at Little Rock—and used to attack its every feature through detailed interpretation of the analogous and interlocking relation between the two.

As Earl Brown snickered in his *Amsterdam News* column of 19 November 1957, "Old Sput has made ['smug, arrogant' Americans] admit that the other guy can pull rabbits out of a hat, too." Reading the satellite as a threat similar to the bomb, Brown commented, "It is possible that Sputnik may make even Faubus cuddle up closer to colored folk for common protection" ("Russia's Sputnik" 6). Fellow *News* columnist Lester Granger agreed that "Sputnik is important . . . because it exposes the myth of an impregnable American superiority" (8). Both Brown and Granger noted that the arms race is partly responsible for recent advances made by the civil rights movement. Brown links "the gains we colored folk have made in the US" with the "Communists [throwing] their weight around" (6) while Granger closes with the opinion that "Any such reevaluation [of race discrimination] is bound to bring more modern attitudes on race, and if it does, Leetle Spootneek is entitled to a lot of the credit" (29).

Others called specific attention to Sputnik as a surveillance device. In the *Courier*, cartoonist Wilbert Holloway drew the satellite bearing witness to a white male figure named "the segregationists" astride a black male figure sprawled on his stomach, a diploma marked "education" loosed from his hands in the assault. The title is "Time to Wake Up, America?" yet a better title might have been "Sputnik is Listening," since, as commented upon elsewhere in these newspapers, Russia's new surveillance devices meant that more than ever America's claims to freedom and democracy must line up with its actions. In a similarly composed cartoon from the *Defender* by the great Chester Commodore, titled "A Mad, Mad Whirl," a "Russian Satellite" orbits the planet, specifically the US, and even more specifically the dizzied figure of Uncle Sam. Another Sputnik-shaped object, named "Integration Problems" whirls across from another direction, making Uncle Sam's disorientation that much worse (see figure 6). Here the message is clear that both Sputnik and Little Rock are twin headaches for hypocritical US leadership, which implicitly find themselves in a powerful, however provisional, alliance. P. L. Prattis noted that the buzz at a UN meeting following Sputnik was not about the Soviet breakthrough but "all the gory details" of the Little Rock incident ("Sputnik and US" 9). An article in the *Afro American* reported that the US Information Agency was having trouble "blanking out" heavy international press coverage of Little Rock ("Little Rock 'sputnik'" 7).

Editorials likewise spoke in scoffing tones, as when on October 19 the *Courier* drew Faubus as a limelight-seeking "hillbilly Governor" who was not smart enough to use Sputnik as an excuse to withdraw himself from the public stage. Instead, accused the *Courier*, Faubus pressed on with spurious charges of national guardsmen invading the Central High girls' gym locker room,

FIGURE 6: Chester Commodore. *Chicago Defender* (19 October 1957). 5. Courtesy of the *Chicago Defender.*

revealing him as yet another "sex-obsessed white southerner" ("Faubus and Sputnik" 8). The *Afro American* enjoyed the jibing Faubus received from a fellow-governor, one from the South no less, when Maryland's Theodore R. McKeldin expressed certainty that "the Arkansas controversy [was] a failing satellite which soon shall have run its course" ("Little Rock 'Sputnik'"). McKeldin called Faubus a "political spotlight sputnik" who postured before cameras to keep his political star from fading. The *News* argued against "$100,000 a day to maintain troops to escort nine Negro children . . . to school" that could have gone to the development of weapons technology ("One Reason" 6), and in a similar vein *Ebony* countered the racist assessment of one Dixie politician—that America's two current problems were "moons [a Sputnik nickname] and coons"—with a rhyme of its own: "it is costing American brain power needed in scientific research to conquer space . . . but being wasted in a futile search for means of avoiding race" ("Race Vs. Space" 90). These editors hoped that the enormity of both the universe now open to exploration and the Soviet thermonuclear threat would put white racial hysteria into proper perspective.

The *Defender* conceded a point to Faubus in a poignant Commodore cartoon from the end of 1957. Pictured is a dazed and lump-headed Father Time handing off to Baby New Year. The old man's comment is ". . . Sputniks. . . . Rockets 'n' everything! But son. . . . *this*"—a rock in his hand marked "Little Rock"—"really rocked me" ("Better Luck"; see figure 7). Yet despite the admission that Faubus scored a hit when even Sputnik and "Unsuccessful Satellite Attempts" could not, the cartoon conveys through its racial designations—a white Father Time addressing an African American Baby New Year with the solicitous endearment of "son"—that black ascension and familial feelings between the races are inevitable in the coming days. While the *Defender* was surely correct that the Little Rock affair was a traumatic event for those directly involved and for African Americans in general, still it and other black newspapers had done their best over the preceding months to alleviate suffering by pointing up a remarkable historical coincidence: yet another US setback in the international atomic contest was worsened by its overlap with an embarrassing low point for this same US leadership in the ever more successful struggle for civil rights.

WRAPPING UP: THE *AFRO AMERICAN'S* CUBAN MISSILE COVERAGE

As noted at the opening of this chapter, the *Afro American* provided no coverage of the Cuban crisis in its 27 October 1962 issue, suggesting that it was a matter of little importance to this paper and its readers. Yet this suggestion is fully undermined by the wide-ranging response provided there in the following weeks, when its coverage outdid all of its counterparts in the top echelon of the

FIGURE 7: Chester Commodore. *Chicago Defender* (28 December 1957). 10. Courtesy of the *Chicago Defender.*

black press. As in the *Defender*, the *Courier*, and the *News* a week earlier, support in the *Afro American* for Kennedy's decision to blockade Cuba was overwhelming; both the editorial staff and those many locals interviewed expressed their intention to "rally 'round" their commander-in-chief at that crucial moment. As per the typical World War II coverage, the *Afro American* made proud reference to "Tan GI's" doing their part to prepare for war, although reporter Dan Day pointed out that now the men serve "in the integrated Armed Services," and "in sharp contrast to the beginning of World War II, a sizeable number of non-whites are now in command positions" (1). As had the Japanese in 1945, the Cubans here play an ambiguous role; they are both ideological adversaries and beleaguered brethren of America's own black underclass, seen as victims of the white capitalist West. Howard University's Dr. Vincent J. Brown complained that "you never can tell what these people [the communist Cubans] will do," while in that same report, another interviewee defended the Cubans who "have already suffered one attempted invasion [the Bay of Pigs landing] and have been constantly threatened with another" ("President Had To" 2; see also Fleming 3 November 1962).

Others, however, supported Kennedy specifically for the role he had played in recent civil rights battles; the soon-to-be-martyred NAACP field secretary Medgar Evers explicitly attached "the Meredith case" to his support for Kennedy's actions against Cuba ("President Had To" 2), while that same day an editorial likened the army preparing to defend the US to the "army [sent] into Mississippi" a few weeks earlier ("Castro and K Went Too Far" 5). The editorial paints Mississippi governor Ross Barnett as an extremist cut from the same cloth as Castro and Khrushchev, all of whom "went too far." While Castro is at one point a "small neighbor" likened to America's "people of color" who bear the brunt of arrogant white leadership, ultimately the editorialist sides with the heroic figure of Kennedy who defends both American shores and American heroes like James Meredith with equal courage and decisiveness.

Ralph Matthews's complex interpretation of the Cuban crisis posited that in fact Khrushchev "won" the recent showdown, yet Matthews's aim is less to score points against white Western leadership than to delineate the many incontrovertible ironies of the Cuban situation. This column provides hard-hitting foreign policy analysis, without necessarily pointing up a race angle. For Matthews, it was Khrushchev who demonstrated courage on this occasion, by stepping away from a confrontation that many others would be "scared not to fight." Now, he noted, US allies might regret hosting American missile bases and adopt a more neutral attitude toward the Soviet Union. Matthews points out that in withdrawing his hardware from Cuban soil Khrushchev lost nothing, since proximity is no longer necessary when conducting modern, long-range guided-missile warfare. If anything, Matthews incisively observes, Khrushchev's withdrawal has only encouraged in US leaders the winner's tendency to fight the "last war," (i.e., the conventionally fought World War II) by acting as a conventional, old-fashioned adversary. In his final movement, Matthews implies his personal gratitude to the Soviet premier and argues that the real winners in the Cuban contest are the still-existent, "grateful peoples of the earth" ("Thoughts on War and Peace").

Again recalling that the *Afro American* was so "elsewhere" to this subject on 27 October that there was no reaction at all, the record also indicates that two weeks later, columnist Matthews was so thoroughly steeped in the nuances and contradictions of the conflict that his long analysis brackets the race angle and stands simply as an outstandingly meaningful treatment of the topic, indistinguishable from any of those found in the mainstream press. The race-inflected coverage of the Cuban Missile Crisis, or any of the atomic mile-stones visited in this discussion, should not be read as preferable to, or, far less, inferior to, the color-blind response from Matthews's column; both kinds of writing instead are essential to indicating the broad range of reaction to the bomb in the African American press and surely to each topic that became im-portant to its editors and reporters. No single political affiliation, nor tone of voice, nor intellectual level, nor angle of significance can be said to character-ize the African American press's coverage of the bomb in these key years be-tween the Japan bombings and the Cuban crisis. From editors' heartfelt pleas for fair hiring and brotherly love, to hard-hitting reporting on issues like Oak Ridge and the Caldwell appointment, to the bracing irony of talented cartoon-ists and the incomparable Langston Hughes, the black press covered (that is, exposed) the bomb from every angle pertinent to its audience, itself a dynamic and wide-ranging body of readers. As per the founding mandate of the black press, the bomb may have never been any more than a "sidebar" to the always-central story of the struggle for civil rights; yet as both profound plan-etary threat and popular American icon it often featured meaningfully in these papers in its own unending complexity—and as an unlikely but no less effec-tive weapon in the rhetorical arsenal of those who crusaded there for equality and freedom.

CHAPTER 4

Against the "Starless Midnight of Racism and War"

African American Intellectuals and the Anti-Nuclear Agenda

Early in Lorraine Hansberry's masterwork *A Raisin in the Sun* (1959), an anxious and distracted Walter Younger reads the paper, as per the playwright's stage directions, "vaguely" and announces to his estranged wife Ruth, "Set off another bomb yesterday" (1.1.6). The average postwar playgoer—and even the skilled contemporary critic (e.g., Matthews 556)—approaching this renowned civil rights narrative might assume that the "bomb" Walter mentions has been directed by racist whites against a black church or residence. Yet in fact Walter refers to an above-ground nuclear test, one of many conducted by the US and USSR throughout the 1950s. As vital as the subject of racial equality was to Hansberry, and the attendant issues of neighborhood segregation and racially motivated terrorist bombing, she also frequently addressed the atomic threat in her essays, dialogues, and dramatic works; in one memorable interview she insisted that we "get rid of all the little bombs—and the big bombs" (*To Be Young, Gifted, and Black* 253–54), and in fact Hansberry—like many peace-loving African American intellectuals of the period—shifted freely between the causes of nuclear disarmament and civil rights from one project to the next, or even within the same work. In *Raisin*, while racially motivated bombing becomes an ever more central issue, the significance of the atomic bomb was so basic to Hansberry's own worldview that her characters take note of related developments, in perfect keeping with their atomic-era context.

Specifically, we discern a nuclear referent in Walter's opening remark because of the way he couches it. Instead of saying "they bombed another church today" or "there was another bombing on the Southside" Walter's emphasis on the "setting off" indicates that this bomb's target is less significant (in the case of a nuclear test it is nonexistent) than are the political and biological hazards involved with the detonation itself. Too, Walter's "vague" comment on the subject, followed by Ruth's response of "maximum indifference" (1.1.6) would hardly make sense if Walter referred to a racially motivated bombing, given the importance of such race-based terrorism to all African Americans during this period. Instead, this item pairs with another that Walter reports in his continued attempt to win over his wife with small-talk safely removed from their immediate domestic travails: "Say Colonel McCormick is sick" (1.1.6). Here he refers to Robert R. McCormick, the arch-conservative publisher of the *Chicago Tribune*;[1] not surprisingly Ruth responds with "tea-party interest"—"Is he now? Poor thing" (1.1.6)—and goes back to scrambling eggs for Walter's breakfast.

While few would question Ruth's indifference to McCormick under even the best of domestic circumstances, the issue becomes whether the bomb figures as similarly meaningless, as removed from Ruth's experience as a struggling but proud African American woman as is the prognosis for some aristocrat. In a later scene the tables are turned when wealthy, snobbish George Murchison awaits the appearance of Ruth's sister-in-law Beneatha (who shares the Younger apartment) and Ruth must preside over her own session of small-talk, "determined to demonstrate the civilization of her family" (*Raisin* 2.1.73). Following a remark about the hot weather—described in the stage notes as "this cliché of cliché's"—Ruth indicates her knowledge of the atomic events she dismissed in a graver but more authentic moment at the opening of the play: "Everybody says [the heat's] got to do with them bombs and things they keep setting off. (*Pause.*) Would you like a nice cold beer?" (2.1.73). No one is surprised to learn that George doesn't "care for beer."

Recent *Raisin* interpreters (e.g., M. Gordon 129) read Ruth's comment here as another reference to racially motivated bombing, yet her jocular tone on this occasion is again hardly conducive to the introduction of such a serious subject about which we see later that Ruth cares a great deal. Too, the race-based reading ignores Ruth's comment about the unseasonably hot weather, popularly feared to have been caused by atomic bombings—and addressed in news media, including African American weeklies such as the *New York Amsterdam News* (see "17 Atomic Bombs" and Chapter 3; more broadly see Deming 113)—since the days of Hiroshima and Nagasaki. Finally, as with Walter's report, Ruth uses the "set off" phrasing to indicate that she is discussing an atmospheric detonation, not any sort of domestic or international targeted attack. Ruth's vague and ungrammatical reference to "them bombs and things" indicates her underlying indifference to and discomfort with the subject of the atom bomb (yet another cliché?), despite her attempt to demonstrate otherwise on the occasion of impressing an upwardly mobile family connection.

Yet George is unfazed by this reference to the bomb, and Ruth might have had a more fruitful conversation on the subject with Beneatha's other suitor, the African intellectual Joseph Asagai, whose solid grounding in self, culture, and history is cast by the play as the preferred alternative to George's superficial emphases on white forms of entertainment and personal appearance. Ruth never has this opportunity, however, and the play thus closes upon remarkable open questions regarding the significance of the bomb for African Americans of this period: did only phonies like George or exotic foreigners like Joseph care about the issue, or is Hansberry's point that any American would take the bomb seriously, were she not so burdensomely distracted by the host of more urgent problems (cramped living quarters, unwanted pregnancy, thwarted dreams) facing Ruth and her family?

Significantly, the family plans their move to escape their long-held, run-down, and overpopulated apartment; while their "ghetto" residence is undesirable in its own right, a "nuclear" reading is also possible: bomb shelter conditions are invoked by this crowded, stressful, deteriorated setting, especially the makeshift image of the Youngers' son Travis sleeping each night on the couch. In accordance with the resonant last line—*"or does it explode?"*—from Langston Hughes's "Harlem (A Dream Deferred)," whence Hansberry borrows the title of her play, the cramped conditions create a powder keg situation; Ruth and Beneatha long to break out of their circumstances, while Walter's nervous, explosive energy menaces his family from the opening moments. Hughes's own poem, written in 1951, is also readable for its "atomic" shadings, echoes of his more explicit response to the atomic age locatable in his popular journalism (see Chapter 3). Even Michelle Gordon's trenchant analysis of the "rats and roaches" (127) infesting the Youngers' tenement dwelling lends itself to an atomic interpretation, since these two species of vermin, thought hearty enough to survive even nuclear Armageddon, have often been rhetorically deployed to depict a nightmarish post-nuclear landscape.

More centrally, *Raisin*'s main plot involves Ruth and Mama's dream of using Mama's insurance money for a down payment on a single-family home somewhere less central to the city. Thus the Youngers are as interested in fleeing their crowded inner city environs, endangered by both crime and nuclear war, as were their white counterparts of the postwar generation (see also Saul 69–70); Walter's dream of staying downtown and opening a liquor store with his untrustworthy friends is presented as ultimately misguided. When racist whites from the suburbs show up to talk the Youngers out of their planned move, Walter is galvanized to do the right thing, opting for a gesture that is simultaneously a strike for civil rights and a precaution taken to protect his family from urban incineration should the nuclear unthinkable occur.

Yet a point of tension in the play between race matters and nuclear fears emerges when the offhanded interest taken in the atomic bomb by Walter and Ruth in the opening scenes is contrasted to the intense focus given to another bombing reported in the papers that hits much closer to home: a racially motivated attack against a black family integrating a white neighborhood. The event is announced by nosey Mrs. Johnson, who crosses the hallway to crow about the dangers imminent in the Youngers' impending move to all-white Clybourne

Park. While this move may shelter them from ever more likely nuclear attack, it invites retaliation from racist neighbors, such that the Youngers—and the play as a whole—are caught within an intractable dilemma: whether it was safer to stay in the city where nuclear attack might never occur, or whether this threat was sufficiently real to play a meaningful role in the personal and political motivations of many postwar African Americans to flee the deteriorating urban core at any cost.

As this example from Hansberry indicates, advocating simultaneously against the bomb and in favor of civil rights could cause conflict or controversy. The ever more dramatic achievements of the civil rights era not only coincided with but frequently competed for attention with each escalation in the nuclear arms race: as per my findings in Chapter 3, the atomic-induced end to war brought massive job loss to the black community; the lackluster civil defense drills of the mid-1950s could not compare with, for instance, the victorious narrative of the Montgomery bus boycott; and the Cuban Missile Crisis in October 1962 shared headlines with the story of James Meredith's heroic integration of Ole Miss. In addition, civil rights leaders may have felt (or may have been encouraged to feel[2]) that foreign policy was outside their purview, and as Marian Mollin has observed, the tactics of some white peace protesters—bohemian dress and comportment, picketing nuclear installations where lucrative, non-discriminatory jobs were available—alienated members of local freedom movements who sought equality by emphasizing middle-class respectability and adherence to conservative values (134, 137–38). So vital were the issues of racial justice and nuclear non-proliferation that it was difficult to not care deeply about both, yet so significant and complex was each that many found themselves alternating between, or having to choose between, the two.

Note for instance that Hansberry's focus on the bomb, which for some including her own recent biographer is "an essentially white intellectual issue" (Cheney, Preface n.p.), may have led black separatists like Malcolm X and Harold Cruse to denounce Hansberry's "left-wing, cosmopolitan, and interracial frameworks . . ." (J. E. Smith 326). Cruse called *Raisin* "a glorified soap opera" and, with respect to perhaps everything from the Youngers' *Tribune* subscription (see note 1 of this chapter) to their implicit "white flight" to the nuclear safe haven of the suburbs, critiqued what he regarded as Hansberry's "quasi-white orientation through which she visualized the Negro world" (283).

Significantly, Hansberry's text stands upon a threshold between the interracialism (including integrated anti-nuclear activism) of the 1940s and 1950s and the race-separatism of later decades. Her detractors look back from the other side of this threshold and call into question a way of seeing things that was assuredly broader but, according to these critics, less effective than would be the single-issue focus they advocated. They also speak from a point in time when the Vietnam War not only began to challenge the notion of interracial harmony as a "simple" domestic issue but also derailed the anti-nuclear focus of earlier pacifist movements both black and white. In the words of Ethel Taylor, a "key person" in the anti-bomb group Women Strike for Peace, "Even though we knew that while the war was going on, the nuclear arms race would continue, we had to make a choice on what issue we would deal with immediately. There was no question it would be Vietnam because this was so urgent" (qtd. in Swerdlow 125). On a parallel track, the undelivered-upon promises of the March on Washington of 1963, the Civil Rights Act of 1964, and the Voting Rights Act of 1965 created their own agenda of urgent problems that distracted African American peace activists from bomb opposition and sometimes even from the commitment to nonviolence itself. If finally atomic disarmament and civil rights traded the places of center and margin in the collective American consciousness during this period, the stock of the former falling as that of the latter rose chiastically across its path, the focus here as throughout will be the key transitional decades of 1945 to 1965, when leading African Americans opposed to the bomb dealt in remarkable ways with the equally vital—sometimes complementary, sometimes competitive—issue of racial equality.

Thus consideration of place and position in this chapter involves the location of both anti-nuclear protest and civil rights struggle on the postwar cultural spectrum. As these two vital issues jockeyed for national attention, so leading figures within the African American community found themselves caught between roles in the fight for one and then the other. As they themselves moved to the center and margin of the "typical" (civil rights-centered) agenda for black leaders in that period, so they may be seen to have occupied shifting points on the American political spectrum. And yet questions of what is "left" and "right"— or what is "black" and "white"—on this spectrum relates to what it might have meant for members of this group to take a position on the bomb itself. Even "standard" (i.e., white-oriented) oppositions needed redefinition on this occasion, since "what kept the race back" versus "what moved the race forward" did not always coincide with "conservatism" and "progressivism" as construed in a traditional (again, often white-oriented) political paradigm.

While the paradoxes of American politics—the vast differences, for instance, between fiscal and cultural conservatives, between liberals and libertarians despite their shared etymological roots—sometimes involve Americans of all races and classes, these paradoxes are complexified when considered in a specifically African American context: for instance, while few would read the image of a white male brandishing a gun on his front lawn as anything other than an expression of cultural ultra-conservatism, black weapon carrying, especially the revolutionary brand advocated in the mid- to late 1960s by Malcolm X, the Black Panthers, and Hansberry herself,[3] is often read as an ultra-leftist attempt to strike out (or even simply defend) against grave social injustice. Yet while we may situate "militancy" and "radicalism" on the political left, these words simply mean "extremism" and may describe the actions of those at either endpoint on the spectrum. The two terms are safely opposed to "moderation," and for many, the moderate approach to civil rights organizing and protest—especially by the late 1960s, but throughout the twentieth century—smacked unacceptably of accommodation.

Radicalism is typically the approach of the younger generation, causing the tactics of the outgoing leadership to seem moderate by its very appearance: when they were first deployed, the nonviolent-resistance strategies of Martin Luther King Jr. (and, a decade earlier, by Bayard Rustin and his cohort at the pacifist Fellowship of Reconciliation) struck almost everyone as revolutionary, even apocalyptic, but after a few years and the advent of Malcolm X, civil disobedience seemed retrograde in comparison (see also Horne, "Black and Red" 5). Beyond (mis)perceptions, civil rights historians have documented the actual centrist, or even rightward, shift of many of the movement's leading figures (most prominently among spokespersons for the NAACP) as the cold war caused conservatism to flourish nationwide. To the degree, however, that the vituperation and violence perpetrated by the radical black Left mirrored the tack taken by the radical racist Right, Rustin, King, and (almost always) Hansberry advocated a rigorous nonviolence that remains for some the true alternative to the American status quo: while, for instance, both the Ku Klux Klan and black militants adopted a fundamentalist religious framework (either Christianity or Islam) to explain and excuse racial hatred and deadly violence, King and the other pacifists discussed in this chapter actually emulated the example of Christ (and his twentieth-century "incarnation," Mahatma Gandhi; see, for example, Farrell 90) and may be read, in this sense at least, as the most radical movement of all.

As this chapter begins, I examine the anti-nuclear activism of early leaders W. E. B. Du Bois and Paul Robeson whose commitments to left politics and world peace could not but compete in some ways with their roles in the civil rights movement. Following, I will discuss the careers of 1963 March on Washington organizer and renowned pacifist Bayard Rustin; Martin Luther King Jr., for whom no introduction is necessary; and Hansberry in her drama, interviews, and nonfiction. Rustin and King deserve great credit for their remarkable stance against the twin evils of the postwar period—racism and the nuclear threat; it is King's Nobel Prize acceptance speech whence comes the title of this chapter. Each successfully integrated (or alternated between) these callings—Rustin in his activist life and King in his sermonic writings—such that for these leaders, as per the example of the Youngers' move to the suburbs, a strike for racial justice was often simultaneously a strike for world peace.

Yet similar to the questions left open in this play, the life of Rustin and the writings of King also indicate complex dilemmas involved in their dual callings: mid-career, Rustin faced the impossible need to be in two places (often on different continents) at once, and for numerous reasons chose finally to commit himself to civil rights activism on American soil full-time. King reached a wide international audience primarily through his writing, which evinced a firm commitment to both peace and equality. Meanwhile, at various key moments appears the tension between the two issues: despite the eloquent use to which King put the trope of "midnight" in his Nobel Prize speech, we locate a rhetorical breakdown between his enthralling vision of a racially harmonious "tomorrow" and the always horrific prospect of the other side of nuclear midnight, which must be avoided at all costs. Of all the thinkers surveyed here, it is Hansberry—notably the only woman in the group—whose commitments to both racial justice and bomb opposition I regard as most consistent, simultaneous, and successfully integrated. In both her life and work Hansberry opposed an ardently pacifist perspective to the dramatic tradition of the white male mainstream by constructing a relentlessly affirming vision of life and survival, literally of the (self-) destructive hand pulling back in time, and by presenting her audience with thought-provoking drama instead of despairing, disabling tragedy. Because Hansberry racialized her thematic tendency toward life-affirmation in this distinctive way, she created a uniquely African American artistic voice that was simultaneously a strike against the cynicism of the nuclear age.

By the late 1960s, when the midnight of racial conflict and political assassination brought only morning's cold light of mistrust and despair, cynicism ran high within the African American community, and leading black intellectuals of a separatist mindset, specifically Elijah Muhammad and John Oliver Killens, saw the bomb primarily as a corrosive sign of the declining white western empire. In the conclusion of this chapter I read the nuclear-inflected apocalypticism of these late-decade thinkers and oppose to this yet another successfully integrated vision of survival in the nuclear age, that of James Baldwin, who responded to the nuclear threat by largely ignoring it, promoting interracial harmony and peace at a local level instead. Finally, each of these writers related the issues of anti-nuclear activism and civil rights in unique and valuable ways. While for late-era intellectuals the bomb was often a mere counterpoint to their committed focus on racial equality, integration-era thinkers sought, and often managed, to address the nuclear threat and the outrage of segregation alternately or simultaneously in their activist lives and artistic output. Even as these causes traded positions of margin and center, the ways in which black leaders wrestled with the dilemmas presented by their dual callings yet particularized and dimensionalized their lives and work.

DU BOIS'S CAMPAIGN FOR PEACE

As an issue of international significance, the bomb was of central importance for some cold war African Americans, even as it was regarded by many others as largely irrelevant to their struggle for civil rights. To the degree that ignoring the bomb was a way of defusing its threat, some African Americans were superior to the bomb on an emotional and intellectual level, even as many remained physically trapped directly in its path. Though in part freed of the "commie" and atomic anxieties that enslaved many of their white counterparts, their emotional energies were not spared but simply channeled—to the breaking point—in other, more urgent directions. Meanwhile, to take a position "on" the bomb, as various prominent African Americans did during the cold war, was to acknowledge one's precarious perch as an American and a world citizen on nuclear arms and arms control at that point in history and to add this frightening realization to a list of other, equally troubling domestic troubles. The remarkable career of world citizen W. E. B. Du Bois, whose long life (1868–1963) enfolded dozens of major episodes in American civil rights and cold war history, helps us to think about the politics of bomb-consciousness for African Americans (and Americans of all backgrounds) during the postwar/cold war period; specifically, Du Bois's suit for peace marked him, incredibly, as an extremist for many Americans in this period.

Du Bois's peace advocacy, which became pointedly anti-atomic as soon as the Hiroshima and Nagasaki bombs were dropped, was a prominent aspect of his long political life; Earl Ofari Hutchinson notes an NAACP resolution in 1932, which already bore "Du Bois' unmistakable imprint" (121) for favoring "world peace, international comity, and disarmament" (qtd. in Hutchinson 121). Despite his sometimes harsh words against communism, for the most part Du Bois "looked benignly and positively on the Communists, and . . . this tendency increased as time wore on . . . ; there was more that united them than divided them" (Horne, *Black and Red* 298, 290). In contrast to other 1930s- and '40s-era fellow travelers (black and white),[4] who drifted rightward or even turned informant by the time of the cold war, Du Bois moved further and further left, at last taking up membership in the Communist Party at the age of 93. One could argue that it was Du Bois's lifelong desire for world peace that pushed him ever leftward, and that it was the specific threat posed by the atomic bomb that aligned him in such pronounced and public fashion with the Communist Party and Soviet Union. Gerald Horne documents the marked leftward shift of Du Bois's politics immediately following WWII, as well as the critical assessment that at this time Du Bois's views made a noticeable lunge to the margin of the civil rights agenda (*Black and Red* 4–5; see also Lewis, *W. E. B. Du Bois* 496–553).

Yet as Horne shows, Du Bois's postwar views were consistent with those of earlier decades: he had always seen the link between war and colonialism or slavery; his experience of WWI only reinforced this sense, and he was keenly observant of the racial dynamics of WWII and the Korean conflict. Before and even during the second world war, Du Bois saw Japan primarily as an oppressed Asiatic race, manipulated into joining the battles of white fascist forces (Horne, *Black and Red* 7; Du Bois, *Newspaper Columns* 650).[5] He viewed Hiroshima and Nagasaki in specifically racial terms and took to heart Truman's threats of using atomic weapons to stop the North Koreans (see Aptheker 8).

He even tended to regard the Russian continent as less European than Asian, even though he used his writing to dissociate "Moscow" from the North Korean offensive.

While it may have been the racial dynamics of the world's first atomic conflicts that drew Du Bois into his battle against the bomb, he soon realized that such tremendous weaponry threatened every earthly inhabitant, regardless of race, and joined the multiracial, multinational effort to forever ban its use. He lashed out—against the bomb and in favor of peace—in columns for *The Chicago Defender* and *The National Guardian* on a regular basis; in a remarkable piece for the *Defender* in early 1946, Du Bois read atomic weaponry as an explicitly white/imperialist phenomenon that would eventually engulf both oppressed and oppressor:

> Is it possible to keep the secret of the loosing of atomic energy, as a monopoly of white folk? . . . If these Colored people ever do, even in small and limited degree, master this language of force, it will be the peoples with massed cities, with sky-scrapers and factories, with piled material wealth, which will suffer all the more easily before desperate men in forest and on steppe, with nothing to lose but their chains. (*Newspaper Columns* 670)

Du Bois incisively reminds us that much white wealth—and many white citizens—remained concentrated in cities during this period, and that the bomb's power would as ably devastate these overbuilt "civilized" environments as it would destroy the "primitive" cultures and natural treasures of the developing world.

In 1950, as the Korean War began, Du Bois directed the Peace Information Center (PIC), helping to generate 2.5 million American signatures for the Stockholm Peace (or "ban the bomb") Appeal. For this, he and his fellow PIC members were declared by the Justice Department to be agents of a foreign government and indicted—Du Bois was 83 at this time—for refusing to register as such. In fact the US peace movement was often situated by its adversaries as "a foreign idea" (Du Bois *In Battle* 56), even when it was a central concern of many Americans, as it was in 1950. Though the charges against Du Bois were dropped shortly, even NAACP executive secretary Walter White asserted that "money from Russia" was behind the PIC (qtd. in C. Anderson 173), demonstrating that few Americans were immune from communist hysteria at that point. Defending Du Bois in the African American weekly the *San Francisco Sun-Reporter*, publisher and anti-nuclear activist Carlton B. Goodlett, MD, asked, "Is 'Peace' becoming a bad word?" He argued that in its attempt to prevent Du Bois from having an opinion on nuclear disarmament, the trial was "a grave threat to civil rights" ("A Grave Threat").

The case against the PIC originated with Secretary of State Dean Acheson, who attacked it as "a propaganda trick in the spurious 'peace offensive' of the

Soviet Union" (qtd. in Du Bois *In Battle* 37). Whether Acheson is quoting or simply making ironic fun of the coinage "peace offensive" is unclear, but it does seem that the Secretary failed to realize the extent of his own implication in the absurdity of this notion. The stringency of his denunciation, and the hysterical reinforcement of these sentiments by the Justice Department, indicates that peace indeed "offended;" it both insulted and threatened a powerful (however narrow) majority of Americans and thus required great courage from even prominent advocates like Du Bois to broach in the public realm. Du Bois's commitment to nuclear disarmament did lasting damage to his public image: branded as a communist by the black and white mainstream, he was shunned by the audiences who for decades had clamored for his work (Marable 122–23). "For the rest of his life," observes Manning Marable, "Du Bois would be treated as a convicted felon in his native land" (122; see also Lieberman "Peace" 97 note 20).

PERMUTATIONS OF PEACE

Indeed, the rhetoric of peace in the postwar era occupied a political spectrum as complex and contradictory as the African American-inflected rightism and leftism just discussed. As C. Wright Mills observed in 1958, "Everybody agrees upon peace as the universal aim—and into it each packs his own specific political fears, values, hopes, and demands" (114). In the Deep South, of course, "peace" meant what it had meant for decades—the status quo of strictly enforced segregation, threatened in the postwar period by "agitators" from the North. In a specific WWII context, "peace" (often followed by the heady but inane exclamation "it's wonderful!"; see Chapter 3) emerged into popular usage as a direct, immediate result of the atom-bombings that ended the war. As the atomic era and its many hazards dawned upon the world stage, even hardcore hawks accessed this spectrum of peace rhetoric, construing peace in terms of weapons-superiority "deterrence" and civil-defense "preparedness" (which brought illusory peace of mind if nothing else). The "atoms for peace" campaign, spurred by Eisenhower's 1953 speech of the same name, appealed to cultural moderates and fiscal conservatives excited by the possibilities of atomic energy and atomic industry. In that same era, the conservative African American essayist Manning Johnson urged that African Americans become "highly skilled or trained to fit into industry during the atomic age" (62).

Peace advocates of other stripes, however, hailed overwhelmingly from the intellectual and radical Left and fought off the stigma of communist ties throughout the cold war.[6] For the average hysterical American of the period, peace was just another word for surrender, and Robbie Lieberman has observed its repeated association with all things "subversive" at this time ("Another Side" 21 and "Peace" 92). African Americans were not immune to this mindset; both the NAACP and A. Philip Randolph's Brotherhood of Sleeping Car Porters distanced themselves from the Stockholm Peace Appeal, so tainted by communist ties had "peace" become in 1950, and Duke Ellington threatened to "sue sponsors of the Stockholm 'peace' appeal if they [did] not withdraw his name from the literature which they [had] circulated" (qtd. in Horne, *Black and Red* 135).

THE PEACE ACTIVISM OF ROBESON
AND THE BROADER BLACK LEFT

Indeed, many peace protesters, Paul Robeson prominent among these, *were* communist or pro-Soviet in inclination and sued for peace so as to protect the war-torn, economically and militarily hobbled Soviet bloc from the incursions of the West in the immediate postwar period. In keeping with his avowed ultra-leftism, Robeson often construed the bomb specifically in terms of bad economics and class warfare. Therefore, the bomb was not only an unthinkable threat to planetary survival but also far too tempting a field of exploration for profit-happy "war-makers" and misguided US legislators who squandered money "for a single H-bomb plant" that should have been spent to improve and desegregate southern schools (376). The bomb industry, noted Robeson, exploited uranium miners in the Belgian Congo (246) and forced US union workers to "participate with their labor unquestioningly in the arms race" (373), such that the bomb was actually a weapon used by American capitalists against American workers (256). Robeson envisioned the masses successfully standing up to the bomb (e.g., 255), saying that "The peoples' will for freedom is stronger than atom bombs" (252). As did Secretary Acheson, Robeson made un-ironic reference to "peace fighters" (374) and retained always his vision of successful class *warfare*, of workers rising up against and striking down capitalists, as opposed to the nonviolent tactics of more religious-minded and civil rights-oriented black intellectuals of the time. As with Du Bois, Robeson's prominent peace activism made him one of the most embattled figures of the cold war period. He was famously targeted by the House Un-American Activities Committee, denied passport privileges throughout the 1950s, and vilified by many within the civil rights movement for both his communist tendencies and his wavering focus on the issue of domestic civil rights. Robeson was one of many peace activists who urged the sharing of atomic secrets with the Russians—a position constituted of a striking blend of left-wing pro-communism *and* hawkish nuclear proliferation.

   In the main, however, he and many in the African American community promoted peace in opposition to the continued imperial presence in colonized Africa. This form of peace advocacy campaigned for nonviolent transition from European rule to self-rule for Africans and saw pan-Africanism as an effective conduit to international community-building, yet another mode of world peace. Coincident with this movement in the US, prominent African political and intellectual figures protested nuclear testing that occurred on colonized soil (e.g., French nuclear testing in Algeria). These charismatic leaders, Ghana's first prime minister, Kwame Nkrumah, chief among them, attracted a large African American expatriate following to their causes, as well as to the "World Without the Bomb" conference hosted by Nkrumah in Ghana in June 1962. The African American actor and writer Julian Mayfield edited a collection of writings that came from this conference; prominent attendees included Du Bois, who was by this point a Ghanaian citizen and who publicly addressed the conferees; *Sun-Reporter* publisher Carlton B. Goodlett; and Selma Sparks and Clarie Harvey Collins, two African American members of Women Strike for Peace (Herring 37, 38).

Yet by far, the peace issue most pertinent to African Americans of this period was the immediate physical threat posed by the Korean and Vietnam Wars—when they felt inclined to oppose war at all.[7] Time and again, the question emerged why Americans of color should risk their lives at the behest of a white-run government from which they felt profoundly alienated. Yet as Simon Hall observes, "black hostility to the war did not translate into active support for the peace movement. Despite widespread opposition to the war within the civil rights movement, . . . the mostly white antiwar leadership was discussing the lack of black participation in 1972, just as it had been in 1965" (11). Meanwhile, Robert Cooney and Helen Michaelowski present a pictorial history of anti-bomb and more generalized peace protest inclusive of both white and African American citizens. As the authors note on one occasion, "The Nashville walk for peace signified to the public what had been true all along: that the nonviolent civil rights movement and the radical peace movement were two aspects of the same struggle" (148).[8]

CIVIL RIGHTS AND PEACE ACTIVISM: DOVETAILS AND DIVERGENCES

Significantly, Du Bois died (in 1963) before the important shift in perspective occurred between the interracialism of the 1950s and early 1960s and the tendency toward race separatism of the mid-1960s and beyond. His anti-nuclear activism thus occurred during an era providing marginally more freedom to act in concert with white pacifists to redefine "white" political issues (the bomb, foreign policy) as international or universal in significance. Too, Du Bois's last war was not Vietnam but Korea, the first large-scale international conflict to follow the atomic bombings of Japan, which unfolded during a series of frightening escalations in both weapons-grade material development and testing by the US and the USSR. Korea was thus very much an "atomic" war not only because it occurred in this context of intense nuclear brinksmanship but also because its participants wondered at all times whether it would go nuclear, as had the war preceding, at any moment. Truman famously remarked at a press conference in 1950 that the nuclear option was not off the table, and it was the completion of that war without resort to Truman's threat that reassured the world, however minimally, that war from now on would not automatically include nuclear weapons. The efforts of Du Bois's Peace Information Center, the Stockholm Peace Accord, and agitation from other pacifist groups such as the Fellowship of Reconciliation, the War Resisters' League (WRL), the Catholic Worker Movement, the Women's International League for Peace and Freedom (WILPF), the Committee for a Sane Nuclear Policy (SANE), and Women Strike for Peace (WSP) encouraged world leaders toward the Limited Nuclear Test Ban Treaty of 1963, just in time for the conventionally fought Vietnam War to commence. For all of these reasons, Vietnam was much less a nuclear war than Korea and yet was even more disturbing an event on its own conventional grounds, due to the length of the conflict and the number of troops eventually involved. Vietnam was thus an "anti-nuclear" war to the degree that war planners thought less automatically about turning to the bomb as an option and to the degree that Vietnam protest drained great stores of energy from the nuclear protest movement. In the context under consideration here, it is the case that conventional warfare took the lives of black Korean War and Vietnam War soldiers in numbers far greater than ultimately unrealized nuclear bombing ever did.

Finally, the various peace movements espousing these multiple peace rhetorics dovetailed with and diverged from the civil rights movement in myriad ways. During World War II, religiously-based and ultra-leftist pacifist organizations agitated for peace and civil rights simultaneously and with seemingly little conflict. Christian minister A. J. Muste's Fellowship of Reconciliation (FOR) and its sub-group the Congress of Racial Equality (CORE) sent interracial student groups peacefully and successfully into segregated restaurants in the early 1940s (see Wittner *Rebels* 66–69); the FOR and the WRL supported conscientious objectors who, as prisoners and work camp inmates during the war, were instrumental in desegregating penal institutions in the US (see Wittner *Rebels* 87–92). Following the war, Gandhian tactics of nonviolent resistance appealed in equal measure to early civil rights leaders such as Martin Luther King and to anti-bomb groups such as the Non-Violent Action Against Nuclear Weapons (NVAANW) who crossed barriers at bomb tests sides in Nevada and the Pacific Ocean (see Wittner, *Resisting* 54–57). Amy Swerdlow reports that for the early 1960s' WSP movement, "The model for their bold action . . . was the civil rights movement—particularly the sit-ins in the South . . ." (19).

Yet others found it difficult, if not detrimental or morally questionable, to serve both masters. For instance, despite its debt to the strategies and goals of the civil rights movement, WSP resisted opening up new fronts (against segregation or Vietnam) because these were seen to threaten the group's original anti-bomb agenda. Swerdlow recounts a 1962 WSP convention that was challenged by a delegation of four African American women from Detroit who arrived bearing signs that read "Desegregation not Disintegration." While this pithy slogan perfectly encapsulated what for many progressives at the time were the day's two most pressing issues, this Detroit contingent was supplanted by four white Detroit women "opposed to the mingling of issues" (90). The convention responded to such "segregationist" sentiments by immediately seating the black delegation, yet "the tension was terrific" throughout the meeting: many white activists felt that the bomb should remain WSP's sole focus, while various black WSP members protested the all-white contingent slated to attend the Ghana conference and argued that "any movement that refused to make a primary commitment against segregation would have no appeal to the majority of African American women" (Swerdlow 91). Instead of solidifying policy on this matter, a committee appealed to Coretta Scott King, a longtime WILPF and SANE member, who was "an earlier and more devoted pacifist than her husband" (Dyson 64, see also Lewis, *King* 305) and who replied with her own pithy observation the following year: "Peace among nations and peace in Birmingham, Alabama, cannot be separated" (qtd. in Swerdlow 92–93). As Swerdlow indicates, it was only mounting pressure to shift focus from nuclear disarmament to the "war abroad" (93) that opened WSP's doors to other issues, including civil rights. Tellingly, WSP's anti-Vietnam crusade became a much more interracial phenomenon (including both African American and Vietnamese women) than its anti-bomb campaign had ever been.

RUSTIN'S DUAL CALLINGS

We have seen that African American intellectuals of the highest echelon—including Hansberry, Du Bois, and Robeson—who fought discrimination and the bomb with equal vigor sometimes met with resistance; one or both of their constituencies questioned the divided allegiances on display in their actions and writings. No biography more meaningfully indicates the dilemmas represented in such dual callings than that of the now largely forgotten but momentously important anti-nuclear and civil rights activist Bayard Rustin. Rustin was born into a Quaker family in West Chester, Pennsylvania, and took up with Muste's FOR as a young man. For this group, he lectured on pacifism to church and community groups, and during the early 1940s his dual commitment to peace and civil rights flourished simultaneously and sympathetically: his refusal to serve during the war in a conscientious objector work camp led to a 28-month prison sentence, during which he led the prison desegregation activities referred to earlier in this chapter (see also Rustin, "Twenty-Two Days"). The bomb itself, however, positioned Rustin at an ideological crossroads that he found himself negotiating and renegotiating for much of the rest of his professional life.

While making the anti-atomic lecture circuit under the aegis of the American Friends Society, Rustin found his late-1940s pacifist work "more dispiriting than satisfying," according to Rustin's biographer John D'Emilio. Impatient with "preaching mostly to the choir" (126) and with the measured response of old guard pacifists to the prospect of universal conscription, Rustin and other radical conscientious objectors developed tactics of Gandhian nonviolent direct action and took these not to anti-bomb rallies but to segregated lunch counters and to interstate bus lines, recently desegregated by a 1946 Supreme Court ruling. (See D'Emilio 133–140, Farrell 91–92, Rustin "We Challenged," and *Brother Outsider.*)

In 1948 Rustin delivered the annual William Penn Lecture to the Young Friends Movement in Philadelphia on the subject of the atomic threat and in 1955 participated in a New York-based strike against the civil defense exercise known as Operation Alert. Deeply shaken by Truman's announcement of the hydrogen bomb in January 1950, Rustin as head of FOR's College Section urged protest to his campus groups, asked Muste to organize a mass-renunciation of citizenship by pacifists nationwide, and directed Caravans for Peace, a summer volunteer program that predated by more than a decade the civil-rights based Mississippi Summer Freedom Project.[9] During Easter Week of that year, he led a "Fast for Peace" that gained significant attention (Mollin 62). Many of Rustin's later engagements on behalf of banning the bomb, however, took him abroad—to India, Africa, the doorstep of the Soviet Union, and often to England—and very shortly a dichotomy emerged between his pacifist work conducted primarily on foreign soil and an at-home workload defined almost entirely by the dynamic and complex civil rights agenda. In 1958 Rustin gave a rousing speech to anti-nuclear protesters gathered in London for a fifty-mile march to the Aldermaston nuclear weapons facility; the enthused response of the British crowds inspired Rustin to push for a march back in the US—but to further the cause of civil rights, not nuclear disarmament. As Lawrence S. Wittner observes, Rustin "was so struck by the [Aldermaston] event that it led him to propose and organize the 1963 March on Washington" (*Resisting*, 49)—very likely his most significant historical achievement. D'Emilio notes that "Rustin was especially taken with the ability of the British movement to mobilize large numbers for rallies and public marches" (314). Yet impressed as he may have been, Rustin was also bound to compare British anti-nuclearism both to meager bomb protests back home and to the always more urgent issue, for black and white Americans, of civil rights.

In the midst of a 1960 campaign co-sponsored by British, American, and African peace activists to head off French nuclear testing in the Algerian Sahara, Rustin received a letter from fellow-civil rights activist Tom Kahn, who was "more than mildly contemptuous of [Rustin's] pacifist ventures" (D'Emilio 284, see also 278): "Dear Bayard: What the hell are you doing in Africa at a time like this? Your colleagues here in the civil rights movement are categorically convinced you should return to New York by the first of January" (qtd. in *Brother Outsider*). The consternation in Kahn's letter is significant: many of his civil rights compatriots saw no link between Rustin's dual vocations and worried that attention given to one would inevitably steal focus and energy from the other. As Kahn's letter makes it seem, Rustin's forthcoming appointment as "Director of the March on Conventions Project" within King's Southern Christian Leadership Conference was designed to lure him away from anti-nuclearism and back toward civil rights. Though at various points leaders from both movements fought over access to Rustin's services, he was as often shunted from one camp to the other whenever his controversial past, including his war resistance but also his remote history of Communist Party affiliation and his life-long identification as a gay man, called his ultimate usefulness into question.

As Kahn's "contempt" of pacifism implies, it was especially the civil rights leaders who cut ultra-masculine profiles (complete with copious womanizing, despite the clerical status attained by many; see D'Emilio 396) and periodically retreated from association with Rustin whenever they homophobically worried that he was not man enough to make it as a movement leader. This would have surely rankled the athletic, confident Rustin, who suffered mightily from each rebuff and from a decades-long inability to live down a morals charge he received in 1953 when found by Pasadena police in the backseat of a car with two other men. While "peace [as] a foreign idea" was a trumped up charge in the case of Du Bois and his Peace Information Center, for Rustin the distinction seemed more and more between a peace movement over-identified as white, "soft," and foreign and a civil rights movement led by masculine black supermen pursuing a uniquely American dream.

Even during moments when national attention was turned toward atomic disarmament, "Rustin was not optimistic about the capacity of the movement to make a difference at home" (D'Emilio 322). Following the 1963 March the contrast between history-making civil rights actions and marginalized peace actions was sharper yet. Rustin returned to Europe and Africa, where he engaged in two pacifist campaigns, an international peace walk and a "peace brigade" dually committed to nuclear disarmament and decolonizing Africa, neither of which bore satisfying fruit. To a British colleague during this time, "Rustin expressed much more enthusiasm about civil rights activity in the United States, where dramatic Freedom Rides that spring had become an international news story, than about anything related to the peace walk" (D'Emilio 312). According to D'Emilio, Rustin deeply regretted each occasion upon which he found himself at a "distance from the center of the action" (324) and more and more came to associate this disenfranchised marginality with the lackluster anti-nuclear movement. Thus, civil rights may have been the more attractive cause not only because he saw it as inherently more important but because rising to prominence in that context would have redeemed his impugned manhood and provided him an opportunity to do what he did best, organize meetings and mass events, on the broadest possible American canvas. While Rustin's position on the bomb—he was radically opposed—was never in doubt, his career epitomizes the tension between two ever more separate commitments to world betterment, between ever more centralized questions of racial equality and ever more marginalized questions of nuclear doomsday that Rustin could not but choose between.

Indeed, a distinction between activist *work* and written *works* enables deeper understanding of the diverse forms of bomb opposition accomplished by Rustin as opposed to King and Hansberry. Though his paper trail is not negligible, Rustin is remembered mainly as a mover and shaker, a globe-trotting activist whose physical presence and total commitment of focus and energy were essential components of the job. Meanwhile, King was an activist-preacher who wrote and spoke to both his congregation and the wider society, and Hansberry was a professional writer cut off by early death from more active forms of community service and whose legacy comes therefore mainly from her marvelous written word. It is Rustin among the three who finally chose to turn definitively from anti-nuclear protest to organizing for civil rights full time, while the writers King and Hansberry moved freely and effectively between these subjects from one written work the next, even, through the power of metaphor, analogy, and other figurative language, militating against racial injustice and nuclear war with the same stroke of the pen. So ultimately divergent were these two issues' causes, effects, and core constituencies, however, that even the flexible and sophisticated medium employed by King occasionally demonstrated a parting of the ways—that is, notable examples of one cause most forcefully advocated at the rhetorical expense of the other.

KING'S METAPHORS AT CROSS-PURPOSES

As incisively as his wife compared world peace to a violence-free Birmingham in the WSP-related anecdote discussed earlier, so King constructed equally memorable parallel constructions to link for his vast American (and world) audience what he regarded as the two most significant threats to his age. On one occasion, he noted that "It is very nice to drink milk at an unsegregated lunch counter—but not when there is strontium 90 in it . . ." (qtd. in Sitkoff 205 and Farrell 95); on another he averred that "it is worthless to talk about integrating if there is no world to integrate in" (qtd. in Lewis, *King* 302) and yet elsewhere confronted his audience with the life-and-death ultimatum not "between violence and nonviolence but nonviolence and nonexistence" (qtd. in Zepp 20). Thomas C. Fleming, chief opinion-maker for the African American weekly the *San Francisco Sun-Reporter*, read the bomb, however nihilistically, as fundamentally enabling of the courageous and daring, civil rights-demanding African

American youth of the period (see Chapter 3). While he cites "such young-sters as Martin Luther King" as leading the charge in this context (25 February 1961, 6), in fact King was less likely to regard the bomb as an opened floodgate than as a moral gatekeeper, enshadowing all human conflicts and thus by its very existence mandating ever-improving relations amongst warring groups. If Fleming linked the growing imminence of nuclear war with the growing dan-gerousness (i.e., challenging effectiveness) of the civil rights movement, King argued that the only way to neutralize the nuclear threat was to shift immedi-ately and universally from antagonism to brotherhood. In his 1964 Nobel Prize acceptance speech, King opposed "this pending cosmic elegy" to a "creative psalm of brotherhood" and vigorously rejected as inevitable "the starless mid-night of racism and war," specifically "the hell of thermonuclear destruction."

King biographer David Levering Lewis reads his Nobel speech as the oc-casion that marked King's broadening view of social concerns (260), when in fact most of the anti-nuclear writings to be examined here came from the pe-riod "during or after the bus protest in Montgomery" (King, *Strength to Love* 11), that is 1955 or the period immediately following.[10] In an article published in 1959 for *Liberation* and reprinted in *A Testament of Hope*, King cited his long record of anti-nuclear activism, including "unequivocally declar[ing] my hatred for this most colossal of all evils, . . . condemn[ing] any organizer of war, . . . sign[ing] numerous statements, . . . and authoriz[ing] publication of my name in advertisements appearing in the largest-circulating newspapers in the country" (*Testament* 34). In fact, there is a remarkable lack of response to King's anti-nuclear writings in particular, and his peace-protesting in the 1950s in general, by King scholars, who define his peace activism almost entirely in terms of Vietnam opposition. In this context, they emphasize the rift created between King and the Johnson administration, whose war this was, as well as between himself and civil rights leaders to his right, who cautioned him against foreign policy embroilments (see, e.g., Darby and Rowley; Dyson chapter 3; S. Hall chapter 3; Long 197–205 *et passim*; McKnight chapter 1; and Wittner, *Rebels* 285).

While these historians do well to analyze the breakdown between peace and civil rights activism as crystallized in the example of King's opposition to Vietnam, it was perhaps his still-great distance from the halls of Washington in the mid- to late 1950s, as well as the lesser fame of many of these marvel-ous sermons from that same period, that enabled King to speak so fluidly and so effectively against the twin evils of that decade. In addition, while Johnson was very much a civil rights advocate, whose distraction by the war in Vietnam greatly disappointed King and other black supporters, Kennedy, despite his weaker record on civil rights, did manage, as King himself noted, to "guide . . . to reality the historic treaty banning atmospheric nuclear testing" (qtd. in Long 149). King's peace statements in a Kennedy context, while less trouble-causing than they were under Johnson, were nevertheless powerful statements whose import is yet to be fully analyzed.

Indeed, it was less often the political platform than the pulpit, where the speaker is predisposed to tackling questions of cosmic survival and salvation, that inspired King to incorporate the threat posed by the bomb into his vision of justice for the nation and the world.[11] In his sermon "Transformed Nonconformist" he likened both peace and civil rights demonstrators to the beleaguered but courageous outsider that Christ himself was (*Strength to Love* 11–12); in "How Should a Christian View Communism?" King critiqued communist atheism yet argued that the only way to rescue the godless and disaffected (be they the Soviet masses or marginalized members of US society) from misguided ideology was to provide the same equality and brotherhood promised by Marxist philosophy. At the end of this sermon, it is not "atomic bombs or nuclear weapons" leveling cities and social relations but justice and democracy that must fulfill the prophecy, "every valley shall be exalted and every mountain and hill shall be made low" (*Strength to Love* 100; see also *The Trumpet of Conscience* 33). In "On Being a Good Neighbor," King drew on the example of the Good Samaritan to stress the international brotherhood of humans, now bound by the bomb in one pact of mutually assured survival or "universal suicide" (*Strength to Love* 23).

Tracing King's theological influences, Ira G. Zepp notes that George W. Davis, King's mentor at Crozer Theological Seminary, argued in similar fashion that "We know now that we must live together or perish. If we will not have one world, we may have no world" (qtd. in Zepp 20). For both Davis and King, therefore, the bomb posed an immoveable mandate to achieve the Christian goals of brotherhood and peace; it functioned as a dreaded alter-apocalypse—an ending to the world *not* ordained by God—and yet also quite effectively as an essential catalyst to better behaviors, as a powerful weapon in the rhetorical arsenal of liberal, peace-loving preachers like Davis and King. Zepp cites the realist/pragmatist writings of Reinhold Niebuhr as another enduring influence upon King, yet the two parted intellectual company specifically over the issue of the bomb: Niebuhr held out war as a preferred alternative to tyranny, as a "negative good" or period of "momentary anarchy" (qtd. in Zepp 159) that must sometimes be weathered so as to increase goodness and fend off sin within the human community. "But [King] then came to the conviction that the destructive power of nuclear weapons was so unlimited that war had ceased being a negative good" (Zepp 166). Taking up the specific example of nuclear war, King debunks war's "momentary" nature: "A world war—God forbid!—will leave only smouldering ashes as a mute testimony of a human race whose folly led inexorably to untimely death" (*Strength to Love* 29; see also *Trumpet of Conscience* 67–68). According to Michael G. Long, for King "the theological sin of total nuclear war is its opposition to the principle of the sacredness of the human personality, more particularly, the God-given (and sacred) right to life" (96).

In other sermons, King critiqued overzealous faith in the power of science, a faith encouraged by mid-century scientific breakthroughs in the fields of "plagues and diseases . . . wonder drugs . . . and physical health" (*Strength to Love* 43). Here King likely refers to yet another headlining current event, the well-nigh miraculous polio vaccine, introduced in 1955. As he likened peace and civil rights activism in another context, in this sermon King presents the challenging opposition between the Salk vaccine and atomic power, two world-altering feats of modern science that are falsely regarded as both being boons to humanity. For King, placing faith in atomic scientists to save the world (for democracy or otherwise) constitutes idolatry of the most spiritually and physically threatening magnitude: "The instruments which yesterday were worshiped today contain cosmic death, threatening to plunge all of us into the abyss of annihilation. Man is not able to save himself or the world. Unless he is guided by God's spirit, his new-found scientific power will become a devastating Frankenstein monster that will bring to ashes his earthly life" (*Strength to Love* 102). On another occasion, he adopted the persona of Paul writing a letter to his followers in America. Herein he lectures,

> Through your scientific genius you have made of the world a neighborhood, but you have failed to employ your moral and spiritual genius to make of it a brotherhood. So, America, the atomic bomb you have to fear today is not merely that deadly weapon which can be dropped from an airplane . . . but that atomic bomb which lies in the hearts of men, capable of exploding into the most staggering hate and devastating selfishness. (*Strength to Love* 128)

Here King argues that the (white, western) arrogance causing America to see itself as superior to all other nations during the cold war was of a piece with the racist superiority modeled toward the disenfranchised within America's own society.

As per the quote from his Nobel speech, and the (anti-) apocalypticism inspired by Davis and Niebuhr, King turned often to the trope of midnight when preaching against the bomb. In "A Knock at Midnight," King's text is Luke 11:5–6, wherein Christ questions his followers, "which of you who has a friend will go to him at midnight" to seek out sustenance for a surprise guest? The surprise guest, of course, is Christ himself, whom the devoted believer must make every effort to receive with an open house and open heart. While the righteous Christian joyfully anticipates this surprise arrival, the "knock at midnight" nevertheless imbues the visitation with a somber, even ominous quality and is akin to the pointing finger of Dickens's Spirit of Christmas Yet to Come and the tolling bell of Donne's "Meditation XVII." Thus King begins this sermon with a warning, "It is midnight within the social order," and immediately defines this social midnight as brought on by "atomic and nuclear weapons that could within seconds completely destroy the major cities of the world" (*Strength to Love* 42). King thus speaks literally of the midnight produced by the dousing of a thousand power grids at the point of nuclear impact as well as the sunless nuclear winter induced by the this same event. King's rhetoric of midnight invokes another icon from the period—the atomic clock developed by the editors of the *Bulletin of the Atomic Scientists* who centered a large clock with hands positioned so many minutes before midnight, depending upon the severity of the current nuclear threat, on the cover of each issue. While surely the Scientists set their clock in motion for the express purpose of never realizing the dreaded midnight hour, King's theological and social narrative is more complex; as a righteous Christian he draws upon the equally enthralling trope of the other side of midnight's "reckoning day," and as a committed civil rights activist he looks as well for "the dawn" of racial equality that "arises from faith in God" (*Strength to Love* 49).

Thus King's campaigns on behalf of world peace and racial equality part rhetorical company with the specific invocation of the social order's midnight hour. In many successive sermons, a better "tomorrow" is envisioned, but such an aftermath is only meaningful in a specifically civil rights context, as the long-sought-after "tomorrow" of perfect freedom and equality. The "dawn" of nuclear midnight is either the world of ashes King envisioned in an earlier sermon or the utopian survival fantasy of the United States rising Phoenix-like from these same ashes, to fly its tattered flag once more. King of course would countenance neither of these mornings-after within the range of his antinuclear sermonizing, yet the midnight-into-dawn narrative—in King's own words, "Good Friday [giving] way to the triumphant music of Easter" (*Strength to Love* 59)—forms Christianity's core tenet, and King drew from this narrative on a regular basis. In "The Death of Evil Upon the Seashore" King even describes "a great cosmic ball of fire" as the setting sun that gives way to "some dark and desolate midnight" (*Strength to Love* 65). Yet here the fireball is no terrifying harbinger of the end of time but is instead "beautiful," (*Strength to Love* 65), natural, and surely supplanted by its rejuvenating counterpart, a light in the east (*Strength to Love* 66), the next morning.

In fact on one occasion, King indeed envisions "survival" of nuclear war in the way the Christian believes he will "survive" his own death—not physically but spiritually reborn, not into this world but into eternity with God. In "Antidotes for Fear," King's text is I John 4:18, wherein "perfect love casteth out fear." For much of the sermon, King distinguishes abnormal (phobic) fears—of, for instance, Russian communists or fellow-Americans of different skin colors—from "normal, necessary, and creative" fears (*Strength to Love* 109) such as those that have led to scientific and medical breakthroughs and, we may assume, that have thus far kept world leaders from inaugurating nuclear doomsday. At the beginning and end of this address, however, King returns to the letter of his biblical passage, wherein the believer is enjoined to face down death—even nuclear annihilation—with courage and confidence in God's saving grace. Thus, "witness our frenzied efforts to construct fallout shelters. As though even these offer sanctuary from an H-bomb attack!" (*Strength to Love* 109). While King is right to question the effectiveness of such undersized preparations, there is a throwing-in-the-towel quality of this address that invites its listener to cease any effort, even legislative or diplomatic means, to fend off nuclear catastrophe. By sermon's end, the seemingly irresolvable conflict between physical survival and spiritual salvation looms large:

> Let us face the fear that the atomic bomb has aroused with the faith
> that we can never travel beyond the arms of the Divine. Death is inevi-
> table. . . . We need not join the mad rush to purchase an earthly fallout
> shelter. God is our eternal fallout shelter. (*Strength to Love* 116)

In the midst of this passage, King envisions a God who "can most assuredly lead us through death's dark night into the bright daybreak of eternal life" (116), taking his audience to the other side of nuclear midnight in a gesture that hews closely to theological doctrine but departs starkly from the messages of world peace and nuclear disarmament delivered by King on so many other sermonic occasions.

HANSBERRY'S INTEGRATED VISION

Both King and Hansberry viewed the bomb through two lenses—as a literal threat to planetary survival (against which both spoke consistently and emphatically) and as a rich metaphor whose power might be successfully harnessed in the fight for justice and equality. For both as well, the dramatically and spiritually satisfying prospect of enduring love (whether divine or human) and the tenaciousness of the human spirit, even in the face of nuclear conflagration, appealed to two writers with abiding faith in the redeemability of humankind. Their optimism may have sprung from different sources—for King the promise of the Gospels, for Hansberry the heights of human artistic and intellectual achievement—but it caused both to hold simultaneously the contradictory opinions that surely human beings could be reasoned away from nuclear war and that surely humanity would prevail, even should such war come. Thus their writing on various striking occasions envisioned and even assented to nuclear Armageddon so as to demonstrate the power of the redemptive love they felt ultimately ruled the universe.

Contrary to the questions raised by her portrayal of Ruth in *A Raisin in the Sun*, the bomb figured meaningfully throughout the course of Hansberry's life;

in interviews and essays Hansberry spoke forcefully against the atomic threat and wrote one of her last full-length dramatic works, *What Use are Flowers?* (1961–1962), in explicit opposition to both atomic weapons and the mood of nihilism they enabled. Eloquently summarizing her most impassioned commitments, including health care for all, racial equality, and maximally engaged artistic expression, Hansberry wrote for *Mademoiselle* in 1960 that "Naturally the first of all longing today is for peace. . . . Intelligence and love of life make debate obsolete; the alternative is a scorched and silent planet" ("Quo Vadis?" 34) In *To Be Young, Gifted, and Black* (1969), a compilation of Hansberry excerpts from the dramatic stage and public platform, "L. H." tells an interviewer that her dream is to "live in a world where some of the more monumental problems could at least be solved; I'm thinking, of course, of peace. That is, we don't fight. Nobody fights. We get rid of all the little bombs—and the big bombs" (253–54).[12] Reviewing the Japanese film *Hiroshima* in 1955, Hansberry called it "one of the greatest propaganda films of our times" ("No More Hiroshimas" 7) and a moving work of art. She wrote appreciatively of the arresting lack of soundtrack that accompanied the moment of the bomb's impact onscreen, as well as the documentary footage of victims and survivors, no matter how difficult to watch, and of peace-marchers making a commemorative pilgrimage to the city each year. In Hansberry's elegant summation, "Coming out of the movie house into the American streets, one repeats [the marchers' chant] with feeling. 'No more Hiroshimas'—anywhere, ever" (7).

Yet when not targeting the threat posed by the bomb in its literal manifestation, Hansberry—like many others writing in this period—borrowed the bomb as a metaphor for explosive energies that could be channeled in more beneficial directions. In a letter to the *Village Voice* on "Strindberg and Sexism," Hansberry critiques the off-Broadway revival of *Comrades* as antiquated and pathetic, akin to "watching King Arthur and his knights diligently hurling their lances against, say—an atom bomb" (172). Here the bomb figures as "the future" or modernity itself, an era of equal rights for women that retrograde playwrights like Strindberg will be unable to fend off. As Hansberry may have sought to harness the power (and threat) of atomic explosiveness in her borrowing of Hughes's poem in *A Raisin in the Sun*, here the bomb is a weapon in the arsenal of yet another beleaguered but inevitably ascendant group, women. In a 1964 issue of *Negro Digest*, Hansberry celebrated the marvels of language as opportunity and challenge for young black writers. For Hansberry, language has been humanity's most effective tool (or weapon) "since our particular group of megatons (or whatever) either fused or split to make this particular world of ours" ("The Nation" 29; see also Carter 153). Urging her audience throughout the address to introduce history into their work, Hansberry fuses contemporary lingo ("megatons") to the pre-historic to indicate the historical range that beckons the modern black writer.[13] Hansberry realized that language would be first threatened and most harmed by any literal manifestation of the bomb, a central theme in *What Use Are Flowers?* (see Carter 154). Yet before and against the dawning of that dreadful day, she appropriated atomic energy in its figurative sense as servant to the causes of justice, equality, and literary excellence.

Hansberry's recurring affirmations of "life" and "future generations" in her writings and especially in her addresses to aspiring youth and black audiences resonate meaningfully and poignantly with the facts of her tragically shortened life (she died of duodenal cancer at the age of 34) and the atomic threat that loomed however silently over all of life in postwar America (see also Carter 3). In her landmark presentation to a group of young black artists in 1959, "The Negro Writer and His Roots," Hansberry sets up a contest between "life" and "despair," the mood adopted by many modern writers in response to the world wars, the bomb, and the existential condition. Hansberry exhorts her young listeners to engage passionately with "the most pressing issues of our time" (3), including anti-capitalism, pan-Africanism, and civil rights, and to emphatically choose the affirmative in "the realm of discussion which haunts the days of humankind everywhere: the destruction or survival of the human race" (11). For Hansberry, despair gives way to both cynicism and complacency, either of which can lead one to conclude that the bomb and its resultant lesser conflicts will be always with us. On its own, complacency enables myriad other false assumptions, regarding racial, gender, and political inequalities that strike privileged members of society as natural and unchanging. Said assumptions feed the most dangerous misconception of all, that "art . . . at its best, CANNOT possibly be 'social'" (4).

Her ideological adversaries in this speech are cynical, despairing sophisticates such as Arthur Miller, Tennessee Williams, and Norman Mailer, whose attitudes of resignation implicitly acceded to the entrenched inevitability of a planetary threat that, for Hansberry, could never be allowed to stand. Her impassioned "wish to live" and for "others to live for generations and generations and generations and generations" ("Negro Writer" 11) vectors out both to her specific audience of young black artists who will do best by their race and "their roots" to carry on and flourish across the decades and to a larger audience of ordinary African Americans, Africans, and other oppressed peoples worldwide, and all who cower in the shadow of the bomb. This larger group will itself survive by "imposing the reason for life on life" ("The Negro Writer" 11), adopting an attitude of life-affirmation that will draw them inexorably and eventually effectively into battle against the bomb.

In an article for the *Village Voice*, "Willy Loman, Walter Younger, and He Who Must Live," Hansberry attached her commitment to survival to decisions made in bringing her most famous dramatic creation to life—and in refusing to kill him off by the end of the play. In purposeful contrast to the doomed figure of Willy Loman, Walter Younger's "typicality is capable of a choice which *affirms* life" (8). Walter's designation as dramatic though not tragic stems from his rich racial heritage, from his ability to "draw on the strength of an incredible people who, historically, have simply refused to give up" (8). Too, this shift implicitly underscores the playwright's hope for planetary survival: when Hansberry reads Walter as "King Oedipus refusing to tear out his eyes" (8), she indulges in a clock-reversing fantasy of literary and political omnipotence, set against the inexorable countdown to nuclear midnight, so oppressively discerned at that moment. Even the implied detail of King Oedipus stopping his hands from tragic self-injury resonates with the hope of stopping and reversing the hands of the doomsday clock, which the *Bulletin's* editors themselves did, every time diplomacy and goodwill managed a successful counterthrust to hawkish rhetoric and international brinksmanship. As opposed to King, whose Christian orientation encouraged the narrative of midnight-into-dawn, here Hansberry implicitly answers the threat to planetary survival inherent in that chain of events, attaching the concept of life-affirmation to the successful stopping of time—or stopping *in* time, before disaster strikes.

Time and again Hansberry criticized the "fashionable despair" ("On Arthur Miller" 174) on display in the writings of her fellow-contemporary playwrights, including Samuel Beckett whose relentlessly bleak *Waiting for Godot* is explicitly targeted by her post-atomic "fantasy" written in the absurdist tradition, *What Use are Flowers?* For Hansberry, unmitigated tragedy, nihilism, and cynicism belonged to the existential pose of white male intellectuals who enjoyed the galling luxury of having absolutely nothing else to complain about besides the supposed meaninglessness of life. In *Flowers* and on many occasions, Hansberry countered such attitudes with her life-affirming vision, "replac[ing] despair with hope, death with life, destruction with rejuvenation" (Cheney 124). She conceded the role of the absurd in the committed dramatist's approach to presenting the human condition in the post-atomic era, yet warned that "attention must be paid in equal measure to the frequent triumph of man, if not nature, *over* the absurd" (*To Be Young* 176; see also "A Challenge" 32). While many times Hansberry herself cried out against the enormity of the nuclear crisis, she never wanted the bomb to become so overwhelming a subject that the artist abdicated his or her "responsibility" ("On Strindberg and Sexism" 171) to speak out.

As Steven R. Carter observes, "elements of the absurd abound in *What Use Are Flowers?* but they are matched throughout with examples of humanity's striving for mastery over nature and life itself" (143). In the story a band of naked, savage, non-verbal children are happened upon by an aged hermit-humanist who fled the incivilities of humankind decades earlier and reappears as the play opens, five years after a world-annihilating nuclear bomb. As in Beckett, the setting is spare and the characters clownish in their rag-tag, unkempt appearance. Yet throughout the story the old man attempts to civilize the children by instilling in them knowledge (of both language and basic physical principles) and love for higher things, including music and "flowers," which have no practical use but once made human life precious and profound. While the hermit dies with much left untaught, immediately following the children's demoralizing return to anarchy when one breaks another's newly invented wheel in a jealous rage, the play ends pointedly on a note of hope, with all of the children, both the wronged and the contrite, reconstructing the vital wheel.

While Hansberry positioned herself firmly against the bomb, the viewpoint in *What Use are Flowers?* is complex. On this occasion, Hansberry's faith in life is so predominant that for her, even following atomic cataclysm, life must, and will, go on. Yet such "fantasies" (to borrow and recast Hansberry's own term) of nuclear survivability, ironically, downplay the magnitude of nuclear war, reassuring readers that no matter how bad things get Americans (and perhaps humans everywhere) will rebound. As worthy as were both her many statements on peace and life-preservation and her critique of pretentious intellectual elitism, it is the case that a more uniformly pessimistic treatment of the post-atomic predicament, of the kind issued from Becket in *Godot* and especially his deeply disturbing, nuclear-themed *Endgame*, may be said to elicit from its audience the stronger pacifist response.

Assessing the overall merits of *Flowers*, biographer Anne Cheney notes that "Hansberry's war is a vague, offstage 'atomic holocaust'" (129), while Charles A. Carpenter refers to the play as a whole as a "modest, sentimentally generalized plea to avoid letting nuclear confrontation occur" (89). Despite these reservations, Hansberry's drama indeed includes haunting effects, specifically its focus on child characters. While these youngsters are readable as "sentimental" indices of rejuvenation and hope for the future, their young age in the play's present day and their veritable infancy—they were a group of five-year-olds—at the moment of atomic holocaust underscores the fragility and vulnerability of the "hope" they embody as well as the pathos and atrocity of child victims in all wars, in the historical instances of Hiroshima and Nagasaki, and in the unthinkable cataclysm of nuclear-induced World War III. Finally, Hansberry's child characters comment more poignantly on the horrors of nuclear war than the flawed and repellent adult men and women of Beckett's *Godot* and *Endgame* ever can. To be sure, Hansberry drew heat from her more militant fellow-intellectuals for taking up the bomb and other "quasi-white" subject matter in her writings and had trouble finding critical or popular success for her final works, including the specifically anti-atomic *What Use Are Flowers?* Yet of the many political and artistic leaders considered in this discussion, it is Hansberry whose position seems most successfully integrated—that is, true on almost every occasion to the dual commitments of planetary survival and equality for all.

MUHAMMAD'S AND KILLENS'S NEW DAY DAWNING

By the late 1960s, the separatist movement led by the Black Panthers, the Nation of Islam, and intellectuals such as Harold Cruse and John Oliver

Killens had reached its zenith; the prospect of an apocalyptic new day looked much less threatening than it had to the sober-minded King, and the bomb's role shifted dramatically in the writings of leading thinkers. In these the Japan bombings were emblems of American hypocrisy and shame (see Cleaver quoting Malcolm X 38, Cleaver 82, Hilliard 122, Newton 40, and "The Power of the People" 23); as with the late-'60s fiction of Chester Himes (see Chapter 2), the persisting nuclear threat was both the corrosive sign of the declining white western empire and—reminiscent of the "segregationist" fantasies of the doomsday scenarists discussed in the introduction—a form of divine retribution poised to strike specifically the white races of the earth. "Babylon" was the name applied to this dying American society, depicted in a political cartoon from *The Black Panther* as a battered, dissipated "pig" bearing weapons of every kind, including a nuclear missile at its foot, and sporting empty symbols of American integrity (the flag, the eagle) and a mouth full of dollar bills (Emury 240; see figure 8). Where the integrationist perspective espoused by Du Bois, King, Hansberry, and others advocated both interracial equality and a realistic understanding of the bomb's indiscriminate destruction of all humankind, leading black separatists counted the bomb as one more reason why African Americans needed to distance themselves from the fates of white Americans and posited, rather implausibly, that the bomb was a white problem that would lead only to white undoing.

While he assiduously avoided references to the bomb itself and many other topical specifics that would detract from the incantatory, mythic power of his sermons, Nation of Islam leader Elijah Muhammad lashed out in speeches and writings at "devil scientists" and their insidious "tricknology," at the boast of the American government that they could "destroy the people of the earth thirty times over" (233), and at the apocalypticism invoked by this war machine itself, the ocean filled with naval vessels and sky filled with planes. Dennis Walker specifically associates the movement's anticipated "collapse" of the West with the fall of the European empire and "the terror and insecurity that Westerners now universally felt in the shadow of the nuclear bombs" (336). On numerous occasions Muhammad created for his audience the vision of a ruined white America and a core of black elect, rescued Rapture-style from the Armageddon promised in Revelations and expected daily by this influential leader.

Muhammad was as indebted to the Bible as he was to the Qur'an and returned again and again to the exegesis of John's final vision, during which he likened America to Babylon—even to the "beast [with] eyes around about" realized in America's numerous "mechanical listening devices" and "powerful telescope[s]" (115)—and promised his listeners that the signs of final days were everywhere. In the early essays of *The Fall of America* (1973), the end of white rule is signaled by everything from meteorological upheaval (hail, tornadoes, and earthquakes) to the spiraling inflation of the early 1970s, gay liberation, student protests, "long, straggly hair" (150), and mini-skirts (127). Yet later in

FIGURE 8: Emury. "Babylon." From *The Black Panthers Speak: Manifesto of the Party*. Ed. Philip S. Foner. 240. Copyright © 1970 by Philip S. Foner. Reprinted by Permission of HarperCollins Publishers.

the collection the references are more pointedly political, as Muhammad critiques America's embroilment in Asia, its contest with Russia, and its meddling in the Middle East. In an eloquent moment, he reads US foreign policy to the letter:

> They command the sea with their powerful navies, parking them off
> the shores of other nations. They secure airbases on their soils to place
> their deadly bomb-carrying planes within easy striking distances of those

whom they fear to be their enemies. Is this not the easy way to make enemies? . . . .

They love meddling in other people's affairs. They are in every fight or war—it matters not with whom or where—but yet crying "Peace! Peace!" with every deadly weapon of war to provoke other nations to war. (169)

A haunting image of "America covered with planes" (124) is summoned throughout Muhammad's writings. It was inspired by Isaiah 18:1, "Woe to the land shadowing with wings," (224), and used to urge his audience to join his movement while there was still time. Muhammad made the daring accusation that white America sought even to destroy itself so as to "destroy her black slave" (222), while his own view of end times involved a similar irony: the very indicators of America's hell-bound sinfulness—its "deadly bombshells held ready to drop on the towns and cities of other nations" (124) and its water and air "polluted by chemico-bacteriologists" (222)—were also the tools of divine retribution, the "cities . . . set on fire" (167) and deadly plagues that would wipe out white America with a bold stroke of poetic justice. "As America has done," Muhammad declares, "so is being done unto her. . . . She has blown their cities to pieces and she has killed their inhabitants" (161).

Muhammad's visions of African American rescue from white apocalypse ranged from the practical to the preposterous. He called for territory within the United States (perhaps the southeastern states) to be turned over to his fellowship for the establishing of a homeland. Were his followers to secure themselves a border against the doomed US, one could conceive of a traditionally fought war involving white America that would not affect this independent political entity, yet even a nuclear war from which the Nation of Islam abstained would result in a period of deadly fallout that of course respects no national boundary. Until the day of independent nationhood, Muhammad preached strict separatism from white society and white cultural forms; he vigorously opposed racial intermarriage and the mimicking of white modes (including revealing clothing and teased out hairstyles) that would indicate continued attachment, that is enslavement, to the oppressor. When he made reference to the "Divine Plagues" (188) on their way to America, Muhammad cast white culture as a contagious disease—perhaps even a sexually transmitted one—that the elect needed to recognize and avoid; one could extrapolate the image of the bomb itself as a telltale pox (of gigantic proportions) on the deceptively attractive body of white American politics and youth culture.

In a notably "atomic" chapter in *The Fall of America*, Muhammad condemns "deadly material manufactured to make war," readable as a reference to the plutonium and other fissionable elements required to make nuclear bombs. He posits that even if white America, with its satellites and advanced weapons technology, were to win a world war fought on human terms, it would never defeat its chosen black adversary, since "It is not necessary for Allah (God) to use mechanical devices" (235), and yet "We have many things out there in space that can be brought into action against America or any other nation today" (235).

Here Muhammad sets the stage for one of his most notable theological concepts, the whirling, fearsome "Mother Plane" based upon a vision had by Ezekiel, during which he looked into the sky and cried "O wheel" (238). According to Muhammad, this enormous vessel, sighted in Canada in the 1930s and elsewhere since then, occasionally visits the earth's atmosphere to replenish its oxygen and hydrogen supplies and is operated by four Original Powers, those of black, brown, yellow, and red. It is as much an escape vehicle for the elect as a weapons-delivery system that on reckoning day will drop bombs over the white cities of the world (238–39; see also D. Walker 49–50). Fantasizing a role reversal for the haves and have-nots of atomic mastery, Muhammad avers that "The Mother Plane carries the same type of bomb on her that our Black scientists dropped on the planet earth to bring up mountains . . . after the earth was created" and that "knowledge of how to do this has not been given to the world (white race), nor will they ever get this kind of knowledge" (240–41). While today these ideas seem implausible to say the least, no one can deny the massive influence wielded by Muhammad and the Nation of Islam during the late 1960s and early 1970s. With the upheavals related to civil rights, Vietnam, women's and gay liberation, and the general sense that the youth of America had cut all ties to the social contract, this was indeed an apocalyptic era, and those in search of answers not surprisingly latched on to the engaging narratives and affirming visions of charismatic leaders.

By the early 1970s, when *The Fall of America* was published, it is not surprising to see that the bomb played only an implicit—though nevertheless powerful—role in the radical apocalypticism of Elijah Muhammad. One could contrast his disinclination to specifically reference the bomb to the pronounced anti-nuclearism of King in his sermons and attribute this difference perhaps to King's Christian (as opposed to Islamic) outlook but especially to his firm commitment to the integrationist aspects of the civil rights agenda. His tendency was to stress inclusion rather than fundamentalist distinctions between the lost and the saved; thus he saw the reality that nuclear weapons, while developed by a culpable few, threatened mass destruction and must be preached against emphatically and pointedly. One could not speak cryptically about the nature of the threat, nor especially could one envision it as a mode of surgically striking divine retribution. In an important respect, Muhammad's self-distancing from both the bomb and white culture is of a piece with what within a US context may be construed as a dissenting faith tradition: he took the radical stances of anti-Christianity, race separatism, and an eager anticipation of nuclear war or whatever means of destruction were to be visited by Allah upon the race of perdition.

All that said, John Oliver Killens was one influential essayist from the late 1960s who indeed specifically implicated the bomb in his argument for radical race separatism. Early in his important manifesto *Black Man's Burden* (1965) Killens diminishes the bomb and its wider "Atomic Age" significance relative to the gains to be made "when most of mankind achieved freedom and human dignity, . . . when racial prejudices became obsolete. For me, this is [not the chauvinistically rendered American Century but] the Freedom Century" (24). Here Killens echoes the humanitarian optimism on display in the writings of Hansberry and King, insisting that justice and equality will prevail over the comparatively puny accomplishments of "who reached the moon first or who made the largest bomb" (24). Later, however, Killens argues that the bomb anticipates and justifies his call for violence-if-necessary, reminding his (white American) audience that "ours" is a violent society, and that the violent reaction of black militants is only the natural outcropping of a long American tradition:

> the fact that we Americans are a nation of violence should give staunch advocates of non-violence pause for reflection. We have always been a nation of violence. Our, rather your, proud forefathers killed off an entire race whom they arrogantly called Indians, though they knew well enough they were not in India. . . . We also dropped the most devastating bombs ever dropped in a military operation, and we dropped them on civilians— in Hiroshima and Nagasaki. Most colored people are convinced that those bombs were dropped there because the people we dropped them on were colored. (118–19)

While Killens, a member of the Armed Forces scheduled for deployment to the Japanese mainland had Japan not surrendered, acknowledges his implication in the atomic bombings, yet they are part of the "proud" tradition that has fostered violent interracial encounters twenty years later. Even the pacifist credo quoted from a fellow-soldier as the war ended—"they should . . . round up all the bloody scientists who know anything about that [atomic] formula and blow their fucking brains out!" (120)—jangles with the violence that Killens persuasively indicates is nothing less than typically, ideally American.

As did Muhammad, Killens saw the bomb as profoundly indicative of the decline of the West: "the Western world [is] dying, though grandiosely, amid pretty slogans of Free Worlds and NATO's, A&P's and SEATO's, New Frontiers and Warsaw Pacts, and H-bombs and earth satellites. The Old World of the West [is] dying over the length and breadth of this death-driven earth" (152–53). In a highly effective rearrangement of world order, Killens posits the "Third World" as the "New World . . . a-borning" (152) and excises it specifically from the ideological warfare hobbling East and West in the cold war (156). While his vision of the new day dawning in recently decolonized nations of the developing world is trenchant, he veers close to the untenable scenarios of Elijah Muhammad when he claims that "the deadly germ killing the West is not necessarily fatal to the other three-quarters of the earth's people. They will fight off this germ . . . and will survive to write the West's obituary" (154–55). Killens has already invoked the contest, in part decidedly nuclear, polarizing the "first" and "second" worlds in that period, and to the degree that Killens envisioned this enlightened three-fourths fending off the nuclear threat, he like Elijah Muhammad speculates upon a geographic and moral immunity with dangerous implications. This text's final reference to the bomb echoes its first, with Killens continuing to valorize the "New World" perspective but on specifically humanitarian grounds:

> Time and again [during sojourns in Africa], I heard variations of that same continuous theme: ". . . You people of the West . . . think to impress us by which of you can make the biggest bomb to cause the most destruction, or which of you will make the first trip to the moon. . . . You of the West have made the greatest progress in technology, and we must learn from you this technology but we will give to the world our own dialogue in human values." (158; see also Gregory 122)

Surely it is only such dialogue, with its stress on the value of human life, that can protect the global South, and the globe in general, from succumbing to the "germs" that threaten planetary dissolution, not the racial or moral superiority posited in other, more fantastic scenarios by Killens himself and the always-apocalyptic Elijah Muhammad.

CONCLUSION: BALDWIN'S NIGHT ON THE TOWN

By the late 1960s, Hansberry (and her pacifist mentor Du Bois) had passed on, black separatism challenged the integrationism of Bayard Rustin and Martin Luther King, and when it was considered at all, the bomb was less a fearful specter than a stigmatizing mark of the West's inevitable downfall. It was perhaps the ideal moment for the striking a-nuclearism of James Baldwin, on display in the early-published but ever more relevant *The Fire Next Time* (1963). In a remarkable scene from this landmark text, Baldwin narrates his encounter with Elijah Muhammad and several followers, who treat him to the same line of argument so strikingly on display in Muhammad's many speeches and writings. As Baldwin phrases the Islamists' assessment of him, "I was black, and therefore a part of Islam, and would be saved from the holocaust awaiting the white world whether I would or no. My weak, deluded scruples could avail nothing against the iron word of the prophet" (*James Baldwin* 327). Bravely, he replies out loud to these assumptions "that *I* did not care if white and black people married, and that I had many white friends. I would have no choice, if it came to it, but to perish with them for (I said to myself but not to Elijah), 'I love a few people and they love me and some of them are white, and isn't love more important than color?'" (327). In the comic aftermath of this momentous encounter, Baldwin acknowledges—to his reader if not to his dinner partners—that "I was, in fact, going to have a drink with several white devils on the other side of town" after the gathering at the home of Muhammad breaks up, and that he "hesitated to give the address" (331) to the young men designated to drive him to his next destination. The incident ends anti-climactically—one might say, with great relief, anti-apocalyptically—when "we arrived in enemy territory, and they set me down at the enemy's door" (333).

Baldwin was as much of a non-believer as a Christian preacher's son could be and made it plain throughout his writings that he "declined to believe in that apocalypse which had been central to my father's vision" (63)[14]—as well as in (if its near-total absence throughout his nonfiction is any indication) the nuclear apocalypse that threatened the world in that era and that so concerned Martin Luther King Jr., whom he greatly admired, and Lorraine Hansberry, who was his dear friend. In some respects, Baldwin's decision to join his white friends for drinks—and to join them if necessary in whatever cataclysm Muhammad envisioned befalling them—instead of a session of anti-nuclear organizing is the ideal response to the atomic threat hanging over his age: even as it tacitly acceded to the difficulty faced by civil rights leaders who divided their time in the service of two causes, yet it may have done as much to maintain world unity as did any of the other valiant gestures made by black and white anti-nuclear activists during this revolutionary period.

CHAPTER 5

Last Man Standing

Sex and Survival in the Interracial Apocalyptic

"When it comes," observed Norman Mailer at a climactic moment in his Beat classic "The White Negro" (1957), "miscegenation will be a terror" (292), and he described this terror in suggestively post-nuclear terms. Though Mailer denounces the bomb and the moods of fear and conformity it has instilled, he deploys the atomic metaphor positively through the later pages, indicating that the existentially selfish "apocalyptic organism" (284) of the Hipster—and of his cultural forebear, the embattled Negro—is both the ironic and the ideal response to the pervasive and unrelenting threat of sudden annihilation in the atomic age: between "instant death by atomic war" and "slow death by conformity," the Hipster chooses "the only life-giving answer . . . to accept the terms of death, to live with death as immediate danger, to divorce oneself from society, to . . . encourage the psychopath in oneself" (277). The Negro outcast has always known "in his cells that life was war, nothing but war" and thus "subsisted for his Saturday night kicks . . . , his orgasm" (279); now that all America discerns itself on the brink of world-ending war, the oracular Hipster is he who has "absorbed the existentialist synapses of the Negro and for practical purposes could be considered a white Negro" (279). The era of atomic nihilism, notes Mailer, both coincides with and encourages black striving for equality and will lead to "matings" between "the Negro" and "the White" and perhaps ignite "the last war of them all . . . between the blacks and the whites, or between the women and the men, or between the beautiful and the ugly . . ." (292). Scott Saul reads the "photographic negative that inverted the white face" on the essay's City Lights edition as having "a space-alien stare, a klieg-bulb keenness" (67). Yet this image is also readable as a racially ambiguous human figure at the atomic flashpoint, nanoseconds before being vaporized into nothingness.

Explicating Hipster lingo, Mailer considers the immediate, explosive nature of the terms "go," "swing," "with it," and "make it" (all potential references to the sex act) and notes that "when the crisis comes, whether of love or violence, [the Hipster] can make it, he can win, he can release a little more energy for himself since he hates himself a little less" (286). Elsewhere this sexual chain reaction is figured as "giv[ing] energy to another" and as "the paradise of limitless energy and perception just beyond the next wave of the next orgasm" (287). While the concept of sex as "energy" emerges in the writing of many psychoanalytic intellectuals of the day, and especially in Wilhelm Reich's notion of the orgone—"a form of tangible, measurable libido that activates all living things" (A. Gordon 49)[1]—Mailer's particular interest in the conversion of matter (human bodies) into not only energy but surplus energy echoes his atomic preoccupation. Another key term, "groove," where likeminded cats meet to get it on together, calls to mind both the "ever-extending radii from the center" of the jazz record and the concentric circles of atomic destruction that were iconic in this era. Finally, Mailer literalizes "dig" in terms both psychoanalytic and atomic: to "unearth" the deepest energies of one's unconscious through "digging" is not to burrow into the bomb shelter of cowardice and denial but to execute a powerful underground detonation: to "allow to come to consciousness a pain, a guilt, a shame or a desire which the other has not had the courage to face." For Mailer, the Negro's explosive sexuality is sought after by the rebel-Hipster, who understands that therein lie the energy, honesty, violence, and creativity essential to survival in an apocalyptic age. While Squares fretted over the atomic-induced end of time, Mailer, like a fundamentalist awaiting the Rapture, searched out and celebrated the Negro's psychopathic, nihilistic focus on "the present," sprung free of its ties to the past and the future.

"The White Negro" thus draws into explosive, (pro)creative relation the twin bogeys of the postwar era—the atomic threat and "the Negro problem"—that this era's predominant white mindset insistently relegated to separate categories. As has been obvious throughout this study, African Americans were as averse to the prospect of nuclear attack as were most white Americans of the period, and would have been as physically, psychologically, and environmentally devastated by such an attack as would have been the lilyest whites. As Mailer suggests, the civil rights movement and the atomic threat have come together, so to speak, to give birth to new possibilities for sexual combination that signaled apocalypse for some and paradise for others. Indeed, both the atomic and the African American represented similar fears (and similar reminders of deep, disconcerting guilt)[2] to the white mind. Both racial integration and atomic destruction were envisioned, for example, as leveling forces that would radically undermine the social and political hierarchies maintained in a white-dominated society, and atomic-doomsday forecasters often spoke of the collapse of "values," "systems," and "institutions" (see the Introduction).

More specific to this argument, both the bomb and "the Negro" functioned analogically in the hysterical white imaginary by threatening "our schools," "our children," and thus "our future" in their respective ways. Mailer pegged the "terror" of interracial coupling to the emerging class of "Negro high school boys brave enough to chance their lives" (292) by having white girlfriends. Despite the apocalyptic dangers brewing therein, by the late 1950s the suburban public school was regarded, ironically, as one of the best-fortified shelters against nuclear attack. Now the post-atomic scenario presented itself as a new world of racially integrated youngsters, sheltering together in the basements of their middle and high schools, without the "guidance" and "protection" (i.e., the resistance to integration) of parents, who, trapped at home amongst hastily assembled basement stockpiles, would fail to survive the bomb's immediate and/or longer-term effects. For many, racial integration—especially the dreaded prospect of interracial sex and marriage—was an "end to the world as we know it" worse than the nuclear alternative; many would have rather had World War III than the apocalyptic free-for-all of interracial coupling envisioned by radical segregationists, and at least one novelist of the atomic doomsday genre (Philip Wylie, see Chapter 1) deployed the bomb in order to, among other things, solve the problem of integration by simply wiping African American characters off the map.

James Baldwin famously rejoindered Mailer's constructions of black male sexuality in his essay "The Black Boy Looks at the White Boy" (1961)—and, one may assume, in the personal interactions shared by the two men and documented to some extent in that same essay. As a reserved, soft-spoken, dapper intellectual, Baldwin embodied the antithesis of both Mailer's sexually rapacious "Negro" and his equally psychopathic "homosexual," yet another manifestation of the Hipster in Mailer's essay. Rightly outraged by Mailer's attack on "the sorely menaced sexuality of Negroes in order to justify the white man's own sexual panic" (230), Baldwin takes Mailer to task for his pessimism as well, refusing to "believe that no one is coming after us" (241). Specifically, Baldwin envisions "coming after us" the future generations Mailer consigned to atomic oblivion in the opening moments of "The White Negro."[3] Because Baldwin refuses to share in Mailer's nihilistic vision, he is thus diametrically opposed to Mailer's cultification of the Now and the total self-absorption this requires and justifies. For Baldwin "responsibility," specifically the major novelist's responsibility to those surely ensuing generations, is primary, and is what Mailer seems to have abdicated in his benighted run for mayoral office, his constant drinking and brawling, and his utterly misguided notions about the black experience. Thus Baldwin's anti-apocalypticism is as meaningful a counterpoint to Mailer's psychopathology of the present as is his status as "Negro" and "homosexual" to Mailer's unmarked race and sexual orientation. His faith in the future and his endorsement of personal responsibility define him in terms anathema to

Mailer's theory, as a Square Negro who—like most of the rest of America at the time—could not help but trust in the basic decency of world leaders to not destroy the planet with atomic power.

Baldwin was as skeptical about imminent nuclear demise as he was—despite being a preacher's son—about the agenda laid out in the book of Revelations; he neither waxed hysterical about the atomic end of the world nor worshipped at the altar of heedless hedonism supposedly sanctioned by this threat. Too, he looked askance at the apocalyptic qualities of interracial sex, having coupled with white lovers himself without Armageddon resulting and, in a remarkable scene from *The Fire Next Time*, countering the Black Nationalism of Elijah Muhammad with the humble but unassailable assertion, "I love a few people and they love me and some of them are white, and isn't love more important than color?" (*James Baldwin* 327; see Chapter 4). Luckily, history has proven Baldwin correct in both of his major claims: the superpowers did not bring about nuclear catastrophe during the cold war, and interracial sex, despite its indeed "catastrophic" rendering in the atomic era, is read less and less as an urgent social "problem" with each passing decade. Yet cultural purveyors of the postwar period—and even into the present day—have adopted the Mailerian view: though World War III and other such disasters will always draws large audiences to a novel or film, their resulting interracial sexual scenarios remain too great a terror to look upon.

SEX AND VIOLENCE ON ATOMIC DOOMSDAY

While Mailer and Baldwin debated the apocalyptic qualities of interracial relationships, sexual and otherwise, others in the postwar era sexualized the bomb itself and the atomic moment in American history while including matters of race only very fitfully in their equations. Contemporary historians have documented the ways in which the bomb was likened to both male sexuality (due to its phallic shape and penetrating trajectory) and female sexuality (through the fads of the atomic "bombshell," the "anatomic bomb," and the "bikini" bathing suit).[4] For David J. Skal, movie posters of the period reveal "a steady equation between out-of-control science and overflowing brassieres" (178–79). From more conservative quarters, parents worried that a generation shadowed by the atom bomb would develop a nihilistic, "what the hell?" attitude when it came to unsanctioned and/or extra-marital sexual activity and even regarded such a "fling" mentality as "understandable" (Lord 100). In addition, the atomic-explosive moment itself was figured as an orgasmic sublime, a massive culmination of self-annihilating desire, in texts as diverse as Erich Fromm's *The Sane Society* (1955) and Stanley Kubrick's *Dr. Strangelove* (1964). More pertinent to my argument here is a tenacious contradiction inherent in the very prospect of sexual activity immediately prior to and following total atomic war: in the nightmare scenario, total sexual anarchy—without regard to race, creed, or class—prevails with "15 minutes to live" and in the bomb's immediate, chaotic aftermath. Yet in the utopian scenario, recovery is frequently figured through the humanitarian—and often jingoistically patriotic—act of procreating, of repopulating the earth with healthy humans and proud Americans once the radioactive dust has settled. Even the "nightmare" prospect of sexual anarchy is fraught with ambivalence, as the envisioned liberation of sexually repressed, racially separated 1950s-era men and women would be impossible to disentangle from the equally likely but truly horrific circumstance of mass sexual assault upon women (of all races and classes) by men (of all races and classes) in the atomic event.

The veiled terminology issuing from doomsday scenarios of the 1950s, '60s, and even '70s, which spoke almost naïvely in terms of minimal violence and maximum sex (i.e., postwar fertility and survival) hardly helped to clarify these matters. Time and again, relying upon the well-worn example of the Cocoanut Grove nightclub fire of 1942, during which 492 were killed and many hundreds more injured, doomsday researchers promised their readers that panic would occur *only* if it were perceived that escape routes were cut off, as in the nightclub whose fire exits were non-functioning. The theory thus ran that, so long as nuclear survivors have clear instructions and goals, ordinary, law-abiding behavior will prevail. Other sociologists of the atomic period extrapolated heavily from the examples of Hiroshima and Nagasaki, where many early observers, John Hersey among them, described the decorous, docile, and altruistic behaviors of Japanese survivors in the immediate atomic aftermath. Thus, forecasts based on the Japanese experience almost always predicted that mainly "fear," "disorientation," and "survivors' guilt" would be psychological reactions to nuclear attack.

While these would surely factor in, they may have been more particular to the cultural context (see Vestermark 15) and ultimately limited sphere of damage that shaped the Japanese experience and may stand alongside the reactions of anger, aggression, and violence that characterize a more violent "peacetime" society such as the United States or that may settle in during any longer-term, more universal nuclear disaster. Others have questioned the use of any historical analogy when forecasting the outcome of nuclear catastrophe. As E. I. Chazov and M. E. Vartanian argue, no previous natural or human-made disaster (not even Hiroshima) can "equal the impact of a nuclear war on the human organism" (156). Instead, they contend that "behavioral and mental disturbances will present one of the main aftereffects of nuclear war. . . . It is expected that one-third of the survivors will be in a state of marked anxiety, characterized by fear, apprehensiveness, irritability, and confusion" (156). Multiple accounts by Japanese survivors in fact corroborate the negative forecasts of Chazov and Vartanian; Michihiko Hachiya reported acute demoralization across Hiroshima following surrender: "How selfishly everyone acted. . . .

Those who wore the aviator uniforms looked like gangsters or cheap politicians. These would enter the little shacks near the station, boldly and obscenely fondle the uncouth girls, and otherwise behave outrageously. The country was in the clutches of the mean and unintelligent" (192). Elsewhere he observed rampant burglary (196) and drunkenness and intimidation (207–8), while Takashi Nagai summed up the situation in Nagasaki: "In general, then, those who survived the atom bomb were the people who ignored their friends crying out *in extremis*; or who shook off wounded neighbors who clung to them, pleading to be saved. . . . In short, those who survived the bomb were, if not merely lucky, in a greater or lesser degree selfish, self-centered, guided by instinct and not civilization . . ." (180–81).

Even discussions minimizing the prospect of panic and antisocial behavior conceded to the widespread belief that "a sudden disaster affecting a large group will typically trigger a wild stampede of hysterical individuals . . ." (Vestermark 6). One researcher, Charles Walter Clarke, MD, who directed the American Social Hygiene Association in the early 1950s, predicted a 1000 percent increase in "V.D." in atom-bombed areas and urged preventative measures to be taken (see also May 81–82 and K. Rose 62). Significantly, Clarke comes close to racializing the post-atomic sexual crisis when he argues that "all kinds of people would be thrown intimately together" (4) in the atomic aftermath, leaving it to his agitated readers to picture the race- and class-mixing he implies.

Such fears were further disseminated in popular texts, such as the atomic survival films *The Day the World Ended* (1956) and *Panic in Year Zero* (1962). Both films demonstrate scenes of hostility and sexual threat following nuclear attack, while *Panic* stages the rape of a young girl at the hands of marauding thugs. Despite the film's own horrified view of such proceedings, its poster campaign lured audiences to the theater with promises of "An Orgy of Looting and Lust" (qtd. in Heffernan 71), and while the film likely has other uses for the term, "panic" as construed by the social scientists describes the actions of the thugs themselves, who lapse immediately into the worst kind of antisocial behavior. In a serious moment from the novel *Mr. Adam* (1946), in which an explosion at an atomic weapons plant sterilizes the world's men, author Pat Frank depicts another sort of post-atomic free-for-all with again dire implications for women. The protagonist's wife predicts total sexual license on the part of men, now "all equipped with built-in contraceptives. . . . Men will continue to live their lives. But to every woman [doomed to a life of childlessness in baby boom America], it will be as if she were already dead" (31–32). Science fiction readers of the mid-1960s might have encountered Philip K. Dick's also seriocomic *Dr. Bloodmoney*, in which the attractive heroine, wandering along the road in bloodied shock immediately following nuclear attack, draws into wordless sexual intercourse the first man she encounters, who conveniently approaches in a VW bus (81, 83). Thus it is difficult to determine, on the utterly unprecedented occasion of massive nuclear attack, whether the lesson supposedly learned in the lone instance of Cocoanut Grove would have prevailed against the subconscious influences of mass popular perception.

Still other American researchers acknowledged the likelihood of wartime violence but declined to correlate these findings with forecasts of wartime sexual assault. In a representative instance, early-1970s researcher Bruce C. Allnutt receives a strongly positive response when he asks a panel of experts whether there would be a post-attack increase in "competitive antisocial behavior, such as looting, hoarding, profiteering, robbery, fighting over resources, etc." (A-31). Yet Allnutt never refers specifically to competition over scarce female resources nor to the prospects of sexual "looting," ignoring as he does the glaring recent precedents of rampaging Russian soldiers during World War II and American GIs in Vietnam. Strikingly, Allnutt and others theorize post-attack antisocial behavior from every angle save one—that which would have affected women and children most severely and which was on the minds of many who construed the apocalyptic moment for mainstream readers and filmgoers.

Since many envisioned post-atomic violence in specifically racial terms (or more generally as a war over resources between the "haves" and "have-nots"), their reticence is laudable to the degree that it staved off hysteria regarding interracial sexual violence. Some feared the atavistic regression of formally "civilized" Americans when subjected to the stress and deprivation of long-term survival (see, e.g., Robinson 220). Others spoke in terms of race and class wars that would erupt either under- or above ground when food and material shortages reached crisis stages so many weeks or months after atomic attack (see, e.g., Janis 66; Katz 222–23, 240; Nordlie 297; and Randall 132). Post-nuclear demographer David M. Heer adds that Negro urban dwellers fleeing cities under nuclear attack would face hostile resistance "in the South" from "native whites" (289; see also Katz 231–32 and Randall 137). Meanwhile, Heer reads the prospect of postwar "fertility" in decidedly constructive terms: he considers post-nuclear birth rates almost exclusively with respect to "marriage" and the many reasons surviving married couples would desire (or not desire) to propagate following nuclear attack (320–25, 370–71). He gives only a brief nod to "illegitimacy"; strikingly, this is framed in terms of the woman's own decision—to "become motivated to rear children without a legitimate father" (385). The specter of post-atomic infertility—crashing birth rates due to radiologically induced sterility—as well as the marked reticence on subjects of sex and violence that prevailed during the era caused Heer and other nuclear scenarists to valorize the prospect of post-nuclear sexual activity, that is to separate the value of sex from the horror of violence in the post-atomic context, even as these continued to be conflated to hysteric proportions in the segregationist context.

Heer envisions a post-atomic US government's "pronatalist" policies, which would encourage survivors to procreate as rapidly as possible, and one of the comic aspects of both Dr. Strangelove's sexual survivalist fantasy at the end of *Dr. Strangelove* and Bill Haley's atomic novelty song "Thirteen Women (and Only One Man in Town)" is the patriotic, pronatalist element of the sexual smorgasbord depicted. Despite its serious subtext, Frank's *Mr. Adam* (1946) is primarily a farce (and a send-up of government bureaucracy in the form of a pronatalist agency called the National Re-fertilization Project) in which the only man still able to reproduce following a world-scale atomic accident is the eponymous shy, gangling redhead (at work in a mine on the day of the explosion). He becomes an object of hot pursuit for every child-starved woman on the planet until a local doctor produces a miraculous seaweed cure. In Philip Wylie's post-nuclear melodrama *Triumph* (1963), the comedy is largely inadvertent, as the men sit around their state-of-the-art shelter and straight-facedly discuss the humanitarian divvying of the surviving women. Waiting in the wings of the post-atomic sexual crisis is that imagined powerhouse of sexual potency, the apocalyptically hip black male. Who better to perform the herculean task of repopulating North America following atomic Armageddon, yet who worse to exacerbate the hysterias of most white Americans of the period, for whom interracial sex was as unthinkable as atomic apocalypse?

DODGING THE QUESTION
IN POPULAR POSTWAR NOVELS

Despite the opportunity presented (or perhaps due to the controversy threatened) in the literary enactment of this equation, both Frank and Dick opt to separate their African American characters from the act if not the subject of sexual reproduction. In *Mr. Adam* the protagonist, the last remaining non-sterile man on the planet, was inspecting lead and silver mines in Colorado the day that "the great new nuclear fission plants at Bohrville, Mississippi [and 'most of Mississippi . . . along with it'] . . . disintegrated in an explosion that made Nagasaki and Hiroshima mere cap pistols by comparison" (23). The narrator comments progressively that "nobody really missed Mississippi. The explosion eliminated [the notoriously racist legislators] Bilbo and Rankin" (24), yet others in the story admit that "the Negro question is particularly vexing" (148) with respect to whether Negro women will be inseminated with Homer Adam's sperm. Much comedy is made about a new civilization of red-haired children, and the implied joke is nastily intensified with the prospect of a new "race" of red-headed mixed-race children resulting from Homer's artificial insemination. While minority groups such as Negroes, Catholics, and Jews clamor to receive Homer's seed lest their populations be wiped out, in fact the mixing with stock as white as Homer's is a sure path to such decimation—one of the dozens of scientific quandaries that this preposterous novel declines to confront. The only black male in the story, a tough-talking numbers runner named Two-Tone Jones, is unmanned by sterility if not impotence. His only role is to query the protagonist, an AP reporter covering the Adam story, about the prospects of artificial insemination since "we [Harlem residents] don't read that part of the papers" that contained the necessary information (55). In *Dr. Bloodmoney*, while the sexual profligacy of the white heroine is expected and encouraged, the novel's only black character, Stuart McConchie, is surprised at the sexual thoughts expressed by his surviving (but terminally injured) white shelter-mate: "Christ, I haven't felt the slightest urge since the first bomb fell; it's like the thing dropped off in fear, fell right off" (102). In each instance here, the prospect of post-nuclear sexual activity for African American characters is suggested only to be dropped, in keeping with officially sanctioned doomsday forecasting published in this period.

The pattern continues in Wylie's *Triumph*, where the question is dodged by presenting only angelically desexualized black male figures in a novel that deals extensively with interracial sexuality in the post-apocalyptic scenario. The novel appeared almost a decade after the much more optimistic *Tomorrow!* (discussed in Chapter 1) and reflects the significant transition experienced by America as a whole from A-bomb to H-bomb technology, from the rigidities of the 1950s to the nascent "broadmindedness" of the early 1960s, and from Wylie's original faith in simple but organized nuclear preparedness to his more cynical but realistic realization that surviving the multi-megaton bombings deliverable by the early 1960s was a one-in-a-million proposition—or more specifically a proposition open only to millionaires (see also Sharp 209). In the earlier story, one black female character plays a starring role on "X-Day" but does not survive into Wylie's utopian, suburbanized day-after. In *Triumph*, the handful of Americans (and visiting internationals) who make it to the implausibly commodious, well-ventilated, and fully stocked shelter of wealthy visionary Vance Farr are a carefully selected band of socially and racially diverse characters. All were strikingly civil to each other before the world ended and only form closer ties in the nuclear aftermath. Significantly, "there can't be any servant-master setup down here! We're all going to have to stand shifts. Cooking. Public-room cleaning. Laundry. Dishwashing. All other chores," cries the millionaire, despite the fact that "my wife won't like it" (58). Wylie suggests here, as did Frank in *Alas, Babylon* (see Chapter 1) that a good nuclear flattening is just what stratified US society needs to achieve democracy once and for all. Throughout, the irony of eventually returning to "civilization," with all of its traditional bigotries and misunderstandings, is the cause behind many of the story's ethical concerns and aborted romances.

Only the scion pledged to Farr's daughter—who turns out to love the Jewish physicist-hero instead—runs off in a stir-crazed lather of paranoid anti-Semitism and succumbs to radiation exposure at story's end. Two men of lower class, a white meter reader named Pete Williams and an Italian-American lothario named Al Rizzo, come across as mercurial and antisocial at first then acquit themselves as loveable team players by mid-story. The women are a veritable Miss Universe pageant of international and locally grown beauties, including the blue-blooded Faith Farr; the African American butler's enticing and "feral" daughter, Connie Davy; a Chinese-American visitor with a good brain and a sweet disposition, Lotus (or Lodi) Li; and a Spanish-Irish siren (whose ethnicity changes to Italian-Irish halfway through the story), Angelica, who is both trashy and good-natured (and an ex-mistress of the millionaire). Wylie's implicit first thesis then is that America can only "triumph" in the face of nuclear catastrophe if its core of survivors—no matter how small—is both socially and racially diverse and willing to befriend, make love, and marry across traditional divides. Meanwhile, Farr's butler, the affable and confident Paulus Davy, has his best moment first, when he enters to welcome Ben, the Jewish intellectual-hero, to the estate and before taking his luggage shakes his hand (11). Ben is "greatly surprised" but pleased to return the gesture; having made his statement, Wiley has little more use for Paulus, who is regarded by the others as too old and grief-stricken over his lost wife to function as any sort of player on the sexual chess board Wiley is otherwise interested to construct.

Yet contra, for instance, repopulating the planet as a sexual subtheme in Heer's research, and contra the copious attention given to sexual activity by Robert Heinlein in his shelter-survival tale of the same era, *Farnham's Freehold* (see Chapter 2), Wylie in this novel is less focused on pronatalism than on the avoidance of sexual anarchy that looms as a real possibility when virile men and curvaceous women become trapped in a shelter. Yet while indeed trapped, they would have been liberated both biologically and socially by the then-newly minted birth control pill, which we can only assume the millionaire-host was farsighted enough to stock in bulk as he did every other possible commodity his guests could wish for. On numerous occasions, various of the men, especially Al and Kit, Faith's arrogant fiancé, lunge after various of the women and are fended off on the flimsiest of pretenses. In one scene, Kit makes the unassailable argument that as an engaged couple, he and Faith are as married as can be under the circumstances; she dodges his advances first by reminding him of all the depressing annihilation that has occurred above ground, then—obscurely—by informing him that the odds of their being the last fourteen survivors in all of America are simply too "preposterous" for her to leave her bedroom door unlocked that night (114–15). Later the lecherous Al is told to "beat it" when he approaches Angelica's door; again, the rationale for turning him out is weak, since these two entered the story as a sexually active couple and since clearly Angelica's sugar-daddy, trapped on the premises with his all-knowing wife, is off-limits. Thus, despite Wylie's obvious interest in exploring the sexual complications inherent in a long-term shelter situation, and despite his progressive willingness to suggest the absurdity of racial and religious bars to marriage, the era's own lingering sexual and racial phobias prevail in every scene; the women remain confirmed in "authentic self-regard" (210) and "propriety" (215), the men never assert the physical superiority that would have ended the matter immediately on countless real-life shelter occasions, and the reader is left with a "wait-and-see" regarding the most provocative interracial romance in the story—between African American, Harvard-educated Connie and white working-class Pete.

Too, it is by now difficult to read Wylie's racial and sexual utopia as anything other than the racialized sexual fantasy it in fact happens to be. With Paulus effectively sidelined, only the white men and George Hayama, the company's savvy Japanese American technician, are left to the fantasies and machinations inspired by the many available women. Not surprisingly, all take lustful interest in the hot-blooded Angelica and the nubile Connie (once even referred to as "feline . . . a black panther" [232]); later, the Japanese American George takes up with the Hawaiian-born, ethnic-Chinese Lodi, after the two have a conversation about the historical animosity between their two nations (i.e., Japan and China). The well-heeled Faith is spared from the clutches of the working-class men but takes the daring step of selecting Jewish Ben over the insufferable Kit; both George and Lodi and Ben and Faith appear to consummate their unions in the story, even though never actually appearing when doing so, and Ben (Wylie's alter-ego) contemplates flings with both Connie and Angelica before relenting to the importuning of Faith. That Faith is lovely and vivacious and Ben is awkward and homely underscores the sexual-fantasy aspect of the story, and Wylie is only willing to take the prospect of post-nuclear interracialism so far—to a place that would have hardly offended most members of the pre-nuclear society who remained, of course, the author's paying customers.

In their very coupledom George and Lodi are linked as an irreducible narrative unit with the same interests (science, math), the same role in the collective (Ben's chief assistants), and the same "oriental" sensibility. At one point, "George and Lodi merely gazed at their chief" (168) as if controlled by the same set of wires; later, George is singled out (by Lodi) as shifty-eyed but endearing: "Every time I feel his black, black eyes fixed on me—and they move so fast you can't see them shift and you will think he's watching someone else, when with no warning you find him gazing at you!" (244). Elsewhere Ben questions the stereotype of the Asian's "unfathomable expression" only to notice that George is fixing him with one now (81). George and Lodi's intense togetherness indicates their deep attachment to each other but also extinguishes their once individual roles and personalities, already rather vaguely realized out of a series of pious stereotypes and clichés. If Wylie attempted at first to call attention to white ignorance of the physical and cultural distinctions between various Asian peoples, by story's end he thoroughly reinscribes this limitation by recasting the two, despite their ethnic difference and romantic attachment, as indistinguishable twins. Another heavily typed figure is the Latin-Italian Angelica, who winds up sexually frustrated due to boredom with all of her male prospects by the end of the story. Clearly, she is made to atone for her oversexed past by finding no suitable partners and being compelled to turn her energies toward mothering the story's two children instead.

Wylie is glowing in his presentation of Connie; she enters the story through the sound of her tennis balls smacking the estate court; despite her father's servant role, she is a thoroughly liberated member of the household—well-educated, multilingual, and of course beautiful. Once in the shelter, she is the group's interpreter of Spanish satellite programming (after Angelica has changed identities from "South American" to "Italian") and teacher of French, as well as Pete's college-level tutor in everything from algebra to geology. As opposed to the oppressively embodied Angelica, Connie has only one sexual moment, when one night, her hair in disarray, she greets Vance, Ben, and George in a diaphanous gown and confesses her attraction to Pete. Following this group's sexually charged but ethically momentous discussion, regarding their return to the civilized world and the necessary euthanizing of any interracial love, Connie heroically decides to break Pete's heart and is rewarded by the men of the story (including the author) by never appraising her with the same collective leer again. Contemplating their own happy prospects for marriage, Ben agrees with Faith that "it was wise and brave of Connie to stop everything between herself and Pete. . . . [I]f we ever got outside, it perhaps wouldn't work. Not yet. Not for another generation or two. So, it better not be continued here" (267). Thus in accordance with the dictates of its era—dictates that have changed little in fifty years—the white and Asian characters are allowed their respectable forms of sexual expression while the more dangerous black and Latina figures are oversexed and/or ultimately denied the prospect of sexual and marital fulfillment.

Regarding their eventual return to the surface, the shelter community is figured explicitly as inter-racial and classless yet also as fragile, temporary, and utterly constructed, unreal. The obnoxious Kit of this story (just like the obnoxious Kit of *Tomorrow!*), dies gruesomely in the throes of a racist harangue, yet the novel implicitly asks whether his unbridled hatred stems from the madness that drives him out of the shelter or is part of the very miasma, like the radiation that kills him, of the outside environment? As the party dreams of rescue (to the implausibly spared southern hemisphere), their return to this environment is explicitly linked to a re-encounter with racist sentiments and racist social structures—with the "normal" order of things that defined each character's pre-nuclear experience. Madness, they all seem to know, would be the interracial coupling occurring throughout the shelter community; that Wylie is sure such bigotries would survive and intensify even in the wake of such a radical readjustment to the world order may be read as either bracingly realist or just the excuse this author needs to perpetuate the racist rhetoric of his own era.

Indeed, the mixed message offered by the band of survivors is replicated in Wiley's macrocosmic vision of the waiting world. *Triumph*'s nuclear war is construed in specifically racial, however physically impossible, terms—that is, as a "white" crisis that obliterates Europe, the United States, Canada, and China, and leaves the global south miraculously unscathed. In a second round of radioactive bombing, at last Mexico and Central America are affected, yet our group of survivors—ultimately those last alive in the entire top half of the planet—know all along that salvation awaits them below the equator, if they can just use their short-wave radio to talk someone into sailing the "hot" waters of the North Atlantic to rescue them. Thus it is a notably brown and tropical world toward which Wylie's survivors look for restoration to the above-ground; a Costa Rican news commentator, watched via satellite on the TV rigged expertly by George, is an early guiding presence, and later the omniscient narrator informs us that racially segregated South Africa is the new pariah in the now ardently pacifist, democratized southern hemisphere. Why then should Connie decline the serious intentions of Pete, if both ethnic pluralism and the general browning of humanity are the post-nuclear future for them all?

Perhaps not surprisingly, the answer lies in the large role played by white-ruled Australia in the final scenes. It is the Australians (the colonizers, not the aboriginals) whom the band of survivors has been waiting to hear from the whole two years of their "immolation," and it is they who come to the rescue and, we may assume, repatriate the survivors to their own white-settled homeland, not to Borneo or Peru. Post-holocaust, the Aussies (and their neighbor New Zealanders) assume a leadership role that the novel never questions. If the South Africans are too racist, the Africans and South Americans are, alas, too "raced" to handle the job, and the middle ground occupied by the peace-loving, progressive, but commonwealth-identified Australians is the landing pad for the rescued Americans and the seat of the new world order. While the outbackers proclaim a gospel of brotherhood and equality, Connie may have known better than all of them—including her author—that a post-nuclear world still run by whites would indeed be "not ready" for the challenge presented by herself and Pete. Meanwhile, the novel's last word on the issue—"perhaps. . . . We, and they, shall see" (275)—is reminiscent of the rhetoric, of "untimely" acts and the need to "wait," condemned by Martin Luther King as he wrote his "Letter from a Birmingham Jail" the same year *Triumph* was published. While King thus debunked *Triumph*'s wait-and-see/we-can-only-hope philosophy before the ink on its first printing had dried, such attitudes remained representative and tenacious. For all of its unspeakable transformation, Wylie's bomb changed nothing, and his band of survivors' potentially revolutionary crossing of boundary lines is a return to the status quo after all.

In its most honest moment, the novel's only black male character besides Paulus Davy plays a central role. He is a striking figure from the "last day" captured on film by a roving photographer and appearing in the course of a sat-ellite news program issued from Costa Rica. In this indeed distressing scene, a white woman is gang-assaulted by three toughs, white characters whom Wiley takes pains to mark as such the only time in the story. A black man, in a mov-ing company uniform, rescues the woman before being shot by yet another white marauder. This character threatens the cameraman then chases down the fleeing, half-dressed female, while her black rescuer lies dying on the pavement. While the survivor group has viewed scenes of destruction, panic, and blood-shed from their underground sanctuary throughout the course of the lengthy news program, it is this traumatic scene of sexual violence that causes them to cry "turn it off" and head individually, "like monks and nuns," as Lodi ob-serves on another occasion (104), to bed. Surely it is this horrifying scene of nuclear chaos that might serve to dampen sexual passion more effectively than any hypocritical appeal to bourgeois "self-regard." It is a pivotal counterpoint to the antipode survivors living chastely and mournfully below the surface, and a rare glimpse of horrific doomsday sexual violence that most writing during this period, from freewheeling Norman Mailer to a host of buttoned-down re-searchers, refused to acknowledge.

Yet the parallel narrative functions played by the heroically nonviolent black actor in this scene and the angelically desexualized Paulus Davy surviv-ing in the shelter below implicate black male sexuality as violent, counter-productive, and apocalyptic in its own way—thus in urgent need of erasure from mainstream narrative. With both of these black male figures, Wylie takes pains to demonstrate their noble sexlessness, just as Heinlein did in *Farnham's Freehold* (especially in its early, "integrationist" scenes) with his houseman Joe. Wylie deserves credit for declining to draw the African American in the video as a marauding rapist, yet the unsexing of his black characters (including Connie) is a double-edged sword: in all cases, they are denied normal sexual urges—we might even argue that at the very end of the world, rough, mean-ingless copulation between strangers would constitute a "normal" physical and psychological reaction—enabling Wylie to emphasize their nobility and self-sacrifice but sparing him (and his readers) the challenge of reading such figures as noble *and* sexual, as physically, explicitly attached to a partner of another race or even a member of their own.

MIXED MESSAGES IN POPULAR POSTWAR FILMS

The six films to occupy the remainder of this chapter, appearing from the heart of the atomic era through the "swinging" 1960s and '70s to the much more "viral" present day,[5] flirt with the prospects of planetary salvation cour-tesy of regenerative interracial sexuality but most often fail to consummate such revolutionary visions. In all but one, the eroticized black lead is male, and significantly it is only the black female costar (Rosalind Cash in *The Omega Man*) paired with a white male lead who experiences post-apocalyptic interracial sex and the redemptive possibilities this entails. Significantly, the films position African American characters no longer as capable domestics (as in the white-authored survivalist fiction discussed Chapter 1), but as broadly empowered civil servants—even "mayors" and chief policy-makers in their geographically extensive but meagerly populated urban terrains. Meanwhile, these black characters remain, despite their increased mobility and newly acquired star status, as members of the Hollywood and American-literary "servant" traditions, providing necessary utilities (lights, water, and marriage-officiating) to white female fellow-survivors yet facing repeated rejection of their implied offer of equally vital sexual services. Several of the films use the cityscape or other locales to challenge traditional notions of black male "criminal" behavior, although each of these challenges fails to sufficiently dismantle the aura of black sexual danger that forms a barrier between the romantic leads. As the years of production roll by, each film provides an ever more sophisticated and disturbing view of the end of the world, enabled by ever-newer technologies, ever more lavish budgets, and filmgoers' ever-larger appetites for mayhem and destruction. Yet despite this increasing familiarity with the apocalyptic scenario—with the end of the world so ubiquitous it is now a staple of the summertime blockbuster—each film's diffidence on the subject of interracial sex sends it hurtling back to the narrowness and moral failing of a bygone era.

The World, the Flesh, and the Devil (1959)

Ranald MacDougall's nuclear-themed *The World, the Flesh, and the Devil* (1959) is the earliest wide-release film in this survey and a suitable index for much of what follows; its tropes and situations were often repeated, intentionally or not, by other film texts belonging to its tradition. Its placement at the height of the integrationist phase of the civil rights movement is also significant, as the interracial cast and production staff refused to present atomic survival as a whites-only affair and instead used their story to counter decades of back-grounding or absenting of black characters and racial themes in Hollywood films. Instead, this film seems to insist, nuclear Armageddon would signal a new, interracial day, with an attractive black Adam in the lead and a willingness to address hot-button topics like racism and interracial sex head-on. The story of an African American miner from Pennsylvania who encounters a frightened white woman in New York following total post-nuclear depopulation, it was a modest commercial success that has gained a critical following over the decades for its striking visual effects, its unique combination of themes, and its star turn by the indeed sexually magnetic Harry Belafonte. Belafonte's landmark concert at Carnegie Hall occurred the year this film was released and marked the apex of his career; the film was a co-presentation of his own Har-Bel production company. Belafonte's involvement—as both actor and decision-making producer—reminds us that unlike an essay, such as that about so-called Negro reality penned by the white writer Norman Mailer, a film is a communal experience in both production and consumption that enabled and required the presentation of more diverse and/or more ambiguous viewpoints. A decade after *The World, the Flesh, and the Devil*, the African American actor Duane Jones starred in George A. Romero's *Night of the Living Dead* (1968) and rewrote much of his own dialogue to make his character Ben sound as educated and cool-headed as Jones himself was (Hardman n.p.). Whether or not they also wrote or produced, the dignified presence of actual black actors taking part in these interracial survival narratives challenged assumptions and invited producers to take political, artistic, and commercial risks that single-authored views of interracial relations did not.

The MacDougall/Belafonte collaboration challenges white hysteria regarding interracial sex, although in many ways it is as confused and contradictory on the subject as the nation itself was in that period. In its first act the film mocks white fear by positioning the elegant Belafonte, of all people, as the marauding black male. After escaping the mineshaft where he was working and became trapped for several days, Belafonte's character Ralph Burton hotwires a car in a showroom and drives it through a broken display window, mimicking "black" criminal behavior, even though it is clear that nuclear disaster has struck, with notions of theft, ownership, and payment similarly obliterated. Getting out to pump gas in the next scene, Ralph has mysteriously changed from his torn, half-open workman's plaid into a gleaming white shirt and suit coat, as if his step up to car ownership comes with an ensemble appropriate to his new station. In said business attire, Ralph reaches New York and storms the empty canyons of Wall Street, shooting a gun (so as to attract fellow-survivors in hearing distance) into the upper reaches of surrounding skyscrapers. His panic, turned paranoia and rage, pushes the irony to limit: "What are you afraid of?" he shouts, as if on the threshold of a southern school or a suburban tract house. "I know you're all staring at me!" Yet now the white inhabitants of these streets are impervious to both integration and racially motivated gunfire: having already done themselves in by their own superior firepower, they have no more to fear from the black man at large.

The film pairs handsome Belafonte with fetching white Inger Stevens, yet when they meet, her first assumption is that he is bent on ravishing her. "Don't touch me!" she screams, and the upstanding Ralph—who is such a straight arrow that in an earlier scene he picked up an overturned trash basket and threw in his empty tin cans—is wounded by the accusation. Ralph comes across as a thoroughly self-realized African American of his time. Despite his growing love for Sarah he understands the barriers between them; at one point, she asks if they could not share an apartment building, and Ralph sagely reminds her that

"People would talk." Sure enough, "civilization" arrives by boat shortly, in the figure of a white male competitor (played by Mel Ferrer); he immediately cuts in on Ralph's time with Sarah and threatens murder if Ralph gets in his way. "World War IV," as Ralph refers to it, is, in confirmation of everyone's worst fears, a race war between two men over sexual access to a white woman.

Sarah's lines, and her motivation, are the most confused and contradictory in the film; in the midst of sexually propositioning Ralph, she throws out a racist comment—"I'm free, white, and twenty-one, and I can do as I please"; throughout, she is equal parts repulsed and attracted and vacillates between these with every look and line of speech. At one point, she weeps over her ruined prospects for marriage, since "there's no one left to marry anyone!" Note how the first problem—there being no (white) man left to (legally) marry is translated immediately into the lack of a proper minister to do the officiating. After a beat, Ralph—who has worked so well to restore the lights, phone service, and a glamorous living standard for the two of them that he is now de facto "mayor of New York"—volunteers to officiate and to do his best to find someone for Sarah to marry, never mind that her best marriage prospect stands right in front of her. Sarah spends much time shouting at Ralph, her anger an inextricable mix of racist arrogance and thwarted desire.

Interestingly, the budding romance between these two unfolds only through the film's heavy-handed romanticizing of nuclear war: Ralph and Sarah are free to flirt with the prospect of perfect union because they have managed to escape both the trauma of catastrophic carnage and their own physical breakdown due to radiation poisoning, both of which are absent. As Frank W. Oglesbee observes, "While there are no live people, there are also no dead ones" (26), and the film's implicit question—"must it take a nuclear war to bring these two together?"—fails to confront the atomic and civil rights issues with anywhere near equal urgency (see also Stafford). Yet the film desexualizes the bond between Ralph and Sarah.[6] There is basically zero chemistry between the two onscreen, so unnerved were the studio executives—though not the cast itself (see Stafford)—by the unprecedented nature of their project, and at last the threat to the couple comes not in the form of deadly fallout but a rapacious white male. Sarah's choice—potentially revolutionary—is dodged disappointingly: she leans toward Ben, the white rival, but in the final frames extends a hand (of mere friendship? of polyandrous sexuality?) to the humiliated Ralph. Reviewing the film during its original run, Albert Johnson complained that it "exemplifies today's approach to the theme of interracialism—vague, inconclusive, and undiscussed" (43), while Hollis Alpert observed that "even in a relatively empty world, the race problem continues. Having brought up the issue, Mr. MacDougall then handles it like an unbearably hot potato" (31). If Mailer hailed widespread interracial sex for the apocalypse it would set off, Baldwin regarded such flights of fancy as irresponsible and recognized that until and unless an actual nuclear war occurs, racist hysteria would maintain "the Negro" as (white) America's worst problem. The flinching of MacDougall's film bore Baldwin out: even nuclear war did not look so bad in the face of the interracial sexual threat (in fact, cinematographer Harold Marzorati made it look quite majestic and serene), and even a nuclear war was not enough to permit the restorative coupling of this revolutionary Adam and Eve.

Five (1951)

More obscure and somewhat earlier was *Five* (1951), written, directed, and produced by the noted leftist radio dramatist Arch Oboler. Oboler's film is credited as the first to imagine the world after nuclear holocaust—and is the first as well to raise the question of race relations in a post-nuclear landscape, an indication that these two issues have been significantly intermeshed in the cultural imagination since the start of the atomic era. Black male sexuality figures implicitly instead of explicitly in this film; white, pregnant Roseanne's missing husband, Steven, we learn from a photo she keeps, is black, and much of her motivation as well as a good bit of the final plot involves her futile search for her absent one-and-only. Each of the two young white male characters on hand in the film's post-nuclear present competes for Roseanne's allegiance with the memory of her missing husband, to whom she faithfully clings on an emotional level, fending off the approaches of both. The kind and well-spoken African American Charles, a bank attendant in Santa Barbara who took refuge in the vault when the blast when off, never learns the race of her former husband nor makes a play for her in the course of the film.

As in *World*, the ugly resurgence of racism comes from the sea; Eric is dragged from the surf following the destruction of his boat; he sports an ambiguous European accent and an arrogant hostility toward Charles and, again as in *World*, inexorably draws the female character into his orbit. As Ben challenged Ralph with violence in the Belafonte production, so Eric challenges Charles as Eric absconds with Roseanne to the city in a faux search for the missing husband; in this case, however, Eric kills Charles, making Oboler's depiction of racism more violent and thus its condemnation more stringent. Oboler's original filmgoers would have been forced to acknowledge the heinousness of Eric's crime—due largely, for better or worse, to the total lack of a sexual threat presented by Charles—yet the modern viewer might observe the ways in which Charles is required to atone for the missing Steven's own "crime," of marrying a white woman in the first place. Thus Roseanne's choice, unlike Sarah's, is not between black and white suitors but between the old ways of bigotry and selfishness and the new, communal, racially integrated alternative offered by the productive alliance between Charles and Michael, the other white man bidding for Roseanne's affections. Roseanne pays for her initial choice of Eric; in the city, she learns of his ruse to lure her away under the false pretenses, and on her solitary trip back to Michael and his idyllic beach house, her newborn dies of exposure. Significantly, and as per the urbophobia on display in many of the science fictions discussed in Chapter 2, she was warned of danger before her trip, as Michael "believes [cities] are the causes and locus of a decadent world that destroyed itself, and which contains the highest concentrations of radiation" (Shapiro 75).

Thus, perhaps Roseanne atones as well for the interracial marriage she attempted in the narrative's prehistory; by film's end, she has been cleansed of her obsession for her lost husband and her foolish infatuation with the swaggering Eric; as opposed to the tightrope act performed by Sarah up through the last frames of *World*, Rosanne clearly chooses—in the figure of Michael—the option of interracial goodwill and cooperation. Yet by this point, there is no more black (or even mixed-race) character with which to integrate the story and the two choose nothing besides the best of intentions instead. Thus as in *World*, *Five* subordinates the realities of post-nuclear survival to the last-man melodrama of racial and romantic triangles, then likewise evades solutions to (and thus the problem of) interracial relations. As with *World*, critics noted the film's implausibly antiseptic setting, wherein "vast clouds of atomic dust . . . reduce the population to skeletons while leaving almost everything else strangely untouched," even while also appreciating "the well-shot, eerie scenes [in which] the heroine visits the ghost city askew in the grotesque attitudes of suddenly interrupted life" (Crowther X1). In *The New York Times*, Bosley Crowther was mainly bored, finding that "that the only drama of even mild consequence in the film is a clash between a white man and a Negro," while the reviewer for *Time* did not even notice this clash, reading Charles and one other survivor as having merely "die[d] off" (X1). Such indifference toward the film's main conflict reveals the reviewer's insensitivity to the fate of Negro film characters, as well as the damage done by the filmmakers' own diffident rendering of its primary social problems.

Night of the Living Dead (1968)

One momentous decade following the Belafonte production, Romero's *Night of the Living Dead* (1968) succeeds where its predecessor failed in certain respects though in others capitulates even more disappointingly to the status quo. Many have hailed the artistic and political achievements of this film—a vividly realized nightmare of zombies attacking a remote middle-American farmstead shot in grainy, documentary-style black-and-white—and the many sequels and remakes that constitute the ever-expanding *Dead* canon; in Stephen Harper's assessment, "zombies function . . . as a *lumpenproletariat* of shifting significance, walking symbols of any oppressed social group" (n.p.). In one key scene from the second installment, *Dawn of the Dead* (1978), the audience is invited "to consider zombiedom as a condition associated with both racial oppression and social abjection . . ." (n.p.). Notably, the franchise has included African

American characters in major and minor roles in each installment. While usually read as the horror classic it is, *Night of the Living Dead* belongs to the atomic genre as well, since it is learned mid-story that hordes of the recently-dead have been revitalized as flesh-eating zombies due to "radiations" from a satellite circling Venus that has gone amok. In the film's original synopsis the hero explains the zombies as "a freak molecular mutation due to man's atomic research" (Russo 33). Also, Kevin Heffernan compares the film to the two atomic survival films mentioned earlier, *The Day the World Ended* and *Panic in Year Zero*, finding several character and situation parallels between *Night* and these predecessors (70). In the later *Dawn of the Dead* an overstressed scientist on an emergency news program suggests dropping nuclear bombs on all major American cities, by way of eradicating the zombie populations concentrated there, taking us back to Harper's equation between the zombie hordes and the "maligned underclasses" (n.p.) of America's inner cities.

In contrast to the sanitized versions of post-apocalyptic devastation presented in the 1950s, *Night*'s graphic scenes of decayed bodies (the zombies' own) and realistically rendered flesh-eating created a storm of controversy, well documented in Roger Ebert's widely noted original review (n.p.) wherein he condemned a faulty MPAA rating system, as well as careless theater owners and parents, who left small children alone with this Saturday matinee to sustain life-changing trauma: "I don't think the younger kids really knew what hit them. . . . This was ghouls eating people up and you could actually see what they were eating . . . I saw kids who had no resources they could draw upon to protect themselves from the dread and fear they felt." Writing for *Variety*, "Beau" seconded this motion, accusing Romero and his film crew, "distributor Walter Reade, and the film industry as a whole" of gross moral turpitude. In its original run, the film therefore generated its very own "social problem" that allowed its breakthroughs on the civil rights front—a confident African American (Duane Jones) in the lead, who strikes out physically at both a white woman and a white man and is supported by the narrative in both acts—to figuratively pale in comparison. In some ways, the lack of controversy—or even lack of much interest—in the fact that a black actor was the lead player was in keeping with the indifference of the filmmakers themselves, who cast Jones without regard to his racial identity, simply because he was the best man for the part (Romero 7). We might say therefore that the film was as radical a departure in horror as it was, in its nonchalance toward multiracial casting, in politics, except that even this film, hailing from the height of a liberal era and violating more expectations than any other in the survey, conforms as do all the others to the code of sexual reticence between black male lead and his available white female costar.

The uneasy partnership between *World*'s Ralph and Sarah is replaced in *Night* by a contest of wills between Ben (Jones) and Barbra (played by the white actor Judith O'Dea); on both occasions, black male industry puts white female hysteria to shame, while simultaneously reenacting a troubling servant-mistress dynamic that I introduced earlier (see also Chapter 1 and Higashi 180 and Williams 26). In *Night* Ben rushes about boarding up the farmhouse they have both taken refuge in, while Barbra clings catatonically to the walls and clutches a large kitchen knife that is more menacing to Ben than to the (white) invaders he keeps at bay. As in the Belafonte film, Ben goes through the motions of black criminal behavior, vandalizing the possessions of the (very likely white) absent rural family whose house he has commandeered, but in fact only breaks up tables and chairs for the wood braces necessary to barricade doors (see figure 9). Strikingly, the ambivalence shown by Sarah in the earlier film, caught between attraction to and animosity toward Ralph, is nowhere evinced by Barbra, who not only fails to gratefully attach herself to Ben but is thoroughly hostile to him. When not staring blankly at the walls, Barbra glares or shouts at him, pummels him with her fists, and becomes furious when he refuses to risk his life to search out her brother Johnny, knocked unconscious in the opening attack and surely (un)dead by now. Both Sarah and especially Barbra belong to Lola Young's category of white women in interracial films of this period who are "implicitly marked as inherently prone to sexual neurosis, . . . [whose] racism is seen as an effect of sexual frustration" (102).

Barbra's monologue in this scene with Ben is her longest in the film; her warm smile at recollection of her last moments with Johnny is an enigmatic mix of sisterly love and sexual reverie, a mood intensified by her seductively

FIGURE 9: Vandalizing for safety, *Night of the Living Dead* (Image Ten Productions, 1968).

announcing that "it's hot in here" and attempting to remove her still-buttoned coat. Barbra informs Ben that when their zombie-attacker approached, she wished him "good evening" and was immediately grabbed by the man who "held me, he ripped at my clothes." Later she moans and pulls at her lapels, reenacting the attack with a mix of fear and longing. In fact her speech is pure fabrication; she never spoke a word to the attacking zombie and was not molested sexually in any manner. Why does Barbra turn simple assault into attempted rape? The scene suggests that Ben's bearing witness brings out the exhibitionist in Barbara, while Ben himself only looks away when she announces she is hot and nervously tells her to calm down as her narrative gets more hysterical and sexual.

Her story builds to a violent climax, complete with the shouting and pummeling referred to earlier. Finally she slaps Ben, who slugs her in retaliation. As per the well-worn cliché, this is just what Barbra needs to pull herself together, as she ceases her tirade and collapses in Ben's arms. He carries her to the couch and opens her coat, whose last button is right over her crotch. In accordance with the dynamic that has prevailed between them from the start, Ben manages with ease something Barbra has been too helpless to do the entire scene, free herself of her confining coat, yet again enacts black "criminal" behavior in his intimate ministrations toward the blond, unconscious woman (see figure 10). For better or worse, this is the only "sex" they will have in the film; shortly thereafter another group of hiding survivors rush the basement stairs and Ben loses his status as "last man standing" until the final frames of the film. As Robin Wood observes, once Ben and Barbra are no longer a prospective survivor couple, Ben "remains unconnected to any of the others, and we learn nothing of his family or background." Since Ben is neither part of a couple (as are two others in the story) nor a family (as are three others), he signifies disruption of the "social order" and must be gunned down like the zombies at film's end (Wood 116). The film's nuclear family is headed by a loudmouth named Harry whose "problem" with Ben is surely racial in part, although it is never named so specifically. While the film pointedly condemns the domineering, hostile attitude of Harry, it takes no similar aim at the equally antisocial caviling of Barbra, whose hysterical-female routine is all but expected by the film's controlling male outlook and evidently all the excuse she needs to be ungrateful, hostile, and abusive to the black man who saves her life.[7]

The dynamic amongst the story's three male survivors resembles that found in Oboler's *Five*, where the interracial friendship between Charles and Michael overrules, and eventually overturns, the racist attitudes of Eric; in *Night*, Ben is joined by a cooperative young man named Tom to outvote the brusque and insulting Harry. Yet whereas the retiring black character Charles is killed off halfway through *Five*, in *Night* it is the white youngster Tom who dies in a mishap with a pick-up truck and Harry who is later shot by Ben in self-defense. Thus Ben freely fends off attack from whites—both living ones and

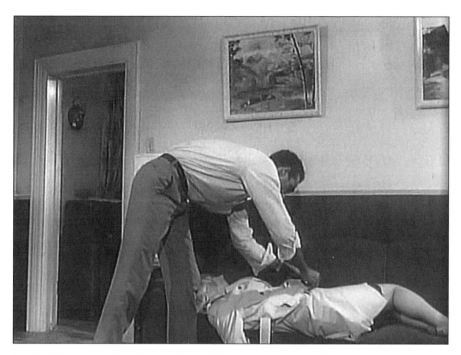

FIGURE 10: Ben servicing Barbra, *Night of the Living Dead* (Image Ten Productions, 1968).

zombies—until he becomes the sole survivor. Meanwhile, his death is as gratui-
tous as was Charles's; where Charles made no overtures to Roseanne and thus
posed no threat to Eric's sexual conquests, Ben is equally (and equally problem-
atically) "harmless"—first for showing no sexual interest in Barbra and second
for simply outliving her. As I argued earlier that Charles is forced to atone for
Steven and Roseanne's interracial marriage, so Ben seems to deserve his own
death—he is shot between the eyes by a white sheriff's posse who mistake him
for a zombie—only through a contrivance of the plot, specifically Ben's out-
of-character error in judgment by which he fails to call out to the approaching
sheriff's clan.

As Ben himself points out, one way to distinguish zombies from people
is their absence of intelligible speech. In the heated racial context of the late
1960s (one that included the assassination of Martin Luther King mere months
before the film's release), Ben's suspicious glare of stony silence is entirely appropriate to the black man's encounter with white law enforcement. Yet in this
case, Ben's principled refusal to ingratiate himself leads to his death. Standing
motionless before the window of the house, he is read by the posse as "no different from" the all-white hordes of zombies now mostly contained (by shots
to the head) by the closing scenes of the film. He is shot mistakenly as one of
them and destroyed democratically on their same funeral pyre. While surely the
film would take a deeply ironic stance upon the manner in which Ben at last
achieves equality with his white fellow-citizens, the sharpness of the political

statement is mitigated by the instigation of a classic horror cliché—of the culpably stupid behavior (often enacted by a hysterical white female) that fatally endangers the actor in question. Such behavior always elicits a sense of got-what-s/he-deserved from knowing members of the audience, who would surely have more sense than to go into the basement, pick up the phone, hide in the closet, or do whatever the benighted on-screen figure has insisted upon doing. Here, the degree to which Ben's death is his own misguided fault undermines the nature of his sacrifice by making it seem avoidable and pointless.

Dawn of the Dead (1978)

As noted earlier, African American male actors have played significant roles in each installment in Romero's *Dead* series. Even when they star as zombies, as in *Land of the Dead* (2005), they quit themselves sympathetically; more often they are smart, effective leaders and striking physical specimens—those fittest to survive in the man-eat-man environment characterizing each film. Exemplary is actor Ken Foree who plays Peter in *Dawn of the Dead*. Many critics have remarked upon the moral and intellectual superiority of Peter to his white male counterparts, Roger and Stephen, each of whom makes a fatal move related to his over-fondness for the mall-turf they have secured for themselves, and all its worthless treasures. As opposed to Stephen who is a poor shot and over-solicitous of his girlfriend Fran, and as opposed to Roger who is sophomoric and gratuitously violent, Peter strikes a balance between masculine prowess and enlightened respect for the only woman in the group. Additionally, he is a head taller than either of the other men, broad in his shoulders and light on his feet; Stephen Harper reads the sexual subtext of Peter and Stephen's raid of a gourmet grocery store, during which the two comically compare the modest loaf of bread found by Stephen to the enormous specimen discovered by Peter. While Foree thus has the physical dimensions that practically destine him for the role of romantic lead—and father of a new civilization—the connection between himself and Fran as they at last escape together is ambiguous at best.

Critics tend to find against their romantic prospects, yet fail to question the film's own unfounded assumptions as they do. Kim Paffenroth at first reads Peter and Fran's pairing in terms of "the forbidden love on screen in 1978 and even in the early twenty-first century, . . . heterosexual romance, love, and sex between blacks and whites, especially between a black man and a white woman" (63). Later, however, she notes that "most importantly, . . . Fran is pregnant with Steve's (white) child, not Peter's. Whatever their relationship may develop into, Peter's first role will be as a stepfather to another man's child" (65). Here Paffenroth adopts the traditional Hollywood (and society-wide) idea that pregnant women are sexually untouchable, that Fran's "(white) child" somehow protects her from Peter's advances or prevents the two from falling in love. Again, this is readable as the film's own take on the final status of their relationship but one that is easily open to challenge. Elsewhere Gregory A. Waller reads these two "not [as] the traditional heterosexual couple" but as forming "potentially a new type of partnership" (321) based on their shared history of oppression in a "racist and sexist society" (322). Instead it is "Fran and Stephen [who] come closest to filling the role of the new Adam and Eve" (321), but with Stephen lying dead with a bullet in his head the regenerative prospects for this Adam and Eve are indeed grim. By contrast, Robin Wood promotes the *Dead* series' subversion of heterosexual romance and the nuclear family. His insistence that "the film eschews any hint of a traditional happy ending, there being no suggestion of any romantic attachment developing between the survivors" (121) has less to do with his inability to see Peter and Fran as romantically involved than with his disinclination to see successful heterosexual couplings anywhere in the film. Corroborating Wood's bleak opinion is the ending originally scripted, in which Peter was to shoot himself in the head and Fran to stand up into the blades of the helicopter that enables their escape; immediately thereafter, the blades would stop rotating, indicating only a minuscule amount of fuel left anyway.

Indeed, the film does little to forge a bond between the two when they are finally alone in the world together. With zombies breaking into their innermost sanctuary, Peter announces that he is staying behind, likely to make a heroic last stand then commit suicide. Fran makes no effort to talk him out of it, only cries out "Oh, my God!" and climbs the ladder to the landing pad. While she hesitates there for several moments, this seems more a suspense device, as the undead charge the ladder and close in upon her, than any gesture of devotion or bereavement. When Peter finally decides to join Fran in the waiting chopper, he inexplicably jumps into the backseat instead of up front beside Fran. While Peter has occupied this left rear seat on each previous occasion in the helicopter, there seems no reason for him to do so again, now that the others are gone. For he has also sat directly beside Fran (also in the backseat—before she learned to fly the chopper herself) on each preceding flight, and to not resume that orientation at this time makes the two seem more estranged than they were upon first meeting. While it is assumed that Fran has the faculties adequate to fly her vehicle until it runs out of gas, one cannot help but question both her mental acuity and her eyesight at this moment; Peter is an ideal mate under any circumstances, yet the film prevents her from seeing this while absurdly sending him to the back of the bus.

The Omega Man (1971)

The World, the Flesh, and the Devil is readable as the unofficial forebear of several films actually descended from another source, Richard Matheson's science fiction novel *I Am Legend* (1954). The first, starring Vincent Price, was *The Last Man on Earth* (1964), and two more recent remakes are *The Omega*

Man (1971), starring Charlton Heston, and *I Am Legend* (2007), starring Will Smith. It is especially these two latter two films that continue the tradition established by *The World, the Flesh, and the Devil* and others considered here by returning in meaningful ways to the subject of interracial relations (sexual and otherwise) in a post-apocalyptic environment. In both *Omega Man* and *I Am Legend*, an interracial couple is posited (and in the earlier film realized) as a fitting response—even solution—to the disaster created when a waste-laying virus runs amok in the human population. (In Matheson's novel, the origin of terrifying vampiric mutations is nuclear [56], changed to a biomedical catastrophe in Price's *Last Man on Earth*. *Omega Man* includes shades of both, attributing the mutations to nuclear and biological warfare between China and Russia.) There are no identifiably African American characters in either Matheson's original novel or the 1964 film version, yet the analogy between the mid-century "Negro Problem" and the story's marauding vampires is clear. This novel also inspired *Night of the Living Dead* (Romero 6), and Heffernan strengthens the link by observing that "Ben's eventual fate . . . recall[s] a passage in the novel *I Am Legend*. One of Robert Neville's drunken interior monologues concerns what he calls the 'minority prejudice' against vampires" (72; see also Waller 275–80). In fact both the novel and the 1964 film version look ironically at the banalities of suburban home life and home maintenance in the face of catastrophic invasion from this unwanted, contaminated "minority element" (31). While in the novel protagonist Neville sympathizes with these pathetic lost souls, the racial connection—and the racial joke—is explicit when he sheds crocodile tears over the vampire who "cannot . . . live where he chooses" and "has no means of support, no measure for proper education, and no voting franchise," then cracks "but would you want your sister to marry one?" (32).

Reversing the gender dynamics of that racist chestnut, Neville himself deals with overwhelming sexual attraction to various female vampires in the novel yet understands that any such coupling would be infectious, even deadly. The taboo nature of the proposition is analogous to the emphatically forbidden act of interracial sex during that period. Also customary for its time, the novel flings about the expression "black" as a reference to extreme evil or doom, as when Neville refers to the (in fact quite pale, bloodless) vampires as "the black bastards" (35) and a hysterical preacher calls the same group "black unholy animal[s]" rising from "black tombs" (113). As opposed to all of the other films discussed in this chapter, wherein African American characters play sexually magnetic roles of heroic proportions, Matheson's novel taps into the hysterical white zeitgeist of his mid-1950s context with his vision of atomic-crazed vampires (urban refugees following nuclear war? urban black children bused to "white" schools?) who invade a middle-class suburb. Fears of sexual mayhem triggered by this invasion are suggested but controlled through Neville's iron fortitude—and through careful exclusion of the prospect of one's "sister marry[ing] one," that is, of any sexual tension between uninfected women and vampiric men.

While the first film adaptation, *The Last Man on Earth*, is largely silent on the issue of race relations in a post-disaster context, its first remake, *The Omega Man*, is intent on consummating the interracial coupling that occurred for the hero of Matheson's novel only by analogy and only in dreams. Specifically, *Omega Man* departs meaningfully from the pattern that has shaped this discussion, in that the lead African American character is female, not male. As per my reading of the sexually significant Connie Davy in Philip Wylie's *Triumph*—and also as per my reading of the lovely mulatta Em in George Stewart's *Earth Abides*, who sexually partners with the white male protagonist to become "Mother of Nations" (see Chapter 1)—here again we find a strong correlation between an attractive black female and the realization of the interracial romance; even in the liberated early 1970s, filmgoers were evidently still more inclined toward the sexual pairing of a black woman and white man than of the opposite racial/sexual configuration. While Lisa (played by the no-nonsense blaxploitation favorite Rosalind Cash) is indeed domineering and tough, she has a softer maternal/sexual side and serves as the typical Hollywood fantasy icon for her (male) viewers and her leading man. Her relationship with her white costar Charlton Heston is frankly depicted, as there is much more nudity in this film—Cash exposes her breasts and backside for a long scene, and the camera found any excuse to shoot Heston with his shirt off—than in PG-13 films of today. Two climactic scenes involve gunfights over possession of Lisa, one between Neville and Brother Zachary, an African American member of the albino-zombie Mansonesque "Family," and one between Neville and the Family's guru, a white man called Matthias. Lisa is thus a universal object of desire, although the Family desires to control her mind while only Neville seems interested to possess her sexually and—as some jokes about the absurdity of birth control pills make clear—start a new world of people in partnership with her. By film's end, Neville has been killed by a spear from the Luddite Mathias, but Lisa—perhaps impregnated with Neville's child—will go on. Interestingly, some reviewers rejected the film's sexual themes, including Tom Shales, who asked that Heston's future contracts eliminate the clause "that says he has to spend much of his screen time in some degree of undress," and Paine Knickerbocker, who read the love affair between Cash and Heston as "simply laughable because its timing is so bad, its execution so banal, so clumsy, so hopelessly obligatory." For many, as with reviewers of *World* and *Five*, the haunting cityscape that figures prominently in the opening scenes was more interesting than the melodrama constituting the main action (see "Summary," Knickerbocker, and Kerbel).

The film echoes several scenes from *The World, the Flesh, and the Devil*, including Neville "stealing" a car and driving it through the broken showroom window and later shouting out for help to an empty world, his voice echoing in broken takes from one abandoned locale to another. (In *World*, a tolling church bell resonates across multiple images of New York's stone lions.) Meanwhile, the irony and comedy of the "marauding male" element is handled differently; instead of the threat supposedly presented by the angry black man storming the city, the film opens with Heston cruising the streets of LA (not New York) in a convertible, enjoying easy-listening jazz on his radio. At one point, he spies a Family member dashing behind some blinds in an office building window. The lilting music is interrupted by the barrage of Heston's automatic weapon, then resumes when the shooting is over. Here, therefore, the joke is inverted; this intriguing man at the wheel does not ascend from thug to humanitarian but instead takes periodic breaks from his role as unruffled playboy to shoot out a few windows. In a scene from *World* mixing comedy and pathos, Ralph flirts with a white mannequin he has pilfered from a department store to keep himself company; echoing this moment Neville finds himself surrounded by several female forms in a lingerie shop, where he also has his "cute meet" with Lisa, who freezes in a provocative pose to escape detection. Yet where *World*'s white mannequins remain stonily indifferent to Ralph's advances, only emphasizing his difference and solitude, for the white male star of *Omega Man*, the encounter with feminine forms underscores Neville's (and Heston's) sex-symbol persona and leads to real human connection.

I Am Legend (2007)

The 2007 version of this franchise, at last named for its originating novel, *I Am Legend* returns the action from Los Angeles not to the suburban hinterland of Matheson's story but the majestic ruins of New York, harking back once more to *The World, the Flesh, and the Devil*. Its villains are a horde of crazed "Infecteds," stricken by a mutated cancer cure and pitted against Will Smith and his female costar. For the first time she is not a helpless blond but the poised and sensible Ana, played by Brazilian actress Alice Braga. Where *Omega* opened with Heston cruising LA to light FM, *Legend* begins with Smith's unidentified character careening through New York in a late-model Ford Mustang—past empty cars, overgrown weeds, and a pervasive atmosphere of urban decay—with a menacing look on his face. His seemingly dangerous behavior recalls Belafonte's shooting spree through the Financial District, while, reminiscent of Ben's early actions in *Night of the Living Dead*, he will soon break into well-appointed houses, though only to commandeer their edible and medicinal contents.

Enhancing Smith's "criminal" profile are the words of the promethean Dr. Alice Krippen, (played by Emma Thompson) who describes her cancer virus to a TV newscaster as "a very fast car driven by a very bad man" that she has managed to transform into a cure—that is, "to replace that [bad] man by a cop." While the story will soon demonstrate the egregious inaccuracy of her boast, in this early scene, a "bad man" is indeed transformed before our eyes into a "cop," as the shot of Smith on a rampage behind the wheel moves left to include his faithful German shepherd (the traditional K-9 patrol partner) on the seat beside him. Whether or not Smith is in fact on some sort of post-apocalyptic police patrol, the dog humanizes the menace he suggests: at the very least, he is a citizen solid enough to maintain a family pet. Sure enough, Sam is his family's dog, left with him by his wife and daughter as they were being swept to safety by a military helicopter on the night of the catastrophic outbreak. And, it is revealed, Neville is not speeding on an angry vendetta or destructive joyride but in pursuit of fresh meat for his dinner, as now wild animals roam freely through the stopped cars and ruined storefronts of lower Manhattan. That Neville refrains from shooting a deer, which suddenly succumbs to attack by a mountain lion, nor even the lion, whose cubs appear at the curb, further validates his character. Clearly he is on the side of life, and the fast car and massive personal armory he wields are read as self-protective only and ultimately unnecessary.

Another citation of Belafonte's film involves the role of (white) mannequins as comic but pathetically inadequate human stand-ins. In *World*, Ralph brings home both a female and male dummy, comically flirting with "Betsy" yet bothered by "Snodgrass's" permanent smug smile, patent indicators of conflicts to come.[8] With yet more pointed racial overtones, Ralph finally determines that "You look at me but you don't see me. You've laughed at me once too often." Their "argument" results in Ralph throwing Snodgrass over the balcony of his high-rise apartment; it is his "death" that draws Sarah from hiding, who cries out in terror at the thought that Ralph himself has gone over the ledge. In *Legend* Neville populates a video store with fashionably dressed mannequins, with which he interacts to comic effect on his daily visits for more DVDs. (Like the multi-talented Ralph, he is a technological mastermind, who has rigged his home with electricity, plumbing, and food supplies despite the ruination around him.) As does Ralph in *World*, Neville flirts with one of the female figures and blows up at a male figure—whom he has named "Fred"—in a key scene in which Fred has been moved from his post in front of the video store, eliciting a panicky outburst from Neville who suddenly realizes that he is not alone.

Legend's mannequins are not only European-featured but are also well toned and painted a stark, flat white. They are therefore eerily suggestive of the film's rampaging Infecteds, who are racialized by their symptomatic "lack of pigment," bald heads, stark Aryan features, and menacing facial gestures (made even more grotesque by digital animation). While their population is large and chaotic, the film confronts its hero with the same adversary—named Alpha Male in the cast list—again and again. Whether this figure purposely stalks Neville or always fortuitously crosses his path, the original impression, this viewer's at any rate, was that Neville encountered—as would happen naturally in this large, unregulated cityscape—random groups of deadly zombies whose main players nevertheless always look exactly alike. The indistinguishable features of what had once been a variety of facial, gender, and perhaps even racial types reads as the diminishing effect of the virus itself, while the filmic effect is to boil these myriad humanoid figures into a monolithic, colorless all-color threat to the African American protagonist. Thus Neville is locked in a decidedly racialized conflict with these zombie figures, primarily through the marked whitening and homogenizing of the adversaries themselves.[9]

Significantly, the film is racialized even to its color scheme. Out in the world of deadly infection—though not infectiousness as Neville has innate immunity—the protagonist is always dressed in black and appears in all subsequent scenes behind the wheel of a black Ford Expedition. At home, specifically in the basement where he has created a fully-functioning laboratory, he moves through a white world (lit by bright fluorescent bulbs) in his white lab coat, having traded his "black" role of rampaging thug for the "white" role of world-class scientist. Of course the film is savvy enough to ironize this dichotomy—for Neville is both the hero-thug and hero-researcher and enacts both roles out of complete selflessness: offered a chance to flee with his family early in the film, he insists on staying at "ground zero" where he can test possible antidotes to KV made from his own blood. In his basement lab, he pursues scientific understanding even when all hope seems lost. Experimenting on a sexually attractive female Infected, whom he has captured and bound to his examination table, Neville undoes the sexual threat posed by the Mad Scientist by substituting infusion for insemination and maintaining strict professional decorum. Following injection with a potential cure, his patient's breasts heave and her face contorts, but the titillation provided to the filmgoer is solemnly ignored by the scientifically neutral Neville, who recognizes her gyrations not as sexual excitement but the throes of death.

Patrick Sharp has studied the theme of technological aptitude—and the morality of good versus bad technologies—in many nuclear texts of the postwar period; though Neville kills his patient during the course of the experiment, he yet wields a technology that is read as morally upright in that it strives for a cure and in that it comes between him and the impulses that any less scientific man might act upon with the sexualized, subjugated female he stands over. Only when he is forced to euthanize Sam following a bite from Infected wolves does Neville lose both his scientist's cool and his humanitarian disposition. He furiously challenges a clan of Infecteds in a vengeful attempt to run them off the edge of the South Street Seaport. At this climactic moment, and reminiscent of a key conflict in Romero's *Night*, interracial hostility is explicit as the black hero pits himself against a gang of maniacal skinheads in a death struggle.

As they overpower him and cause his SUV to pitch into the river, Neville is rescued by the soulful South American Ana, yet again arriving by water and guiding a white American boy to what she hopes is a safe haven in Vermont. Ana is as sexy and available as she is earnest and maternal, yet curiously this modern film is as reticent with respect to consummating the sexual prospects of the black male hero as was the Belafonte film many decades ago. *Legend* defuses the sexual spark between Neville and Ana by introducing a key piece of ancient history just as she enters the scene. In a flashback, Neville revisits the fateful night of his wife and daughter's departure. In an earlier reenactment, we saw their helicopter clear the ground and made the assumption that they were somewhere safe and waiting for him; in the second flashback, we see that in fact moments after its ascent the helicopter collides with another departing chopper and spins into the water. Although Neville has known this tragic story all along, it is only introduced here for the first time. The audience grieves for the loss, and Neville's grief is fresh as well; he assumes a monkish disinterest in Ana that turns into anger at her naïve faith in a northern safe zone. Just before his final encounter with the Alpha Male and the other Infecteds—he will do them in with a self-sacrificing hand grenade—Neville stashes Ana and the boy safely in a coal chute, passing her a vial of his own curative blood. Echoing the earlier scene with his experimental Infected, he functions as Ana's doctor instead of her lover; the gesture is a weak figuration, and no substitute whatever, for the restorative sex act they might have engaged in but inexplicably fail to do.

CONCLUSION: WHEN COOL IS NOT HOT

It is a tradition for black characters in Hollywood films (and even, evidently, in independent films like Romero's) to never lose their cool, even when the world is about to end. Even the contemptuous Brother Zachary from *Omega Man* is never seen engaging in any of the ridiculous scenes of attack and ambush that occupy the cult's minor characters; Lisa makes some narrow escapes and has some good action sequences but is too tough and streetwise to ever descend into the emotional breakdown or the foolish missteps characteristic of panic behavior. Of course *Night of the Living Dead*'s Ben dies for being too calm and collected to call out to the approaching sheriff's men—in Mailer's parlance we could read this as a literal instance of tragic hipness—and Duane Jones, Ken Foree, and Will Smith all turn in determined but understated performances in their respective *Dead* and *Legend* films. Fittingly, they are all rewarded with survival-'til-film's-end for keeping cool heads in difficult situations, although such remarkable coolness never pays out into the expected hotness—the sexual attractiveness that would win them the companionship of these films' attractive leading ladies.

Indeed, the disinclination of Will Smith's Dr. Neville to partner with the beautiful and willing female set in his path mirrors regrettably the same lack of interest that cloaked the figure of angelic Paulus Davy back in Philip Wylie's novel of forty years previous. Notably, both men's persistent grief over the death of beloved wives prevents them, so the story goes, from making new connections, even though such connections might prove vital to the survival of humankind. While many another narrative has used the device of the assuredly dead wife (instead of the simply missing but possibly still alive wife) to enable the story's Good Man to love again, in both cases here the wife's passing is a permanent barrier between the heroic African American figure and the fertile women at his fingertips. In each of the texts considered in this chapter, the sexual magnetism—or at least the moral superiority—of the black male protagonist is on display; in many cases, this alluring figure elicits a pointedly sexual response from the blond, white female counterpart in his charge (e.g., Sarah, Barbra), only to send her panic-stricken into the arms of the white male love interest (even, as in Barbra's case, if this is her own brother) by story's end.

As Mailer observed at the beginning of this discussion, the black male figure is an unstoppable source of vital energy—in the case of Belafonte's Ralph, Duane Jones's Ben, and Will Smith's Neville, this involves actually keeping the lights on—but in all cases this energy flow is cut off before it can reach the regenerative sexual parts of the women the civilization in question depends upon his coupling with. As with Wylie's African American characters in *Triumph*, "sexuality" and "nobility" are mutually exclusive categories for the film leads, with noble self-sacrifice winning out over sexual self-interest and securing these lead characters' heroic profiles thereby. Instead, the black male figure fuels the sexual prospects of the white characters in the story, much as I had observed the black characters functioning mainly as servants in the cause of white post-nuclear survival in Chapter 1 (see also Gabbard 6–9, 150). Ralph, as de facto Mayor of New York, literally presides over the union of Sarah and Ben, in *Five* Charles gives his life so that that Roseanne can partner first with Eric and then Michael, and Smith's Dr. Neville fathers a new nation of uninfected survivors but only clinically, not sexually speaking. Thus the specifically sexual potency of these characters is repeatedly underscored, but this sexual energy must be rerouted through the bodies of the story's white survivors, a theme that has regrettably varied little since the inception of the atomic age sixty years ago.

Conclusion

"Don't Drop It, Stop It, Bebop It": Some Final Notes on Race, Place, and the Atom Bomb in Postwar America

In January 1951, the Los Angeles R&B artist Frankie Ervin recorded "I'd Rather Live like a Hermit," in which he informs some "jive cats standing on the corner" that they had "better find some place to hide, / Because when those bombs start falling, / You gonna jump right out o' your hide." Ervin's "Hermit" is one of dozens of atomic-themed novelty songs performed by African American gospel, R&B, and pop acts—and a memorable Calypso band from Bermuda, the Talbot Brothers—during the postwar decades; in this same time period white gospel groups as well as country, rockabilly, and folk singers recorded scores more, and at least one of these tunes, the hugely popular "Jesus Hits Like an Atom Bomb," was originally recorded by Lowell Blanchard's white gospel group but became a staple amongst black gospel artists from then on. Yet Ervin's single stands out in this array for being one of the few to address the bomb as an actual threat and to suggest appropriate reaction ("i.e., find[ing] some place to hide"). Notably the Talbot Brothers also look directly upon zero hour by announcing that they have "just heard from a little bird / that they're going to drop the atomic bomb." In response, each is planning to "run, run, run, like a son of a gun / I don't know where I'm going to go, / but I'm really going to run."

While it is not possible, within the silent medium of printed text, to audition the hard-driving R&B styling of Ervin's tune, nor the toe-tapping rhythms of the Talbot Brothers' flat-out delightful "Atomic Nightmare" (1957), one can discern from the lyrics themselves that the artists in each are having a bit of fun, in keeping with the lighthearted, social-satiric tradition of the novelty song, even when the subject is nuclear attack. In Ervin's "Hermit," the racial dynamic is especially pronounced, such that not simply human survival but the specific survival of African Americans is at stake: the "jive cats" on the corner are enjoined to hide, the listener is later referred to as "brother" (who "better dig just what I say"), and a specifically urban audience is addressed as a whole, who "better get out of that city, / When the bombs come tumbling down." Throughout this book, the urban setting has been read for both its concentration of African Americans and US ethnic minorities and its likelihood as ground zero during nuclear attack. In "Hermit" Ervin sings that the doom of heavily African American cities such as LA is imminent and that he will be forced to flee to "the woods" as a "hermit," two traditionally white habitations that suggest as well the incineration of modern black culture and identity. Though Arthur "Big Boy" Crudup sings also in 1951 that "I might dig myself a hole / Move my baby down in the ground," by the end of the song his baby has rejected the prospect of shelter existence and left the blues singer bereft of all comforts—"My baby leavin' me and I'm leavin' out my home"—due to atomic emergency.

Finally, however, such serious subject matter in a song ultimately intended for bumping and grinding or snapping and tapping—and as always for chart-topping and million-selling—is a rare phenomenon, as the vast majority of atomic novelties of the postwar period looked obliquely upon the atomic threat when they considered the atomic as threatening at all. As was the case with various contributors to the black press during this period (see Chapter 3) and various black intellectuals who spoke out as well (see Chapter 4), the bomb was often an effective metaphor for modernity, scientific enlightenment, democracy, and equality, or—on the flipside of this proposition—unbridled sexuality or political derring-do. As many of the writers and thinkers discussed in this book looked to the dawn of the atomic age to bring an all-around fairer tomorrow, so the entertainers and artists considered in this conclusion accentuated the hip, swinging, and/or sexually fulfilling aspects of the atomic "boom" in their popular songs. These diverse approaches will therefore helpfully summarize many of my main arguments regarding the African American response to the bomb throughout this project—and restate once more that the African American position on this subject was multifold and ever-changing.

The emphasis in popular music on the sexual and romantic prospects afforded by entry into the atomic age is not surprising. While various atomic-era novelists, filmmakers, social scientists, and ordinary Americans looked with concern, even hysteria, toward an atomic-doomsday sexual free-for-all, it is only Norman Mailer—and Bill Haley and his Comets—of those discussed so far who eagerly anticipate this event. Indeed, Haley's "Thirteen Women (and Only One Man in Town)" is one of the many atomic novelty songs whose main purpose is not to frighten or inform but to get people up on the dance floor—and in the mood for sexual activity after their night on the town. If almost all popular music is about romance failed or successful, the artists who produced postwar-era atomic pop were no exception. Performances by black artists of the 1950s and 1960s ran the gamut from the lilting tones of Little Caesar's "Atomic Love" (1953) and the harmless doo-wop of the clean-cut Cuff Links's "Guided Missiles" (1956) to the more suggestive stylings of Linda Hayes, who covered Amos Milburn's "Atomic Baby" (Milburn 1950, Hayes

1953) with a sultry flattening of the "a" in "atomic," and Fay Simmons whose diversely futuristic (and regrettably never-released) "You Hit Me Baby Like An Atomic Bomb" (1954) celebrates "a radioactive feeling in my knees," "flying off into space," "supersonics," and "find[ing] a new world." When she sings to her baby that their atomic lovemaking will enable them to start a "super race," we are returned to the get-even dreams of Langston Hughes, who fantasized in his columns for the *Chicago Defender* about the atom bomb leaving behind a race of African supermen (see Chapter 3) and to the broader theme of atomic power leveling class distinctions in US society.

In several of the atomic novelties issued by both black and white artists of the period, the atomic metaphor is all but dispensed with once the trendy bomb-themed title has done its attention-getting work. H-Bomb Ferguson, so named by his producers for his explosive singing style, produced the R&B styled "H-Bomb Rock" (1952), which refers only once to "that rockin' bomb" and repeats its one-line refrain "Rock, H-Bomb Rock" so frequently (every other line) that it soon becomes meaningless. The Jewels's "B. Bomb Baby" (1956) is another R&B track whose main point is to extol the virtues of the eponymous baby who is "not too short" and "not too tall." Though the listener may pause to wonder what a "B. Bomb" is in the first place, this listener soon stops caring and returns to enjoying the danceable beat. Various instrumentals of the period, including Dexter Gordon's "Bikini" (1947) and Clarence "Gatemouth" Brown's "Atomic Energy" (1949), bore no special significance to their atomic context beyond the topical title; as Bill Geerhart, whose comprehensive overview of atomic music in this period has been essential to my research at every stage in this conclusion, reports, "most of the songs recorded for small jazz labels of this era had no titles when they were recorded—artists would simply record and then abdicate the naming process to producers" (213), who applied any name they thought would sell. The Slim Gaillard Quartette's early, jazzy "Atomic Cocktail" (1946) is loaded with references to its immediate post-Hiroshima moment but is, like these later tunes, notably indifferent to the atomic threat, or even to the particulars of atomic power. Geerhart observes,

> while Hiroshima and Nagasaki still glowed, the attitude of this comical tune mirrors the blissful ignorance of the western world to the true horror unleashed on Japan. Additionally, [Gaillard's] lyric, "*push a button, turn a dial, your work is done for miles and miles*" reflects the popular notion of the day that the bomb had ushered in a carefree new era of easier living—not to mention killing—through science. (90)

Like the more romantic fare from singers of the 1950s, Gaillard's piece sets a swinging mood with his tribute to the atomic cocktail, which lounges nationwide hastened to concoct while Americans remained in the throes of victory celebrations.

Yet another thematic tradition is the patriotic (even jingoistic) homage to the bomb, its deleterious effects on the "Japs" that enabled World War II soldiers to come home when they did, and later in the atomic cra its message sent to the new enemy Stalin, frequently referred to in condescending fashion as "Joe."[1] It was especially white country and gospel performers who adopted this swaggering style with respect to American exceptionalism and vigorous anti-communism.[2] Yet just as various members of the black press adopted a jingoistic stance immediately following the close of the Second World War, so, for instance, did country blues artist Homer Harris who mock-laments the plight of "poor Tojo [who] had to find a place to hide" at the end of "Atomic Bomb Blues" (1946). As Guido van Rijn, another valuable resource for this conclusion, observes, "Tojo personified the Japanese foe for the blues singers and there are many blues records referring to him, but very few which mention Emperor Hirohito" (30). Though the title (and tone) of Harris's piece suggest sadness about the bomb's detonation, in fact the soldier-narrator assures his baby that he is physically safely (and, we may assume, staunchly politically) "behind the atom bomb" and coming home to her soon. As I have considered the importance of place and positioning with respect to the atomic threat since the introduction to this book, Harris's lyric makes it plain that the pro-atomic position—backing the bomb all the way, or perhaps even riding it to Western victory—contrasts the anti-atomic viewpoint that, as in the lyrics of Frankie Ervin and Arthur Cruddup, emphasizes the plight of those positioned beneath the bomb, directly in its path.

As in the black press, however, overtly bomb-loving viewpoints are rare within the canon of postwar African American popular music; even when Roosevelt Sykes addresses "Sputnik Baby" to "Mr. Khrushchev," it is not in order to threaten him with atomic destruction but to brag about how his girlfriend is "faster" and more stylish than any "hound / dog crew"—a reference to "Laika, the first canine cosmonaut" (Geerhart 90)—the Soviets will ever put into orbit. While Louisiana Red challenges both Khrushchev and Castro to a fight, the weapon brandished is pointedly not a hydrogen bomb but "a bat / with your head for a ball," since Red insists in this Missile Crisis track that the two communist dictators dismantle their atomic arms. Titled "Red's Dream," the song is yet another get-even fantasy during which the singer imagines being asked for advice by JFK and telling the president that he can run the country, but "I'm going to run the Senate / Oughtta make a few changes / With a few soul brothers in it." Yet as in the African American press, when the Cuban crisis inspired the call to "rally 'round" JFK in patriotic tones reminiscent of the immediate post-WWII moment, Bo Diddley's gung-ho "Mr. Khrushchev" (1962) works almost as propaganda for the Armed Forces, opening with "I think I want to join the Army (hut 2, 3, 4) / I think I want to go overseas (hut 2, 3, 4)." Diddley reminds his listeners that "JFK can't do it by his self" and echoes the mantra of preparedness planners, to "keep on alert" and protect families whether from home or abroad. In "Overseas Blues," "Memphis" Willie Borum remembered in that same era how glad he was when MacArthur told Eisenhower that the atomic bombing of Japan meant that "Your boys don't have to come." Meanwhile, there is almost no explaining "Hammers and Sickles," a romantically vocalized side from the Charades that comes so late in both the anti-nuclear and civil rights eras (1966) that its right-wing jingoism seems utterly misplaced. With lyrics complaining that "hammers and sickles would see freedom dead" and kissing off the girl in "Teen Angel" fashion with "Don't cry as I leave you tonight / I don't want to go but I'm sure that you know / That our country's in danger and I need to fight," the Charades also effected a "white" vocal style with careful pronunciation and dramatically drawn out notes. One wonders if this group's name is a telling indicator—that the act was some sort ironic put-on of styles long past.

Coincidentally, the period of 1945 to 1965 has been termed a "Golden Age" for both pulp science fiction (see Chapter 2) and gospel music; as with the science fiction, the bomb may have been instrumental in the postwar boom in gospel. No less a personage than Thomas A. Dorsey, bedrock of the Chicago-gospel movement, suggested to Lerone Bennett Jr. that "the 'transitions of time' are largely responsible for the return to the gospel tradition. . . . 'It's the age. The Atomic Age. People are scared. They want something to turn to'" ("The Soul of Soul" 118, 120). Thus the gospel tradition, as we saw in some of Martin Luther King Jr.'s remarkable sermons in Chapter 4, presents itself as a haven from anxiety and has little room in it for doom and despair. As King placed faith in God as the "eternal fallout shelter," so various gospel acts in the late 1940s and early 1950s established a relationship between the atomic threat and the power of God that took a variety of permutations. Here I mean to nuance the worthy readings of several commentators already published on this subject, including atomic novelty specialist Geerhart, blues scholar van Rijn, and country music expert Charles K. Wolfe, who refer almost always to this relationship as "metaphorical." While it is the case that several country, blues, and gospel songs directly identify the bomb as a modern manifestation of "God's mighty hand," in many instances, this relationship is less harmonious than dissonant.

The contest, if you will, is on display in the title of Arval Hogan and Roy Grant's (aka Whitey and Hogan's) country hit, "There is a Power Greater than Atomic." As Wolfe records, this piece was written in direct response to Fred Kirby's early instant classic, "Atomic Power," in which the bomb is indeed referred to as "brimstone fire" and as issuing directly from God. While the conservative message in Kirby's song is plain—God wanted us to destroy "the Japs"—Whitey and Hogan step even further to the right by, according to Wolfe, writing a "deliberate sequel" to their friend Kirby's song and recalling their audience from daily cares to spiritual matters. The effect, however, cannot but be to diminish if not undermine the "atomic power" so fervently praised by Kirby and by many God-fearing Americans of the era. Whitey and Hogan almost taunt atomic scientists, "So when you're planning power that will melt away the sod, / Don't forget there is no power to equal that of God." Later they recall the "targets left" during the Bikini tests of 1946, when "only five of ninety target ships were sunk" (Wolfe 114). Wolfe observes that "two Americans especially impressed with the ships' survival were Whitey and Hogan" (114), such that one must wonder how this song—let alone their faith—might have fared differently had the ratio been any better. At any rate, we will hear this challenging, even troubling, refrain in many of the black gospel performances to be examined as well: when a devout musical group insists that the bomb is "nothing" compared to the mighty power of God, the listener already thoroughly versed in the realities of atomic destruction must take a great leap.

One of the earliest African American gospel acts to record an atomic theme was the widely regarded, jubilee-styled Golden Gate Quartet, whose "Atom and Evil" (1947)—from its comically punning title on—has more in common with a laid back, jazzed up vocal such as Gaillard's "Atomic Cocktail" than with the "brimstone" motifs and intonations of the typical gospel hymn; Horace Boyer points out that jubilee groups were often "heavily influenced by popular music" (34). The ultra-cool harmonies are reminiscent of the Mills Brothers' (a noted Gates influence [Buchanan 15]), and the lighthearted lyrics—"Now if Evil gets Atom, 'twill be such a shame / "Because a-plenty of big shots are playin' that dame"—seem almost heretical, even though standard fare in the jubilee format. Other jubilee elements, such as the vocal colorings—the refrain "boom, boom, boom, boom" plucked out in syncopated fashion by the bass singer like notes on a stand-up bass and the closing "doom, doom, doom, doom!" pealed out in harmonic thirds—seem simply too much fun for a gospel rendition of the end of the world. As with Gaillard's early "Atomic Cocktail," it is as if the seriousness of the atomic threat had simply not fully dawned upon the performing artists of the immediate postwar period. Though they do it very differently than did Whitey and Hogan, this song also tends to diminish the threat posed by the bomb through its plentiful wit and verve (see also Buchanan 12–16).

Two black gospel songs from the early H-bomb era enlarge the "God's holy weapon" theme introduced by Kirby in his early "Atomic Power." While an oft-repeated word in the Strangers Quartet's "The Atomic Age" (1949) is "peace," the song's final verse, which provides the basic narrative of World War II, explicitly equates this peace with "the atomic," revealed by God "to man" (i.e., to Americans) and instrumental in realizing His declaration that "dictators shall not stand." The top-rated Pilgrim Travelers debuted the notably militaristic "Jesus is the First Line of Defense" (1951), which gets tangled up in all of the biblical contradictions involving the "Christian soldier" and "might makes right." Without a note of irony, the Travelers sing "We're gonna build

big armies and arm to the teeth, / Tell the other nations that we want peace."
In both the Strangers' "Atomic Age" and in this "battle of Jericho"-themed
track from the Travelers (see van Rijn 37), God refers to Himself as the "Prince
of Peace" right before blowing the reds to kingdom come.

While the title of Swan's Silvertone Singers' "Jesus is God's Atomic Bomb"
certainly bespeaks a metaphoric relationship between the two entities named
therein, the lyrics reveal that this is another contest song, the Victor of which
we do not have to wonder about. Early on in this majestic ballad, the Singers
make the distinction plain: "the blast in Japan . . . can kill your body / But the
Lord can kill your soul," while in more merciful guise, He "Shook the grave,
causing death to run," winning out over the bomb's power to kill. Another contest song from this canon was also its greatest hit, "Jesus Hits Like an Atom
Bomb," originally recorded by the white gospel group Lowell Blanchard
and the Valley Trio (1950) but performed successfully by numerous African
American acts into the present day. Geerhart notes that the Pilgrim Travelers's
version is considerably "less harsh than the Lowell Blanchard country version" (148), that the Blanchard rendition is "full of brimstone and acts as an
admonition to those who are more concerned about earthly peril (caused by
the Bomb) than the second coming and salvation" (72). Yet I find Blanchard's
version to be much peppier and more danceable—complete with instrumental breakdown between several stanzas—than the more urgently intoned renditions performed not only by the Travelers in 1951 but by the Soul Stirrers
and Charming Bells in 1950 and even by the Blind Boys of Alabama as the
title track of their 2005 release *Atom Bomb*. Notably, each African American
version dispenses with musical accompaniment. By far the most popular style
(effected by the Travelers, Stirrers, Bells) is *a cappella*, and even the Blind Boys
add only a restrained drum beat. In 2004 Chanticleer (a UK-based, multiracial
a cappella group performing often in the in the American folk and Negro spiritual traditions) hewed closely to the Travelers's rendition, regarded by many as
definitive.

Despite their diverse stylings, each version of this song stages the now familiar contest between worldly cares (even those so profound as to involve the
end of the world) and the focus on "my Lord" that should be every Christian's
priority. The song's refrain, "Everybody's worried 'bout the atomic bomb / But
nobody's worried about the day my Lord will come," laments the false-idol
features of the atomic threat, whose anxieties can be set aside with the proper
metaphysical perspective. The refrain continues, "When he'll hit! like an atom
bomb," suggesting that this jealous God will stage an atomic-style end of the
world expressly to punish those who let atomic fear distract and depress them
in their ordinary lives. All versions of this song also climax with the admonition to "seek King Jesus" to find "Peace, happiness, and joy divine." In the war
context evoked by the song as a whole, the equation of Jesus with peace is as

multifaceted as were the permutations of "peace" examined during my discussion of W. E. B. Du Bois in Chapter 4. In the lyric here the suggestion, almost SF style, is that of an alternate universe surrounded by faith where no war can exist, or of an armored indifference to planetary demise due to the blessed distraction of Christian faith. Finally, "peace" suggests to all Christians the blissful harmonies (or unending silence) of the hereafter; in a specific (and ironic) atomic context, one could say that when the last being has succumbed to the last bomb blast, there will at last be total peace. The inference is clearly that individual attempts at peace-making are a waste of time and perhaps even an insult to the omnipotence of God; all versions reinforce the point by informing listeners that "He'll fight your battle if you keep still," the "battle" being not war itself but puny human attempts to preserve and elongate human history, such as peace activists' "battle" against the bomb.

With respect to the African American cultural context in which these gospel renditions were recorded, this call to turn away from atomic distractions resembles the request made by leaders within the civil rights movement to not allow political flashpoints like the Cuban Missile Crisis to derail the growing momentum of the "rights fight" (see Chapter 3). Throughout this project I have been as interested in examining the tension between the competing causes of anti-nuclearism and civil rights as I have their moments of mutual advancement, and gospel music, with its heavy emphasis on the spiritual over the material, was a form of black cultural expression just as conducive to turning from the atomic threat. As indicated above, the bomb is a worldly "care" similar to any false idol strewn across the path of humans' life journey; to worry too much about the bomb—or to worry at all—is a sin, these performers suggest, creating as they seek to solve a profound ethical dilemma.

The latest in this tightly clustered array of atomic hits by African American gospel groups is "Atomic Telephone" (1952), originally recorded by a white country ensemble, the Harlan County Four, but followed soon after by the Spirit of Memphis Quartette's version, which was also popular. Wolfe argues that the atomic thrust of the song is weak; beyond the gospel-themed title (linking it to other Christian classics such as "The Royal Telephone" and "God's Radio Phone,"), "No mention is made of 'atomic' in the song; there is no hint of atomic bombs or atomic holocaust. 'Atomic' functions solely as a religious adjective" (119). Yet I cannot but disagree with Wolfe's assessment, as the song is not only thoroughly preoccupied with an atomic-induced end of the world but also recalls the most rhetorically effective uses to which King put the bomb in various of his sermons and theses. In these, the bomb is no metaphor for God's power but a literal manifestation of the greatest moral dilemma in human history; for King in his writings, God has absolutely no relationship to the atomic bomb, metaphoric or otherwise; He hates it as He hates all forms of violence and death and challenges humans themselves to do all it takes to stave off their impatient, hubristic, self-engineered reckoning day. The theology of "Atomic Telephone" appears most clearly in the opening stanza, performed (in the Spirit's version) in the marvelous "shouting" style by a powerful solo voice:[3]

> Some people wanna use [atomic power] to destroy everything
> Bu-UT God didn't mean it like that
> He wants it used for the good of all mankind!

The song's recording date coincides with the optimism of the early Eisenhower administration, regarding the powerful but positive uses toward which atomic energy could be put. As an energy source, an industrial sector, even a tool in medicine, atomic power—in Eisenhower-era parlance, "atoms for peace"—promised rewards and relief, and this spirited introduction poses a moral contest between "some people [who] wanna use it to destroy everything" and God's desire for healing, peaceful uses. The refrain continues this implicit reference to atomic energy as "it," emphasizing its potential to do good but only by divine intervention: "with one sweep of power / known by God alone." The reference to human ignorance of divine will might be rephrased in this context to suggest that man has no idea how awful atomic war would be, that this is therefore a fruit of the Tree of Knowledge best left untouched. As well, the song's name is not just a catch phrase tapping into the "atomic" and "telephone" trends in gospel performance. Instead, it presents the striking image of Christians getting on the "atomic telephone" specifically to consult with the Almighty regarding atomic power. The connection, the song implies, is excellent, as God's anti-weapons message is clear: as King regarded the atomic threat as humanity's most effective impetus to understanding and brotherhood, so the terrain of "Atomic Telephone" includes the figure of God setting a great challenge, and a great opportunity, in humans' path.

In the year of the Cuban Missile Crisis, the moment widely regarded as the closest the world has ever come to the brink of nuclear war, jazz master Charles Mingus recorded "Oh, Lord, Don't Let Them Drop That Atomic Bomb on Me" (1962). Mingus biographer Gene Santoro calls the piece "another of his acidly parodic blues-singing interludes" in the tradition of "Fables of Faubus," which Mingus wrote in response to the Little Rock integration crisis, aimed this time at "the cold war scenario of Mutual Assured Destruction" (186). While the piece is largely instrumental, in fact the music itself—combining styles of blues, honky-tonk, slow drag, and funeral dirge—is spot-on coincident with the atmosphere of its title, and Mingus enlarges upon the piece's blues influence by lacing in a lamenting lyric. He opens with a spoken introduction to this live recording—"We'd like to do a piece titled, "Oh, Lord, Don't Let them Drop that Atomic Bomb on Me"—and wryly accents the word *me*, as if to emphasize African Americans' greater likelihood of being targeted during nuclear attack, as well as to remind his white audience that he and his racial community must be included in the broader vision of atomic jeopardy, preparedness, and survival obsessing thinkers and writers in that period.

As the title also indicates, the entire song is something of a prayer, an anguished calling out to the Lord to do all He can to swerve the course of history away from the destruction that seemed imminent in the early 1960s. Mingus's most inspired line begs the Lord to "don't let 'em drop it, stop it, bebop it," suggesting that God borrow some strength from Mingus's own powerful art form—or, in cruder parlance, to screw it or do just about anything He can think of—to stave off the nuclear inevitable. Contrasted to the reverent tones of the formal quartets of the 1950s, Mingus's more modern address to the Almighty is a howl of despair and anticipates the "attitude problem" of Sun Ra and his Arkestra whose featured lyric for the early-1980s "Nuclear War" is "It's a mother fucker, don't you know / they push that button, your ass gotta go." As opposed to Frankie Ervin, "Big Boy" Cruddup, and the Talbot Brothers, who looked with a lighthearted resignation—or at least the resolve to play on 'til the end—upon the prospect of atomic war, these later jazz and pop artists combine an awareness of the nuclear threat with a liberated mindset that allowed singer and song itself to treat the subject with due seriousness, or at least profound cynicism.

Reading these later arrangements thus, I do not mean to value them above the earlier musical responses, as I consider almost every one of them appropriate to their respective early, mid-, or late atomic moments and as valuable indicators of the vast range of atomic sentiment within the African American community and across postwar American popular culture as a whole. Their notes of hope, despair, indifference, and exuberance are the ideal soundtrack to a specific era in twentieth-century American history, as well as to the major themes presented for examination in this book: the opacities and opportunities constituted by the atomic threat with respect to every aspect of planning, survival, and societal recovery; the vital importance of position (physical, intellectual, political, spiritual, and artistic) vis à vis the bomb itself; and the ever-shifting nature of the relationship between anti-nuclear protest and the struggle for civil rights attempted (and sometimes failed) by some well-meaning white authors and filmmakers, as well as many leading African American intellectuals, journalists, and artists in the postwar era. Each of the texts discussed in this book has presented its vision of an atomic-inflected reckoning day, some fancifully freed of the racial and cultural diversity that has characterized the American experiment since its inception, others resulting more realistically in a nuclear alternative (or even a nuclear aftermath) that challenges its survivors to build a tomorrow more firmly guided by equality, brotherhood, and peace.

Notes

Introduction

1.   Urban theorist Robert Goldston referred to the megalopolis as simply "the explosion of the city" (154); he concluded his anti-suburban treatise from 1970 on an apocalyptic note: "megalopolis is doomed. . . . Its existence is incompatible with human life and will therefore be terminated in the interests of human survival. Possibly by the conflagration of war" (181). While still nuclear-inflected, it is a softer terminology—the suburban "boom," the "mushrooming" of the suburbs—that has been applied to the rapidly developing exurban environment (see also D. Rose 26–30).

2.   Yet in addition to their solid construction, schools were often the only locus of civil defense awareness and drilling in otherwise indifferent or un-mobilized urban and suburban environments (Weart 15–16).

3.   Deen and Browning's assessment of post-nuclear survival is especially upbeat regarding the benefits of sheltering in large, high-rise structures (82–83), suggesting none of the downsides considered in other texts referenced in this discussion.

4.   See also Hayes and Leyson, whose WWII-era survival guides described civil defense for conventional, not atomic, bombs but who even then questioned the adequacy of tenement houses and "modern apartments" (Hayes 58–61) and "older types" of buildings (Leyson 69) during an air raid. Leyson places great faith in the structural soundness of modern office buildings, but regards most apartment housing, subways, and "shelters that have been built" (65) as inadequate urban shelters. He even worries that privately-built, suburban shelters would be useless against most conventional bombs, unless these shelters were "sixty to eighty feet beneath the surface of the ground" (70). Postwar, atomic-ready shelters were regarded even by their advocates as expensive and difficult to build (Hassard 87; Martin and Latham 256–61, 264, 271; Ring 78–79).

5.   See Weart 13; also, Martin and Latham observe that in 1961 only $532 million was spent on civil defense, less even than the Congressional appropriation of $620 million, although both of these sums pale in comparison to the $19 billion spent annually on military defense during this period (262–63, 265). Hassard noted similar patterns of de-funding the Federal Emergency Management Agency (FEMA) in the early 1980s, while "[o]nly the funding for the protection of the leadership and continuity of government seems to have escaped [budgetary cutbacks]: in fact, it was increased from $140 million to $155 million" (87).

6.   Notably, the white middle-class was not the only group enjoined to "run toward the fire" in a nuclear emergency. McEnaney shows that civil defense planners sought to mobilize America's industrial forces by inspiring (or contractually obligating) them to man their machines throughout or immediately after a nuclear

attack, so as to re-establish America's military and economic superiority as quickly as possible (126–34). Yet the majority of unionized, skilled, "essential" workers at this point were white, so that, even as members of the working class, African Americans were still considered expendable in the nuclear scenario.

7. See also *Town of the Times* (1963), in which African American characters (mainly children) are featured very briefly, and *The Day Called X* (1957), a network television staging of Portland, Oregon's successful preparation for attack, in which an Asian-American girl of primary-school age plays a brief featured role. Notably, one film appearing late in the CD era, *Occupying a Public Shelter* (1965), features an unnamed black male character who surely integrates the shelter during his several scenes yet is carefully segregated at all times as well: this character functions as the communication specialist who immediately moves to a reserved seat at the radio desk in the shelter control area, away from the white shelterees identified as ordinary citizens. He spends all of his scenes at his radio controls with his back to the group, interacting amiably with other (white) shelter managers but never eating, sleeping, or talking with the rest of the occupants.

8. P. Boyer has read an array of hopeful speculations, based on the promise of unlimited atomic energy, whose politics also tend to match those of the speculators themselves. For instance, "the splitting of the atom, exulted a 1946 Socialist Party pamphlet . . . had 'made it possible to transform nature into the servant of man, giving him food infinitely beyond the capacity of the human appetite, clothing far more abundant than he can wear, homes for all to fill our streets with palaces'" (114; see also 164). Here atomic energy promises the classless society feared by others who analyzed the physical and societal "leveling" threatened by nuclear apocalypse. Others on the intellectual left envisioned dystopia resulting even from so much abundance; they lamented the onslaught of automation, mass unemployment and boredom, and the rise of a "highly complex technocratic economy" that would in fact reinforce class division (See P. Boyer 141–43).

9. Sterling Brown wrote in 1945 that "dissatisfaction with Jim Crow [was considered] tantamount to subversiveness" (373) by anxious whites, and a racist character in Himes's *If He Hollers Let Him Go* (1945) informs protagonist Bob Jones that "this isn't any time for private gripes [about racial discrimination]. . . . In order to beat fascism we got to have unity" (107).

Chapter 1

1. Both Merril and Wylie had science fiction fan bases, while Wylie was also a prolific writer for the mainstream whose articles on dozens of topics, prosaic or prophetic, appeared in a variety of magazines and whose *When Worlds Collide* was a successful Hollywood film. His "Crunch and Des" fishing stories inspired a mid-1950s TV series, and his polemical *Generation of Vipers* made him a household name in the 1940s and 1950s. His concept of "momism," misunderstood or not, encouraged a generation of male writers already under the misogynist influence of Freud. While *Tomorrow!* was dismissed in "Books of the Times" as "slapdash" and "shrill" (Poore 14 Jan. 1954), it was praised in the *Book Review* as "among [Wylie's] best" and having a "stunning impact" (Peterson 4–5). That the reviewer was no less a personage than Eisenhower's chief Civil Defense administrator, Val Peterson, indicates the "importance" of this book for its time (in the preparedness sector at any rate), even while Peterson may lack the credentials to vouch for its literary

merit. Like Wylie, Frank was a journalist and sportswriter whose comic nuclear fable *Mr. Adam* (1946) was a bestseller and fortune-maker, allowing Frank to work primarily as a novelist from then on (see discussion of this novel in Chapter 5). A condensed version of *Alas, Babylon* appeared in *Good Housekeeping* (March 1959), shortly before the novel was released. Merril's text was adapted and retitled *Atomic Attack* for the *Motorola TV Hour* in 1950, starring Phyllis Thaxter and Walter Matthau. Frank's *Forbidden Area* (1956) was episode #1 in the prestigious *Playhouse 90* series, with *Alas, Babylon* produced for the show in 1960.

2. On Wylie, see Bendau and especially Keefer, whose brief but informative biography describes Wylie's roller-coaster career and prodigious textual output. Keefer acknowledges that "Wylie has never been taken seriously by critics" and speculates as to why: "he wrote 'potboilers' for a living; even worse, he set down his books at an incredible rate—a short story in a morning, a novelette in a long day, a novel in ten—and he made fun of those who claim that writing is a slow and painful search for the perfect word" (156).

3. Jon has a fairly small role in the story, so is not analyzed in-depth in this discussion. Contra the reading I advance here, he is both non-ethnic and an "outsider" to the bomb's harmful effects, as he clearly spends the narrative traveling through contaminated zones yet arrives at home in the story's last moments with only a survivable gunshot wound to the arm. We can perhaps attribute Jon's biological fortitude to the fact that he is the man in the family, while his white female family members display the typical feminine susceptibility to the bomb's effects.

4. In the revised edition of this novel (though "restored" is the more accurate term; Merril and Pohl-Weary 99–100), published for a British press fifteen years after the original, Jon does not escape from New York but dies of the bullet wound he makes it home with in 1951. His death paves an even wider way for Dr. Levy as Gladys's next husband.

5. Atkins, who makes this same observation, feels that the gesture is intentional, that the "image of the home as claustrophobic prison has a dual agenda" (190).

6. Lenore Bailey, the story's white heroine is Wiley's feminine ideal—gorgeous, talented in math and science, and commonsensical. As opposed to her social-climbing mother, Lenore spends wisely and loves Chuck, the poor boy next door, even though the wealthiest man in town bids for her affections. Not surprisingly, she is a "geigerman"—that is, actively involved in the most dangerous sector of civil defense—and has a heroic moment testing a "hot" pile of rubbish for some waiting fireman, after the bomb explodes. Her low moments are always surprising departures from her sterling character, revealing her mother's influence but primarily added in for plot complication: the night before the bomb, for example, she makes Chuck take her out of "that Chink spot" where they were eating so that she can reject his marriage proposal for financial reasons (105).

7. In the same year that my article on this subject appeared in the *Journal of Modern Literature*, Sharp (198–204) drew similar conclusions about this novel.

8. Often viewed as a world apart from the rest of the country—with respect to its expensive real estate, its rushed and rude inhabitants, its utterly unique cultural spectrum, and even its self-perpetuated air of elitism and separatism—New York is simultaneously the US city most often by far represented as typical (or as "the ultimate") in media representation internationally and in countless American novels, films, and television programs. Especially after the solidarity-inducing catastrophe of 9/11, when New York's Rudolph Giuliani became "America's Mayor," the rest of

the country clasped the city to its "heartland," although architectural historian Page has also read 9/11 as a culmination or realization of "the fantasies, nightmares, and premonitions of New York's destruction that have pervaded New York and American culture for more than a century" (168). Reviewing novels and films whose climactic action is the obliteration of New York, Page quotes from Joaquin Miller's *The Destruction of Gotham* (1886) to argue that "only when Manhattan has 'burned and burned and burned to the very bed-rock' is the apocalypse complete" (169). In Page's estimation, "New York has always embodied the most troubling and longstanding tensions in American history and life: the ambivalence toward cities, the troubled reaction to immigrants and racial diversity, the fear of technology's impact, and the tensions between natural and human-made disaster" (171).

9. My reading departs from that of Sharp, who argues that the Henrys "contributed by providing whites with knowledge about farming, fishing, and moonshine. Their contributions were portrayed as useful only after the community had lapsed into a state of nature" (216). Despite their continued enforced subservience, the Henry family, I contend, supplies the ignorant white characters with the technical know-how that allows them to live not only in health and safety but with a notable portion of modern convenience.

Chapter 2

1. See del Rey 10 and Clareson, who remarks frequently on "the topicality of science fiction" (16).

2. Although his writers did not always have to agree, Campbell published a year earlier Poul Anderson's "Logic," in which a character echoes this claim: "It'll be a new culture . . . scattered towns and villages, connected by airlines so fast that cities won't need to grow up again" (56).

3. The opposite phenomenon is on display in the work of Robert A. Heinlein, who frequently identified major characters in his novels, including *The Star Beast* (1954), *Starship Troopers* (1959), *Tunnel in the Sky* (1965), and *I Will Fear No Evil* (1970), as "black." While readers, most famously Samuel R. Delany, have expressed appreciation for these identifications (see Scholes and Rabkin 188), so subtle are they that many readers fail to notice.

4. In his essay "Harlem is Nowhere" (1948), Ellison displays the typical American's mixed reaction to the dawn of the atomic age; he is glad that Harlem "men whose grandparents still believe in magic prepare optimistically to become atomic scientists" (322) yet likens the "cosmic destruction lurking within an atomic stockpile" (324) to the psychological chaos that threatens this same Harlem community cut off from the support of social institutions. Similar, and similarly spare, references are made in letters to Albert Murray (*Trading Twelves*, e.g., 97, 116).

5. Tal stresses the low-tech ethos of African American futurist novels, which "make use of old technologies in new and unexpected ways" (68). His example from *Plan B* involves less the guns themselves than the "sophisticated social mechanism for door-to-door delivery [of flowers] in 1960s Harlem . . . reemployed in a new and revolutionary cause" (69).

6. The disparities in Himes's views between his discussion with Williams in 1970 and with Fabre in 1983 are many. Likely the passage of thirteen years and the decline of race-based radicalism in this time account for some of the differences, yet the markedly different venues matter as well: with his fellow black expatriate

Williams, originally preparing the discussion for publication in *Amistad I*, Himes may have felt he could speak more candidly than he could with his white, French, long-time associate Michel Fabre, who published his interview in a mainstream journal about detective novels. See Walters 216.

7. Meanwhile, in the novel's memorable first chapter, Tang snidely remarks that T-Bone was "*so arrogant in bed he acted like his dick was made of solid uranium*" (6).

8. Himes recast chapter 21 as the short story "Prediction" and published it in his *Black on Black* in 1973. He repurposed chapter 1 as "Tang" for that same collection.

9. The hero of Colson Whitehead's recent *Zone One* (2011) reads as a distant cousin of the sweetly heroic Lobey. Mark Spitz (a nickname bestowed upon an otherwise unidentified protagonist related to a nasty racial joke about black people being unable to swim) is the resolutely "mediocre" (148) hero of a post-apocalyptic universe. Herein zombies of a distinctively cinematic stripe (Whitehead admits his marked indebtedness to Romero's *Night of the Living Dead* and its understated African American hero; see Keehn) threaten and finally breach frantically installed barricades around lower Manhattan. As in the work of Delaney, Whitehead sets nuclear war usefully, almost benignly, in his hero's distant past; in pre-plague times, he and his father bonded over nuclear survival films (120), and these scenarios reassure him as he lives through his own age's disaster that he is destined to live on, as do the lowly but indestructible cockroaches of atomic-survival narratives (134). Like Lobey and Delany's other brown heroes, Mark Spitz's racial identity as African American is largely incidental to his character, announced off-handedly late in the story, and no barrier whatsoever to his taking up with a white lover, Mim, a Jewish woman with whom he shares an idyllic but tragically abbreviated episode mid-story. Mark Spitz's B-averageness (56) pointedly removes him from the categories of both dangerous thug and magical negro; in fact, pre-plague Mark Spitz is an ordinary suburban kid from Long Island, admiring his beloved uncle's urban lifestyle. Thus as in Delaney's work, *Zone One* is devoutly urbophilic, its hero working assiduously with his military-sponsored sweeper team toward the personal goal of resurrecting beleaguered New York and all the low- and middle-brow pleasures it once afforded for his personal inhabitance (103).

10. Like Hansberry, Delany has been faulted for his integrationist views by more militant-minded contemporaries. See Dery 189–90 and Tucker 53. Notably, they echo complaints of Blish and the old guard that Delany's scenarios—this time of interracial harmony—were simply too "fantastic" to believe.

Chapter 3

1. In February 1956 Lucy began the graduate-level library science program yet was expelled on spurious grounds three days later. After a hostile attempt by white students to block Lucy's entry into class, the University stated that it could not guarantee her safety and removed her from campus. Following a lawsuit filed on her behalf by the NAACP, the University accused Lucy of slander and permanently expelled her. James Hood and Vivian Malone were the two students who successfully integrated Alabama in 1962.

2. This layout, for the *Courier*'s National Edition, differed somewhat from the City Edition, which featured the Cuban Missile Crisis more prominently.

3.   Also silent on this day, and fairly muted in subsequent weeks, was the *San Francisco Sun-Reporter*, yet interestingly, *Sun-Reporter* publisher Carlton B. Goodlett, PhD, MD, distinguished himself as deeply committed to nuclear disarmament. During the early 1960s, Goodlett was as well-traveled in the cause of world peace as were W. E. B. DuBois and Bayard Rustin (see Chapter 4). He attended, addressed, and/or reported on multiple ban-the-bomb conferences in the early 1960s, including the World Congress for General Disarmament and Peace, which met in Moscow in July 1962 (Goodlett, "World Congress"); the World Without the Bomb Conference in Accra in September 1962 ("Accra"); the World Conference Against the A and H Bombs in Tokyo in October 1962 (Randolph); and a local meeting to recap various peace conferences ("Four Speak"). In a well-received column from July 1962 (reprinted in the Spring 1963 issue of *Freedomways*), Goodlett lamented the lack of interest in nuclear protest within the US, compared to the excitement generated by the topic abroad. As did his popular columnist Thomas C. Fleming (in his column of 25 February 1961), Goodlett argued that African American youth, who had striven so heroically to achieve equality in recent years, deserved to enjoy the fruits of their labors "in a world secure and disarmed" ("The Task"; see also Patterson).

4.   See for example, "Army Missile Profs," "Atom Bomb Guards," "Atom Scientists," "Negroes Who Help Conquer Space," and "Radioactive Gold."

5.   Skewing my sample to the densely populated Northeast, I must confine to this footnote a brief reference to two noted African American activist-journalists of the Midwest and West, Erna P. Harris, who founded and edited the Wichita weekly *The Kansas Journal* for three years before World War II, and Charlotta A. Bass, the illustrious Los Angeles newswoman-turned-politician who headed the *California Eagle* for forty years. Both women's commitment to peace activism (not limited to anti-nuclearism) was life-long yet ironically was also responsible for provisionally or permanently derailing their journalism careers; Harris's WWII-era opposition to the draft caused her entire advertisement slate to decamp as war commenced and the *Journal* to fold immediately thereafter; ten years later, Bass's opposition to the Korean conflict and close association with Paul Robeson and W. E. B. Du Bois resulted in her appearance before California's state-level HUAC committee and the financial crisis that forced her to sell her interest in the *Eagle*, which itself closed in 1964. Harris's final decades were spent in northern California where she occupied a leadership role in the Women's International League for Peace and Freedom (WILPF) and became a noted advocate of far-left causes. The Co-op stores where she served as a board member in the 1950s "were the first to check vegetables for cesium-137 and strontium-90," since, as Harris commented in an interview in the 1980s, "we don't know what even a little bit of radiation will do" (Dougherty n.p.; see also "Erna P. Harris" folder, WILPF Papers, Swarthmore College Peace Collection). Following her departure from news publishing, Bass ran for Los Angeles City Council and Mayor and for US Vice President on the Progressive Party ticket in 1952 (see Cairns, chapter 3).

6.   Because of its need for daily content, the *World* regularly published from wire services that provided news and features with no discernible African American angle. It thus addressed the bomb far more often than did the more locally focused African American weeklies but often with less relevance to black community. The *World* also provided a somewhat conservative editorial slant; there was heavy coverage of local religious meetings and visiting preachers, for whom

the bomb and its metaphors—e.g., "God's Atom Bomb" ("Bishop") and "atomic prayer bomb" ("Macon")—were favorite topics. The typical mix of alarmism and boosterism characterized the editorials, where readers were exhorted to prepare for World War III by following Civil Defense guidelines (see "Awakening," "Bomb Shelters," "Civil Defense Still Needed," "Civil Defense to the Fore," "Civilians," "Is Nobody," "Just What," "Moving On," "On Bomb Shelters," "Prepare," "Remember," and "Watch"). Of all the papers surveyed for this chapter the *World* had by far the most numerous references to the "imminence" of "World War III" (see e.g., "Public is Warned"). While joining the weeklies in condemning the appointment of segregationist Florida governor Millard Caldwell as Eisenhower's head of Civil Defense, the *World* provided also a lengthy interview with Caldwell himself, who promised therein to treat all Americans as citizens and put their safety first (see Lautier). See also note 12 in this chapter.

7. In their publication of multiple editions and their regular coverage of doings in diverse and far-flung communities, the weeklies targeted readerships far beyond their geographic points of origin. Washburn observes that recirculation amongst friends and family members accounted for three to six times the official war-era circulation rate of 1.8 million (177), and historians have credited *Defender* publisher Robert S. Abbott's WWI-era "Great Northern Drive" with "single-handedly" engineering the Great Migration (qtd. in De Santis 13; see also E. Gordon "The Negro Press," 208, Washburn 87–94). As reported by Washburn, "the Bible was the only publication that was more influential than the *Defender* with the black masses" (95). As a boy in Kansas, Langston Hughes recalled developing his race consciousness by the "flaming headlines" and "stirring" editorial style of the *Defender* issues reaching his doorstep (qtd. in De Santis 13, 14).

8. Not surprisingly, these same writers took a generally pacifist stance against bomb testing in the immediate postwar period; *Defender* columnist Earl Conrad argued that repeated testing was mainly an experiment by which to normalize atomic bombings and pave the way for future wars ("May Atom Bomb" 15). See also Badger, Cayton, and "H-Bomb Reaction," all of which protest atomic testing against the dark-skinned peoples of the Pacific. Meanwhile, see also Goode, who takes a sanguine view of the Bikini detonations, relative to the historical incident of Mont Pelée's eruption in 1902 (10).

9. Kinchy's excellent article on "Race and the Bomb" accesses an archive very similar to the ones I draw from in this chapter and in Chapter 4. However, our emphases are different and several of my conclusions diverge markedly from those she presents.

10. Bus rides were indeed an occasion of racial conflict at Oak Ridge during the war. See Johnson and Jackson 115 and Olwell 21.

11. Recent histories of Oak Ridge corroborate Waters's and Anderson's original findings. See Johnson and Jackson 111–18, 122, 126, 212–15; Olwell 20–24; Steele 198–203; and Walkowitz 241. Olwell tells the hair-raising story of an African American truck-driver named Ebb Cade, who entered the Oak Ridge hospital in 1945 with multiple limb fractures following a road accident and came out as an unwitting guinea pig to the facility's experiments with human exposure to plutonium (49).

12. By contrast, the *Atlanta Daily World* gave frequent, favorable coverage to various citywide school evacuation drills in the 1950s, despite the fact that in Atlanta, as in Chicago and New York, air raid sirens were frequently inaudible in black neighborhoods (see "54,000"). It likewise refrained from calling attention to the

comically undersized nature of the drills it covered; one year only a handful of schools had actually to remove their children from campus, and the transportation for one group was "33 cars" and "four buses," which not surprisingly had absolutely no trouble following their short route to the appointed staging ground ("Five Hundred"). Instead, the *World* plumped for Civil Defense in numerous editorials (see note 6 of this chapter), in coverage of a "Survival March" coincident with Pearl Harbor Day of 1959 ("Giant Parade"), and in notices of annual Operation Alert days (e.g., "Radio, TV").

13. Rosa Lee Ingram was a Georgia sharecropper and widowed mother of twelve who was accused with two of her adolescent sons of the 1947 murder of their white neighbor John Ethron and sentenced to death. This was later commuted to life imprisonment at the urging of women's and civil rights groups. The facts of the case remain in dispute; see Gellman 254, Horne "Civil Rights" 151, Klarman 280, Lorence 136, and Waligora-Davis 57–58.

Chapter 4

1. The reference indicates that the Youngers' morning paper is the middle-class *Tribune* where McCormick's well-being would have been front-section news, instead of the *Sun-Times* favored by Chicago's Southside working classes for decades. Very likely, Hansberry's own affluent Southside family were *Tribune* subscribers, and Hansberry either failed to correct for the class difference between herself and her characters or subtly indicated the sophisticated reading interests of this poor but respectable family for pointed political reasons.

2. Historians have argued that US policymakers pressured civil rights leaders to focus narrowly on civil rights and leave foreign relations to white national leaders. See Gaines "From Black Power" 259–60; S. Hall 40–41 *et passim*; Lieberman, "Another Side" 21; and Von Eschen.

3. The Black Panthers, who were well versed on the Constitution's provisions for gun ownership, stormed the California State Senate in May 1967 to protest a law being passed against gun-carrying in public places. Armed to the teeth, they ran into the Assembly hall and read their "Executive Mandate Number 1," which castigated a litany of crimes perpetrated by the US throughout its history, including "the dropping of atomic bombs on Hiroshima and Nagasaki" (Seale 358–59). Hansberry's spirited statements on rights assertion include the following: "it is no longer acceptable to allow racists to define Negro manhood—and it will have to come to pass that they can no longer define his weaponry" (*To Be Young* 213). Later in that same letter to a young white male interlocutor, "Negroes must concern themselves with every single means of the struggle: legal, illegal, passive, active, violent, and nonviolent. . . . They must harass, debate, petition, give money to court struggles, sit-in, lie-down, strike, boycott, sing hymns, pray on steps—and shoot from their windows when the racists come cruising through their communities" (*To Be Young* 213–14).

4. See C. Anderson on the career of Max Yergan, a one-time head of the communist-fronting National Negro Congress who turned FBI informant during the cold war, also Anderson on NAACP executive secretary Walter White. See Kornweibel on the changing attitudes of *Messenger* editor A. Philip Randolph, and the rightward swings of the *Messenger* itself in its later years (144, 169, *et passim*). On Harold Cruse, see Hutchinson, who notes that Cruse was once a correspondent for the communist *Daily Worker* but quit the party in the late 1940s "because it

manipulated blacks" (249). Whether Cruse's departure from communism to Black Nationalism constitutes a move to the right or the left is open to question.

5. Eisenhower shared Du Bois's concern during the Quemoy-Matsu crisis and the French-Indochina conflict during the post-Korea mid-1950s. As K. Rose reports, "Eisenhower . . . told his advisers, 'You must be crazy. We can't use those awful things [atomic bombs] against Asians for the second time in less than 10 years. My God'" (36).

6. Ironically, there was much animosity among these various peace factions. As Wittner reports, "A. J. Muste, considered the dean of American pacifists," regarded a vote for Progressive Party candidate Henry Wallace as a vote for the communist party (*One World* 202). Meanwhile, communists railed against the SANE peace group founder Norman Thomas whose "one world" movement was "but a reflection . . . of the aspirations of American foreign policy to dominate the world" (qtd. in *One World* 202).

7. Horne notes that throughout this period NAACP leadership took a moderate, pro-government/anti-communist stance and that A. Philip Randolph, president and founder of the Brotherhood of Sleeping Car Porters, "supported the war down the line" (*Black and Red* 130). Randolph made history during World War II by threatening strikes if Roosevelt refused to establish fair employment practices in the war industries. The threat worked, and for Randolph, war became an important occasion for equalizing work opportunities and demonstrating patriotism through heroism in battle.

8. See also Deming, who narrates an encounter with racist whites as an integrated peace walk made its way through the South in early 1962: "It is my own conviction that these men listened to us as they did, on the subject of peace, just *because* Robert Gore [the group's lone African American participant] was traveling with us. . . . It snatched [the nuclear issue] from the realm of the merely abstract" (115). While the situation is readable as tokenism at its most exploitative, Deming nevertheless implicitly acknowledges how peace activists depended in this instance upon the literal prospect of racial integration to "bring home" to complacent Americans the revolutionary nature of a world freed from the nuclear threat.

9. Describing his proposal to Muste as purposely "rash," Rustin suggested something dramatic, if not citizenship renunciation then lying down in front of the gates at Los Alamos and going to jail, to impress a complacent citizenry with the urgency of the problem ("Hydrogen Bomb Protest"). Rustin copied more than twenty people on the memo, several of whom wrote back to decline participation in his various bold schemes, especially the one involving giving up citizenship. Documentation of Rustin's opposition to the hydrogen bomb can be found in the Fellowship of Reconciliation Records (DG 013), Swarthmore College Peace Collection (Box D52, Folders: "Bayard Rustin Files, College Section," "FOR Program Staff / Bayard Rustin—College Section," and "Hydrogen Bomb Protest").

10. As early as the late 1940s, King's father used the pulpit to warn against the bomb; an item in the 16 October 1947 issue of the *Atlanta Daily World* reported on a recent meeting of the Atlanta Baptist Association, addressed by Dr. M. L. King, who placed atomic energy amongst "liquor traffic" and "division among church organizations" as leading causes of concern (Marke 1).

11. From a completely different sort of pulpit, a sound-living column that he wrote for *Ebony* magazine during this same period, King doled out opinions about child-rearing and advice to the lovelorn, counseled homosexuals (unfortunately, to "see

a good psychiatrist" to help break the "habit" ["Advice for Living" January 1958]), and addressed the serious matters of racism and the bomb. In December 1957, he responded to a questioner about banning nuclear weapons with emphasis and eloquence: "It cannot be disputed that a full-scale nuclear war would be utterly catastrophic. . . . War must be finally eliminated or the whole of mankind will be plunged into the abyss of annihilation" ("Advice for Living" 120).

12. While there is no date attached to this quotation, surrounding material is dated 1964, indicating that "little bombs" may refer to conventional warfare bombings going on in Vietnam at the time and/or the terror campaign of church bombings undertaken by white supremacists in Birmingham, Alabama, in 1963. Thus Hansberry may be seen to align the fight against nuclear arms with that against race hatred in both Vietnam and the American South.

13. Similarly, Eldridge Cleaver used nuclear terminology to hail the salvific effect of black popular culture: "the Twist, superseding the Hula Hoop, burst upon the scene like a nuclear explosion, sending its fallout of rhythm into the Minds and Bodies of the people. . . . The Twist was a guided missile, launched from the ghetto into the very heart of the suburbs" (197).

14. I am aware that this assertion runs counter to the widespread critical tendency to emphasize the "apocalyptic" and "prophetic" aspects of Baldwin's writing, especially his nonfiction. Copious attention has been paid to Baldwin's *Fire Next Time*, even though many readers (e.g., Leeming *James Baldwin* 214) concede that the "Jeremiah-like" rhetoric does not flare up—with the quote from the Negro Spiritual that contains the book's title—until the very last lines of this lengthy work. Closing *Fire* as he did, Baldwin surely samples from the apocalyptic tradition, but the remainder of this text displays the measured, ironic, philosophic tones that are typical for his style. Some hear apocalypticism in Baldwin's work, when what is more correctly discerned is anger or righteous indignation; these differ markedly from the visions, predictions, and condemnations that belong to the specifically apocalyptic. Porter's book-length study of Baldwin is titled *Stealing the Fire*, and the cover of Q. Miller's recent reassessment features licking flames, causing it to resemble Muhammad's entirely different and overtly incendiary *The Fall of America*, whose cover also boasts a flames motif. Hardy labors to make the case, yet what is deemed initially the divine retribution of apocalyptic "themes and rhetoric" (79) dissolves fairly quickly into natural and historic "inexorability" (80–81). See also Brooks; Campbell 144–45 et passim; Ellis; Howe; and Leeming "Forward" viii–ix.

Chapter 5

1. Reich belonged to an influential brace of post-Freudians who—building from but reacting to Freud's *Civilization and its Discontents* (1929)—rejected Freud's theory of the inevitability (and necessity) of societal repression. Reich, along with Herbert Marcuse, Norman O. Brown, and R. D. Laing were a few of the many intellectuals of the mid-1950s and early 1960s who sought to excavate buried instincts so as to maintain individual and collective mental health (see also Zaretsky). As A. Gordon notes, "According to Laing, 'normal' people are crazy because they have adjusted themselves to a mad contemporary civilization: 'What we call "normal" is a product of repression, denial, splitting, projection, introjections, and other forms of destructive action or experience'" (48). Reich influenced Mailer in

this period, yet while "Reich . . . never talked very much about violence, except as another instance of the perverse behavior into which a sex-denying civilization drove individuals," by contrast "Mailer want[ed] to remove *all* social restraints" (A. Gordon 41) and refused to distinguish between the violence and sex instincts that Freud himself linked together in *Civilization.*

2. Psychiatrist Helen Swick Perry consulted Gunnar Myrdal's exhaustive study of race relations in the United States, *An American Dilemma* (1944), in her discernment of American/white guilt regarding the atom bomb. For Perry, postwar Americans avoided discussion of the bomb because of their deep-seated feelings of guilt for having initiated atomic warfare against the racially other nation of Japan (229–30).

3. Also responding to "The White Negro," Baldwin's close friend Lorraine Hansberry located the apocalyptic not in Mailer's preposterous vision of a sexual free-for-all but in the unlikely event that Mailer and his white readership would ever "think of the Negro quite as he is, that is, simply as a human being. That *would* raise Havoc" (*To Be Young* 199). Echoing Baldwin, Hansberry pled, "Norman, write not of the greatness of our peoples—yours or mine—in the *past* tense" (*To Be Young* 201).

   In Baldwin's nonfiction in general, specific references to the bomb are spare. At the end of "Notes for a Hypothetical Novel," Baldwin regards "the Cadillac, refrigerator, atom bomb, and what produces it . . ." (*James Baldwin* 230) as the glibly rendered paraphernalia of modern life. The only other atomic reference located in my searches occurs in his poem "Staggerlee wonders," remarkable for its broad inclusion of then-current events, including the Vietnam War and Patty Hearst. In section 3 of the poem, Baldwin mocks hypocritical white liberalism: "Neither (incidentally) / has anyone discussed the Bomb with the niggers: / the incoherent feeling is, the less / the nigger knows about the Bomb, the better." (*Jimmy's Blues* 17).

4. See May 95–98; P. Boyer 11–12; and Hendershot chapter 6.

5. In *Enemies Within,* I traced the tendency of cold war films remade in the AIDS era to transpose the atomic threat into a viral threat. *The Omega Man* and *I Am Legend* both mutate the nuclear origins of the crisis in the novel from which they are adapted into viral epidemics.

6. Bogle describes Belafonte as "lack[ing] conviction and humor" in the film and concludes that "his venture into motion pictures was a disappointment in the 1950s" (191). In the earlier *Island in the Sun* (1957), Belafonte's character David Boyeur with his white love interest (played by Joan Fontaine) "seems to have a good come-on but surely audiences wanted to accuse him of false advertising. All Mavis (and an expectant audience) got from this rebel-rouser was a lot of talk" (190–91). Bogle has valuably discerned categories into which black actors and characters were placed in film history; for him, Belafonte "fell into the black buck category. . . . But if a black buck is not going to be daring or flashy or uninhibitedly sexy, then what good is he?" (190).

7. Many have emphasized the marked improvement in Romero's female characters from *Dawn* on; see for instance Grant and Paffenroth. Each of Paffenroth's chapters have a section discussing sexism in Romero's films—both the sexism on display in them and, later, the sexism satirized by them.

8. The triangulation is reinforced when Belafonte treats his audience to a rendition of his hit song "Gotta Travel On," to which he accompanies his vocals on folk guitar. Ralph sings a verse about "waiting around for you to change your mind" to Betsy,

then a second verse about promising to "soon be on my way" to Snodgrass. Again, this is a close summary of the plot to unfold in the film's final scenes: before devolving into their final gun battle, Ben attempts to coerce Ralph to leave town.

9. See also Dyer (60–62), who reads the whiteness of the zombies in Romero's *Dead* trilogy, specifically the film's equation of whiteness with death and the link between the zombies in *Dawn of the Dead* (even the black and Latino zombies, whose faces are intensely powdered) with the mall's mannequins, "all of whom are white" (62).

Conclusion

1. An interesting point of confusion involved equally casual references to Senator "Joe" McCarthy, who is regarded as a hero by, for instance, the Kavaliers in "Get that Communist, Joe."

2. See (or hear) for instance Roy Acuff's "Advice to Joe," Hank Williams's "No, No, Joe," Ray Anderson's "Stalin Kicked the Bucket," and Jackie Doll's "When They Drop the Atomic Bomb."

3. While my research could not confirm this, the performer is likely Silas Steele, identified by Heilbut as a member of Spirit in the early 1950s and described as a "powerhouse . . . [whose] thunderous baritone could shake a church" (47).

Works Cited

Abernathy, Robert. "Single Combat." *Magazine of Fantasy and Science Fiction* Jan. 1955: 62–70.

"A-Bomb City to End Bias." *Pittsburgh Courier* 2 Jan. 1954: 1.

"Accra: To Give us 'A World Without a Bomb'?" *San Francisco Sun-Reporter* 1 Sept. 1962: 12–13.

Acuff, Roy. "Advice to Joe." Columbia, 1951. Sound recording.

"'Air Raid' Reveals Need for Volunteers." *New York Amsterdam News* 16 Feb. 1952: B1+.

Allen, Danielle. "Ralph Ellison on the Tragi-Comedy of Citizenship." *Ralph Ellison and the Raft of Hope: A Political Companion to* Invisible Man. Ed. Lucas E. Morel. Lexington: U of Kentucky P, 2004. 37–57.

Allnutt, Bruce C. *A Study of Consensus on Psychological Factors Related to Recovery from Nuclear Attack.* McLean: Human Sciences Research, Inc., 1971.

Alpert, Hollis. "All this and Heaven, Too." *Saturday Review* 2 May 1959: 31.

Altman, James W. "Laboratory Research on the Habitability of Public Fallout Shelters." *Symposium on Human Problems in the Utilization of Fallout Shelters.* Washington, DC: National Academy of Sciences/National Research Council, 1960. 157–66.

Amis, Kingsley. "Starting Points." *Science Fiction: A Collection of Critical Essays.* Ed. Mark Rose. Englewood Cliffs: Prentice-Hall, 1976. 9–29.

Anderson, Albert. "Dr. Bethune Named to Defense Staff." *Atlanta Daily World* 9 May 1951: 1.

Anderson, Carol. *Eyes Off the Prize: The United Nations and the African American Struggle for Human Rights, 1944–1955.* Cambridge: Cambridge UP, 2003.

Anderson, Poul. "Logic." *Astounding Science Fiction* July 1947: 51–76.

———. "Prophecy." *Astounding Science Fiction* May 1949: 52–58.

Anderson, Poul, and F. N. Waldrop. "Tomorrow's Children." *Astounding Science Fiction* Mar. 1947: 56–79.

Anderson, Ray. "Stalin Kicked the Bucket." Kentucky, 1953. Sound recording.

Anderson, Trezzvant W. "*Courier* Expose [*sic*] of Atomic City Shames Nation." *Pittsburgh Courier* 28 Apr. 1949: 1+.

———. "Government-Owned Atom Bomb Birthplace: Dixie's Race Pattern Dominates Oak Ridge." *Pittsburgh Courier* 9 Apr. 1949: 2.

———. "H-Bomb Project Reeks with Bias." *Pittsburgh Courier* 7 July 1951: 5.

———. "Hideous Housing Treatment Sickens Stoutest Stomachs." *Pittsburgh Courier* 16 Apr. 1949: 6.

———. "New Dirty Deal in A-Bomb Birthplace." *Pittsburgh Courier* 1 Oct. 1949: 1+.

———. "New Scandals Rock Oak Ridge: Trickery in A-Bomb Birthplace Puts Dems on Spot." *Pittsburg Courier* 8 Oct. 1949: 1+.

Aptheker, Herbert. Introduction. *In Battle for Peace: The Story of My 83rd Birthday.* By W. E. B. Du Bois. Millwood: Kraus-Thomson Organization Limited, 1976.

"Are We Prepared for Peace?" *Baltimore Afro American* 18 Aug. 1945: 1.

"Army Missile Profs: Negro Soldiers Play Vital Role in Shaping US-Allied Missile Defense." *Ebony* May 1961: 94–98.

Atkins, Eliot J. "Judith Merril." *Canadian Fantasy and Science Fiction Writers. Dictionary of Literary Biography, Vol. 251.* Detroit: Gale, 2002. 185–96.

"Atom Bomb Bias." *Pittsburgh Courier* 20 Oct. 1951: 6.

"Atom Bomb Forces End to Racial Strife—Epstein." *Chicago Defender* 1 June 1949: 9.

"Atom Bomb Guards." *Ebony* Mar. 1948: 39–42.

"Atomic Bomb Brings Fear of Cave Life, Joblessness." *Baltimore Afro American.* 18 Aug. 1945. 17.

"Atomic Entertainment Next Sun. Night." *Atlanta Daily World* 26 Aug. 1945: 3.

"Atomic Fashion Show." *New York Amsterdam News* 30 May 1953: 12.

"Atom Scientists." *Ebony* Sept. 1949: 26–28.

"Awakening the Civil Defense Interest." *Atlanta Daily World* 13 June 1954: 4.

Badger, John Robert. "Signs of the Drift to War." *Chicago Defender* 13 July 1946: 15.

Baldwin, James. "The Black Boy Looks at the White Boy." *Nobody Knows My Name: More Notes of a Native Son.* By Baldwin. New York: Dial P, 1961. 216–41.

———. "The Fire Next Time." *James Baldwin: Collected Essays.* Ed. Toni Morrison. New York: Library of America, 1998. 291–348.

———. *Jimmy's Blues: Selected Poems of James Baldwin.* 1983. New York: St. Martin's P, 1985.

Bartter, Martha A. "Nuclear Holocaust as Urban Renewal." *Science Fiction Studies* 13.2 (1986): 148–58.

Beau. Rev. of *Night of the Living Dead. Variety* 16 Oct. 1968. Rpt. in *Film Facts* 11 (1968): 442.

"Behind the Men Who Made the Atomic Bomb Were These Women." *Baltimore Afro American* 18 Aug. 1945: 15.

Bendau, Clifford P. *Philip Wylie and the End of an American Dream.* San Bernadino: Borgo P, 1980.

Bennett, Lerone, Jr. "Auburn Ave., West Side on City's 'Critical Defense List.'" *Atlanta Daily World* 24 Aug. 1952: 1.

———. "The Soul of Soul." *Ebony* Dec. 1961: 111+.

Berger, James. *After the End: Representations of the Post-Apocalypse.* Minneapolis: U of Minnesota P, 1999.

Bethune, Mary McLeod. "Threat of Atomic Attack Demands Everyone Be Alert." *Chicago Defender* 3 Feb. 1951: 6.

Bibb, Joseph D. "Gone with the Bomb." *Pittsburgh Courier* 8 Oct. 1949: 17.

Birnbaum, Michele. *Race, Work, and Desire in American Literature, 1860–1930.* Cambridge: Cambridge UP, 2003.

"Bishop Busy Man." *Atlanta Daily World* 6 Oct. 1945: 3.

Blanchard, Lowell, and the Valley Trio. "Jesus Hits Like an Atom Bomb." Mercury, 1950. Sound recording.

Blind Boys of Alabama. *Atom Bomb.* Real World, 2005. Sound recording.

Blish, James (writing as William Atheling Jr.). *More Issues at Hand.* Chicago: Advent, 1970.

Bogle, Donald. *Toms, Coons, Mulattoes, Mammies, and Bucks: An Interpretive History of Blacks in American Films.* 4th ed. New York: Continuum, 2001.

"The Bomb and Bias." *Pittsburgh Courier* 29 Sept. 1951: 6.

"Bomb Shelters or Dispersion?" *Atlanta Daily World* 4 Nov. 1950: 6.

Booker, M. Keith. *Monsters, Mushroom Clouds, and the Cold War: American Science Fiction and the Roots of Postmodernism, 1946–1964.* Westport: Greenwood P, 2001.

Booker, Simeon. "Ticker Tape U.S.A." *Jet* 21 Feb. 1963: 12–13.

Borum, "Memphis" Willie. "Overseas Blues." Prestige/Bluesville, 1961. Sound recording.

Boyer, Horace. *The Golden Age of Gospel.* Urbana: U of Illinois P, 2000.

Boyer, Paul. *By the Bomb's Early Light: American Thought and Culture at the Dawn of the Atomic Age.* New York: Pantheon, 1985.

Bradbury, Ray. *The Illustrated Man.* 1951. New York: William Morrow, 2001.

———. Introduction. Bradbury, *Illustrated* v–ix.

———. "The Other Foot." 1949. Bradbury, *Illustrated* 38–55.

Brelis, Dean. *Run, Dig, or Stay: A Search for an Answer to the Shelter Question.* Boston: Beacon P, 1962.

Bresee, J. C., and D. L. Narver Jr. "Improved Shelters and Accessories." *Survival and the Bomb: Methods of Civil Defense.* Ed. Eugene P. Wigner. Bloomington: Indiana UP, 1969. 194–224.

"Briefly Noted: Fiction." *New Yorker* 4 Apr. 1959: 166–67.

Brooks, A. Russell. "James Baldwin as Poet-Prophet." *James Baldwin: A Critical Evaluation.* Ed. Therman B. O'Daniel. Washington: Howard UP, 1977. 126–34.

Brother Outsider: The Life of Bayard Rustin. Dir. Bennett Singer and Nancy D. Kates. California Newsreel, 2002. Film.

Brown, Clarence "Gatemouth." "Atomic Energy." 1949. *Atomic Energy.* Blues Boy, 1984. Sound recording.

Brown, Earl. "Russia's Sputnik." *New York Amsterdam News* 10 Oct. 1957: 6.

———. "Timely Topics." *New York Amsterdam News* 19 Jan. 1946: 8.

Brown, Sterling A. "Count Us In." *Primer For White Folks.* Ed. Bucklin Moon. Garden City: Doubleday, Doran and Company, 1945. 365–95.

Buchanan, Samuel Carroll. *A Critical Analysis of Style in Four Black Jubilee Quartets in the United States.* Diss. New York U, 1987. Ann Arbor: UMI, 1987.

Burns, Ben. "Teaching for Tolerance." *Chicago Defender* 18 Aug. 1945: 14.

Burroughs, Margaret Goss. "Peace is Wonderful." *Atlanta Daily World* 24 Aug. 195: 2.

Cairns, Kathleen. *Front-Page Women Journalists, 1920–1950.* Lincoln: U of Nebraska P, 2003.

Campbell, James. *Talking at the Gates: A Life of James Baldwin.* Berkeley: U of California P, 1997.

Campbell, John W. "How to Lose a War." *Astounding Science Fiction* Nov. 1959: 6+.

———. "Megopolis." *Astounding Science Fiction* Feb. 1948: 5–6.

Carpenter, Charles A. *Dramatists and the Bomb: American and British Playwrights Confront the Nuclear Age, 1945–1964.* Westport: Greenwood P, 1999.

Carter, Steven R. *Hansberry's Drama: Commitment Amid Complexity.* Urbana: U of Illinois P, 1991.

"Castro and K Went Too Far." *Baltimore Afro American* 3 Nov. 1962: 5.

Cayton, Horace. "American Foreign Policy is Outdated Because it Thinks in Terms of Whites." *Pittsburgh Courier* 10 July 1954: 6.

Charades. "Hammers and Sickles." Monument, 1966. Sound recording.

Charming Bells. "Jesus Hits Like an Atom Bomb." Selective, 1949. Sound recording.

Chazov, E. I., and M. E. Vartanian. "Effects on Human Behavior." *Aftermath: The Human and Ecological Consequences of Nuclear War.* Ed. Jeannie Peterson/AMBIO. New York: Pantheon, 1983. 155–58.

Cheney, Anne. *Lorraine Hansberry.* Boston: Twayne, 1984. Twayne's United States Authors 430.

Christopher, Nicholas. *Somewhere in the Night: Film Noir and the American City.* New York: Free P, 1997.

"Civil Defense Ignores Medics, Other Leaders." *Baltimore Afro American* 27 Aug. 1955: 5.

"Civil Defense in Harlem." *New York Amsterdam News* 3 Feb. 1951: 6.

"Civil Defense Still Needed." *Atlanta Daily World* 23 May 1954: 4.

"Civil Defense to the Fore." *Atlanta Daily World* 16 Feb. 1954: 6.

"Civilians in the Next War." *Atlanta Daily World* 3 Jan. 1951: 6.

Clareson, Thomas D. *Understanding Contemporary Science Fiction: The Formative Period (1926–1970).* Columbia: U of South Carolina P, 1990.

Clarke, Charles Walter. "VD Control in Atom-Bombed Areas." *Journal of Social Hygiene* 37.1 (1951): 3–5.

Cleaver, Eldridge. *Soul on Ice.* New York: Ramparts, 1968.

Cochran, David. "So Much Nonsense Must Make Sense: The Black Vision of Chester Himes." *Midwest Quarterly* 38.1 (1996): 11–30.

Commodore, Chester. "Better Luck 1958" (cartoon). *Chicago Defender* 28 Dec. 1957: 10.

———. "A Mad, Mad Whirl" (cartoon). *Chicago Defender* 19 Nov. 1957: 5.

Conrad, Earl. "The May Atom Bomb Experiment." *Chicago Defender* 16 Feb. 1946: 15.

———. "Open Letter to President Truman." *Chicago Defender* 18 Aug. 1945: 14.

———. "That Unscientific Word Race." *Chicago Defender* 15 Dec. 1945: N. pag.

Cook, Fannie. "An Atomic Approach to Racism." *Negro Digest* Aug. 1946: 23–24.

Cooney, Robert, and Helen Michaelowski, eds. Marty Jezer, original text. *The Power of the People: Active Nonviolence in the United States.* Philadelphia: New Society Publishers, 1987.

Cousins, Norman. "Shelters, Survival, and Common Sense." *No Place to Hide: Fallout Shelters—Fact and Fiction.* Ed. Seymour Melman. New York: Grove/Black Cat, 1962. 174–75.

Cripps, Thomas. *Slow Fade to Black: The Negro in American Film, 1900–1942.* New York: Oxford UP, 1977.

Crowther, Bosley. "A Touch of 'Art': 'The Scarf' and 'Five' Betray an old Taint." *New York Times* 29 Apr. 1951: X1.

Crudup, Arthur "Big Boy." "I'm Gonna Dig Myself a Hole." RCA Victor, 1951. Sound recording.

Cruse, Harold. *The Crisis of the Negro Intellectual.* New York: William Morrow, 1967.

Cuff Links. "Guided Missiles." Dootone, 1956. Sound recording.

Darby, Henry E., and Margaret N. Rowley. "King on Vietnam and Beyond." *Phylon* Mar. 1986: 43–50.

Dawn of the Dead. Dir. George A. Romero. Laurel Group, 1978. Film.

The Day Called X. Film. Dir. Harry Rasky. CBS Public Affairs, 1955. Web. Prelinger Archives. *archive.org/details/DayCalle1955.*

Day, Dan. "Tan GI's Playing Top Roles in Crisis." *Afro American* 3 Nov. 1962: 1+.

The Day the World Ended. Dir. Roger Corman. Golden State Productions, 1955. Film.

Deen, Thalif, and Earl S. Browning. *How to Survive a Nuclear Disaster.* Piscataway: New Century Publishers, Inc., 1981.

Delany, Samuel R. *Babel 17.* New York: Ace Books, 1966.

———. *The Einstein Intersection.* New York: Ace Books, 1967.

———. *The Fall of the Towers.* 1963–1965. Boston: Gregg P, 1977.

———. *The Jewels of Aptor.* 1962. Boston: Gregg P, 1976.

———. "The Necessity of Tomorrows." *Starboard Wine: More Notes on the Language of Science Fiction.* By Delany. Pleasantville: Dragon P, 1984. 23–35.

———. "Racism and Science Fiction." *Dark Matter: A Century of Speculative Fiction from the African Diaspora.* Ed. Sheree R. Thomas. New York: Warner, 2000.

del Rey, Lester. *The World of Science Fiction, 1927–1976.* New York: Garland, 1980.

D'Emilio, John. *Lost Prophet: The Life and Times of Bayard Rustin.* New York: Free P, 2003.

Deming, Barbara. *Prison Notes.* New York: Grossman, 1966.

Denning, Michael. "Topographies of Violence: Chester Himes' Harlem Detective Novels." *The Critical Response to Chester Himes.* Ed. Charles L. P. Silet. Westport: Greenwood P, 1999. 155–68.

Dentler, Robert A., and Phillips Cutright. "Social Effects of Nuclear War." *Nuclear Information* July 1963: 1–10.

Derleth, August. "The Dark Boy." *Magazine of Fantasy and Science Fiction* Feb. 1957: 53–64.

Dery, Mark. "Black to the Future: Interviews with Samuel R. Delany, Greg Tate, and Tricia Rose." *Flame Wars: The Discourse of Cyberculture.* Ed. Mark Dery. Durham: Duke UP, 1994. 179–222.

De Santis, Christopher C., ed. *Langston Hughes and the* Chicago Defender: *Essays on Race, Politics, and Culture, 1942–62.* Urbana: U of Illinois P, 1995.

Dick, Philip K. *Dr. Bloodmoney.* 1965. New York: Vintage/Random, 2002.

Dickson, Gordon R. "Black Charlie." *Galaxy Science Fiction* Apr. 1954: 123–37.

Diddley, Bo. "Mr. Khrushchev." Checker, 1962. Sound recording.

Disch, Thomas M. *On SF.* Ann Arbor: U of Michigan P, 2005.

Dodson, Rebecca Stiles. "African Women Rise That They Might Live." 17 Apr. 1954: 15.

———. "Chicago Women Act for Peace." *Chicago Defender* 6 Feb. 1954: 16.

———. "'Steps to Peace' Planned by 'Women for Peace.'" *Chicago Defender* 26 Feb. 1955: 15.

———. "They Fight Together So As Not to Die Together." *Chicago Defender* 25 Sept. 1954: 16.

———. "Women Want to Live." *Chicago Defender* 20 Nov. 1954: 15.

Doll, Jackie, and his Pickled Peppers. "When They Drop the Atomic Bomb." Mercury, 1951. Sound recording.

Doreski, C. K. "'Kin in Some Way': *The Chicago Defender* Reads the Japanese Internment, 1942–1945. *The Black Press: New Literary and Historical Essays.* Ed. Ted Vogel. New Brunswick: Rutgers UP, 2001. 161–87.

Dougherty, Larry. "Activist Harris Recalls Her Life Fighting Racism." *The Daily Californian* 26 Feb. 1986: N. pag. In the Women's International League for Peace and Freedom (WILPF) Records (DG 043), Swarthmore College Peace Collection. Series III, A, 1; Box 4A; Folder: "Erna P. Harris."

Du Bois, W[illiam] E[dward] B[urghardt]. "Atom Bomb and the Colored World." *Chicago Defender* 12 Jan. 1946: 13.

———. *In Battle for Peace: The Story of My 83rd Birthday.* New York: Masses and Mainstream, 1952.

———. *Newspaper Columns: Vol. 2, 1945–61.* Ed. Herbert Aptheker. White Plains: Kraus-Thomson Org. Ltd., 1986.

Duck and Cover. Film. Dir. Anthony Rizzo. Federal Civil Defense Administration/ Archer Productions, 1951. Web. Prelinger Archives. *archive.org/details/ DuckandC1951.*

Dunbar, Eve. "Black is a Region: Segregation and Literary Regionalism in Richard Wright's *The Color Curtain. Representing Segregation: Towards an Aesthetic of Living Jim Crow and Other Forms of Racial Division.* Ed. Brian Norman and Piper Kendrix Williams. Albany: SUNY P, 2010. 185–200.

Durham, Richard. "Negro Needs Atom Bomb More than Russians, Says Ex-Slave." *Chicago Defender* 1 Dec. 1945: 1+.

Dyer, Richard. "White." *Screen: The Journal for the Society for Education in Film and Television* 29.4 (1988): 44–64.

Dyson, Michael Eric. *I May Not Get There With You: The True Martin Luther King, Jr.* New York: Free P, 2000.

Ebert, Roger. "The Night of the Living Dead." Rev. of *Night of the Living Dead,* dir. George Romero. *Chicago Sun-Times* 5 Jan. 1967. Web. *rogerebert.suntimes.com.*

"Eleanor." *Atlanta Daily World* 31 Jan. 1952: 2.

Ellis, Cassandra M. "The Black Boy Looks at the Silver Screen: Baldwin as Moviegoer." *Reviewing James Baldwin: Things Not Seen.* Ed. D. Quentin Miller. Philadelphia: Temple UP, 2000. 190–214.

Ellison, Ralph. "Harlem is Nowhere." 1948. *The Collected Essays of Ralph Ellison.* Ed. John F. Callahan. New York: Modern Library, 2003. 320–27.

———. *Invisible Man.* 1952. Intro. Ralph Ellison. New York: Vintage/Random House, 1981.

———. "A Special Message to Subscribers." 1980. *The Collected Essays of Ralph Ellison.* Ed. John F. Callahan. New York: Modern Library, 2003. 351–55.

———. *Trading Twelves: The Selected Letters of Ralph Ellison and Albert Murray.* Ed. Albert Murray and John F. Callahan. New York: Modern Library, 2000.

Emshwiller, Carol. "A Day at the Beach." *Magazine of Fantasy and Science Fiction* Aug. 1959: 35–43.

Emshwiller, Ed. Cover Illustration. *Magazine of Fantasy and Science Fiction* Aug. 1959.

Emury. "Babylon" (cartoon). *The Black Panthers Speak.* 1970. Ed. Philip S. Foner. New York: Da Capo P, 1995. 240.

Ervin, Frankie, with Austin McCoy and his Combo. "I'd Rather Live Like a Hermit." Mercury (unissued): 1951. Sound recording.

Fabre, Michel. "Chester Himes Direct." *Conversations with Chester Himes.* Ed. Michel Fabre and Robert Skinner. Jackson: UP of Mississippi, 1995. 125–42.

Fabre, Michel, and Robert Skinner. Introduction. *Conversations with Chester Himes.* Ed. Michel Fabre and Robert Skinner. Jackson: UP of Mississippi, 1995. ix–xiv.

Farrell, James J. *The Spirit of the Sixties: Making Postwar Radicalism.* New York: Routledge, 1997.

"Faubus and Sputnik." *Pittsburgh Courier* 19 Oct. 1957: 8.

Feiffer, Jules. *Crawling Arnold. Horizon: A Magazine of the Arts* 4.2 (Nov. 1961): 49–56.

Ferguson, H-Bomb. "Rock, H-Bomb Rock." Atlas, 1952. Sound recording.

"54,000 School Children 'Saved' from Atom Attack." *Atlanta Daily World* 1 May 1957: 1.

Five. Dir. Arch Oboler. Arch Oboler Productions/Columbia Pictures, 1951. Film.

"Five Hundred Students in Mock Evacuation." *Atlanta Daily World* 19 May 1955: 1.

Fleming, Thomas C. "Weekly Report." *San Francisco Sun-Reporter* 25 Feb. 1961: 6.

———. "Weekly Report." *San Francisco Sun-Reporter* 30 Sept. 1961: 15.

———. "Weekly Report." *San Francisco Sun-Reporter* 18 Nov. 1961: 12.

———. "Weekly Report." *San Francisco Sun-Reporter* 28 Apr. 1962: 10.

———. "Weekly Report." *San Francisco Sun-Reporter* 3 Nov. 1962: 10.

———. "Weekly Report." *San Francisco Sun-Reporter* 22 Dec. 1962: 10.

Foertsch, Jacqueline. *Enemies Within: The Cold War and the AIDS Crisis in Literature, Film, and Culture.* Urbana: U of Illinois P, 2001.

"Food For Atom Attack." *New York Amsterdam News* 20 Oct. 1951: 10.

Ford, Douglas. "Crossroads and Cross-Currents in *Invisible Man.*" *Modern Fiction Studies* 45.4 (1999): 887–904.

"Four Speak Out for Peace." *San Francisco Sun-Reporter* 20 Oct. 1962: 7.

Fowles, William A. "Extended War." *Atlanta Daily World* 19 Aug. 1945: 4.

Frank, Pat. *Alas, Babylon.* 1959. New York: Harper/Perennial, 1999.

———. *Mr. Adam.* Philadelphia: J.P. Lippincott, 1946.

Franklin, H. Bruce. *Robert A. Heinlein: America as Science Fiction.* New York: Oxford UP, 1980.

———. *The Victim as Criminal and Artist: Literature from the American Prison.* New York: Oxford UP, 1978.

Fritz, Charles E. "Some Implications from Disaster Research for a National Shelter Program." *Symposium on Human Problems in the Utilization of Fallout Shelters.* Washington, DC: National Academy of Sciences/National Research Council, 1960. 139–56.

Gabbard, Krin. *Black Magic: White Hollywood and African American Culture.* New Brunswick: Rutgers UP, 2004.

Gaines, Kevin. "From Black Power to Civil Rights: Julian Mayfield and African American Expatriates in Nkrumah's Ghana, 1957–1966." *Cold War Constructions: The Political Culture of United States Imperialism, 1945–1966.* Ed. Christian G. Appy. Amherst: U of Massachusetts P, 2000. 257–70.

Geerhart, Bill. Essay. *Atomic Platters: Cold War Music from the Golden Age of Homeland Security* (five CDs, one DVD, 291-page guidebook). Ed. Bill Geerhart and Ken Sitz. Hambergen, Germany: Bear Family Records, 2005.

Gehman, Richard B. "How Negroes live in Atom City." *Negro Digest* Oct. 1948: 4–8.

Gellman, Erik S. "Civil Rights Congress." *Encyclopedia of US Labor and Working Class History, Vol. 1.* Ed. Eric Arnesen. New York: Routledge 2007. 253–54.

Gerstell, Richard. *How to Survive an Atomic Bomb.* Washington, DC: Combat Forces P, 1950.

"Giant Parade to Feature Civil Defense Week Here." *Atlanta Daily World* 4 Dec. 1959: 1.

"Giant Youth Program at Denson's Temple." *Atlanta Daily World* 12 June 1948: 3.

Golden Gate Quartet. "Atom and Evil." Columbia, 1947. Sound recording.

Goldston, Robert. *Suburbia: Civic Denial.* New York: MacMillan, 1970.

Goode, William. "When Nature Topped the Atom Bomb." *Negro Digest* Dec. 1946: 8–10.

Goodlett, Carlton B. "The Task of the Peacemakers." *San Francisco Sun-Reporter* 28 July 1962: 8.

———. "USA Peace Movement and the Negro Revolt." *San Francisco Sun-Reporter* 14 Dec. 1963: 14.

———. "World Congress for General Disarmament and Peace Meets in Moscow." *San Francisco Sun-Reporter* 28 July 1962: 10–11.

Gordon, Andrew. *American Dreamer: A Psychoanalytic Study of the Fiction of Norman Mailer.* London: Associated UPs, 1980.

Gordon, Dexter. "Bikini." Dial, 1947. Sound recording.

Gordon, Eugene. "The Ashes of Death." 5 July 1958: N. pag. Eugene Gordon Papers. Schomburg Center for Research in Black Culture, box 5, folder #7: "Another Side of the Story."

———. "Fallout Shelter—Ideas for a Fiction Story." MS. Eugene Gordon Papers. Schomburg Center for Research in Black Culture, box 4, folder #6: "Notes for Stories."

———. "The Negro Press." *American Mercury* Aug. 1926: 207–15.

Gordon, Michelle. "Somewhat Like War: The Aesthetics of Segregation, Black Liberation, and *A Raisin in the Sun.*" *African American Review* 42.1 (2008): 121–33.

Granger, Lester. "Manhattan and Beyond." *New York Amsterdam News* 26 Oct. 1957: 8.

Grant, Barry Keith. "Taking Back *The Night of the Living Dead:* George Romero, Feminism, and the Horror Film." *Wide Angle* 14.1 (1992): 64–76.

Graves, Lem, Jr. "Admit Oak Ridge Bias: Atom Chiefs In Explanation to *Courier.*" *Pittsburgh Courier* 15 Oct. 1949: 1+.

"A Grave Threat." *San Francisco Sun Reporter* 6 Oct. 1951: 8.

Gregory, Dick. *The Shadow that Scares Me.* New York: Doubleday, 1968.

Grossman, Andrew D. *Neither Dead Nor Red: Civilian Defense and American Political Development During the Early Cold War.* New York: Routledge, 2001.

Gup, Ted. "The Doomsday Blueprints." *Time* 10 Aug. 1992: 32–39.

Hachiya, Michihiko. *Hiroshima Diary: The Journal of a Japanese Physician, Aug. 6–Sept. 30, 1945.* Ed. Warner Wells. Chapel Hill: U of North Carolina P, 1955.

Hagan, Roger. "Community Shelters." *No Place to Hide: Fallout Shelters—Fact and Fiction.* Ed. Seymour Melman. New York: Grove/Black Cat, 1962. 176–92.

Hager, Hal. Afterword. *Alas, Babylon.* 1959. By Pat Frank. New York: Perennial Classics, 1999.

Haley, Bill, and his Comets. "Thirteen Women (and Only One Man in Town)." Decca, 1954. Sound recording.

Hall, Simon. *Peace and Freedom: The Civil Rights and Antiwar Movements in the 1960s.* Philadelphia: U of Pennsylvania P, 2005.

Hancock, Dean Gordon B. "Louisiana Loosens Up." *Atlanta Daily World* 17 Oct. 1951: 4.

———. "Peace, It's Blunderful!" *Atlanta Daily World* 11 Dec. 1945: 6.

Hansberry, Lorraine. "A Challenge to Artists." *Freedomways* 3.1 (1963): 31–35.

———. "The Nation Needs Your Gifts." *Negro Digest* Aug. 1964: 26–29.

———. "The Negro Writer and His Roots." 1959. *The Black Scholar* 12 (1981): 2–12.

———. "No More Hiroshimas." *Freedom* May-June 1955: 7.

———. "On Arthur Miller, Marilyn Monroe, and 'Guilt.'" 1964. *Women in Theater: Compassion and Hope.* Ed. Karen Malpede. New York: Drama Book Publishers, 1983. 173–76.

———. "On Strindberg and Sexism." 1956. *Women in Theater: Compassion and Hope.* Ed. Karen Malpede. New York: Drama Book Publishers, 1983. 171–73.

———. "Quo Vadis?" *Mademoiselle* Jan. 1960: 34+. Lorraine Hansberry Papers, 1947–1988. Schomburg Center for Research in Black Culture, box 58, Folder: "Quo Vadis?"

———. *A Raisin in the Sun: A Drama in Three Acts.* New York: Samuel French, 1959.

———. *What Use Are Flowers?* 1961–1962. *Les Blancs: Collected Last Plays.* Ed. Robert Nemiroff. New York: Vintage/Random House, 1994. 227–61.

———. "Willy Loman, Walter Younger, and He Who Must Live." *Village Voice* 12 Aug. 1959: 7–8.

Hardy, Clarence E. *James Baldwin's God: Sex, Hope, and Crisis in Black Holiness Culture.* Knoxville: U of Tennessee P, 2003.

Hare, Nathan. "Can Negroes Survive a Nuclear War?" *Negro Digest* May 1963: 26–33.

Harlan County Four with the Delmore Brothers. "Atomic Telephone." King, 1951. Sound recording.

"Harlem Escapes As A-Bombs 'Hit' City." *New York Amsterdam News* 26 Sept. 1953: 4.

"Harlem Left Out of A-Bomb Shelter Plans." *New York Amsterdam News* 6 Jan. 1951: 5.

"Harlem's CD Units Await Citywide Drill." *New York Amsterdam News* 3 Nov. 1951: 1+.

"Harlem Shelters." *New York Amsterdam News* 3 Mar. 1951: 6.

Harper, Donna Akiba Sullivan. *Not So Simple: The 'Simple' Stories by Langston Hughes.* Columbia: U of Missouri P, 1995.

Harper, Stephen. "Zombies, Malls, and the Consumerism Debate: George Romero's *Dawn of the Dead.*" *Americana: Journal of American Popular Culture* 1.2 (2002). N. pag.

Harris, Homer. "Atomic Bomb Blues." Columbia (unissued), 1946. Sound recording.

Harris, Trudier. *From Mammies to Militants: Domestics in Black American Literature.* Philadelphia: Temple UP, 1982.

———. *Saints, Saviors, Sinners: Strong Black Women in African American Literature.* New York: Palgrave, 2001.

Hartman, Saidiya V. *Scenes of Subjection: Terror, Slavery, and Self-Making in Nineteenth-Century America.* New York: Oxford UP, 1997.

Hassard, John. "Maintaining Perceptions: Crisis Relocation in the Planning of Nuclear War." *Civil Defense: A Choice of Disasters.* Ed. John Dowling and Evans M. Harrell. New York: American Institute of Physics, 1987. 85–104.

"Hats Off to Branch Rickey." *Chicago Defender* 10 Nov. 1945: 14.

Hayes, Linda, with the Red Callendar Sextette. "Atomic Baby." Hollywood, 1953. Sound recording.

Hayes, William H. *Bombs, Buildings, and Shelters: ARP [Air Raid Protection] for the Home.* New York: Columbia UP, 1942.

"H-Bomb Reaction." *Chicago Defender* 9 Oct. 1954: 2.

Heer, David M. *After Nuclear Attack: A Demographic Inquiry.* New York: Praeger, 1965.

Heffernan, Kevin. "Inner-City Exhibition and the Genre Film: Distributing *Night of the Living Dead.*" *Cinema Journal* 41.3 (2002): 59–77.

Heilbut, Anthony. *The Gospel Sound: Good News in Bad Times.* 1971. New York: Limelight Editions, 1992.

Heinlein, Robert A. *Farnham's Freehold.* 1964. New York: New American Library/ Signet, 1965.

Heise, Thomas. "Harlem is Burning: Urban Rioting and the 'Black Underclass' in Chester Himes's *Blind Man with a Pistol.*" *African American Review* 41.3 (2007): 487–506.

———. *Urban Underworlds: A Geography of Twentieth-Century American Literature and Culture.* New Brunswick, NJ: Rutgers UP, 2011.

"The Hell Bomb." *New York Amsterdam News* 10 Apr. 1954: 18.

"Helping Hands?" (cartoon). *New York Amsterdam News* 15 Sept. 1945: 6A.

Hendershot, Cyndy. *Paranoia, the Bomb, and 1950s Science Fiction Film.* Bowling Green: Popular P, 1999.

Henderson, Paul S. "7,000 Employed at Atomic Bomb Plant." *Baltimore Afro American* 18 Aug. 1945: 1+.

Herring, Frances W. *The World Without the Bomb: Story of the Accra Assembly.* Berkeley: Women For Peace, 1962.

Hersey, John. "A Reporter at Large—Hiroshima." *The New Yorker* 31 Aug. 1946.

Hicks, Heather J. "Hoodoo Economics: White Men's Work and Black Men's Magic in Contemporary American Film." *Camera Obscura* 53/18.2 (2003): 25–55.

Higashi, Sumiko. "*Night of the Living Dead:* A Horror Film about the Vietnam Era." *From Hanoi to Hollywood: The Vietnam War in American Film.* Ed. Linda Dittmar and Gene Michaud. New Brunswick: Rutgers UP, 1990. 175–88.

Hilliard, David. "The Ideology of the Black Panther Party." *The Black Panthers Speak.* 1970. Ed. Philip S. Foner. New York: Da Capo P, 1995. 122–23.

Himes, Chester. *Blind Man with a Pistol.* 1969. New York: Random House/Vintage Crime, 1989.

———. *If He Hollers, Let Him Go.* 1945. New York: Signet, 1971.

———. *My Life of Absurdity: The Later Years. The Autobiography of Chester Himes.* 1976. New York: Paragon House, 1990.

———. "Negro Martyrs are Needed." *Crisis* May 1944: 159+.

———. *Plan B.* 1969. Ed. Michel Fabre and Robert Skinner. Jackson: UP of Mississippi, 1993.

———. "Prediction." 1973. *The Collected Stories of Chester Himes.* New York: Thunder's Mouth P, 1990. 420–25.

———. "Tang." 1967. *The Collected Stories of Chester Himes.* New York: Thunder's Mouth P, 1990. 407–11.

"Hint Jim Crow Bomb Shelters in New Orleans." *Chicago Defender* 3 Feb. 1951: 1.

"Hit Caldwell Appointment. *New York Amsterdam News* 31 Mar. 1951: 8.

Holloway, Wilbert. "Time to Wake Up, America?" (cartoon). *Pittsburgh Courier* 19 Oct. 1957: 1.

Holmes, Dwight. "Lights and Shadows." *Baltimore Afro American* 25 Aug. 1945: 4.

Horne, Gerald. *Black and Red: W. E. B. Du Bois and the American Response to the Cold War, 1944–1963.* Albany: State U of New York P, 1986.

———. "Civil Rights Congress." *Organizing Black America: An Encyclopedia of African American Associations.* Ed. Nina Mjagkij. New York: Garland, 2001. 151–52.

The House in the Middle. Film. National Paint, Varnish, and Lacquer Association (in cooperation with the Federal Civil Defense Administration), 1954. Web. Prelinger Archives. *archive.org/details/Houseint1954.*

Howe, Irving. "James Baldwin: At Ease in Apocalypse." *James Baldwin: A Collection of Critical Essays.* Ed. Keneth Kinnamon. Englewood Cliffs: Prentice-Hall, 1974. 96–108.

Hughes, Langston. "Charged with Atoms, Simple Takes Charge." *Chicago Defender* 10 July 1954: 11.

———. "Harlem (A Dream Deferred)." *Montage of a Dream Deferred.* New York: New York: Holt, 1951. 74.

———. "How Jim Crow Will Jim Crow Air Raid Shelters Be, Asks Simple." *Chicago Defender* 20 Mar. 1954: 11.

———. "Joyce Discusses Hats and Bombs With Jesse B. Simple." *Chicago Defender* 17 July 1954: 11.

———. "Simple and the Atom Bomb." *Chicago Defender* 18 Aug. 1945: 13.

———. "Simple and the Secret." *Chicago Defender* 23 Mar. 1945: 14.

———. "Simple's Selfish Peace." *Chicago Defender* 15 Sept. 1945: 14.

———. "Simple Supposes What Would Happen If Our People Were Immune to Atom Bomb." *Chicago Defender* 29 Oct. 1949: 6.

———. "Simple Views the News." *Chicago Defender* 5 Jan. 1946: 10.

———. "VJ Night in Harlem." *Chicago Defender* 25 Aug. 1945: 12.

———. "Week by Week." *Chicago Defender* 30 Nov. 1957: 10.

———. "When the Atom Comes, Negroes Go Out, Says Simple." *Chicago Defender* 27 Feb. 1954: 11.

Huntington, John. "Science Fiction and the Future." *Science Fiction: A Collection of Critical Essays.* Ed. Mark Rose. Englewood Cliffs: Prentice-Hall, 1976. 156–66.

Hutchinson, Earl Ofari. *Blacks and Reds: Race and Class in Conflict, 1919–1990.* East Lansing: Michigan State UP, 1995.

I Am Legend. Dir. Francis Lawrence. Warner Brothers, 2007. Film.

"Ike's Highway Program." *New York Amsterdam News* 31 July 1954: 14.

"Interview with Karl Hardman and Marilyn Eastman." *Homepage of the Dead.* Oct. 1997. Web. *www.homepageofthedead.com/films/night/interviews_1.html*

Jackson, Jay. "So What?" (cartoon.) *Chicago Defender* 15 Sept. 1945: 15.

———. "So What?" (cartoon.) *Chicago Defender* 2 Nov. 1945: 5.

Janis, Irving. "Psychological Problems of A-Bomb Defense." *Survival and the Bomb: Methods of Civil Defense.* Ed. Eugene P. Wigner. Bloomington: Indiana UP, 1969. 52–78.

Jewels. "B. Bomb Baby." RPM, 1956. Sound recording.

Johnson, Albert. "Beige, Brown, or Black." *Film Quarterly* 13.1 (1959): 38–43.

Johnson, Charles W., and Charles O. Jackson. *City Behind a Fence: Oak Ridge, Tennessee, 1942–1946.* Knoxville: U of Tennessee P, 1981.

Johnson, Manning. *Color, Communism, and Common Sense.* New York: Alliance, Inc./ Stuyvesant P, 1958.

Johnson, Wayne L. "The Invasion Stories of Ray Bradbury." *Critical Encounters: Writers and Themes in Science Fiction.* Ed. Dick Riley. New York: Frederick Ungar, 1978. 23–40.

"Judge Compares Racial Prejudice to Deadly Atomic Bomb." *New York Amsterdam News* 25 Aug. 1945: 2-B.

"Judge Wendell E. Green Lauds Bud Billiken." *Chicago Defender* 25 Aug. 1945: 9C.

"Just What is the Meaning of Air Raid Signals?" *Atlanta Daily World* 8 May 1954: 6.

Katz, Arthur M. *Life After Nuclear War: The Economic and Social Impacts of Nuclear Attacks on the United States.* Cambridge: Ballinger Publishing, 1982.

Kavaliers. "Get that Communist, Joe." Republic, 1954. Sound recording.

Kearney, Reginald. *African American Views of the Japanese: Solidarity or Sedition?* Albany: SUNY P, 1998.

Keefer, Truman Frederick. *Philip Wylie.* Boston: Twayne, 1977. Twayne's United States Authors 285

Keehn, Jeremy. "Six Questions for Colson Whitehead." *Harper's Weekly.* Online Commentary. July 1, 2011. *harpers.org/blog/2011/10/six-questions-for-colson-whitehead.*

Kennedy, Stetson. "New Civil Defender is Old Jim Crower." *New York Amsterdam News* 3 Feb. 1951: 2.

Kerbel, Michael. Rev. of *The Omega Man. Village Voice* 26 Aug. 1971. Rpt. in *Film Facts* 14 (1971): 495–96.

Ketterer, David. *New Worlds for Old: The Apocalyptic Imagination, Science Fiction, and American Literature.* Bloomington: Indiana UP, 1974.

Killens, John Oliver. *Black Man's Burden.* 1965. New York: Pocket Books, 1969.

Kinchy, Abby J. "African Americans in the Atomic Age: Postwar Perspectives on Race and the Bomb, 1945–1967. *Technology and Culture* 50.2 (2009): 291–315.

King, Martin Luther, Jr. Acceptance Speech. 1964. Nobelprize.org. *nobelprize.org/ nobel_prizes/peace/laureates/1964/king-acceptance.html*

———. "Advice for Living." *Ebony* Dec. 1957: 120.

———. "Advice for Living." *Ebony* Jan. 1958: 34.

———. *Strength to Love.* New York: Harper and Row, 1963.

———. *A Testament of Hope: The Essential Writings of Martin Luther King, Jr.* Ed. James M. Washington. New York: HarperCollins, 1986.

———. *Trumpet of Conscience.* New York: Harper and Row, 1967.

Kirby, Fred. "Atomic Power." Performed by the Buchanan Brothers. RCA Victor, 1946. Sound recording.

Klarman, Michael J. *From Jim Crow to Civil Rights: The Supreme Court and the Struggle for Racial Equality.* New York: Oxford UP, 2004.

Knickerbocker, Paine. Rev. of *The Omega Man. San Francisco Chronicle* 26 Aug. 1971. Rpt. in *Film Facts* 14 (1971): 495–96.

Kornweibel, Theodore, Jr. *No Crystal Stair: Black Life and the* Messenger, *1917–1928.* Westport: Greenwood P, 1975.

Kuttner, Henry, and C. L. Moore (writing as Lewis Padgett). "Beggars in Velvet." *Astounding Science Fiction* Dec. 1945: 7–46.

Lapp, Ralph E. *Must We Hide?* Cambridge: Addison-Wesley P, 1949.

The Last Man on Earth. Dir. Sydney Salkow. Associated Producers/API, 1964. Film.

Lautier, Louis. "All Lives in Danger From Atomic Attack, Caldwell." *Atlanta Daily World* 4 Jan. 1951: 3.

Leeming, David. Foreword. *Reviewing James Baldwin: Things Not Seen.* Ed. D. Quentin Miller. Philadelphia: Temple UP, 2000. vii–ix.

———. *James Baldwin: A Biography.* New York: Knopf, 1994.

Leigh, David J. *Apocalyptic Patterns in Twentieth-Century Fiction.* Notre Dame: U of Notre Dame P, 2008.

Lewicky, Zbigniew. *The Bang and the Whimper: Apocalypse and Entropy in American Literature.* Westport: Greenwood P, 1984.

Lewis, David Levering. *King: A Critical Biography.* New York: Praeger, 1970.

———. *W. E. B. Du Bois: The Fight for Equality and the American Century, 1919–1963.* New York: Henry Holt, 2000.

Leyson, Burr. *The Air Raid Safety Manual.* New York: E. P. Dutton, 1942.

Lieberman, Robbie. "'Another Side of the Story': African American Intellectuals Speak out for Peace and Freedom during the Early Cold War Years." *Anticommunism and the African American Freedom Movement: "Another Side of the Story."* Ed. Robbie Lieberman and Clarence Lang. New York: Palgrave, 2009. 17–49.

———. "'Peace and Civil Rights Don't Mix, They Say': Anticommunism and the Dividing of US Social Movements, 1947–1967. *Peace Movements in Western Europe, Japan, and the USA during the Cold War.* Ed. Benjamin Ziemann. Essen: Klartext, 2008. 91–106.

Lifton, Robert J., and Greg Mitchell. *Hiroshima in America: A Half Century of Denial.* New York: Avon Books, 1995.

Loeb, Charles H. "Loeb Reflects on Atomic Bombed Area." *Atlanta Daily World* 5 Oct. 1945: 1+.

"Lone Negro Describes Life in Bomb Shelter." *Pittsburgh Courier* 25 June 1960: 9.

Long, Michael G. *Against Us, But For Us: Martin Luther King and the State.* Macon: Mercer P, 2002.

"A Look at Atom and Evil." *Ebony* Apr. 1951: 94–95.

Lord, Mrs. Oswald B. "Today's Crisis and Tomorrow's Families." *Journal of Social Hygiene* 37.3 (1951): 99–108.

Lorence, James J. *A Hard Journey: The Life of Don West.* Urbana: U of Illinois P, 2007.

Louisiana Red. "Red's Dream." Roulette, 1962. Sound recording.

Lundquist, James. *Chester Himes.* New York: Frederick Ungar, 1976.

MacCannell, Dean. "Baltimore in the Morning . . . After: On the Forms of Post-Nuclear Leadership." *Diacritics* 14.2 (1984): 33–46.

"Macon Minister Heard in Atlanta Message Sunday." *Atlanta Daily World* 22 July 1947: 3.

Mailer, Norman. "The White Negro." *The White Negro.* New York: City Lights, n.d. N.pag.

"'The Man' Hauls Out a New One: Atomic Threats." *Chicago Defender* 1 June 1946: 3.

Manring, M. M. *Slave in a Box: The Strange Career of Aunt Jemima.* Charlottesville: UP of Virginia, 1998.

Marable, Manning. *Black Leadership.* New York: Columbia UP, 1998.

Margolies, Edward, and Michel Fabre. *The Several Lives of Chester Himes.* Jackson: UP of Mississippi, 1997.

Marke, Loo Koo. "King Delivers Stirring Address to Atlanta Baptist Association." *Atlanta Daily World* 16 Oct. 1947: 1.

Martin, Thomas L., Jr. and Donald C. Latham. *Strategy for Survival.* Tucson: U of Arizona P, 1963.

Matheson, Richard. *I Am Legend.* 1954. New York: Tom Doherty Associates, 2007.

Matthews, Kristin L. "The Politics of 'Home' in Lorraine Hansberry's *A Raisin in the Sun. Modern Drama* 54.1 (2008): 556–78.

Matthews, Ralph. "Thoughts on War and Peace—Do We All Die This Year or Next?" *Baltimore Afro American* 12 Aug. 1961. Rpt. *Freedomways* Fall 1961: 282–84.

———. "Watching the Big Parade." *Baltimore Afro American* 25 Aug. 1945: 4.

May, Elaine Tyler. *Homeward Bound: American Families in the Cold War Era.* New York: Basic Books, 1988.

McEnaney, Laura. *Civil Defense Begins at Home: Militarization Meets Everyday Life in the Fifties.* Princeton: Princeton UP, 2000.

McIntosh, J. T. "Eleventh Commandment." *Magazine of Fantasy and Science Fiction* May 1955: 78–114.

McKittrick, Katherine, and Clyde Woods. "'No One Knows the Mysteries at the Bottom of the Ocean.'" *Black Geographies and the Politics of Place.* Ed. Katherine McKittrick and Clyde Woods. Toronto: Between the Lines, 2007. 1–13.

McKnight, Gerald R. *The Last Crusade: Martin Luther King, Jr., the FBI, and the Poor People's Campaign.* Boulder: Westview P, 1998.

"Memo to Mr. Millard F. Caldwell." *Chicago Defender* 27 Jan. 1951: 6.

Merril, Judith. *Shadow on the Hearth.* Garden City, NY: Doubleday, 1950. Rpt./Rev. ed. London: Roberts & Vinter, 1966.

Merril, Judith, and Emily Pohl-Weary. *Better to Have Loved: The Life of Judith Merril.* Toronto: Between the Lines, 2002.

Milburn, Amos. "Atomic Baby." Aladdin (unissued), 1950. Sound recording.

Milicia, Joseph. Introduction. *The Fall of the Towers.* By Samuel R. Delany. 1963–1965. Boston: Gregg P, 1977. v–xxi.

Miller, Quentin D., ed. *Reviewing James Baldwin: Things Not Seen.* Philadelphia: Temple UP, 2000.

Milliken, Stephen F. *Chester Himes: A Critical Appraisal.* Columbia: U of Missouri P, 1976.

Mills, C. Wright. *The Causes of World War Three.* New York: Simon and Schuster, 1958.

Mingus, Charles. "Oh, Lord, Don't Let Them Drop that Atomic Bomb on Me." *Oh Yeah.* Atlantic, 1962. Sound recording.

"Miss Voters League Leads Bilbo Fight." *Atlanta Daily World* 13 Dec. 1946: 1.

"Mock A-Bomb Warning Fizzles in Chicago." *Chicago Defender* 26 June 1954: 12.

Mollin, Marian. *Radical Pacifism in Modern America: Egalitarianism and Protest.* Philadelphia: U of Pennsylvania P, 2006.

Morel, Lucas E. "Ralph Ellison's American Democratic Individualism." *Ralph Ellison and the Raft of Hope: A Political Companion to* Invisible Man. Ed. Lucas E. Morel. Lexington: U of Kentucky P, 2004. 58–90.

Morrison, Toni, ed. *James Baldwin: Collected Essays.* New York: Library of America, 1998.

"Moving On the Alert Time." *Atlanta Daily World* 23 Nov. 1957: 6.

Muhammad, Elijah. *The Fall of America.* Chicago: Muhammad's Temple of Islam No. 2, 1973.

Muller, Gilbert H. *Chester Himes.* Boston: Twayne, 1989. Twayne's United States Authors 553.

Nagai, Takashi. *We of Nagasaki: The Story of Survivors in an Atomic Wasteland.* New York: Duell, Sloan, and Pearce, 1951.

"Negroes Subject to Added Peril in A-Bomb Attack." *Jet* 10 Apr. 1952: 21.

"Negroes Who Help Conquer Space." *Ebony* May 1958: 19–21.

"Negro Friends Cost White Engineer Atomic Post." *Jet* 5 Nov. 1953: 3–4.

"Negro Sailor Relieves Boredom in Shelter Test." *Jet* 15 Mar. 1962: 10.

Nemiroff, Robert, ed. *To Be Young, Gifted, and Black: Lorraine Hansberry in her Own Words.* Englewood Cliffs: Prentice-Hall, 1969.

"A New Low in Thinking." *Chicago Defender* 15 Sept. 1945: 14.

Newton, Huey. "In Defense of Self-Defense: Executive Mandate Number One." 1970. *The Black Panthers Speak.* Ed. Philip S. Foner. New York: Da Capo P, 1995. 40–41.

The Night of the Living Dead. Dir. George A. Romero. Image Ten, 1968. Film.

"N.O. Bomb Shelters Integrated." *Pittsburgh Courier* 3 Nov. 1962: 1.

Nordlie, Peter G. "Societal Recovery." *Survival and the Bomb: Methods of Civil Defense.* Ed. Eugene P. Wigner. Bloomington: Indiana UP, 1969. 283–307.

"Now—The Battle for Jobs!" *Chicago Defender* 25 Aug. 1945: 12.

"Nuclear Attack Fallout Shelter Now Available." *Chicago Defender* 15 Aug. 1959: 11.

Oakes, Guy. *The Imaginary War: Civil Defense and American Cold War Culture.* New York: Oxford UP, 1994.

"The Oak Ridge Disgrace." *Pittsburgh Courier* 23 Apr. 1949: 14.

Occupying a Public Shelter. Film. US Army and Office of Civil Defense, 1965. *Atomic Platters: Cold War Music from the Golden Age of Homeland Security / Disc 6 (DVD) Target You: Cold War Educational Films from the Golden Age of Social Security.* Ed. Bill Geerhart and Ken Sitz. Hambergen, Germany: Bear Family Records, 2005.

O'Donnevan, Finn. "Uncle Tom's Planet." *Galaxy Science Fiction* Dec. 1954: 56–69.

Office of Technology Assessment. *The Effects of Nuclear War.* Washington, DC: Congress of the US, 1979.

Oglesbee, Frank W. "*The World, the Flesh, and the Devil.*" *Nuclear War Films.* Ed. Jack Shaheen. Carbondale: Southern Illinois UP, 1978. 25–30.

"Ole 'Satchmo' Shook the World." *Chicago Defender* 5 Oct. 1957: 10.

Olwell, Russell B. *At Work in the Atomic City: A Labor and Social History of Oak Ridge, Tennessee.* Knoxville: U of Tennessee P, 2004.

O'Meally, Robert G. *The Craft of Ralph Ellison.* Cambridge: Harvard UP, 1980.

The Omega Man. Dir. Boris Sagal. Warner Brothers, 1971. Film.

"On Bomb Shelters." *Atlanta Daily World* 29 Sept. 1961: 4.

"One Reason." *New York Amsterdam News* 12 Oct. 1957: 6.

"On Target." *Baltimore Afro American* 3 Mar. 1963: 4.

Operation Cue. Film. US Federal Civil Defense Administration, 1955. Web. Prelinger Archives. *archive.org/details/Operati01955.*

Our Cities Must Fight. Film. Dir. Anthony Rizzo. US Civil Defense Administration/ Archer Productions, 1951. Web. Prelinger Archives. *archive.org/details/ OurCitie1951.*

"Our Underground Shelters." *New York Amsterdam News* 12 Aug. 1950: 6.

Padmore, George. "Africa Holds Key to Atomic Future." *Chicago Defender* 8 Sept. 1945: 4.

———. "Morals of Whites Dropped With Atom Bomb, Say Africans." *Chicago Defender* 8 Sept. 1945: 4.

Paffenroth, Kim. *Gospel of the Living Dead: George Romero's Visions of Hell on Earth.* Waco: Baylor UP, 2006.

Page, Max. "Creatively Destroying New York: Fantasies, Premonitions, and Realities in the Provisional City." *Out of Ground Zero: Case Studies in Urban Reinvention.* Ed. Joan Ockman. Munich: Prestel, 2002. 166–83.

Panic in Year Zero. Dir. Ray Milland. American International Pictures, 1962. Film.

Parrinder, Patrick. *Science Fiction: Its Criticism and Teaching.* London: Methuen, 1980.

Patterson, William L. "Reader Replies to the Task of the Peacemakers." *San Francisco Sun-Reporter* 11 Aug. 1962: 8.

"Peace?—It's Not So Wonderful!" (cartoon). *Chicago Defender* 25 Aug. 1945: 12.

"Peace Picketers" (photo). *Baltimore Afro American* 10 Nov. 1962: 5.

Peeks, Edward. "'End Madness!' Peacemongers Cry." *Baltimore Afro American* 10 Nov. 1962: 5.

Peplow, Michael W., and Robert S. Bravard. *Samuel R. Delany: A Primary and Secondary Bibliography, 1962–1979.* Boston: G.K. Hall, 1980.

Perry, Helen Swick. "Selective Inattention as an Explanatory Concept for U.S. Public Attitudes Toward the Atom Bomb." *Psychiatry* 17.3 (1954): 225–42.

Peterson, Val. "They Said It Would Never Happen. . . ." *New York Times Book Review* 17 Jan. 1954: 4–5.

Pilgrim Travelers. "Jesus Hits Like an Atom Bomb." Specialty, 1951. Sound recording.

———. "Jesus is the First Line of Defense." Hollywood, 1951. Sound recording.

"Pittsburghers Speak Up." *Pittsburgh Courier* 4 Nov. 1961: 10.

Plant, Sandra Whitten. "The Integration of Oak Ridge High School." *These Are Our Voices: The Story of Oak Ridge, 1942–1970.* Ed. James Overholt. Oak Ridge: Children's Museum of Oak Ridge, 1987. 385–92.

Poore, Charles. "Books of the Times." *New York Times* 15 June 1950: 29.

———. "Books of the Times." *New York Times* 14 Jan. 1954: 27.

Porter, Horace. *Stealing the Fire: The Art and Protest of James Baldwin.* Middletown: Wesleyan UP, 1989.

"The Power of the People." 1970. *The Black Panthers Speak.* Ed. Philip S. Foner. New York: Da Capo P, 1995. 23–24.

Prattis, P. L. "Sputnik and US." *Pittsburgh Courier* 12 Oct. 1957: 9.

———. "'Supposin'" Piece Ponders How Things Might Have Been Had Russia Gotten the A-Bomb First." *Pittsburgh Courier* 15 Oct. 1949: 14.

"Prepare For the H-Bomb." *Atlanta Daily World* 1 Apr. 1955: 4.

"President Had to Do It" *Baltimore Afro American* 3 Nov. 1962: 1+.

"Protest Use of Atom Bomb" (photo). *Chicago Defender* 15 Aug. 1959: 1.

"Public is Warned of Civil Defense Needs in this Area." *Atlanta Daily World* 18 Feb. 1951: 1.

"Race Vs. Space." *Ebony* Mar. 1958: 90–91.

"Radioactive Gold." *Ebony* July 1949: 63–66.

"Radio, TV, To Go Off Air During Defense Exercise." *Atlanta Daily World* 3 May 1960: 8.

Randall, Nan. "Appendix C—Charlottesville: A Fictional Account." *The Effects of Nuclear War.* Office of Technology Assessment. Washington, DC: Congress of the US, 1979. 124–38.

Randolph, Robert. "Japan Holds 8th Peace Meet." *San Francisco Sun-Reporter* 20 Oct. 1962: 6.

Redding, J. Saunders. "A Second Look." *Baltimore Afro American* 8 Sept. 1945: 4.

"Religious Group Heads for Hills for World's End." *Atlanta Daily World* 19 Aug. 1961: 3.

"Remember Your Civil Defense." *Atlanta Daily World* 26 Oct. 1962: 4.

Ring, James W. "Sheltering from a Nuclear Attack." *Civil Defense: A Choice of Disasters.* Ed. John Dowling and Evans M. Harrell. New York: Am. Inst. of Physics, 1987. 77–85.

Rivera, A. M., Jr. "Drop Race Bias, Not Atom Bomb." *Pittsburgh Courier* 9 Dec. 1950: 1+.

Robeson, Paul. *Paul Robeson Speaks: Writings, Speeches, Interviews, 1918–1974.* Ed. Philip S. Foner. New York: Brunner/Mazel, 1978.

Robinson, Mary E. Response. *Symposium on Human Problems in the Utilization of Fallout Shelters.* Washington, DC: Natl. Acad. of Sciences/Natl. Research Council, 1960. 220–22.

Rogers, Hubert. Cover Illustration. *Astounding Science Fiction* Mar. 1947.

Rogers, J. A. "Atom Bomb May Disclose That Civilized Man Is Headed Back to the Caves." *Pittsburgh Courier* 1 Sept. 1945: 7.

———. "Each Time White Folks Get Into Trouble the Negro Gets Closer to His Goal." *Pittsburgh Courier* 8 Oct. 1949: 17.

———. "History Shows." *Pittsburgh Courier* 7 Jan. 1956: 9.

Romero, George A. Preface. *The Complete* Night of the Living Dead *Filmbook.* By John Russo. New York: Harmony Books, 1985. 6–7.

Rose, David. "The Mycologically Strange: Fungi and Myxomycetes in Surrealism, Fantasy, and Science Fiction (Part 2)." *Fungi* 2.3 (2009): 20–34.

Rose, Kenneth D. *One Nation Underground: The Fallout Shelter in American Culture.* New York: New York UP, 2001.

Rose, Mark. *Alien Encounters: Anatomy of Science Fiction.* Cambridge: Harvard UP, 1981.

———. Introduction. *Science Fiction: A Collection of Critical Essays.* Ed. Mark Rose. Englewood Cliffs: Prentice-Hall, 1976. 1–7.

"Russia and the A-Bomb." *Baltimore Afro American* 1 Oct. 1949: 4.

Russo, John. *The Complete* Night of the Living Dead *Filmbook.* New York: Harmony Books, 1985.

Rustin, Bayard. "Twenty-Two Days on a Chain Gang." *Down the Line: The Collected Writings of Bayard Rustin.* Ed. C. Vann Woodward. Chicago: Quadrangle Books, 1971. 26–49.

———. "We Challenged Jim Crow." *Down the Line: The Collected Writings of Bayard Rustin.* Ed. C. Vann Woodward. Chicago: Quadrangle Books, 1971. 13–25.

Sallis, James. *Chester Himes: A Life.* New York: Walker and Company, 2000.

———. "In America's Black Heartland: The Achievement of Chester Himes." *The Critical Response to Chester Himes.* Ed. Charles L. P. Silet. Westport: Greenwood P, 1999. 127–38.

Santoro, Gene. *Myself When I am Real: The Life and Music of Charles Mingus.* Oxford: Oxford UP, 2000.

Saul, Scott. *Freedom Is, Freedom Ain't: Jazz and the Making of the Sixties.* Cambridge: Harvard UP, 2003.

"Say Negroes More Prone to Atomic Burns." *Jet* 14 Nov. 1957: 29.

Schaub, Thomas. "Ellison's Masks and the Novel of Reality." *New Essays on Invisible Man.* Ed. Robert O'Meally. Cambridge: Cambridge UP, 1988. 123–56.

Scholes, Robert, and Eric S. Rabkin. *Science Fiction: History, Science, Vision.* New York: Oxford UP, 1977.

Schuyler, George. "Views and Reviews." *Pittsburgh Courier* 18 Aug. 1945: 7.

Seale, Bobby. "Seize the Time." *The Eyes on the Prize Civil Rights Reader: Documents, Speeches, and Firsthand Accounts from the Black Freedom Struggle, 1954–1990.* Ed. Clayborne Carson et al. New York: Viking, 1991. 348–61.

"See Complete Annihilation If Atom Bomb Strikes Stuyford." *New York Amsterdam News* 3 Feb. 1951: B1+.

Seed, David. *American Science Fiction and the Cold War: Literature and Film.* Edinburgh: Edinburg UP, 1999.

"See Quick Peace as End to FEPC." *Atlanta Daily World* 12 Aug. 1945: 1.

"Separate Races in Bomb Shelters." *Chicago Defender* 20 Apr. 1960: 3.

"17 Atomic Bombs Would Completely Destroy Boro." *New York Amsterdam News* 25 Aug. 1945: 1.

Shales, Tom. Rev. of *The Omega Man. Washington Post* 19 Aug. 1971. Rpt. in *Film Facts* 14 (1971): 494–95.

Shapiro, Jerome F. *Atomic Bomb Cinema: The Apocalyptic Imagination on Film.* New York: Routledge, 2002.

Sharp, Patrick B. *Savage Perils: Racial Frontiers and Nuclear Apocalypse in American Culture.* Norman: U of Oklahoma P, 2007.

Sheckley, Robert. "Human Man's Burden." *Galaxy Science Fiction* Sept. 1956: 95–108.

"Should Parents Spare the Rod?" *Atlanta Daily World* 9 Nov. 1962: 2.

Sidel, Victor W., H. Jack Geiger, and Bernard Lown. "The Physician's Role in the Post-Attack Period. *New England Journal of Medicine* 266.22 (1962): 1137–45.

Simmons, Fay. "You Hit Me Baby Like an Atomic Bomb." Reco-Art Studios (unissued), 1954. Sound recording.

Sitkoff, Harvard. *The Struggle for Black Equality, 1954–1992.* New York: Hill and Wang, 1993.

Skal, David J. *Screams of Reason: Mad Science and Modern Culture.* New York: W. W. Norton, 1998.

Skinner, Samuel J. "Let's Think." *San Francisco Sun-Reporter* 11 Nov. 1961: 17.

Slim Gaillard Quartette. "Atomic Cocktail." Atomic, 1946. Sound recording.

Smelser, Neil, J. "Chapter II: The Social Dimensions of Nuclear Attack." *Vulnerabilities of Social Structure: Studies of the Social Dimensions of Nuclear Attack.* Ed. S. D. Vestermark. McLean: Human Sciences, Research, Inc., 1966. 207–63.

Smethurst, James. "'Don't Say Goodbye to the Porkpie Hat': Langston Hughes, the Left, and the Black Arts Movement." *Callaloo* 25.4 (2002): 1225–36.

Smith, Jessie Carney. "Rebecca Stiles Taylor." *Notable Black American Women, Book II.* Ed. Jessie Carney Smith. Detroit: Gale Research, 1996. 631–35.

Smith, Judith E. *Visions of Belonging: Family Stories, Popular Culture, and Postwar Democracy, 1940–1960.* New York: Columbia UP, 2004.

Smith, Martin A., and William E. Eliason. *The Family Survival Handbook.* New York: Belmont Books, 1961.

Snead, James. *White Screens, Black Images: Hollywood from the Dark Side.* Ed. Colin MacCabe and Cornel West. New York: Routledge, 1994.

"Some Atom Bomb Targets." *Chicago Defender* 13 Aug. 1949: 6.

Sontag, Susan. "The Imagination of Disaster." 1961. *Science Fiction: A Collection of Critical Essays.* Ed. Mark Rose. Englewood Cliffs: Prentice-Hall, 1976. 116–31.

Soul Stirrers. "Jesus Hits Like an Atom Bomb." Hollywood, 1950. Sound recording.

Spirit of Memphis Quartet. "Atomic Telephone." King, 1952. Sound recording.

"Splitting the Atom of Race Hate." *Chicago Defender* 18 Aug. 1945: 13.

Stafford, Jeff. "*The World, the Flesh, and the Devil.*" *Turner Classic Movies.* 9 May 2008. Web. *www.tcm.com/this-month/article/95535%7C0/The-World-the-Flesh-and-the-Devil.html.*

"State Issues Booklet on 'Fighting' A-Bomb." *New York Amsterdam News* 23 Sept. 1950: 28.

Steele, Valeria. "A New Hope." *These Are Our Voices: The Story of Oak Ridge, 1942–1970.* Ed. James Overholt. Oak Ridge: Children's Museum of Oak Ridge, 1987. 198–203.

Stewart, George R. *Earth Abides.* New York: Random House, 1949.

Still, Larry. "The Spotlight is Diverted, But Rights Fight Goes On." *Jet* 8 Nov. 1962: 14–17.

Stonier, Tom. *Nuclear Disaster.* Cleveland: Meridian/World, 1964.

Strangers Quartet. "The Atomic Age." Coleman, 1949. Sound recording.

Summary. *The Omega Man. Film Facts* 14 (1971): 494.

Sun Ra and Arkestra. "Nuclear War." *Nuclear War.* Music Box, 1982. Sound recording.

Swan's Silvertone Singers. "Jesus is God's Atomic Bomb." King, 1950. Sound recording.

Swerdlow, Amy. *Women Strike for Peace: Traditional Motherhood and Radical Politics in the 1960s.* Chicago: U of Chicago P, 1993.

Sykes, Roosevelt. "Sputnik Baby." House of Sound, 1957. Sound recording.

Tal, Kali. "That Just Kills Me: Black Militant Near-Future Fiction." *Social Text* 20.2 (2002): 65–91.

Talbot Brothers of Bermuda. "Atomic Nightmare." ABC, 1957. Sound recording.

"Theater." *Baltimore Afro American* 1 Sept. 1945: 8.

Thomas, Sheree R. "Introduction: Looking for the Invisible." *Dark Matter: A Century of Speculative Fiction from the African Diaspora.* Ed. Sheree R. Thomas. New York: Warner, 2000. ix–xiv.

Town of the Times. Film. Department of Defense/Wilding Production, 1963. *Atomic Platters: Cold War Music from the Golden Age of Homeland Security / Disc 6 (DVD) Target You: Cold War Educational Films from the Golden Age of Social Security.* Ed. Bill Geerhart and Ken Sitz. Hambergen, Germany: Bear Family Records, 2005.

Trodd, Zoe. "In Possession of Space: Abolitionist Memory and Spatial Transformation in Civil Rights Literature and Photography." *Representing Segregation: Toward an Aesthetic of Living Jim Crow, and Other Forms of Racial Division.* Ed. Brian Norman and Piper Kendrix Williams. Albany: SUNY P, 2010. 223–43.

Tucker, Jeffrey Allen. *A Sense of Wonder: Samuel R. Delaney, Race, Identity, and Difference.* Middletown: Wesleyan UP, 2004.

Turner, Patricia A. *Ceramic Uncles and Celluloid Mammies: Black Images and Their Influence on Culture.* New York: Anchor, 1994.

Twagilimana, Aimable. "Alienation as Narrative Strategy in Ralph Ellison's *Invisible Man.*" *Alienation.* Ed. Blake Hobby. New York: Bloom's Literary Criticism, 2009. 101–10.

United States. Natl. Education Assn., Natl. Commission on Safety Education, and American Assn. of School Administrators. *A Realistic Approach to Civil Defense: A Handbook for School Administrators.* Washington, DC: GPO, 1966.

van Rijn, Guido. *The Truman and Eisenhower Blues: African-American Blues and Gospel Songs, 1945–60.* London: Continuum, 2004.

Vestermark, S. D. "Chapter I: Social Vulnerability and Recovery as Analytic Problems." *Vulnerabilities of Social Structure: Studies of the Social Dimensions of Nuclear Attack.* Ed. S. D. Vestermark. McLean: Human Sciences, Research, Inc., 1966. 5–203.

"V-J Day and the Atomic Bomb Kiss" (photo). *New York Amsterdam News* 25 Aug. 1945: 2A.

von Eschen, Penny M. *Race Against Empire: Black Americans and Anticolonialism, 1937–1957.* Ithaca: Cornell UP, 1997

von Glahn, George A. "A World of Difference: Samuel Delany's *Einstein Intersection.*" *Critical Encounters: Writers and Themes in Science Fiction.* Ed. Dick Riley. New York: Frederick Ungar, 1978. 109–31.

Vonnegut, Kurt. "Harrison Bergeron." *Magazine of Fantasy and Science Fiction* Oct. 1961: 5–11.

Waligora-Davis, Nicole A. "W. E. B. Du Bois and the Fourth Dimension." *NewCentennial Review* 6.3 (2007): 57–90.

Walker, Dennis. *Islam and the Search for African-American Nationhood: Elijah Muhammad, Louis Farrakhan, and the Nation of Islam.* Atlanta: Clarity P, 2005.

Walkowitz, Carol. "Nuclear Families: Women's Narratives of the Making of the Atomic Bomb." *Transformations: Thinking Through Feminism.* Ed. Sara Ahmed et al. London: Routledge, 2000. 235–49.

Waller, Gregory A. *The Living and the Undead: From Stoker's* Dracula *to Romero's* Dawn of the Dead. Urbana: U of Illinois P, 1986.

Walters, Wendy W. "Limited Options: Strategic Maneuverings in Himes's Harlem." *The Critical Response to Chester Himes.* Ed. Charles L.P. Silet. Westport: Greenwood P, 1999. 201–20.

Washburn, Patrick S. *The African American Newspaper: Voice of Freedom.* Evanston: Northwestern UP, 2006.

"Watch Your Civil Defense—Be On the Alert." *Atlanta Daily World* 16 Sept. 1961: 6.

Waters, Enoch P. "Atom Bomb Birthplace City of Paradoxes: Negro Kids Can't Go To School At Biggest Brain Center." *Chicago Defender* 29 Dec. 1945: 1+. Rpt. as "Atom City Black Belt." *Negro Digest* Feb. 1946: 81–84.

———. "Inside Oak Ridge: Negroes Live in Modern 'Hoovervilles' at Atom City." *Chicago Defender* 5 Jan. 1946: 1+.

Weart, Spencer R. "History of American Attitudes to Civil Defense." *Civil Defense: A Choice of Disasters.* Ed. John Dowling and Evans M. Harrell. New York: American Inst. of Physics, 1987. 11–32.

"What Goes On . . . In the Most Important Little City in the World." *Pittsburgh Courier* 2 Apr. 1949: 1.

"What Motorists Should Do in An Atomic Attack." *New York Amsterdam News* 9 Aug. 1952: 30.

"Which is Greatest Menace, Bilbo or Atomic Bomb?" *Chicago Defender* 16 Feb. 1946: 14.

White, Walter. "Atom Bomb and Lasting Peace." *Chicago Defender* 8 Sept. 1945: 13.

———. "Race for Atomic Control Makes FEPC a 'Must' for U.S." Chicago Defender 17 Dec. 1949: 7.

Whitehead, Colson. *Zone One*. New York: Doubleday, 2011.

Whitey and Hogan (aka Arval Hogan and Roy Grant). "There's a Power Greater Than Atomic." Performed by the Buchanan Brothers. RCA Victor, 1947. Sound recording.

Wilcox, Johnnie. "Black Power: Minstrelsy and Electricity in Ralph Ellison's *Invisible Man.*" *Callaloo* 30.4 (2007): 987–1009.

Williams, Hank. "No, No, Joe." MGM, 1950. Sound recording.

Williams, John A. "My Man Himes: An Interview with Chester Himes." 1970. *Conversations with Chester Himes.* Ed. Michel J. Fabre and Robert E. Skinner. Jackson: UP of Mississippi, 1995. 28-82.

Williams, Tony. *The Cinema of George A. Romero: Knight of the Living Dead.* London: Wallflower P, 2003.

Williamson, Jack. "The Equalizer." *Astounding Science Fiction* Mar. 1947: 6–55.

Winkler, Allan M. *Life Under a Cloud: American Anxiety About the Atom.* Urbana: U of Illinois P, 1993.

Wittner, Lawrence S. *One World or None: A History of the World Nuclear Disarmament Movement through 1953.* Stanford: Stanford UP, 1993. Vol. 1 of *The Struggle Against the Bomb.* 4 vols. 1993–2003.

———. *Rebels Against War: The American Peace Movement, 1933–1983.* Philadelphia: Temple UP, 1984.

———. *Resisting the Bomb: A History of the World Nuclear Disarmament Movement, 1954–1970.* Stanford: Stanford UP, 1997. Vol. 2 of *The Struggle Against the Bomb.* 4 vols. 1993–2003.

Wolfe, Charles K. "'Jesus Hits Like an Atom Bomb': Nuclear Warfare in Country Music, 1944–56." *Country Music Goes to War.* Ed. Charles K. Wolfe and James E. Akenson. Lexington: UP of Kentucky, 2005. 102–25.

"Women, It's Up To Us." *San Francisco Sun-Reporter* 7 July 1962: 10.

Wood, Robin. *Hollywood from Vietnam to Reagan.* New York: Columbia UP, 1986.

The World, the Flesh, and the Devil. Dir. Ranald MacDougall. HarBel Productions/ MGM, 1959. Film.

Wylie, Philip. *Tomorrow!* New York: Holt, Rinehart, and Winston, 1954.

———. *Triumph.* Garden City: Doubleday, 1963.

Young, Lola. *Fear of the Dark: "Race," Gender, and Sexuality in the Cinema.* London: Routledge, 1996.

"You Save These Rules—They May Save Your Life." *Pittsburgh Courier* 10 Feb. 1951: 13.

Zaretsky, Eli. "Norman O. Brown, 1913–2002." *Radical Philosophy* 118 (Mar./Apr. 2003). N. pag.

Zepp, Ira G. *The Social Vision of Martin Luther King, Jr.* 1971. Brooklyn: Carlson Publishing, 1989.

Index